This
Much
is True

This Much is True

Miriam Margolyes

JOHN MURRAY

First published in Great Britain in 2021 by John Murray (Publishers)
An Hachette UK company

12

Copyright © Miriam Margolyes 2021

The right of Miriam Margolyes to be identified as the Author of the Work has been asserted by her in accordance with the Copyright, Designs and Patents Act 1988.

A CIP catalogue record for this title is available from the British Library

Hardback ISBN 978-1-529-37988-4
Trade Paperback ISBN 978-1-529-37989-1
eBook ISBN 978-1-529-37991-4

Typeset in Minion Pro by Hewer Text UK Ltd, Edinburgh
Printed and bound in Great Britain by Clays Ltd, Elcograf S.p.A.

John Murray policy is to use papers that are natural, renewable and recyclable products and made from wood grown in sustainable forests. The logging and manufacturing processes are expected to conform to the environmental regulations of the country of origin.

John Murray (Publishers)
Carmelite House
50 Victoria Embankment
London EC4Y 0DZ

www.johnmurraypress.co.uk

For Heather

and

in memory of my mother and father

Contents

Introduction   1

Daddy   4

Mummy   12

Enter Miriam   21

We Are a Fortress Family   25

Going to School   38

Oh, Miriam!   48

Families   52

Showing Off   61

The Facts of Life   67

Latin Lessons   75

Dinner with Isaiah Berlin   79

Nude Modelling for Augustus John   85

Miriam Kibbutznik   90

Cambridge   97

Adventures in Academia   109

Footlights   113

Saved by the Beeb   117

Swinging London   129

The Importance of Voice   134

Sexy Sonia   138

Women Are Better than Men: Discuss   142

Heather	150
Coming Out	157
Life on the Road: *Fiddler on the Roof*	164
Going on the Stage: A Masterclass of Sorts	175
The Joys of Being an Understudy: *The Threepenny Opera*	186
When a Play Goes Wrong: *The White Devil*	194
Getting into Character: *Endgame*	202
PG Tips and the Caramel Bunny	208
To Dub or Not to Dub	218
Banged up in Bow Street	222
Money Talks	229
Too Fat to Go to Bed With	238
My First Time on Broadway was . . . *Wicked*	246
Call Me Gert and Leave Out the Rude Part	250
In Therapy	260
Only Connect	266
Blood Will Tell	273
Two Spikes Would Be an Extravagance!	276
It is a Far, Far Better Thing	290
Taking America by Storm	300
Please Do Not Wear Shorts	307
My Turn to Fail	312
Adventures in Cinema	319
Working with Scorsese: *The Age of Innocence*	330
Romeo + Juliet	335
Would You Like to Go to Disney World?	342
Harry Potter	345
Down Under	353

Contents

A New Habit	361
Being Jewish	367
Choosing My Side	376
Speaking Out	384
A Right Royal Reception	388
Spliced	397
Getting Older	400
Dirty Talk	409
The Final Curtain	414
Acknowledgements	419
Credits	423
Index	425

Introduction

Suddenly I am eighty. How can that possibly be? Eighty is OLD! Eighty means maybe five, maybe ten years left. Where did my life go? There's much I still want to do. What have I learnt? Have I done the best I could? Have I made a difference? Those are the questions that rush at me.

I am writing this book in an attempt to make sense of my life, to take stock. It's been a full, if chaotic, eighty years. I was born in 1941 at the darkest moment of the war; my parents were convinced that Britain was about to lose. Despite this, the Holocaust and its horrors didn't really impinge on my childhood; it's only later I've come to realise how powerfully and inescapably that shadow has become part of my life.

Growing up in the post war period, with loving parents, I skipped from moment to moment. I've travelled through every continent bar Antarctica, I've slept with a curious variety of humans. I entered a precarious profession where a short, fat, Jewish girl with no neck dared to think she could stand on a stage and be successful. I've completed over five hundred jobs and relished every minute of them. But have I merely skimmed the surface? Why do I still feel so unsure about things? Might a certain level of uncertainty be a good thing? Complete confidence carries smugness alongside – and I do *not* want that. Smugness shows on stage; when you can see a performer admiring their delivery of a certain line, it kills the performance stone dead. It's possible that my insecurity is the very quality that connects me to everyone else. I don't hide my vulnerability. I don't know how.

From the beginnings of my coherent existence, a common thread has been the ease with which I could connect with others. Latterly I've found the joy of using that gift to make documentaries and *listen* to others, rather than talking myself.

I'm quite sure you picked this book up hoping I'd make you laugh. That's what I seem to have become best known for. I lack the filter others possess and out of my potty mouth pop filthy sexual anecdotes, verbal and physical flatulence on a grand scale. I swear, I fart, I draw attention to things best left unremarked – and it seems it's made me popular. Please don't think I'm unaware of my duty to both entertain and shock you, but I won't allow my book to be just dirty talk. Let me tell you the truth about myself, too.

When asked, I said I had never made an attempt to write anything down before. This is not entirely true: when I was nine, in 1950, I wrote my autobiography in a large, blue book without lines. I wish I could find it, but in one of the many moves of my life, that youthful testament disappeared. Since then, I have simply lived my life to its fullest – until 2020 trapped me in Tuscany for eight months and I finally had the time to write it. With help from my loyal friends, many of whom have known me for most of that life, I've been piecing things together and teasing out memories from the deepest recesses of my mind. It's been a fascinating process.

My partner of fifty-three years, Heather, finds such spilling out of all one's deepest, most personal thoughts and fears, excruciating. She said: 'Now, don't let this book be like one of your Graham Norton interviews where all you do is talk smut – it's got to be about things that matter, Miriam.' Heather is a serious person.

Well, I can't please everyone all the time. But I honour the Truth. And within these pages, you will only find Truth, or at least *my* Truth. There will be some smut inevitably, and it might be a bumpy ride, but I promise you the REAL Miriam Margolyes.

Daddy

Daddy was extremely handsome as a young man, despite being below average height. He had a high forehead, glossy black hair, a ravishing smile and a little moustache. He looked rather like Charlie Chaplin. He was a very fine doctor, well-mannered, with a profound sense of right and wrong, and a strong Glasgow accent he never lost. He was an observant Jew and he had no vices – a dram of whisky after the stars came out on *Shabbos* (Sabbath) was all he ever drank. He smoked the occasional cigar, never cigarettes. But he was a weak man. He was basically afraid: afraid of confrontation of any kind, afraid of being overlooked, and yet unable to push himself forward. Of course, he didn't need to: my mother, Ruth, did all the pushing. I think she crushed him a little with her energy and ambition.

Genealogy is my passion: it's being a detective in history. I have no family, no children, no husband, no parents, no brothers and sisters. Genealogy offers me the family I never had. I'm not a lonely person, but I need to investigate the past and find out about lost cousins. It's how I discovered that Mummy's fear of childbirth was based on fact, not just family lore. And when Daddy ended up with dementia he forgot everything from his past, and so it has always been very important for me to remember where he came from . . . Let me tell you about the Margolyes family.

Like many Scottish second-generation immigrant Jews, Daddy was born in 1899 in the great Glasgow slum, the Gorbals. He grew up in poverty in Govanhill, a short walk from the city centre on the south bank of the Clyde. The first born child of Philip Margolyes and Rebecca née Turiansky. I never met my paternal grandfather; he died in 1937, but I did get to know my grandmother, Rebecca, quite well, as she lived till 1959.

Grandpa Margolyes was born in 1874 in a small *shtetl* called Amdur (now Indura) in Belarus, which at that time was part of the Russian Empire. Anti-Jewish feeling started to gather and grow and by 1880 large numbers of poor Jews had made their way across Europe. Many European Jews arrived in Scotland as a stopping post on their way to America. They spoke no English, had no idea about Scotland and probably got out at the port of Leith in Edinburgh, thinking it was New York, the *goldene medina* they dreamed of reaching. The sea captains encouraged them to disembark so they could return more quickly for another boatload of immigrants. They ended up staying, settling mainly in Glasgow, and in particular in Govanhill and the Gorbals.

When my grandfather came to Scotland around 1887, his first job was as a peddler: a traditional Jewish trade, because it requires little capital. Grandpa Margolyes was an itinerant seller of the small gems and trinkets you might find in gift shops. We Jews call them *chatchkes*. He used to put his wares in a pack on his back and traipse around the lowlands of Scotland selling to the miners' wives. He was a quiet, sweet man, liked by his customers who sensed his gentle integrity; they would save up and buy from him each time he came their way. Eventually, after many hard, precarious years plying his trade among the mining communities, he'd saved enough money to be able to buy a small premises in Glasgow in St Enoch Square, and he opened his own jewellery business. The shop was called James McMenamin: he bought it from a Scotsman and never changed the name. While the business did well, he was by no means a millionaire. I still have the well-made wooden coin box from his shop, with scooped holes for farthings, halfpennies, pennies, shillings and sixpences, from before the time cash registers were used, with their pinging drawers to hold the coins.

Philip and Rebecca married in 1897 when they were both twenty-three, and Daddy was born two years later in 1899, when they were living in a tiny, two-room tenement apartment in Allison Street, Govanhill. Then followed Daddy's three siblings: two sisters, Doris (b.1901) and Evalyn, who was always known as Eva (b.1903), and a brother Jacob (Jack), the baby of the family (b.1906). As the family grew, they were sleeping six in a single, cramped room. My father told me he suffered from rickets as a child, a disease of malnutrition and lack of sunlight; he had bow legs as a result.

It was an orthodox Jewish upbringing. Philip and Rebecca were 'frummers'* – pious and observant people. Philip was in thrall to the seriousness of his nature. He was deeply earnest, the kind of man who would never have dreamed of being unfaithful – that would have been unthinkable. (It was my *maternal* grandfather who was the bounder and fucked about, but more on that later.) The Margolyeses kept all the most rigorous strictures of the ultra-Orthodox Jewish faith. It was a *kosher* home life – *Shabbos* began at sundown on a Friday evening and ended only on the appearance of three stars in the sky on the following night. During this time, no work, including no

---

* Not *meshuganeh frummers* – there *is* a difference.

cooking nor reading of any text other than the Jewish scriptures was permitted, nor, later, when the family finally had electricity, could anyone so much as switch on a light.

Daddy told me that as a young man in Glasgow, one Friday night he arrived home and discovered that he'd left his front door key behind. He couldn't press the electric doorbell, which would have infringed the Sabbath rule of not creating a spark, and so he had stood outside in the cold for half the night, and nearly caught his death with a very bad chill as a result. I hope he knocked on the door, but these were big houses and no one can have heard him, so he just stood there, shivering in the sub-zero Glasgow night. Of course, to me that is extraordinary, but that's what he and his family were like.

He might have told me this story to try to explain the culture clash between his family and ours. It would be a source of profound sadness to him to know that I no longer believe in the Jewish faith, although so powerful are the traditions I was taught that I still fast on Yom Kippur, our Day of Atonement, observe the rules of Passover and keep the dietary laws. I have never eaten bacon, although I am told I would love it. I will live and die a Jew, with my culture intact but minus the religion that is at the heart of it.

Daddy's parents spoke and read Hebrew, but they were not formally educated. They were poor but determined that their children would enjoy every benefit of a Scottish education. Daddy was especially bright; as a schoolboy, he won a scholarship to attend Hutchesons' Grammar School in Govanhill. He did so well that he became 'Dux of Hutchie' (*dux* is Latin for 'leader') – a title given to the highest-ranking student in academic, arts or sporting achievement. He always intended to go to university; he was a serious little chap, as you can see from his photo.

By the time Daddy's secondary education came to an end, Grandpa Margolyes's jewellery shop was clearly successful, and the family had moved out of the tenement building on Allison Street to Aytoun Road, in the comparatively upmarket suburb of Pollokshields. The family were still tenants, not well enough off to own their own home, but clearly Grandpa's determination to better the family's prospects and hard work had paid off, and his business was thriving, if not booming. Some years later, Grandpa Margolyes did buy a wonderful house just a short walk further up Aytoun Road. They named it 'Pearl House' (Margolyes means 'pearl'), and had the words engraved on the gate-posts. My grandparents lived out the rest of their lives and died at home in Pearl House. I went there for my holidays as a child and it's always been one of my favourite places in the world.

As the eldest son, my father – Joseph – might comfortably have stepped into his father's shoes at James McMenamin. Daddy, however, had never wanted to go into the family business; he wanted to become a doctor. He had always known that this was his vocation and in 1917, he took the entrance exam at Glasgow University. So it was my father's younger brother, Uncle Jack, who went to work in the shop. Eventually, in 1937, when my grandfather died, Jack inherited the business and he did very well. In fact, Uncle Jack ended up dying an *actual* millionaire.

One morning in 1917, when Daddy was eighteen, he received his call-up papers. It was three years since the beginning of the First World War, and not one of the young men the family knew who had gone off to fight had come back. My grandfather was all too aware that the life expectancy of young officers in the trenches was about six weeks. He was desperate to keep Joseph at home. He telephoned to make an appointment with the commander of the 4th Glasgow Battalion of the Highland Light Infantry, and went to see him that afternoon.

Imagine this little man, a small Jew in his best suit, foreign-looking with a darkish complexion, knocking on the door of the commander's office.

'Come in.'

Philip entered and in front of him, behind a desk, sat a very upright, Scots officer, in full uniform.

The officer said, 'Sit down. What can I do for you?'

My grandfather spoke haltingly, in broken English: 'Firstly, I want to thank you very much for seeing me this afternoon. My son has received his papers to join your regiment and go to France. Sir, he is the thing I love most in the world, my firstborn, my beloved son.' (It always makes me cry when I tell this story.) My grandfather continued, 'I come here to ask for something. It is a very big thing. But I must ask. I want you to take my son's name off the draft. We want him to grow up; he is a fine young man, the first member of our family to go to university, to Glasgow University. He has won a scholarship to study medicine, but if he goes to France that cannot be, because you know and I know that he will not survive. But I cannot just *ask* for something. I must also *give*.'

My grandfather paused, put his hand in his pocket, and when he took it out, there was a glistening diamond lying in the palm. 'This is the most precious jewel in my warehouse. It is not completely flawless, but it is nearly flawless. And I beg that you should take this – *please* take this – please – in exchange for the life of my son.'

I tell this story in my one-woman stage performance, *The Importance of Being Miriam*, and when I reach this moment in the show I pause, and ask the audience, 'What do you think happened?' One night in Adelaide, I overheard two Scottish women talking after the show. One said to the other, 'Did you hear what she said about the commander? That's unthinkable! No Scottish officer would dare to take a bribe.'

But he did and my father's name was taken off the draft. And if he hadn't, I might never have existed. So Daddy survived and thrived and became a doctor.

In those days, to be a doctor (or a lawyer) was the acme of Jewish achievement. It was what every immigrant Jewish family wanted for their child. University was a tough experience for Daddy. Anatomy was a particular disaster for him and he had to take the exam twice.

Daddy graduated in 1926, and then he left Scotland because he wanted to experience life. His first job was as a ship's surgeon, on the Paddy Henderson line, plying between Glasgow and Rangoon. He looked very dashing in the white merchant seaman's uniform, but no one had explained all the rules of shipboard life. Once the ship gets into port, apparently it's the captain's job to issue the command: 'Haul down the yellow flag!' – meaning that the ship is free from disease. As ship's surgeon, Daddy thought it was *his* job, so in a very loud voice, on the top deck, he shouted, 'HAUL DOWN THE YELLOW FLAG!' From the crew's amusement and evident derision, he realised he'd made a gross error. He never forgot the shame he felt and was always severely shy in company, afraid to stand out in any way. That was part of his temperament and he could never understand my delight in being different. He wanted to blend into his surroundings. I never did.

He said Burma (now Myanmar) was enchanting and beautiful, and I think it was that trip that gave him the gentle attitude he always had towards Asian people. Once settled in Oxford, he became the doctor for all the Indian restaurants. His Indian patients particularly appreciated his care of them and we were greeted as honoured guests, we never had to pay; Daddy particularly appreciated that!

On his return to Scotland, Daddy decided to go to London as a locum at a local surgery in East Ham. He got a house in Plaistow and engaged a housekeeper, Miss Shrimpton, to cook and look after him – she stayed with my father and later joined the marital household, only leaving when the house was bombed and my parents left for Oxford. In London, Daddy hoped to settle down and lead the conventional life of a respected doctor.

He was never a sportsman and pointedly despised football and cricket, but a sports club was a place to meet respectable girls. Jews were not welcome at most sports clubs but in a huge place like London he discovered that there were Jewish ones to join instead. And so it was at a Jewish tennis club in south London that Joseph met my mother, and everything changed.

Mummy

Without a doubt, the most important person in my life was my mother. Perhaps she still is. She died in 1974 when I was thirty-three, but she has never left my side. She bound me to her, quite deliberately, with emotional hoops of steel.

Mummy was short and stout, with wavy grey-white hair, piercing blue eyes, a high forehead and a generous mouth. (She looked a lot like Gracie Fields, whom she admired greatly.) Her hands were expressive, with perfect nails and soft skin. Her wedding ring was white gold; she had several beautiful diamond rings, the one I loved best was a solitaire dazzler set in black onyx. She stood very straight and was always telling me to do the same – shoulders back, head erect, no slouching.

She was the most intelligent yet untutored woman that I ever met. In other circumstances, she could have been the head of a company or leading the government, but she came from a poor background, and she was always conscious of that. Like Charles Dickens, she had sprung from the lower-middle class. It's an uncomfortable situation: hampered by poverty and strongly aspirational, she observed keenly the class distinctions which exist in England. She wanted to speak well and meet 'the best people'. She was anxious always to separate herself from the 'common'. The odd thing was that she was endlessly generous to anyone poorer than herself. But she was squeezed in the trap of 'class' – and feared being at the bottom of the social scale. She was a passionate and determined social climber. Her dictum: 'It's not what you know, it's *who* you know, that counts.'

My mother, Ruth Sandeman Walters, was born on 24 January 1905 in Walton Road, Kirkdale, Liverpool, where my grandfather Sigismund 'Siggi' Sandeman had a second-hand furniture business, although he put himself down on the census as an auctioneer.

Jews have lots of names: their birth name, their Yiddish name and, sometimes, the name they chose when they came to England and wanted to anglicise themselves. During the First World War, my grandfather changed the family name from Sandeman to Walters, in order to avoid anti-German feeling: this sentiment was so strong that even the British royal family discreetly shifted their name from Saxe-Coburg to Windsor.

Siggi's parents, Simon and Hanna Sandmann (note the original spelling), came from a small town, Margonin, in the lake district of Western Poland. Grandpa Margolyes came from Amdur (now Indura) in Belarus. I visited there in 2006 while making a BBC Radio 4 documentary called *Sentimental Journey* with Arthur Smith, to see if any traces of my family remain. There are none. All the Jews were obliterated in 1941, when the Nazis arrived and the Final Solution was put into practice.

Grandpa Walters was born in Middlesbrough in 1867; in fact, he has the distinction of being the first Jew to be born there. In those days, Middlesbrough was in Yorkshire, and Siggi was very proud of being a Yorkshireman. He was one of eight siblings: Doris, Rose Rachel, Jacob, Elizabeth, Charles, Solomon and Augusta.

In April 1892, Siggi – a draper – married Flora Posner, the daughter of Jacob Posner, a furrier. Flora was a teacher at the famous Jews' Free School in Bell Lane, Spitalfields, the Eton of the East End. Siggi and

Flora had four children: Mummy's older sister, Gusta (short for Augusta); Doris, second eldest; then my mother, Ruth; and a brother, Jacob, who died as a baby because the nurse dropped him out of the pram. Not intentionally, of course – it was an accident.

Shortly after Mummy was born, the family moved to south-east London where my grandfather was one of the founders and first president of the South East London synagogue in New Cross. The building still stands next to the old fire station, but it's now a Mormon temple. He opened a furniture shop in Church Street, Camberwell, but I think he hoped for more. Much later on, Grandpa Walters went into property, quite successfully, and their last house in Underhill Road, Dulwich, is now worth two million. I wish we'd kept it! Flora and Gusta opened a smart dress and hat shop called Madame Flora in Rye Lane, Peckham. It was such a substantial premises that it was later sold to C & A Modes.

My family story illustrates the archetypal trajectory of a working-class Jewish immigrant family: first, a peddler, then in trade, then in the professions, and then, with me – the third-generation immigrant – in the Arts.

There was always, perhaps, the hint of a leaning towards performance, all the way through my mother's side, because Grandpa not only fancied himself as an auctioneer, but was also an amateur magician of great skill. He had many books on magic and was always performing tricks. He would flourish an egg out of my ear, throw a pack of cards in the air and catch the one I'd named. Siggi was open, funny, handsome and disgracefully charming. He had the same manipulative charm that I've got. Apparently my great-grandfather also had it, and Mummy certainly did. I think there must have been a 'charm gene' in my maternal line. When you have it, you *know* you have it, and you must be very careful not to misuse it. My great-grandfather did misuse it, and most likely my grandfather did too, because everybody seemed to adore him uncritically. (My grandmother Flora did not, however. She was a little sour, perhaps because she knew her beloved Siggi had an eye for the ladies. My cousin Ethel told me he was a devil with the salesgirls in his wife's shop, and 'screwed everything that moved'.)

Last year I discovered beyond all reasonable doubt that Siggi had enjoyed an extramarital fling in 1918. This is how I found out: a man in Swindon, Derek Austin, wrote to me suggesting that we were possibly first cousins: we had both shared our DNA on a genealogical website, and a match had shown up. At first, I was bewildered at this discovery of an unknown relative; I phoned and asked him if he was Jewish. He and his brother had talked and as far as they both knew, there was no Jewish blood in their family. We worked out that his grandmother had lived around the corner from my grandfather in south-east London. He had an affair with this woman, she had a child, and that child had grown up and got married and had two sons. So Derek and I are indeed half first cousins.

I invited him, his wife, Ingrid, and daughter to visit me in London; we had a wonderful day together, bonding and sharing. I am sad to say Derek died shortly afterwards, but I'm still in contact with his family and intend to remain so.

Of course, my dear grandfather could never have imagined that his peccadillo would be discovered over a hundred years later, long after his death in London in 1945 at the age of seventy-eight. Genealogy makes those kinds of family secrets much harder to hide.

There are more colourful characters in my maternal family line. I was in the General Register Office looking for my grandfather's father, Simon Sandeman, on the 1881 census (the first indexed census) and when I found him, next to the name were the letters 'CONV', for 'convict'. It turned out that Simon had a shop in Leicester. In the local directory of 1878 he was listed as a 'wholesale retail jeweller and clock dealer', but in the previous year he had been jailed for fraud and receiving stolen goods, and in the 1881 census, he was serving a seven-year sentence with hard labour, in Parkhurst Prison on the Isle of Wight. Hard labour not only meant the treadmill, just like Oscar Wilde, but that Hanna had to bring up seven children all alone in London, far away from her husband. Grandpa Walters was only ten years old when his father went to prison.

When I first started tracing my family tree, my cousin Buffy, Auntie Gusta's daughter, brought me a couple of photographs from a box she had found in her attic. One of them showed a man dressed in a smart coat, sporting a diamond tie pin and a fine Astrakhan fur hat. No one in my family could tell me anything about him, nor did we have a date, nor know where the photograph was taken. But when I saw my great-grandfather's mugshot taken in jail before his sentence, I realised it was him.

Many of my ancestors emigrated to South Africa in the nineteenth century, so I got in touch with Paul Cheifitz, who comes from Cape Town and who is a specialist on South African Jews. Paul confirmed that shortly after his release from jail, Simon and his wife Hanna had emigrated to South Africa. Two of his daughters had also gone to live there with their husbands in the 1880s, and their families are still there. Presumably he'd had his portrait taken in a studio in

Johannesburg and he had sent it home to England to show his family how well he had done for himself – finally. There is also a photograph of his wife, my great-grandmother Hanna, dressed equally elegantly in black silks, pearl earrings and a fine black hat with an ostrich feather.

Of course, some of my family were not thrilled to learn of our great-grandfather's criminal history. I, however, am absolutely delighted. I am fascinated by the vagaries of my ancestors' lives. I found out that great-grandfather Simon was not the only person with a dubious past. His son, my great-uncle Charles, a senior member of the Durban Synagogue Committee, received a summons for keeping whores in his room in a Johannesburg hotel, described as a 'resort for thieves, drunkards and unsavoury clients'.

On a slightly less sleazy note, I also discovered that four granddaughters of 'the criminal' were music hall artists. The most successful was Bertha, who moved with her German husband, Max Otto Bierman, to Leipzig before the Second World War, where they performed acrobatics and comic songs in a troupe called The Three Ardos.

———

Doris, the second eldest of Flora's children, was the angel of the family. She was brilliant at school and won a scholarship to Goldsmiths College. She would have been the first member of the family to go to university, but she developed meningitis during the First World War and died, aged just seventeen. Like her father, Mummy never got over it; she talked about her sister Doris often, with tears. It was the tragedy of the family. Her other sister, Auntie Gusta (cousin Buffy's mother), was absolutely beautiful – auburn-haired, willowy, and elegantly sexy. Mummy loved her too, but she wasn't special in the way that Doris had been.

When my mother left school at fourteen, she went to work as a salesgirl in Flora's shop. She relished her time working there, delighting in her selling skills, cajoling and sweet-talking a customer until they *had* to buy. One of her stories related how at the end of a day when she'd sold nothing, a woman came into the shop. Mummy was determined to make a sale. The woman tried on hat after hat; Mummy was losing patience. Finally, she jammed a hat on the customer's head and twisted it harshly to get the decoration at the front. The woman screamed, tore the hat off and shouted as she ran out of the shop, 'They do people in, here!'

Mummy was in her mid-twenties when she met Daddy at the Jewish tennis club. She noticed this dapper Scottish chap with his bright face and little moustache – but, more importantly as far as my mother was concerned, she appreciated his status: he was not merely Jewish, but a Jewish *doctor*. My mother confessed that she didn't love my father at first when she married him; she wanted him because she wanted a doctor as a husband. I don't know if he ever knew that and, of course, I never told him, but Mummy told *me* because we told each other everything. She told me that she grew to love him and always said he was a good man and a good husband. He was an honourable person and that was the thing that she loved about him. He had complete honesty, decency and integrity. Mummy recognised that. If he found money in the street, for example, he would take it to the police. I'm not sure Mummy would have, but he would. He was also always scrupulous about his income tax. We weren't particularly well off, but he always said to me, 'Never dodge the taxes! Never cheat the government.' That was one of his criteria for living a decent life.

They got engaged in 1930. At the crowded engagement party at Siggi and Flora's house, her beloved parrot, Polly, collapsed in the heat and was found expired at the bottom of his cage the next day. He used to squawk, 'Polly wants a butty!' (a Merseyside expression for a piece of bread and butter), one of the few remnants of Liverpool in my mother's life.

The wedding reception was held in the Porchester Hall in Bayswater, on the other side of London from the synagogue in New Cross – an absurd expense. The music was supplied by Nat Gonella and his band, the top Jewish orchestra for weddings. The theme of the reception was 'floral and coral', while the bridal party's clothes, chosen by Mummy, were inspired by *Little Lord Fauntleroy*. The honeymoon, chosen by Daddy, was in Norway, sailing up the fjords. They spent their wedding night in the Grosvenor Hotel – very posh. It was the only time in their lives that they went abroad together.

My grandmother Flora wasn't happy. On the morning of the wedding, Grandma said to Mummy: 'Well, you've made your bed and you must lie on it.' She didn't like my father, because she felt he thought he was a cut above them socially, but that's a spiteful thing to say to your daughter on her wedding day. That's what my grandmother could be like, and yet she was all sweetness and light where I was concerned. She *adored* me.

Mummy married Daddy and raised her social status in a single stroke, which is what she intended to do. They went to live at my father's house in Terrace Road, Plaistow, where he was in single-handed practice as a GP. Their household was completed by a wire-haired terrier called Bonny and Daddy's loyal housekeeper, Miss Shrimpton.

Mummy was the rock in my life. It was not that I didn't love my father, but he was quiet, and she was not. In some senses, they were incompatible. They came from very different strands of Jewish life. Mummy was the most vivid person I have ever known. She was an overflowing, ebullient, seemingly confident and, if I'm honest (and I must be), slightly vulgar person, while my father was totally buttoned-up, very Presbyterian and hemmed in by all the orthodoxy of Judaism to which his family subscribed. My mother was more of a free spirit: accomplished and brave and fearless.

While undeniably much more like my mother, I remain a strange mixture of them both to this day.

Enter Miriam

Daddy was forty-two when I was born, in 1941. Ruth, my mother, was thirty-seven; they were relatively old to be having a first child. But it was deliberate: most newly married couples try to have children, but for ten years my parents tried *not* to. It was my mother's wish. Two of her cousins in South Africa had died in childbirth, and she was terribly afraid it was a family curse and that the same fate would befall her. So, for eleven years after their marriage no child was born. But, eventually, at the beginning of the Blitz, to Mummy's despair, she conceived. I was told it was the terror of an air raid pounding above the cellar where they were sheltering that allowed Daddy in – and me to be born. Mummy always said that was why I had curly hair. She wanted desperately to have an abortion, but it was against the law and no one would do it. So, she held on to me and never, for the rest of her life, let me go.

It was in early 1941, when Mummy was four months pregnant with me, that my parents were bombed out. Their house in Plaistow had a direct hit. They lost everything. They fled to Oxford, because people said that Oxford would never be bombed. And it never was. Apparently, Hitler had planned that it would be his capital when he won the war, because it was such a beautiful city. The other, more pragmatic, reason why we ended up in Oxford was that their car, a Morris Oxford, was already in a garage there for repair, so they left London on a train and came to Oxford with nothing but the clothes on their backs. They found a room to rent on the Cowley Road for £2/10s (two pounds and ten shillings) a night. That was a lot of money in those days: Oxford people were greedy and exploitative and fleeced the refugees and the people who had to escape from London during the war.

My parents came to Oxford very much as 'outsiders', and it has always been an unfriendly city to outsiders. It's not a warm, welcoming place. It's a cold, assessing place, and it is also an antisemitic one. As a Jew *and* a Scotsman with a strong Glaswegian accent, Daddy must have felt especially incongruous.

Eventually, they found a flat in Banbury Road, North Oxford, and I was born on 18 May 1941 in the Elizabeth Nuffield Maternity Home on the corner of Beech Croft Road. It's now an old people's home.

The name Miriam means 'bitter', 'star of the sea' and 'longed-for child', but the meanings were immaterial. Mummy named me after her favourite aunt, her mother's sister – a dark, pretty little woman, who died a widow in 1933. I was a much prized, spoilt, golden child; my parents' *only* child, the centre of their worlds. They were determined I should have every advantage they'd been denied. They wanted to make sure I'd be accepted, that no door would be shut to me. And it was a very secure upbringing. I never felt underprivileged. I always felt that I was important, because I was to my parents. Everything I did fascinated them: I always had their undivided attention and their all-consuming, unconditional adoration.

Just the three of us: it was passionate, close, indulgent. Mummy[*] often said, 'We are a fortress family.' That was her expression, and I

---

[*] I would never have said 'Mum and Dad' – it was always 'Mummy and Daddy'. It was North Oxford, you see.

don't for a second regret my closeness to them because they gave me so much confidence. The umbilical cord was never completely cut, metaphorically speaking: I still feel connected to them long after their deaths.

My earliest memory is of sitting in my pram, sucking my thumb, in the front garden of our flat on Banbury Road. A woman came up and said, 'If you do that, a bogeyman will cut it off.' I was only two, but I thought, 'That woman's mad. How stupid of her. Of course there isn't a bogeyman. No one's coming.' I was immediately sceptical, and convinced I was right.

Nothing has changed.

I was four when the war ended, in 1945. Mummy decided that Victory in Europe Day must be marked in some way. 'We'll make tea and sandwiches for the bus crews,' she announced. I had no idea what this meant, but I was clearly involved. Trestle tables were set up outside the house and all morning we made sandwiches; Mummy was the best sandwich-maker I've ever known. She sliced tomatoes and onions frighteningly thin, but cheese was generously applied. Our home-made gooseberry jam from the garden was spread with cream on delicious scones. The plates were piled high; we had cakes too, bought from the Cadena Cafe in Cornmarket Street, whose patisseries and cream-filled chocolate doughnuts were legendary. She lifted me up to hand the goodies to the conductors and the bus drivers in their cabs. It was a glorious memory; we were released from the horrors of the war and everyone wanted to celebrate.

Mummy composed a song, the 'Victory Song'. I remember only the first line: 'Now victory is here . . .' One day we went to the New Theatre, and the whole orchestra played her song. Daddy and Mummy and I sat in the front stalls, rigid with pride.

Mummy used to say, 'You don't know what life was . . . what we had before the war.' That phrase 'before the war' implied a kind of paradise time when everything was as it should be. It was clearly a way of life that had disappeared for ever.

We Are a Fortress Family

Our 'fortress' was a ground-floor and basement flat on Banbury Road, between Beech Croft Road and Moreton Road. It was awful – very damp and dark; Mummy called it 'the hovel'. She hated living there and from the moment they moved in, she planned and schemed to get out of it. But Daddy didn't make enough on his own to rescue them.

In those days, doctors in general practice were paid per capita; leaving Plaistow had meant saying goodbye to a profitable practice. It wasn't easy to start from scratch. As soon as they arrived in Oxford, Daddy put up his brass plate on the door of the surgery he rented in Cherwell House, a fine Georgian residence backing on to the river at St Clement's, and hoped that patients would come. Eventually, they did, but then Magdalen College decided to demolish the house (Robert Maxwell's publishing empire, Pergamon Press, replaced it – a hideous concrete structure). For a while, Daddy had no surgery at all and saw patients at our house, but Mummy fought Magdalen College on his behalf and, after a fierce struggle, secured a small but pleasant property opposite the back door of the college at 4 Longwall Street. That was where Daddy practised medicine until he retired.

Gradually, single-handedly, Daddy built up his practice. Later on, in 1948, when the National Health Service came into existence, my father welcomed it wholeheartedly. Despite voting Conservative, he believed in the principle of social welfare, in the idea of looking after his patients from the cradle to the grave. The hierarchy in private medicine enraged him; everybody bowed down to the hospital consultant. Daddy reaped satisfaction from treating his patients, and had no further aspirations. He was an old-style family doctor carrying a little Gladstone bag, complete with stethoscope and otoscope; he took time to listen to his patients; he got up in the middle of the night to attend house calls because it was his vocation – making money was never Daddy's objective.

Mummy might not have had a formal education, but she understood people. She was shrewd; she was businesslike. Daddy was none of those things. He was a high-minded physician with a love of words and scholarship. So, while I was still a baby and they were still trying to establish a proper living in Oxford, Mummy was constantly thinking of ways to make money and escape from 'the hovel'. She asked herself: 'What is it they have here that they don't have in other places?' The answer? Students. Thousands and thousands of students. She knew that not all students live in college, and those that didn't needed accommodation.

Mummy requisitioned the upstairs rooms in Daddy's surgery at Longwall Street for letting to students, carrying out her favourite maxim: 'Make every post a winning post.' Then Grandpa Walters gave her a loan and she started out with one house in Old High Street, Headington, eventually going on to own about seven – all rented out to students. Mummy was considered to be the best landlord in Oxford. (She was adamant that she was never to be called a landlady – she was a landlord.) Much later, when I was in my teens, I became her cleaner. I used to have to go and scrub the houses out between tenancies. Some of the students were tidy and some were not. I remember that Tariq Ali left owing Mummy £100. I keep meaning to tell him, and one of these days I'll get hold of him. (Or maybe he'll pay up if he reads this book!)

We had a classy list of tenants, including the writer Ferdy Mount – in his autobiography, *Cold Cream*, I feature, along with my mother. We also housed Jacob Rothschild, 4th Baron Rothschild, OM, GBE, CVO, FRCA, the British peer and investment banker; Rachel Pakenham, the third daughter of the 7th Earl and Countess of Longford, who became Rachel Billington (Mummy particularly loved her); Paul Betjeman (son of John); and Robert Maclennan, the future MP. There was also Francis Hope, a very wonderful writer, who died in the Turkish Airlines plane crash in 1974.

Mummy always knew immediately if someone was lying, whereas Daddy was more trusting of people's inherent good character. She was very canny in all sorts of ways: a fascinating mixture of business acumen and emotional sensitivity.

Sympathetic, funny, sharp as a tack – Mummy loved business: selling, making money, that was her pleasure. She was good at it, and good at being the boss. And so, whenever they had any difficulties, or if there was confrontation in any sort of situation, Daddy would say, 'You speak, Ruth.' And she would. I remember the rage I felt at his weakness. I used to despise him for that. It made me furious that he wouldn't stand up and speak for himself, but he had no confidence and didn't feel that he would prevail in any argument. Mummy fought for all of us and made all the big decisions in the family.

Mummy was extremely house-proud, and she did all the housework in the nude. It was a tad discomforting for our maids and au pair girls, but she liked to get it done, then have a bath. Mummy always had somebody to help in the house. Even when she was a child growing up in south-east London, my grandmother had employed a maid, Lizzie. To Mummy, it was an essential part of modern life. She was quite a tough employer, but always kind. When I went to Cambridge in 1960, she wanted a young person in the house, and started to have live-in au pair girls instead of maids. They were all innocent young things from various European countries, and her nudism most definitely upset them at first, but they got used to it. There was Marie Claire from France, Boyte from Norway, Simone from Sweden (we became friends and I went to stay with her family in Stockholm – her father was the *stadsfiskal*), but the most treasured one was Mummy's first au pair, a sweet young girl from Vercelli in northern Italy, Francesca Franco. Her father was a rice farmer; I remember when he brought us a large sack of rice as a present, it lasted for a year. Franca was quiet, studious and ambitious. I was delighted when it was clear Mummy saw her as another daughter. They remained close and even after Mummy's death, Franca became like a sister to me. In fact, I invited her to represent my mother and join me and my beloved cousin on Daddy's side, Penelope Lerner, when Prince Charles presented me with the OBE at Buckingham Palace in 2002. Franca is still one of my closest friends; and her son Paolo is a glorious young man. I want them in my life for ever.

As Daddy was far more straight-laced than Mummy, I don't know how he reacted when he first discovered my mother's penchant for dusting the picture rails nude. He joined the qualities of being Jewish and being Scottish together – a formidable combination. A sombre, emotionally reserved man, he was measured, entirely moderate in every respect. He would always say, 'Miriam, behave yourself.' Of course, I haven't, alas. He was a man who found it difficult to express joy, whereas my mother was a forthrightly joyous person. She was also tempestuous, *un*measured and *im*moderate in almost every aspect of her personality – and her habits.

They both agreed, however, that I must be educated. They encouraged my reading and studying from an early age. I liked Enid Blyton's *Sunny Stories* and Miss Blyton's oeuvre in general; I didn't have an elevated literary world. I joined a library; in those days, local councils put money into libraries and the Oxford City Library was magnificent. I used to get through about six books a week. I loved stories set in girls' schools; I think I read nearly all fifty-seven of the *Chalet School* series: *The Exploits of the Chalet Girls, The Chalet School Triplets, Excitements at the Chalet School, A Genius at the Chalet School*, etc. etc. etc., by Elinor Brent-Dyer. I especially enjoyed the 'Dimsie' books by Dorita Fairlie Bruce, or *The Girls of St Bride's, That Boarding School Girl*, and *The Best Bat in the School*, etc., in her long-running St Brides and Maudsley series featuring Nancy Caird.

Daddy was not artistic; he went to the theatre only because Mummy insisted. He thought films and theatre were unnecessary, slightly absurd. He was tone-deaf, a legacy he passed to me which I could have done without. He didn't notice pictures, or other works of art. When he was in his nineties, living with me in London, I commissioned Anne Christie to paint his portrait. He didn't like the finished picture – 'I look so small,' he complained. It hangs behind me as I type – I love it. Daddy did enjoy the radio, and listened every night when he came home from surgery. *It's That Man Again* was a great favourite and, later, when television was permitted to enter the house,[*] *Dad's Army*. He never told jokes but he was a terrible tease. I hated being teased, and he never stopped.

Mummy appreciated literature, but she especially loved going to the ballet and the theatre. She insisted that she and my father continued to go to the theatre in Oxford every week as they had done in London, and they had permanent seats at the New Theatre Oxford (now the Apollo).

When I was five, my parents took me to my first pantomime, which was *Aladdin*. Of course I loved it, but I was very frightened of the wicked wizard, Abanazar. I had nightmares every night for a week. Finally, my parents decided to take me backstage to meet the actor, so that I would see for myself that he was only pretending. That's the magic word – pretending. It is the beginning of imagination.

Mummy also adored music. Her favourite singers were Conchita Supervía, the Spanish mezzo-soprano, and Gracie Fields. My mother insisted on having a piano, and she and I used to sing music-hall songs together. We often sang 'Sally', Mummy sitting at our Blüthner baby grand piano in the drawing room, tears rolling down her cheeks. I used to ask her, 'Mummy, why are you crying?' and she'd say, 'I can't help it. It's so beautiful.' And now I'm exactly the same: I weep uncontrollably at a piece of music, an operatic aria, even a military band marching past. She filled my memories. Filled my heart. And she always will.

---

[*] We didn't have a television for a long time: my parents felt it would distract me from study and so deprived themselves and me.

I loved Daddy, no question; he was a dear, dear man and it's from him that I get my love of words, but we never understood each other. Mummy flooded me. She was fun to be with and so we were always in cahoots, in that sense.

Every morning when I wasn't at school – weekends, or holidays – when Daddy was up and going off to work, I'd go to my parent's bedroom and climb into Mummy's bed. They had two beds pushed together. Mummy always slept naked and I liked hugging her generous adipose tissue. We talked about *everything*. It was during one of our bedroom talks that she told me she had not been in love with Daddy when they married. We had unlikely conversations: politics, people in synagogue and what they were wearing, what furniture Mummy wanted to buy, or about the tenants in her houses. I loved hearing about life in London before the war, and her days as a sales girl in Madame Flora. I had no filter with her. We talked about school and the people that I went to school with and what they were doing. There was no subject that was taboo; we were completely open with each other and we would often just lie in helpless giggles. Mummy had big plans. She was always talking about moving out of 'the hovel' and building our 'family home' – what the bathrooms were going to be like and what the size of the kitchen would be.

The time she spoke of most, though, was when her parents moved to Underhill Road, in Dulwich. They had previously lived in Camberwell, which was considered a lower-class area at the time – Dulwich was a step up. From the beginning, Mummy instilled in me who were the people to be friends with and who were 'common' (and so to be avoided). My ear became attuned early to the minute gradations of class, indicated by a thickening and mangling of the vowels, a dropping of the consonants. She also talked often about who, amongst our acquaintances and Daddy's patients, she considered to be 'the best people'. She had that concept in her mind, which I think a lot of poor people have – that there actually is such a thing as *the best people*, but by that she didn't mean the socially important. She actually meant the sort that *I* would call the best people: the thinkers, the philosophers, the historians – because the life of the mind was very important to my mother.

At the same time Mummy enjoyed making money. It allowed her to indulge her passion for fine things. She always wore the original 4711 Eau de Cologne. She often wore a cape instead of a coat and I remember my embarrassment sometimes when she came to school. As a child, you want your parents to fit in with everyone else's parents – Mummy never did. Now, of course, I'm very proud of her individuality. She liked to wear Cuban heels, duster coats, and in the days when fur coats were politically acceptable (not that she would have cared), she had minks, ermines and a glorious leopard-skin coat, all made for her by one of my father's patients, Sam Dimdore, a furrier from London who had also settled in Oxford during the war and had a shop in High Street. His wife Lil made the best cheesecake I'd ever tasted. She had multiple sclerosis and was a sad figure, always seated in the back of the dark shop. Later, their son, Mervyn, contracted the same disease. I knew early of tragedy.

Mummy despaired of my lack of style. 'Take a pride in your appearance,' she would say repeatedly. I never did. Growing up, I hated our necessary, but often fruitless, shopping trips. I detested the shopkeeper telling us, 'I'm afraid we've nothing in her size.' And so we went to Miss Norridge, Mummy's dressmaker just off Walton Street in the centre of Oxford. More than anything, though, I wanted to have a man's suit, male in every particular. Was I 'butch' as a little girl? No – I simply wanted not to have to wear dresses. Now, I adore the little summer frocks I have, always made to the same pattern. There is a subtle difference between a frock and a dress. Mine are all 'frocks'. They've all been made for me by various wardrobe mistresses on every film and play I've ever done. I look like a throwback to the 1950s, but they're comfy and suit me and they ALL have pockets. Pockets are essential in my life, and every garment I own must have them.

When I look back to the 1940s when I was a child, it seems an impossibly distant landscape, much simpler, less adorned. The only times we left Oxford was to see family or to go on holiday. Most of our times away were spent in Scotland with my father's family. These were not exactly relaxing breaks: my mother really didn't like my father's family and they didn't like her. She thought they were hard and mean; they thought she was vulgar.

My father's brother, Jack, had married an Irish girl called Muriel and they had one daughter, my cousin Philippa, whom I adored for most of my life. I think Auntie Muriel was far more vulgar than Mummy. My mother called her 'the scum of the Liffey'. And she was a *Jewish* Irish girl! I remember Mummy saying to her once, 'When you go past a dustbin, you don't lift the lid.' I don't know what that means but it is obviously an insult.

Uncle Jack and Auntie Muriel came down from Glasgow to Oxford to visit me when I was very little. I must have been about one and still in my playpen in the back garden at Banbury Road. I wasn't wearing a nappy and I had done a poo on the ground. This nice lady, Auntie Muriel (actually, she was a complete cunt, but I didn't know that because I was only a baby), came over to the playpen and said, 'Oh, what a sweet little lovely.' I must have thought, 'What a nice, friendly lady!' because apparently I toddled over to my recently laid turd, picked it up and gave it to her. To her credit, she was polite: she accepted my gift, saw what it was, gave a great scream and then ran away. I think that was it, as far as Auntie Muriel and I were concerned. She never showed me much affection after that.

One holiday, when I was about nine, I stayed with Uncle Jack, Auntie Muriel and cousin Philippa in their home in Albert Drive. My parents were staying around the corner in Aytoun Road with Auntie Eva, Uncle Harold and Grandma Margolyes. I was in my bedroom and I remember vividly that Muriel came in and shut the door behind her, then she stood in front of it, her back against the door, the way they do in Hollywood movies. She said to me in her Irish accent, smiling slightly: 'Your mammy doesn't love you.'

What a shocking thing to say to a child; I knew that even then. I replied, 'Of course she does. What do you mean?' She said, 'No, your mammy doesn't love you, because if your mammy loved you, she'd buy you nice clothes, and she'd do your hair nicely and then you'd look nice, but you don't look nice. So your mammy doesn't love you.' Such a statement could have been incredibly destructive for a child, but I had complete confidence in my mother's utter devotion to me. I replied, 'Oh, don't be ridiculous. Of course, she loves me. You're quite wrong about that.' The power of our 'fortress family' meant that I knew she was talking rot and that for some reason – beyond my childish comprehension – she wanted to hurt me. Nothing more was said – then or ever. She opened the door and I went out. I told my parents, and it merely confirmed their opinion of Muriel Margolyes, née White. I never stayed there on my own again.

This didn't affect my friendship with Philippa, their much loved only child who was a few years older than me. Our only wobble came when I picked up the phone to her boyfriend who was so taken with my educated voice and cut crystal tones, that he couldn't stop talking about it. I was around thirteen and seventeen-year-old Philippa was not amused at all: 'Och, what sort of conversation did you have with him?' I said, 'I don't know, I can't remember, I just answered the phone.' She said, 'Well, he thinks you're pretty hot stuff but you're just a schoolgirl.' But I found that so funny that eventually she burst out laughing too.

My other aunt in Scotland, my father's sister, Evalyn (always called Auntie Eva) was wonderful. As a child, I loved staying with her and her husband, Uncle Harold, who was also a doctor. He had a charming personality, urbane and comical, with a little moustache and smiley eyes. His great passion was watching wrestling on television. We didn't have a television when I was little, so it was a great treat to watch the wrestling with him; he taught me all the moves. He would point them out, and I remember that I was very impressed by the Boston Crab. (It's a hold that is very difficult to get out of, in case you ever need it.) I became quite the expert; we would sit together watching a match, and I would say, 'Oh, look at that, Uncle Harold! He's just pulled off the Boston Crab! (Or the Half Nelson Choke, Cobra Clutch, or Tongan

Death Grip, or whatever feat had just been performed.) And Uncle Harold would proudly say, 'Yes, that's it, Miriam. You're right there. He's got him.'

Auntie Eva was jolly and kind and had enormous breasts – obviously a family trait. I can remember her washing her bosoms in the bathroom at the basin, lifting up the pendulous flaps and sponging beneath them. I gazed fascinated, but doubted I would ever have such encumbrances. How wrong I was!

Once she asked me, 'Miriam, do I have a Scottish accent?'

'Yes, Auntie Eva, you do.'

She was a little put out. 'Och, I do not,' she replied.

How wrong she was!

—

Perhaps in response to these tense times in Pollokshields, in addition to Mummy's burgeoning property empire in Oxford, my parents bought a small house by the sea in east Kent, in Kingsgate, a suburb of Cliftonville, which is itself a suburb of Margate. My first holiday, that is to say my first seaside holiday, was to set the pattern for all my most enjoyable childhood excursions.

I was four and a half. We drove from Oxford to Kingsgate in the Standard Eight car – a most unreliable and cluttered vehicle, it stood for years in our front garden unused, until someone bought it for £50 and called it 'vintage'. It took six hours, going through the Blackwall Tunnel, which had white tiled walls and a roaring sound and went under the River Thames. On the way we stopped for fish and chips in Lewisham; wrapped in newspaper (it always tasted better, why did they change the law?) with liberal dashings of salt and vinegar eaten sitting in the car. Then on to Percy Avenue, a long ribbon of a road ending with a clifftop and THE SEA.

I'd been promised that I would see THE SEA, would swim in it, and make sandcastles in the sand. Daddy had bought me a bucket and spade and I was told to wait till the morning. But, of course, I was up before my parents – I wasn't going to wait for them to awaken, I needed to see this phenomenon for myself. So, at about 8 a.m., having dressed myself, I opened the front door and down the road I went.

Soon I couldn't help noticing a huge, blue expanse facing me at the bottom of the street. It seemed to go right up to the sky. I had never seen anything like it before and I remember that blinding moment of recognition, that light breaking into my brain: 'Of course! This must be THE SEA.' I headed onwards to the edge of the cliff and, at that moment, heard screams from behind me up the street, and turned to see my distraught mother racing towards me. 'Miriam, Miriam, stay where you are, don't move, you bad girl, what are you doing, don't move, don't move!'

We both got over it, but I never forgot my first sight of the sea, its immensity and sparkle, the sound and the smell. I've loved it ever since. Much later, when I was thirty-six, I bought the nearest house to France to gaze at it always: across that same English Channel, for me as magical as any ocean.

And now I never get spanked for getting up early and rushing towards it.

Going to School

When I was little I was ravishing. I was glorious – truly gorgeous, impish and mischievous and adorable. I have no doubt at all that I would have fallen in love with myself. When I look at photographs of myself as that little girl, and then I look at myself now, I think, 'Oh, dear!' but that's what happens. You have to take the rough with the smooth.

In 1945, when I turned four, I started at Greycotes School, which was a good private day and boarding school for girls in north Oxford. I was only there for half a year. It had a reputation, I learned afterwards, of receiving girls who hadn't got into Oxford High School and might be classed as 'slow learners'. Mummy may have known this and been all the more determined to get me into Oxford High School at the first opportunity.

The headmistress of Greycotes, Mrs Cunliffe, was tall and kind. Greycotes had a meadow. I'd never heard that word before, but it turned out to be a large patch of green behind the high wall of the school, minutes away from 'the hovel'.

I liked going to school; I have always needed other people around me. We walked in a crocodile; I'd never heard that word, either. Greycotes has receded from my mind, but there is still a Cunliffe Close off Banbury Road. I think Mrs Cunliffe would be delighted about that.

Later that year, Mummy removed me from Greycotes, as she had heard there was a vacancy in the preparatory department of Oxford

High School. The war had just ended and times were hard, but somehow my parents found the money to pay my school fees, first in the preparatory department, which was in St Margaret's Road; and then in the junior school in another building; and then later I moved into the 'big school' on Banbury Road.

The preparatory department of Oxford High School comprised three forms: lower kindergarten (Miss Franklin), upper kindergarten (Miss Farrands), and transition (Miss Fuller). Miss Franklin was a dear woman. She had white hair and a broken nose; she always wore a thick, blue tweed suit and seemed capable. Afterwards, we discovered her lover was Miss West, the senior school games mistress. They retired at the same time and stayed together until they died.

We had a Swiss student supply teacher, with plaits wrapped around her head like Heidi. Her grasp of English was insecure: I giggled at her pronunciation of *oven* – 'OFF-VEN,' she said over and over again. I was helpless with laughter. I've always loved accents. There were only two boys in the prep department: Mark Turner, who was ginger with big teeth, and very tall Robin Houghton. I saw Mark having a pee when I opened a loo door once, thinking it was empty, and was AMAZED to see him standing up with his back to me. 'Boys are *odd*,' I thought.

The Prep. Dep (as it was known) was a happy place; they were excellent teachers and took care of us. There was milk in little bottles – we could have it hot or cold. The only drawback was that every day after lunch, we had 'rest'. We lay on the floor under blankets and were supposed to sleep. I hated it. I couldn't sleep – I've always been a bad sleeper and we were boisterous and noisy, pinching each other and sniggering.

In the transition year, we had a concert. I recited, 'Some one came knocking/At my wee, small door . . .'* Apparently, I was rather good, showing off at an early age.

In autumn 1948, my form moved to the junior school in Bardwell Road, near the famous Dragon School. Miss Temple was the first-form mistress. Her worn, lined face topped with iron-grey hair could have been formidable, but she was the sweetest soul; clearly, she loved teaching and my memories of her are entirely positive. However, Miss Chase, who took the lower second, was the one I loved. I don't know why I loved her so much. I can't remember anything about her, or any reason why I should have felt so desperately, passionately involved, other than she had golden hair, a white face and red cheeks, like an apple. It was Miss Chase who was responsible for my first orgasm, when I was eight. I was walking past her house in Banbury Road with my mother and as I approached it, I felt this overpowering heat in my loins that was deeply pleasant and rather exhausting. She wasn't even in sight! There was no friction – it was simply the power of longing and desire. I don't think you ever know why you feel such passion for people. It is inexplicable. It's been like that ever since.

Miss Plummer taught Scripture. I stayed for the Old Testament lessons only, at my parents' request. Everyone in her class remembers Miss Plummer going up and down the rows of desks intoning: 'The Assyrian is the Lord's rod, the Assyrian is the Lord's rod' over and over again. Drama was part of her teaching method, and she would re-enact the Covenant between God and Man, clasping her hands tightly

---

* 'Some One' by Walter de la Mare.

together; then to show how the Covenant was severed, she pulled her clasped hands violently apart. I still remember that the sign of the First Covenant is circumcision (but Miss Plummer avoided any re-enactment of that).

The teacher I hated, truly loathed – and I suspect it was mutual – was Miss Palser. Ugly, with a mouth too full of teeth and slightly over-weight, she was a cruel sniper of a woman. My parents suspected she was an antisemite, although she treated my non-Jewish form-mate, Valerie Rowe, with the same cutting sarcasm. Valerie left after a term of Miss Palser. She took every opportunity to make me feel small and inadequate, doled out frequent bad reports and detentions, and often reduced me to tears. When I was asked to donate to a retirement present for her, long after I'd left the school, I refused.

From the junior school we moved to the lovely old buildings at Banbury Road. This had been the original Oxford High School, founded in 1875 but now it held only the senior school. There was a tuck shop opposite: great excitement when sugar came off the ration in September 1953. My favourite was sherbet with a liquorice straw in the middle of the packet, through which the sherbet was violently sucked.

It was in that old building in Banbury Road that the bulk of my schooldays were passed. From the lower fourth to the third year sixth I was with the same form-mates, the same teachers. It was a powerful, female world and it satisfied every need I could have for learning and for companionship.

Finally, while I was in senior school at Oxford High, we moved from Banbury Road into the new buildings in Belbroughton Road. ('Belbroughton Road is bonny, and pinkly bursts the spray/ Of prunus and forsythia across the public way.' That, for your delectation, is from a Betjeman poem about Belbroughton Road.)

―――

Mummy was entirely right. Oxford High School wasn't just any school: it had pretensions. It would have been a difficult job to be headmistress there because the parents would always have thought they knew better: the dons of Oxford are a conceited bunch. But our imposing headmistress, Vera Stack, had a proper respect for academia. When Sir Arthur Norrington, Master of Trinity, came to the school – his daughter, Pippa, was a pupil – Miss Stack practically genuflected. Pippa was a very tall, slim, clever girl, who looked rather like Virginia Woolf; she became head girl. One exciting day her corsets were found in Lost Property. The news ran through the school, inflaming everyone but only enhancing her popularity.

Miss Stack always put Gown before Town, and her social and intellectual attitudes permeated the school. 'Scholarship girls' from the county, who entered after passing the eleven-plus exam, were conscious of being second-class citizens, although I'm ashamed to say I never realised that until many years later when, at one of our old girls' reunions, Catherine Bowley said, 'You never asked us to your parties.' Yes, I was a snob too.

The school also had a sense of itself as academically pre-eminent, perhaps because many of the pupils were daughters of dons, including J. L. Austin, the philosopher; J. R. R. Tolkien, the writer; Russell Meiggs, whose subject was ancient history and who looked like Wild Bill Hickok; and William Walsh, another philosopher, whose daughter

Catherine was in my form – she came to stay with us when her mother was having a hysterectomy, and she was quite surprised we didn't wear gloves at teatime.

Catrina Tinbergen, in the form above me, became a good friend. Her father, Niko Tinbergen, won the Nobel Prize in 1973 for Physiology. Deh-I Hsiung's father wrote a successful play *Lady Precious Stream* performed in London and on Broadway. Teachers told us later that our form was a remarkable year and I think it must have been. It is those form-mates who made my life at Oxford High School so glorious – I can name them all without a pause. I think of them often and cannot ever express how happy their friendships made me, how deeply I am in their debt for the fun we had – the walks home from school with Catherine Pasternak Slater (niece of Boris, the writer) and Anna Truelove, my particular chums – and the discoveries of Life we shared.

After school, I would often go to Catherine's house in Park Town, full of her grandfather Leonid's oil paintings, and listen to her mother and her two handsome brothers, Michael and Nicholas, playing Scriabin on the piano. Her mother, Lydia, would make us borscht and I was allowed, for a while, a glimpse into the Russian intellectual environment. Mrs Pasternak Slater was determined her children would go to Oxford. They all went; they all got starred Firsts and were brilliant and, to Anna and me, fascinating. Lydia was a distinguished poet in her own right so she found me unbearably trivial. But Catherine laughed at my jokes – she still does.

Anna's parents were much racier: Anna called her parents by their first names – Joan and Sidney (Mummy thought that was rather shocking). They were remarkable personalities: Sidney Truelove, jokey with a bushy moustache, was a specialist in ulcerative colitis at the Radcliffe Hospital; Joan was larky and elegant and beautiful. She lived to be nearly one hundred and never lost her humour and vitality. Anna and Catherine continue to live in Oxford; they are still precious to me.

I will be forever grateful to my parents for paying for my schooling – I wasn't clever enough to win a scholarship, and the gift they gave me has lasted my entire life. It was a special place and it will always hold a special place in my heart.

Despite this, my parents often had to visit the school and apologise for me. I was a *very* naughty schoolgirl – more of which later – and I was always being dismissed from class and sent to stand outside Miss Stack's office. Vera Stack was tall and buck-toothed, with a huge but controlled bust. We would say, 'Ms Stack was stacked.' Her efficient brassiere held her gigantic bosom in check – once encased, it didn't budge. She wore severe, tailored suits rather than dresses. I doubt she ever had a boyfriend in her life; she was born to be a teacher and she knew it. Miss Stack had been the head of studies at Holloway Prison and she brought some of that penal institution's techniques back to Oxford High School. She was stern, and had genuine authority – you felt that you were in the presence of a general. She didn't chat to us, but she knew the name of every child in the school. Her sister, Peggy Stack, had been one of the founders of the League of Health and Beauty – one of the first mass keep-fit systems to be devised and used in the UK. (Mummy was a member and I think it was from there that she got the idea of nude housework. 'This "skin-airing" should be practised daily with nothing on – in private,' wrote Mollie Bagot Stack, the leading light of the League.)

Peggy Stack used to give concerts at the school, singing songs like 'There's a Hole in My Bucket' and 'A Frog He Would a-Wooing Go' ('with a rowley, powley, gammon and spinach'), her fingers clasped in front of her, both thumbs and index fingers lightly touching. But Miss Stack's true passion was for Robert Browning; on her retirement she wrote an excellent book on the letters of Robert and Elizabeth Browning. I was quite frightened of her, but not frightened enough to be well-behaved – Miss Stack had grey hair by the time I left. When Mummy died, she wrote me a most beautiful letter in her immaculate, immediately recognisable handwriting.

Many years later I was highly entertained to read my own mock obituary in our OHS form magazine of the time.[*]

And now we must say our goodbyes to M*R**M who has inflicted the school with her presence since she was a happy member of the lower kindergarten. She has offered the school many proofs of her abounding energy and versatility. Her name has always been the first one entered in the Report Book since she was eligible for reports; her familiar face, framed in that flowing aura of raven locks greeted the Detention Mistress on countless Thursday afternoons and I myself have often had the pleasure of calling her to my room. She was School Boxing Champion from 1953 – 1955 during which time three of her challengers were sent to the Churchill [hospital]. Her merry

---

[*] An archive lovingly preserved by Biddy Peppin, another valued old school chum.

voice booming along the corridors has cheered many a despairing examinee and enlivened many a flagging Hockey team, often at the same time. We send our best wishes and love to M*R**M in her new career as Probation Officer and hope she will often come and see us again in her official capacity.

I can't imagine why the authors asked to remain anonymous.

⁓

I wanted to stand out, to be odd and talked about. It worries me now that my behaviour may just have been a therapy for my insecurities, but no such introspection deterred me then. I carried a collection of stones around with me for a while and would spend a long time, dramatically arranging them on my desk at the start of lessons and loudly introducing them to the class. 'This [half-brick] is Methuselah, he's sensitive, please don't upset him.' I had become the form wag, and people laughed at my exploits; even at sports – indeed, especially at sports – where I was spectacularly inadequate; if a team were being chosen, I would always be the last to be picked. I realised early on that making people laugh was as useful as athletic skill. The only way I could score at hockey (I played in the left inner position) would be to run in a funny way or shout out rude things. My opponents would be forced to stop because they were in paroxysms of laughter and then I'd be off with the ball, dribbling clumsily in the direction of the goal. I didn't have to engage in the unseemly hurly burly of a tackle and I was quite fast. I've always seen myself as a little, darting thing but now, alas, I have to admit that vision is wholly incorrect.

I realised then, I suppose, that laughter was like love and, then as now, I can't get enough of it. When I asked Liz Hodgkin, still one of my closest friends, what I was like at school, she said I was always asking: 'Do you like me?' I desperately wanted to be liked. I'd do almost anything to be liked.

I haven't changed. ·

Oh, Miriam!

At school, I wore my hair in great glossy bunches on either side of my head, and I was *naughty*. My hair was naughty, too. For the whole of my life, my hair has caused comment – sometimes envy, sometimes revulsion. Mummy used olive oil to try and tame it. It certainly gave it a shine, but it could have imparted an odour. I remember in the third form, Valerie Scott said loudly, 'Your hair smells.' I punched her to the ground and she had to go to hospital. Thankfully, she's still a valued chum.

I answered back in lessons. When Miss Willetts came in and said briskly, 'Right!', I said loudly and immediately, 'Left!' I was sent out for that. Most teachers got used to it, and my classmates egged me on to do the things they might not have dared to do themselves.

In the upper fifth, I decided to stage a 'dare'. I pretended to faint in the playground. It was a fine day, during our fifteen-minute morning break, after which everyone went back up to the form rooms. But not me. As I collapsed onto the asphalt and lay flat on my back, I could see my form-mates above, peering out of the windows, giggling, wanting to see the results of my 'faint'. There was a pause while teachers were summoned. Miss Jackson, the maths teacher, arrived: 'Get up, get up, Miriam!' Then she kicked me and said, 'Oh, she's just shamming.' Miss Jackson, who was an extremely nice woman apart from The Kick, was one of the teachers you remember. She was very tall, straight up and down, no chest or hips to speak of, legs like tree trunks encased in very thick lisle stockings, and she always wore a light brown tweed suit.

But I continued to lie there on the ground, eyes closed, in my pretend swoon. This went on so long that the teachers who had gathered started to get really worried. By the end of break, it seemed as if the whole school was standing at the windows, watching to see what would happen next. I lay still, occasionally moaning but, eventually, Miss Brown (biology – memorable for her extraordinary hair style: two sharply etched rolls on each side of her otherwise cropped head) who was wonderfully tender-hearted, came and said, 'Come and lie down, Miriam.' I had to lie down in the quiet room with a cup of hot water (I never drank tea and still don't) until it was decided I had suffered no ill-effects and could return to the classroom. I was greeted with acclamation; and it seems everyone who was there remembers this jape.

Another time, in Miss Willett's French class, I dressed up as a French lady who had come to inspect the school for her daughter. I borrowed Mummy's best fur coat and her court shoes, and I tripped into the classroom, saying in a very thick French accent, 'Oh, I'm zo veery sorry to interrupt everyzing. I am veery interested in how you teach ze French in ze school.' I rolled my r's in a pretty good approximation of a French accent. The whole class was writhing with laughter and even Miss Willetts tried not to smile as she said, 'Come along, Miriam, you're wasting time.' To which I replied, 'Oh, zo you do not vant me to stay? Well, zen, I will go.' And with a flounce of Mummy's fur coat, I stepped out into the hall (and into yet another detention).

On one frightful occasion, I saw a child bending over in the corridor in front of me and, of course, I rushed up to the presented bottom and gave it a resounding THWACK! The figure straightened up and, to my horror, I saw it was not a child but Miss Maddron (head of French). Miss Maddron was one of the special ones: she was tiny and slim, but carried herself very straight and wielded immediate and powerful authority. She wasn't much taller than the shortest child, but taught brilliantly and had everyone's undivided attention. The abject shock on my face was enough to clear me of any impertinence, and not a word was said as I fled up the corridor. I liked her tremendously; I wasn't very good at French, but I did try.

Later, just as I was leaving to go to university, Miss Maddron told me, 'You were naughty, Miriam, but you were never wicked.' I hope that is true, although I remember once in the lower third putting up my hand in the biology lesson and saying, in between hysterical giggles, to Miss Keay, our rather buttoned-up teacher: 'Please, Miss Keay, what are [snigger, snigger, giggle] t-t-t testicles?' Of course, I knew what they were, but I just wanted to hear how she replied, which was, unsurprisingly: 'Miriam, don't be silly.'

The school prank I enjoyed most of all happened in gym class. We had been reading about the Greeks tricking the unsuspecting Trojans during the siege of Troy and this had given me the idea for my own wooden horse episode. Our school vaulting horse was constructed in a pyramid shape in a series of wooden tiers, which you could remove or add to in order to make it lower or higher, with the padded suede-leather 'saddle' on the top for vaulting. My accomplices and I took the saddle off, I climbed in and the top was replaced, leaving me concealed and snug inside. By the time Miss Leonard, the gym teacher, came into the gym hall asking 'Where's Miriam?' my classmates were already in paroxysms, which, of course, flummoxed the poor soul. I had a perfect view of the unfolding scene from my hiding place, through the grab holes in each of the wooden tiers. My chums could see my eyes darting about, but Miss Leonard didn't notice a thing – she had no idea I was in there. It was exquisite fun. I moved the horse just an inch or so. I could see that Miss Leonard was aware that it had moved, but didn't quite believe it. Every so often, I would shuffle the horse forward a little more, inch by inch, watching her increasing befuddlement at every movement. She couldn't work out what was happening.

Our lumbering game of Grandmother's Footsteps was one of my best bits of naughtiness. Miss Leonard did bear the brunt of a good deal of my more boisterous behaviour. I can still remember the weariness in her voice – despair tinged with resignation – as she reacted to my antics: 'Oh, Miriam! Oh, Miriam!' In fact, it was the usual response to most of my activities at school – 'Oh, Miriam. *Oh*, Miriam! Oh, *Miriam!*'

No other pupil would match me in my outrageousness until Tatty Katkov came to Oxford High School. I was always in detention. I *always* got caught. I remember when I was given a detention for a Thursday afternoon for some transgression or other, I was obliged to say truthfully, 'Oh, I'm sorry I can't do then, as I'm already booked for a detention on Thursday. But I could fit Friday in . . . ?'

Families

Mummy loathed 'the hovel' passionately, and was so desperate to have her own house, she decided she was going to build one. She bought a patch of land at the top of Banbury Road and hired an architect to draw up ambitious plans. We moved to it in 1951, when I was ten, Grandma Walters (my maternal grandmother) coming too. It was Mummy's dream: she had been the driving force behind the plan. Daddy merely followed in her wake – we all did.

It was an attractive mock-Tudor house at the top of Banbury Road, right on the roundabout. For some years after the war, no domestic building was allowed, but Mummy had hassled the authorities so much that a building permit had been granted. Unfortunately, the architect she chose, Major Knight, was an idiot. He'd been recommended but he was hopeless. Construction had been going on for some time before he noticed they'd forgotten the staircase – so much for supervision, one of an architect's main tasks. Building materials were left unprotected in the rain and finally Mummy realised the fireplace had been omitted. But, once completed, it was a handsome property, fronting onto Banbury Road but set back from its noise.

Outside the kitchen window was a wrought-iron garden seat, which had belonged to my grandparents (it sits now in my south London garden). There were apple trees and gooseberry bushes and roses and it had a fine, broad driveway built by council workers Mummy snaffled from their official duties one summer's day. The kitchen itself was far too small (again, post-war stipulations limited kitchen size) but it contained enough cupboards and work surfaces, a gas cooker and a fridge. There were bathrooms on both floors.

Just outside the kitchen, Mummy had made sure I had a little 'den' – my own personal work space. I decorated it with pictures of the Queen from floor to ceiling. I was a huge fan of the Queen's. I remember on 2 June 1952, standing at my bedroom window and saying, 'This is Coronation Day, and you must remember this all your life.' And I have. It was a very important event in our family and, lacking a TV, we went to watch it at Mrs Harwood's house. She was one of Daddy's patients, a sweet lady who every year made Daddy a huge and delicious Christmas cake.

At the top of the first flight of stairs, Mummy had designed a large, stained-glass window of a shepherdess. When the sun shone through the glass, it gave a rosy glow to the stairs and hallway. A small bronze statue of a naked woman holding a glass lantern was on a shelf by the window.

Daddy's surgery was on the ground floor to the right of the porch, full of books and his old-fashioned medicine cabinet. A hand basin was inset in a little alcove. He put his plate up at the entrance, but he continued to have a surgery at 4 Longwall Street until he retired in 1969, at the age of seventy.

Upstairs there were four bedrooms: Grandma's, mine, the au pair's and my parents' – their bedroom suite was my mother's choice, fashioned in a garish bird's eye maple hardwood, it was hideous: a hectic yellow, and gigantic. A large bathroom was in pink and blue terrazzo mosaic, modern then but definitely a period piece now. For my bedroom, Mummy had gone to High Wycombe, furniture capital of England, and had bought a conventional walnut suite. I hated it: it bore no relation to what I needed or liked. The headboard of my single bed was absurdly styled; I've always disliked headboards. Nothing else there was to my taste. In the living room there was an Esse stove, with little see-through doors giving the room focus and considerable warmth. Eventually, we had a TV there and a canteen of cutlery, a wedding present from Daddy's parents.

The house was Mummy's castle. We all enjoyed the space, the garden, and having two lavatories. Her special delight was the parquet flooring throughout – in a herring-bone pattern, and partially covered in the drawing room by a Chinese blue and beige carpet, made of a material that Mummy called 'unwashed silk'. That's where the piano went – and The Cherub. The Cherub was a six-foot-high Cupid in Carrara marble, on a turntable you could move with one finger. Cupid was seated on a pair of doves, reaching for an arrow from the quiver on his back. It was a piece of high Victoriana which I imagine my grandfather had purchased in an auction. Mummy loved it and so Daddy accepted it. Now I gaze at it with pride in my kitchen in Clapham. At one time, I thought of selling it and Phillips auction house advised me it would fetch £50,000. I entered it in the auction, but then realised I couldn't bear to part with it. From America, I telephoned Phillips and withdrew my cherub from their auction. They were furious and understandably charged me for the publicity they'd arranged to help the sale. But I never regretted it. Cupid will stay with me until I die. It represents home.

After Daddy came to live with me in London, I decided to sell the Oxford house. A local dentist, Mr Pick, bought it and subsequently sold it on to a development company. It has now been pulled down for horrible flats. If I'd known he was that sort of man, I would never have sold it to him.

———

Just across Banbury Road from us was the Cutteslowe Estate. A 'class wall' was built between the bottom of Carlton Road and the beginning of the estate, because it was not thought appropriate that North Oxford should have to deal with 'hoi polloi' living in what they considered to be vile council housing. That's what Oxford was like when I was growing up – and it hasn't changed much. Oxford is a place that pushes people away, which has divisions – divisions of class, divisions of intelligence. It's a place of harsh judgements and little compassion. The wall was finally pulled down in 1959, but snobbery is harder to demolish.

I know that my parents keenly felt discriminated against in many situations, and yet I don't think they ever considered moving away, chiefly because I was at Oxford High School. They always put my well-being before theirs and made many sacrifices for me.

When I started to become the person that the High School created, it was a complicated situation for my parents. My mother had come from a lower middle-class background, but by becoming a doctor my father was now middle class, and so my mother had remade herself. She did a lot of charity work, and gave parties for the synagogue. And they *always* voted Tory. They wouldn't, or couldn't, consider anything else.

Once I was at Oxford High School, however, I would confront them about their voting Tory. Through school, I had formed strong friendships with people like Anna Truelove, Catherine Pasternak Slater and Liz Hodgkin, that have lasted all my life. The Hodgkins, in particular, were an intellectual family: Hog's grandfather (she was called Hog at school) had been Provost of Queen's College, and spending so much time in the company of Liz's large and vociferously opinionated household led me to question aspects of my upbringing.

I have been friends with Liz since we were eleven. After school, we both went to Newnham College, Cambridge (Old Hall), and have remained close ever since.

Liz lived with her parents, her two brothers, and her aunt and five cousins, in one of those vast, Victorian houses close to the school in Woodstock Road. Liz's father was Thomas Hodgkin, the Marxist historian of Africa at Oxford, while her mother was the Nobel Prize winner Dorothy Hodgkin. There were only three female Nobel Prize winners for chemistry: one was Marie Curie, one was Irène-Joliot Curie, and the other was Dorothy Hodgkin.

Dossie, as everyone called her, had been Margaret Thatcher's tutor at Somerville College. Like me, Dossie didn't seem to care about the clothes she wore or her appearance; her focus was science. She would hum softly under her breath all the time, but in addition to being a wife and mother of three children, she discovered the structure of insulin and vitamin B12 and so cured pernicious anaemia. She was gentle and hospitable, and I had no idea till much later that she was a genius. I just liked her enormously.

The Hodgkins were relaxed and liberal-minded parents; theirs was an open house and I fell in love with the whole family, as only children often do. One grandmother lived near Stratford-upon-Avon so the Hodgkin family went to see Shakespeare quite often. One time they

invited me along, too. When I said, 'Oh, thank you so much for inviting me,' Liz's father, Thomas, laughed and said, 'It's always nice to have
a free seat in the front row.' That's what it was like having me around,
he said: you didn't need to go to the theatre, with me you already had
a front row seat.

It was at the Hodgkins' house that I first listened to music in a room
with other people. At home, we never listened to classical music and I
found the idea of doing so alarming. After supper, the family would
gather around the gramophone and play records. One evening, I was
told we were to hear Tchaikovsky's sixth symphony, the 'Pathétique'.
After supper I joined the circle of listeners. No one spoke. That was the
first frightening thing: not a word was uttered – the idea of being in a
room with people and NOT SPEAKING had never even crossed my
mind. No one spoke for the entire length of the piece. I was amazed
and discomfited. I didn't know what to do, where to look. Eventually,
I tried to forget the absence of conversation and concentrated on the
music. It was lovely, and I did enjoy it, but that initial embarrassment
remains a powerful memory.

But what most drew me to the Hodgkins and has held me to Liz
ever since was politics. Liz and her family taught me that through
politics you could *change* things. They joked that I came into their
household as a far-right Conservative candidate, who believed in
hanging and capital punishment (like my parents) and eventually, by
the sixth form, they had transformed my way of thinking. They
educated me about Palestine, for example. And that was a difficult
one. It still is hard.

To Mummy, the Hodgkins exemplified 'the best people', and yet
they were Communists. When they met, my parents liked them very

much, but because Mummy and Daddy were aspiring middle class, they were suspicious of anyone or anything with even a whiff of left-leaning sympathies.

———

Mummy's sister, Auntie Gusta, died young in April 1950, at just fifty. She had married an absolute shit of a man, a timber merchant called Ben Tosh, originally Benjamin Toshinski. They had settled in Dulwich and had three children. My cousins were all quite a bit older than me: Doris Tosh who was born in 1926, Jack (Jacob) Tosh was born in 1923, and the aforementioned cousin, Buffy, was born in 1928. Subsequently, after they buried Gusta, Grandma Walters, who had been living with Gusta and Ben, came to live in Oxford with us. It was a sad time for Mummy, because she had lost her only surviving sibling and by this time Grandma had advanced bowel cancer and was very frail. My mother looked after her and nursed her until her death in January 1953, aged eighty-eight.

In her will, my grandmother left everything to my mother – she inherited about £18,000, which was rather a lot back then. Uncle Ben and his children, my first cousins, accused my mother of forcing my grandmother's hand in making her will and filed a civil claim of 'undue influence' against her.

From that point on, the case cast a shadow over my childhood. While this nastiness was unfolding, Mummy and Daddy continually went to London to consult lawyers; and my mother became stressed and upset. She would come home quite broken after these days with the solicitors, and it was awful to see. It aged her terribly, because of course she was fighting a lie. Mummy didn't use undue influence in order to secure her mother's estate. Mummy adored Grandma and Grandma loved Mummy and when Gusta died, understandably she wanted to live with us; just as it was natural to want to leave her money to her only surviving child.

One of the accusations levelled at my mother was that she prevented my cousins from visiting their grandmother. A lie! They came once to see her and she refused to see them. She disliked them because they made fun of her slowness, and mocked her. In court they alleged that I was the gatekeeper, shoving them away at the front door and that I was twenty-one years old. I was actually eleven.

It was reported in the *Oxford Mail*, and Mummy was badly advised by a solicitor who persuaded her to make a settlement, telling her: 'If you go ahead with this case and you lose it, you'll lose everything. If you make a settlement, at least you'll keep something.' As I said, it was about £18,000, so it was a considerable sum, but not an utter fortune. Anyway, Mummy listened to this solicitor and so the case never actually went to trial. The whole matter was eventually settled but the judge told my mother that she had not been well served by her solicitor. He actually said that in court.

It was a dark time; and afterwards I didn't have much of a relationship with any of my Tosh cousins. For over fifty years we didn't speak. I never forgave my uncle for accusing my mother; he knew very well she had been a loving daughter and there was no foundation for the charge. He didn't like my mother because she thought he had been a bad husband to her sister.

I found my cousins again because I wanted to sort out my family history. I couldn't do that if I didn't speak to them, and so I went to see

Gusta's daughter, Buffy, who had a dress shop in Conduit Street in London, right next to the Westbury Hotel. I walked in one day and said, 'Do you know who I am?' She looked at me and said, 'Oh, my God. Of course I do!' And since then, we've been the closest of friends. She's in her nineties now and I love her.

Throughout my childhood and most of my adulthood, we were not a united family in the wider sense. We three – Mummy, Daddy and me – had to be together. My mother wanted us to be open only to each other and to nobody else.

Of course, by writing this book, I'm doing exactly the opposite. Mummy often quoted her grandmother's warning, spoken in a German accent: 'Never trust anyone until hair grows in the palm of their hand.' As we all know, hair *never* grows in the palm of your hand. It's a shocking lesson to teach a child, and sadly it is one that I have accepted. I trust everyone until they let me down, and then I never trust them again. But I don't close myself off from people and I never have. Mummy and my father always felt that we were surrounded by enemies. I don't agree. I've accepted that there are enemies, but I've always known that my friends are my fortress, and for that I'm grateful.

Showing Off

I used to have huge pashes on people; we called it being 'cracked' on someone. The violence of the language is completely appropriate, as this was much worse than a mere 'crush' – it was a pulverising experience. I even wrote a little essay in 1954 on the subject entitled, 'People I Have Been Cracked On (or rather, People On Whom I Have Been Cracked)', which, happily, like my mock obituary, has been preserved for posterity in our handwritten form magazine.

Nobody minded these infatuations of mine. We didn't know much about lesbians. We didn't know what lesbians did, although we speculated about the home life of Miss Mather and Miss Tilston. They were known to be a couple, but what that actually entailed was never specified; we didn't talk about it much, we just knew that they did things that shouldn't be done by women to each other. We giggled about it because we knew that sex was something you giggled about. Miss Mather taught German and Miss Tilston taught chemistry. Miss Tilston was pretty and had red hair and a bad temper. Miss Mather was dour, with a triangular face and an extraordinary hairstyle – a version of a 1950s Victory roll at the side of her head. She really did look quite strange. I promise a chapter on lesbians later.

My life revolved around school and my school friends and I was very happy. Despite my continuing naughtiness, I was elected Form Leader one term and when we got to the sixth form I was made a prefect. I couldn't understand why the dons' daughters, who seemed cleverer and much better behaved than me, were not afforded that honour. But I wasn't going to argue. Perhaps they thought that they could turn the naughty person into, well, a *good* person – and it would be a clever way of controlling me. The scheme worked: I became as bossy as any *gauleiter*, ruling with a rod of iron, demanding complete silence when the bell rang.

Our teachers were from the generation who could have lost their boyfriends in the war. We speculated endlessly about their lives outside the school gates. Miss Davis (History) was mimsy and prim and wore white, ill-fitting blouses and a skirt. To our great delight, she had the habit of storing her hankies in her knickers – we kept an eye out for their swift retrieval when she had a cold. She was the epitome of a spinster. Her passion was Charles the First. She described his execution so vividly that we saw his shirt blowing in the breeze as he ascended the gallows outside Whitehall. When she evoked this scene, all her juices flowed and she sparkled. I think it's because of Miss Davis that I've always been a royalist, even though my broader politics tend in the other direction. She made me see kings and queens as real people, as flawed, interesting characters and not as the representation of privilege and repression.

Our music teacher, Mrs Archer, was a burly, formidable woman, one of the school's few married teachers. Her husband ran a profitable removal firm, Archer Cowley, so she didn't need the money, but taught for the sheer joy of it. Every morning, she would oversee hymn practice. I have always been tone-deaf, which Mrs Archer spotted. I was told firmly to mime during hymn practice. Despite that, Mrs Archer liked me – I think she appreciated my wildness and saw me as a free spirit.

English was always my favourite subject. Our first English teacher was Miss Bartholomew. She loved Shakespeare so much that little beads of spittle formed into froth at the corners of her mouth when she read the plays aloud. She taught Dame Maggie Smith, who remembers her well. When she left Oxford High School she became head-mistress of Norwich High School for Girls. I was in touch with her until she died, a most splendid woman.

Joan Gummer succeeded her – tough shoes to fill, but she was also an excellent teacher. In different times in her life, she had been both a nun and an actress. She still looked like a nun, with a pale face, an ethereal expression and light blue eyes. She had studied at RADA, had a keen sense of drama and she directed the school play. I had a rapport with her, I think because she could sense that I was a performer and not just a show-off. Miss Gummer had a big influence on my attitude to the theatre, because she loved it too, although being deeply religious she had renounced it. She was a devout Catholic and truly believed in its dogma and its strictures, but her single-mindedness, her focus, is what I will always remember. She talked with flair and joy about Keats and the Romantics and we inherited her enthusiasm. She had a curious custom: when she quoted poetry or read from a play, she would turn her head and expose her noble profile to us, gazing into the middle distance. We would giggle, because it was a self-conscious gesture that must have come from her time as an actress. Perhaps somebody once told her, 'Goodness, you've got a sensational profile.' It was a dramatic thing to do, though I don't know if it would work in church. She was inspirational.

———

I once described myself as 'extremely unintelligent', but I no longer think it's sensible for me to say that I'm *extremely* unintelligent. I can't do intelligence tests and I'm completely innumerate, for example, but I can remember telephone numbers easily, so perhaps a more accurate self-assessment would be that I am a *little* bit thick. I did have some talents, though. Liz says that they all knew that if there was a public speaking competition, our house at school (East) would win because of me. I loved public speaking. And I always wanted to win – desperately. One year my speech was about *Deirdre* – the Jacob Epstein bronze torso that stood above the pool in the courtyard outside the staff room. I thought my speech had been very poor and I was in a paroxysm of despair, but we still won the cup. Apparently, I did it almost without notes and that was how I first realised that I could entertain by talking, and that was pleasing.

In the sixth form, there were often soirées at Liz's house. Even the teachers would come to the Hodgkins' parties and do charades. I have a strong memory of Miss Jackson saying, 'I don't mind being a camel.' But charades made me nervous. I felt that a spotlight was shining on me because I was supposed to be good at acting, and the expectation spoilt it for me.

The school plays were, of course, *my* chance to shine. My school friends now tell me that I was always a brilliant actress, and that even then they knew that everything was going to work out. The pleasure of making people laugh was exquisite and intense. And school provided my audience from the beginning to the end.

Every day, I used to walk to and from school along Banbury Road. Daddy insisted on it and my parents wouldn't buy me a bicycle; I didn't own one until I went to Cambridge. It wasn't a particularly long journey, but trudging up and down that same stretch of road every day, past Squitchey Lane, past the parade of shops, past Lodge the Jewellers where Mummy had her rings cleaned, and Axtell's the Chemist (Gillian Axtell was in the form below), I would invent little plays and voice all the characters, striding along, talking animatedly to myself. People would notice me and I could see them wondering: 'What is she doing? What is she talking about?' Without knowing it, I was honing the improvisational skills often taught in drama schools; I was flexing my imagination. It would stand me in good stead later, when I went for my audition for BBC radio drama.

In 1958, I played Gertrude in our school play of *Hamlet*. Miss Gummer directed, and Nina Katkov was Hamlet. Nina was spellbinding – a true star. She was tall and beautiful, with dark eyes and honey-coloured, curly hair. I was in love with her, but I knew I had to keep that secret. I hope I did. She moved quickly and gracefully; she had a natural feel for the text. When she was on stage, no one else existed. I wasn't jealous, just in awe. She was a magical person, mercurial and compelling. She died aged twenty-five in 1970. I mourn her still.

As Brutus in *Julius Caesar*, my toga kept slipping off, revealing rather more bosom than Brutus was normally expected to have; some parents in the front row showed alarm. On another occasion, in the junior school, when I was Bottom in 'The Dream' I forgot my words, but I didn't crumble or hesitate – I just made up some nonsense and carried on.

When I was young, acting was just showing off. As you grow older, you realise the responsibility you have towards the writer and their text, and to the audience. You come to understand it's not all about you.

The Facts of Life

I was the first person in my class to have periods; I was eleven. It came as a surprise. Mummy wasn't prudish (after all, she did her housework in the nude) but she hadn't expected menstruation to erupt so early in my life and hadn't yet mentioned it. I don't know when people are supposed to become aware of such things; Miss Keay in upper third biology did cover sperm and testicles, ovaries and fallopian tubes etc., although we never felt involved. It was not *our* bodies under the microscope.

So I was worried when I found blood in my knickers; I told Mummy at once. 'Oh, my goodness, you've started your periods,' she said, and rushed to tell Grandma. 'Darling, you're very young but it's all right. It's perfectly normal, everybody has them and you just have to deal with it.' Mummy had never heard of Tampax (invented in 1931!) – she decreed do-it-yourself sanitary towels. We went to the chemist, Mummy bought masses of cotton wool and gauze, and we had a practice session in the kitchen as she taught me to make my first sanitary towel. 'Just pop it in your knickers,' Mummy said cheerfully, in a Joyce Grenfell voice. It was a nuisance; a bloody awful business, in every sense.[*] But Mummy had a Dickensian solution for period pains – gin.

---

[*] I was lucky, in a way, because for most of my life I haven't had periods. I had fibroids and so my womb was removed when I was thirty-four. I was thrilled – I didn't want to have periods, I thought they were awful, and then after that that was the end of them.

Apparently, when she was little, Grandma had supplied gin to help Mummy's pains and she was continuing the tradition. I developed a real taste for gin, which I've never lost.

Mummy used to call it being 'poorly', so, of course, it always had a negative connotation. It was worrying because when you were playing hockey, you didn't want blood to come through your clothes and be seen. That was always the major anxiety when you had a period. We used to worry about it a lot, and think, 'Can people smell it? Does it show?' It was the thing you wanted to hide more than anything. You didn't want anyone to see you changing a sanitary towel or dealing with its disposal. Eventually, I discovered I didn't have to make my own any more: ready-made sanitary towels were available at the chemist. Much later on, after I left Cambridge, Tampax arrived in my life. A friend shouted instructions through the loo door in a Soho restaurant. Even with her help, I suffered greatly as I inserted and left the cardboard sheath inside me, too; she hadn't explained it was merely the cover and the real deal was inside.

Mummy wrote a note to tell the school of my startling female development. Miss West, our games mistress, was extremely embarrassed by the whole thing. It was her unfortunate duty to discuss the matter with all who menstruated. She was one of the Oxford High School lesbians and wore divided skirts. I was given a note to go and see her. I turned up wondering what I'd done wrong, as that was usually what a note to see a teacher meant. Miss West gave an awkward snigger and said, 'Miriam, I think we must have a little chat about how to, er . . . manage your periods.' I could see she was embarrassed; I wasn't at all. Miss West took a deep breath and resolutely continued, 'In the pavilion . . . there are no, er . . . incinerators. So, on the days when we are playing hockey and you have your, er . . . period, I am afraid you will have to bring some newspaper to school and [snigger] wrap your . . . er . . . sanitary towel in a newspaper and, er . . . take it home [snigger] . . . in your satchel.' (It was a sublime moment of high comedy. I related it to Dawn French in her series on comedy, and when Jennifer Saunders cast me in *Jam and Jerusalem* she allowed me to resurrect Miss West and her snigger.) Possibly I was the first one that had to face that conversation; before, when people had periods, they simply didn't play hockey. I've no idea how other girls dealt with the problem until incinerators or those dreadful, smelly sanitary bins were brought in, because no one ever talked about it.

Neither Mummy or Daddy ever talked to me about the facts of life or any aspect of sex – that simply wasn't discussed or mentioned. I learnt about the facts of life in that famous teaching arena: the school bike shed. SEX was the major topic. On certain days, our sports pavilion was let out to a boys' school and once, when walking past, I saw a completely naked man walk across to the showers – in profile, with his dick sticking out in front. I think that was probably the first time I'd ever seen a penis, and I didn't like it. And I never have.

At school, I was with the more snobbish group that didn't have boyfriends, but we wanted them nonetheless. I used to spy on couples going off for little snogs. There was a particular bridge near Kidlington under which couples would lie and cuddle, and I used to stalk them. I'd lie in the bushes quite close by so I could observe their amorous scufflings. I suppose I got some pleasure out of it. Often I'd go with another girl. I don't think we ever actually surprised anyone *in flagrante*, but it was close.

I was a well-developed girl – my breasts were large and lustrous, thrusting my nipples through the school jumper to the consternation of practically everyone. I remember an American soldier clapping his hands over them in the street when I was about twelve. He didn't hurt or frighten me; I think he might have been drunk as his pals pulled him away from me before anything got nasty. I was quite flattered by the attention. Two of my father's patients molested me. One had a motorbike and took me for a spin into the country. He stopped the bike, took me into a field and asked me to stroke his inflamed member. I did so willingly, stirred by the experience but not shaken. After I told my parents, I was never alone with him again.

When I was in the sixth form, my first boyfriend was a portly Indian gentleman who spotted me, a schoolgirl, collecting for the blind in Cornmarket, and approached me – most respectfully. He asked my father if he could take me to the pictures. Daddy consented and we went to the Scala in Walton Street. He took me out a few times; we never kissed, and I didn't fancy him at all, but the rest of my form at Oxford High School all seemed to have boyfriends, so I think peer pressure was the initial motivator.

I then fell in with a group of other older men. I met them when I modelled at the Ruskin School of Art. I used to go along and stand or sit there, fully clothed, facing the class. Standing or sitting still for a long time could, of course, sometimes get a bit boring, but I met and had coffee with the artists, and I quite enjoyed that. One was a retired army officer in his seventies, of impeccable bearing – my parents thought he was delightful – called Major Harding. He was aptly named as he was an experienced groper, but not scary. His advances were gentle and almost affectionate. He talked about my eyes a great deal, and then moved on to my breasts. He asked if he could stroke them. I was seventeen, well brought up, but what woman doesn't like having her breasts stroked? I responded merrily to Major Harding and when it became clear to him that I wouldn't fuck but I would suck, we were on a roll. We met often to go to the cinema, or for Sunday tea parties. His pleasure gave me pleasure and proved the template for my sexual activities until I was initiated into the joys of lesbianism.

I did a great deal of sucking off because I seemed to be good at it, and it was all I *could* do. I remember a lusty Hungarian student who once achieved orgasm seven times in a session – so good for him, so tiring for me. I wasn't going to fuck, you see. I knew I wasn't going to do that, because I had promised my parents I wouldn't. They were highly conventional and deeply moralistic. They couldn't imagine a relationship outside marriage, and had impressed on me that I mustn't have sex: pregnancy would result, and their hopes and dreams for my future happiness would be destroyed.

The subject of sex was difficult for my parents, especially where I was concerned; and, indeed, possibly where they were concerned, too. In those days, a respectable female could not give vent to sexual longings; intercourse resulted in unwanted children, and masturbation was 'dirty'. That's how it was in the fifties and sixties. Jewish girls were known for sucking off: the man is satisfied and we don't get pregnant. Oral skill enhances your popularity and, if I'm honest, I think I enjoyed the power it lent me.

—

Growing up, I had no fear of people. I would go up to strangers and talk to them; I still do. I like taking the initiative and striking up relationships with people who seem interesting. On my walk from school one time, I noticed a beautiful woman: I think she worked in Webbers, or Elliston & Cavell's, one of the two old Oxford department stores. I went up to her and I said, 'I think you are the most beautiful woman I've ever seen.' I was in my school uniform wearing my school hat; she looked at me with great pleasure: no doubt it was a nice thing to be told. But I meant it: she *was* beautiful, with perfect make-up. On other occasions, I used to meet a local tramp who was often to be found on Banbury Road. I remember noticing his pungent smell and dirty feet, but he smiled amiably and was entirely unthreatening. Other people's lives are always gripping. I didn't know I would one day make a living from being inquisitive, but it stems from a genuine and powerful curiosity about the world.

Another time, again coming home from school along the Banbury Road, I noticed a handsome man walking in front of me. I accosted him just beyond South Parade, and started talking to him. We talked for a long time. He was a beautiful young Anglo-Russian called Anton Vinogradov and I fell very much in love with him, almost immediately.

He lived somewhere in North Oxford, and so, after that first encounter, every day after school as I walked home, I would wait to see if he was around; he was quite often. He didn't approach me; I picked *him* up. He was a passive volunteer in my pursuit.

Anton was a postgraduate student at Oxford – educated, Jewish, English and, more importantly, he was actually a decent man. He was the apotheosis of what my parents wanted for me and I was very much my parents' child so I longed to please them. And there must have been some sexual feeling, though I doubt there was on his part. However, I felt that I loved this man. His soul interested me, and I have not been interested in very many men's souls (but more on that topic later). I thought about him obsessively, all the time.

I threw myself at him in a way that must have been quite alarming. Looking back, I'm not sure how much happened between us, because it wasn't real. It was merely a projection of my romantic soul, and absurdly one-sided. To be precise, I'm sure that nothing below the waist actually happened. He was in no way a groper; I knew gropers, of course. Who doesn't? (Groping is worth a whole other chapter.)

As I said, I sucked off lots of people, but I didn't suck off Anton. All the bike-shed encounters with prick and mouth – as opposed to foot and mouth – were totally sexual. They were not about emotional connection, they were about sexual gratification, about lust. With Anton it was emotional; it was romantic, and intensely so. I had never experienced that before with a man and I never have since. (There was a Chinese professor of journalism in Shanghai for whom I felt a twang, but that's it.) And I was in love with him because, when he ended it, I can remember the feeling of being annihilated – a pure, wrenching grief and loss.

I think he liked me and thought I was engaging and intelligent but, obviously, I was a schoolgirl, not a particularly pretty schoolgirl, and he was married. That clinched it; he felt at a certain point that he had to put the kibosh on it, and he did. He took me to tea somewhere in North Oxford and he told me that he thought it was not right for me to feel so passionately for him.

When he said it, I knew it was sensible and final, and the fact that he had a wife and a child confirmed the finality. I've always felt slightly moral about that sort of thing; it's pretty shitty to interfere in a marriage. He was right to put an end to it, but that didn't stop it from hurting.

After that, I put the whole infatuation behind me. I didn't fight the decision. I didn't chase him. I've often wondered what happened to him. He's not an important figure in my life, but in my memories he is unique. He would probably be astonished if he ever reads this, to think that I still hold a candle for him. Actually, I'll rephrase that – *carry a torch*, albeit a very dim, flickering one.

Latin Lessons

My education was the focus of my home life: Mummy and Daddy desperately wanted me go to university. Ours was a Jewish household: academic achievement was considered important; it had always been a way to pull yourself out of the depths. In that city of academics, Mummy wanted me to belong to that social and intellectual elite to which they were clearly not given access. It wasn't just any university Mummy wanted me to attend; it had to be Oxford or Cambridge, because, she said, 'That's where you meet the best people.'

For Mummy, the *most* important thing was that I should be educated, and the matter of my education was *her* decision; Daddy kept quiet. Mummy would talk over everyone and everything. She often said, 'I know there are things that people will speak about and I won't understand. That's why I want you to go to university.' She wanted me to be able to talk to anybody about anything. I hope she would be proud now, because although I know I disappointed her in some ways – I never took a pride in my appearance, I can't sing, I can't dance and I never gave her the grandchildren a child should – at least I *can* talk to anyone about anything.

Around the time I met Anton in the Lower Sixth, it was time for college entrance. We had an excellent Latin mistress, Miss Frisby. Her particular sartorial peculiarity were pockets outside her skirts. She would put her hands in those pockets and flap them up and down. She called people 'deary' when she was cross. I liked her but she thought I was a frightful show-off. I wanted attention, just like a child. I confess I have never lost that pathetic need to be the centre of attention.

Everybody knew that my Latin wasn't strong enough and that it might be a stumbling block in my university ambitions, so Miss Frisby advised my parents that I should get extra coaching. They made some enquiries and arranged extra tuition with C. E. Stevens, the professor of Latin and Greek at Magdalen College, who was affectionately known as 'Tom Brown'.

Tom Brown was a charming and interesting man who had got married late in life to a fierce Russian lady. He had a set of rooms in Magdalen College where I used to go every week. He was big and burly, smoked a pipe and wore the sort of clothes that a country gentleman would wear, including a good tweed jacket with leather-patched elbows. He would stand in front of the fire, puffing his pipe, and talk about the Greeks and Romans as if they lived around the corner.

One day, some months after I had begun my tutorials, we were sitting in his study, me tussling with my Latin exercises, and he said he wanted to tell me something.

Naturally I thought that he was going to say that he'd fallen in love with me, because that's what you think when you're a seventeen-year-old girl. Instead, he said, 'I want to be a woman.' I was flabbergasted. I had seen no sign of this and I couldn't quite believe it. He then said, 'May I go on?' Of course I said yes. He said, 'Do you know what I'm wearing under my trousers?' He pulled up his trouser leg – he was wearing stockings. I showed my surprise, and he said, 'Have you noticed how smooth my skin is?' I said, 'Well, no, not really.' Though he did have a very good complexion.

He asked me to follow him. He took me to his bedroom, and showed me his dressing table, 'Look at all my creams, that's why I have such smooth skin, because I use all these lotions.' His dressing table was like the vanity table of an actress. It was covered with emollients and perfumes and various unguents for the body, for the face, for the eyes, anti-wrinkle preparations, and every possible beauty formulation you could think of. I was astonished. Then he said, 'Haven't you seen how small my feet are?' And he showed me his feet.

I didn't quite know how I should respond to the sight of these perfectly normal-sized feet, so I said, 'Well, honestly, Tom, I've never really thought about it.' I wasn't disgusted. I was fascinated and rather surprised – very surprised, in fact.

He replied, 'I want to be a woman. I've always wanted to be a woman since I was a little boy. I used to go into my mother's cupboard and take out her dresses and wear them and look at myself in the mirror. I know that I'm meant to be a woman. I shouldn't be a man, it's all wrong.' He was practically crying. 'I have this pole, which makes me a man, and I don't want it. I want to cut it off. I don't want it.'

'May I tell you my real name?' He told me his true name was Agatha.

At that point, it was really hard not to laugh because Agatha isn't exactly the most glorious female name, but he said, 'May I write to you as Agatha, Miriam?' Naturally I said, 'Of course.' He wrote me letters as Agatha and we were friends until he died.

Eventually, I told my parents about what Tom Brown had told me and they were amazingly non-censorious. They accepted it; they did ask if he had touched me inappropriately, though it wasn't called that back then. Obviously, the college authorities didn't know, but I think his wife did and she didn't mind. She accepted it too. She loved him, and he was a respected don and he made her a home.

I'm a repository of many confidences. People often tell me private things about themselves or about things that have happened to them that they haven't told anybody else, because they trust me, and this was one of those times.

Many women come to lesbianism later in life, after marriage and children. I have been the confidante of a surprising number of 'straight' women, who fall in love with a person not a sex – and now it's easier for them to follow their emotions and find happiness. It delights me.

Like Anton, Tom was someone whose soul interested me. I believe he liked me very much and he wanted me to know the real Tom Brown. I have always felt it an honour to be allowed to see into another's soul. I cherished my friendship with Tom until he died; it is the vulnerabilities in people, rather more than their strengths, which allow us to love them.

Dinner with Isaiah Berlin

When the time came to apply to university, a form was required from school, and I had to find a sponsor – somebody who would support my application and vouch for my academic promise and moral repute. Very often it was the headmistress who fulfilled this role. As Miss Vera Stack was perhaps not my biggest fan, Mummy came up with an alternative solution to secure my sponsorship.

One evening, she said to Daddy: 'Isn't one of your patients Isaiah Berlin?'

Daddy replied, 'Yes.'

When Isaiah Berlin came to Oxford, he brought his parents with him, and while his father, the erstwhile head of the Riga Association of Timber Merchants, was fluent not only in Yiddish, Russian and German, but also French and English, his Russian-speaking mother, Marie, was fluent in only Yiddish and Latvian. And because Daddy was quite probably the only doctor in Oxford who spoke Yiddish, he had become the Berlins' family doctor.

She said: 'Joe, I want you to invite Isaiah Berlin for supper and I want him to sponsor Miriam for her college entrance.' She couldn't have known that he was a Fellow of All Souls and Oxford's most important intellectual figure. Yet, with remarkable instinct, my mother had fixed upon the perfect sponsor for her daughter.

Daddy said, 'Don't be ridiculous, I'm not asking him to dinner. I'm a professional person. I can't ask a patient to do that!'

But Mummy insisted: 'You will, and I will cook a wonderful Jewish meal' – which she did. She was a good, plain cook. And so, Sir Isaiah Berlin* did come to supper, and I was there at the table with Mummy and Daddy. It was just the four of us – and he was utterly charming. I think he was amused to be invited, although I don't think Daddy had been able to bring himself to explain the real reason for this impromptu dinner invitation. 'Would you come to supper? And by the way . . .' That was simply against his nature: Daddy was a moral person. Mummy was an opportunist.

We sat down to eat, and we soon found that Isaiah Berlin, though friendly, was completely unintelligible. He was a brilliant man, but so thick was his accent that you did not understand anything he said – you simply couldn't grasp a single word, not a word! Conversation was difficult therefore (an understatement), but nonetheless he was charming. So, there we were, all smiling and convivial, me pretending to follow whatever in God's name he was talking about – and Mummy rose to the occasion. She just came straight out with it. 'This is our daughter, Miriam. She's leaving school, and obviously we're putting her in for college entrance. It would be wonderful if you could be her sponsor.'

The meal was excellent, and we all had a very pleasant evening. Before he left, Sir Isaiah signed the sponsorship forms that Mummy had reminded me to bring back from school. It was done and dusted.

Getting into university was (and is) a fraught process; all of us at school knew we *had* to get a degree. I waited nervously for news from my chosen colleges. But when the principal of Somerville College,

---

* He had been knighted the previous year.

Oxford, and the principal of Newnham College, Cambridge, looked at my form, and saw that Isaiah Berlin had sponsored me, I was home and dry. No college principal in the world would have turned down someone sponsored by the country's premier intellectual. Today it would be as if I was the protégée of Simon Schama and Mary Beard.

And so, thanks to Isaiah Berlin (and Mummy), I braced myself for the famously exacting grilling by the Oxbridge dons.

In those days, there was a direct train between the two towns; you would do your interviews at Oxford, then get on the train to Cambridge and do your interviews there. In my compartment on the train going to Cambridge, I met an interesting girl, Diana Devlin. She was going to Girton College and I was going to Newnham. We immediately hit it off, and she said to me, 'What do you think you'll do when you finish?' 'Well, I really would like to be an actress,' I replied. And she said, 'Oh, my grandma was an actress,' and I thought, 'How ridiculous.' In an offhand way, I said, 'Oh, yeah, who's that?' And she said, 'Sybil Thorndike.' I shrivelled with embarrassment; what a slap in the face. 'That'll teach you, Miriam,' I thought to myself. Diana recovered from my gaffe; we continued to our respective colleges and remained close friends until she died last year. We often laughed about that first meeting and my crassness. I miss Diana deeply: after Cambridge, she had a distinguished career as an arts administrator at the Guildhall School of Music & Drama and was Sam Wanamaker's partner in creating the Globe Theatre. A rare and charming woman, irreplaceable in my life.

On arrival at Newnham, we were directed to the English department's Director of Studies. I was nervous but armed with the information that if I used the word 'ambiguity' (that was a tip being passed around at the time), I'd be certain to get in, I felt I could deal with an oral examination. I'd stipulated that I wished to specialise in Anglo-Saxon, so was interviewed by Dorothy Whitelock. She was white-haired, a little fierce but seemed interested in why I'd chosen this more obscure part of the English Tripos. I didn't really know – I wanted to understand the roots of the language, and I enjoyed the narrative power of *Beowulf*, which was the only Anglo-Saxon text I'd read. Somehow, I convinced her I would be worth her time.

Another scheduled interview was with the principal of Newnham, Ruth Cohen, at the principal's lodge. This modern house, built in 1958, is in Newnham Walk, a quiet road near Old Hall. My appointment was for 3 p.m. The problem was that the house was so modern, I couldn't find the front door, nor any bell to announce my presence. I banged for a while on what I thought might be a door, I walked around peering in high glass windows, I called out nervously and tapped on the walls, hoping to hear something hollow. Punctuality is important; I was already late and somewhat desperate. Finally, in an unexpected place, a door opened and Miss Cohen emerged. 'Oh, thank goodness,' I said, 'I couldn't find the front door.' Luckily, she laughed. 'It's not the first time people have got lost,' she said. I immediately felt at home and the interview became a genuine conversation.

At Oxford it was very different. My interviewer at Somerville was Rosemary Syfret. If ever there were a masculine woman, she was it. She had a loud bass voice, and wore tweeds. 'Do you like Milton?' she'd barked. I *did* like Milton and could honestly say so. 'DAMN GOOD POET' she'd boomed, slapping her thigh like a principal boy in pantomime. This convinced me Somerville would not be the place for me. I may have been a lesbian without knowing it, but that kind of academic was not to my taste.

Some months later, the day that we got the news was one of the happiest of my life. All of us who had been successful were summoned to the headmistress's study to be told our fate. Miss Hancock was Miss Stack's successor, a pleasant woman from Liverpool GPDST, but totally without her predecessor's authority and presence.

The telegram from Newnham College had come to my house but I had already left for school. Mummy had opened it and seen that I'd been accepted, but she rightly guessed that I would want to hear the news with the other girls at school. So, instead, she rang the school, unselfishly allowing *them* to tell me.

We stood in a line in front of Miss Hancock's desk and, one by one, she asked us to repeat our results aloud. We fully understood the importance of the occasion. We knew that it was a door opening, a moment of unalloyed happiness, undiluted by any other anxiety, an amazing sensation of triumph and fulfilment that I shall never forget. I had made it. I had got into university, alongside my closest friends, Catherine Pasternak Slater and Anna Truelove, who were the two cleverest girls in the class. I was never academically bright compared to them; I knew that I was a poor third, but now I could say, 'Miriam Margolyes: Exhibition to Newnham, Cambridge.' They were going to Oxford, I to Cambridge. But that separation did not dim our friendship, which flourishes and nourishes me to this day.

I was simply and purely proud of myself. And when I got home, Miss Stack, from retirement, had sent a telegram saying, 'Heartiest congratulations'. She'd sent one to all of us – classy to the end.

I'd also, it turned out, been accepted at Somerville College,

Oxford, but Newnham had offered me an Exhibition, which is a minor scholarship that meant I got to wear a longer gown than if I'd come in as a commoner, and I would have more status. Thus, I turned down Somerville and plumped for Newnham. I'm absolutely sure I made the right choice.

Nude Modelling for Augustus John

In May 1960, just a few days before I turned nineteen, I watched a television programme called *Face to Face*, in which a television journalist called John Freeman interviewed the octogenarian Welsh artist Augustus John.

The conversation with Augustus John was riveting because it was filmed at his home in Fordingbridge, Hampshire, in rooms chock-a-block with half-finished oil paintings and rough sketches, and huge rough-hewn sculpted busts. I was enthralled by him. He was a big man, good to look at – he had an untidy, bushy beard and bright, twinkling eyes. He would have been in his eighties then, but vigorous and naughty, and he had a mischief about him which I relished. He seemed the epitome of a great living artist.

I'd left school and was earning pocket money modelling for the students at the Ruskin School of Art. But Augustus John was clearly the real deal and suddenly I thought, 'Why don't I model for him?'

I found out the name of his house in Fordingbridge: Fryern Court. I don't know how I found his address; I probably looked it up in a phonebook or something, because that's how you found out about things then – and I wrote him a letter. I said that I was writing to suggest that I model for him, that I was eighteen, with experience in modelling, and it would be such an honour to pose for him.

A few days later, my mother received a phone call from Dorelia McNeill, Augustus's common-law wife and model for both Augustus and his sister, Gwen. You could tell within seconds (certainly Mummy could) from Dorelia's clipped, cut-glass tones that she was from the upper classes and someone with social status. I hadn't told my parents that I was going to write to him, because I didn't think that anything would come of it, but as it turned out Mummy was charmed by Dorelia; so charmed, that she didn't demur when the ground rules were firmly laid out: 'You know, I think my husband is doing a painting of some bathers, so it would have to be a nude portrait.'

I have never understood why my parents agreed to let me do it. I think Mummy must have found out that he was a very famous painter, because as I have said, she was quite the social climber and delighted by celebrities. Daddy might have disapproved but, ultimately, when he saw the determined females ranged against him, he gave way and he did as he was told.

I stipulated that my parents were to deliver me to the house in Fordingbridge and then they must go away and come back a couple of hours later to drive me back. That's what we did.

Beforehand, I practised taking off my clothes quickly in my bedroom. I remember that I wore a blue and white polka-dot dress, which had, as it were, easy access and I could get it on and off without fuss. I didn't wear stockings, just some socks and my sandals. So off we drove – it took over two hours to get there but when we arrived at his beautiful old house – a big country manor – my parents, at my request, dumped me on the doorstep and drove away.

I rang the doorbell. Nothing happened for about ten minutes, and I was beginning to get rather anxious, when suddenly from around the side of the house came a very strange, tiny old lady with fine, wispy, white-grey hair, wrapped in a Mexican blanket.

She saw me and said, 'Oh, hello. Have you been waiting long?' She rang the doorbell again, and Augustus John came to the door and opened it. He was smoking a pipe, and he was tall and imposing with that full white beard and the shock of straggling snow-white hair I remembered from the television. He wore what I used to call dungarees – it was a boiler suit made out of denim – and he had a little, dark, flat cap like a beret on his head.

I said, 'Hello, I'm Miriam.'

Augustus John said, 'Oh, yes. Come in, come in!'

He seemed very well-to-do and commanding, with a great booming voice. The house was dark, messy and muddled. Dorelia insisted, 'We must have some tea before we start.' So, we three went into the kitchen. I sat down nervously and Dorelia said, 'Do you like bread and jam?' And I replied, 'Yes.' She carved me a couple of slices of brown bread and covered them with jam – and it was nice jam, homemade, although I was so anxious that I remember finding it hard to swallow. Then – and this is the thing I really remember – I noticed on the wall there was a painting of a woman sitting in a chair with her back to us. Augustus John said, 'Do you like that painting?' I said, 'Yes, I do, I do like it. Very much.' He said, 'Well, my sister Gwen painted that, and one day people will come to realise she was a much better painter than I am.' And he was right, I think they have.

He asked me if I knew how to play shove-ha'penny. I'd never heard of it and said so. He brought out a little board and taught me how to play it. I've never played it since. He asked a bit about me – what did I want to do, and what was I doing, but I can't truly remember much else of the conversation because I was so wonderstruck. I was very much in awe of this man who seemed to fill the landscape – he really was a big chap. Some people dwindle with age, but he didn't seem to: he was still immensely physical, and very present.

After this slightly awkward chat, Augustus said, 'Right, well, we'll take you into the studio now.' We went out of the house and into the studio, which was an extraordinary white modernist construction at the bottom of the garden, with two storeys and a strange, curved, snailshell-like staircase. His studio space was on the ground floor. It had a high ceiling, tall windows with clean, white upholstered window seats (where, I supposed, his models must have posed), and lots of dazzling light. Like the house, it was higgledy-piggledy and not at all tidy.

Augustus said, 'I'm doing a study of bathers by the sea. You might as well take your clothes off now.' And so, without any curtain or anything, I speedily divested myself of my polka-dot dress in front of him. This was the moment I'd been waiting for; I was nervous but excited too, in a good way. I'd never stripped for anyone before, certainly not for a strange man. I wasn't wearing a bra. I wanted to keep everything simple. I took off my socks and shoes, then finally my knickers, and I stood there naked, feeling quite embarrassed, hoping my plumpness wouldn't put him off.

Augustus John looked at me, stroked his beard contemplatively, and said, 'Very nice. Very nice.' Then he said, 'Your skin takes the light.' I thought that was a fine compliment; I treasure it still. Then he said, 'Good! Well, I think what I'd like you now to do is to climb that ladder.' And I thought, 'Blimey, I wasn't expecting that!'

I looked to where he'd indicated and there was a library ladder, which had steps and a pole you could hold on to. He wanted me to go up and down it. I walked over to the ladder and somewhat awkwardly

I clambered up and down. All the while, Augustus John stroked his beard and stared at me. Then he started to draw. I suppose I was there for a couple of hours doing different poses – not all on the ladder. He didn't talk much when he was drawing as he was concentrating, but he was always avuncular, like a humorous uncle, gentle and so sweet. It was a wonderful experience and I cherish it, and one that I later recounted to Michael Holroyd, his biographer.

I remember little of the journey back. Of course, my parents were very interested to know if Mr John had behaved himself. And he had. I had nothing untoward to report on that front, because he'd comported himself quite impeccably. I'm not sure that I shouldn't be insulted that he didn't attempt at least a quick grope, or whether it was Dorelia's watchful eye that ruled out any unseemly advances, because I later discovered that Augustus John's insatiable sexual appetite had allegedly resulted in his fathering up to one hundred offspring. Supposedly, whenever he walked down the King's Road in Chelsea, he would pat any passing ragamuffin on the head 'in case it's one of mine'.

I wrote to him again afterwards, and very sweetly he wrote back and said that it had been very nice to meet me and that he'd like to do some more sketches. But shortly after that, in 1961, he died. I have those letters somewhere. And I never did see the drawings. I don't know what happened to them. They must be somewhere in his oeuvre.

I'm so glad I had the courage to do that. But possibly the thing that clinched the deal was that I said I would do it for free, because most people would have expected money in return. So, the lesson of this story is, I suppose, that it's sometimes worth taking off your clothes for nothing.

Miriam Kibbutznik

Being Jewish, I've been lucky enough to have two distinct linguistic influences in my life – English, obviously, because I was born and brought up in Britain, but the cadences of Yiddish are also deliciously familiar. As a little girl, I was always hearing the sounds of people whose first language was not English. As the only Yiddish-speaking GP in Oxford, the many refugees from London and abroad who found my father did so with relief. For many, German was their mother tongue, but they didn't want to speak that language anymore; it reminded them of the Nazis and how they had suffered at their hands. They preferred to speak English, albeit brokenly, with the German-Jewish accent which, whenever I hear it, brings back a vanished milieu. My father's patients would try hard to be English and would say things like, 'How are you? Very nice to meet.'* When we brought *Gertrude Stein and a Companion* to the Hampstead Theatre Club in 1985, I heard those same accents in the theatre foyer and all over Swiss Cottage. Death has silenced those voices now but I remember them and love to imitate them so they live again.

Mummy and Daddy did talk about the war – not in huge detail, but as a child you somehow glean things when something serious is going on. There were ration books and lines of POWs in blue uniforms

---

* One of them, Mrs Kemp, used to say, 'Dr Margolyes, I put my leg down!' – instead of 'I put my foot down.'

marching down Cornmarket, but I didn't really know what had happened until much later on. Once I was old enough to understand, it cast a shadow from which I have never escaped.

Obviously my parents' friends and father's patients weren't all Jewish but, nonetheless, I was steeped in Jewishness. Every time somebody came on television, Mummy would say, 'He's Jewish.' We were thrilled when Frankie Vaughan got to number one in the hit parade. He was called Vaughan because his grandmother said to him, in her thick Yiddish accent: 'Frankie you are my number vone [Vaughan] grandson.' I still look at every cast list at the end of television programmes to see who's Jewish.

I even had a Jewish penfriend, through the *Jewish Chronicle*'s Children's Page. We corresponded for some years. She lived in South Wales, in a little town called Tonypandy. There was once a flourishing Jewish community in South Wales. Merthyr Tydfil has one of the loveliest synagogues in Britain, now disused, but do visit if you can; sheep graze nearby high up, overlooking the town. Whenever I can, I visit synagogues; as religion dwindles and congregations age, the synagogues close. I want to keep alive the past and support parish churches in the same way. Religion isn't important to me, but I want to acknowledge the people who took on the challenge of continuing their heritage in a strange land.

When I started at Oxford High School, Mummy went to see Miss Stack and announced: 'We have our own religion and I don't want Miriam to attend lessons about the New Testament.' Now I regret that I'm ignorant of Book Two. I could have read it for myself – I never did. During assembly, which was Christian where hymns were sung, or during choir practice, the few atheists and Jews at the school used to go to another classroom. We read poems, which the teachers thought was a punishment, but actually it was a pleasure. We were always very aware of being Jewish, and I never let anyone forget it. That's still true.

When I was in the First Form, one of the other children said to me, 'You killed Christ.' I said indignantly, 'I didn't.' And she said, 'Yes, you did! You're a Jew and you killed Christ.' I was upset and I went back home and told Mummy. Straight away, without a second's pause, she said, 'Right, I'm going to the headmistress.' She always confronted things head on. She arrived at the school and marched right up to the office. I don't know what she said to Miss Stack. It wasn't the child's fault, after all, she'd just heard it from her parents, but she never said anything like that again.

———

From my earliest memory, a little blue collection box made of tin and decorated with a star of David, marked 'The Jewish National Fund', sat in our hallway. Every Jewish household had one, and everybody put coins into it, and it all went towards the charity collection for the building of the Zionist dream.

As soon as I was old enough I wanted to go to Israel; I bought the lie that we were all taught as young Jews, that the Arabs had no right to be in Israel, that Israel is an amazing country which should belong only to the Jews, where clean water flowed in places that had never had it before. European Jewry had been almost obliterated, but here was a country where they survived, where they flourished, where they were in charge of things – it meant life: it was the future; it was hope.

I was in my late teens when I first went to Israel. It had become a popular pastime for young Jews to volunteer for work on Israeli *kibbutzim*. I had become friendly in Oxford with the niece of one of my father's patients, a girl called Naomi Assenheim, born in Israel of Romanian parents. She was staying further up the Banbury Road with her uncle during her holidays. She lived in the Galil (Galilee), on a *moshav* (a less rigorous socialist construct than a *kibbutz*). She completely believed in the system. The accepted version of the *kibbutz* was that it was a rural settlement, peopled largely by Russian immigrants, who worked hard on the land. Children were separated from parents and brought up by other members of the community. It was pure socialism in action, an experiment in communal living. I wish the system had continued: the *kibbutznik*s were idealistic, decent people. They didn't hate Arabs, and perhaps Israel would have developed differently if their energies had fuelled the land.

Naomi suggested that I go to a *kibbutz* in the Negev desert called Urim, so I did. I was frightened of flying, so I went by boat. I was quite a larky girl, on my own on an intrepid adventure, and I loved the experience of sailing, but my cabin was down in the bowels of the ship and very noisy and smelly. All the officers looked handsome in their white naval uniforms and one of them noticed me: travelling solo, with big breasts. He came over to me as I was sitting on the deck, reading. 'Do you like this perfume?' he asked, and showed me an enormous bottle of scent. He sprayed a bit on my wrist. 'It's lovely,' I said. He smiled, 'It's yours.' I demurred but he made me take it. He insisted I spray it liberally all over myself. It was jolly nice.

Then he said, 'We have a cabin up on the top deck looking to the sea, with its own porthole. Would you like this cabin?' 'Oh, is it available?' I asked. He said, 'Sure, I'm an officer. I can arrange it.'

'Oh, how lovely of him!' I thought.

I asked an orderly to schlep all my luggage up several decks and all that day I flounced about the cabin, enjoying its facilities, luxuriating in my good luck.

After supper in the first-class dining room, I went to bed. At about two o'clock in the morning, I woke with a start. The officer had let himself into the cabin. 'What are you doing?' I cried. 'Oh, darling, you didn't think I'd send you to this cabin and you would be all alone . . .?' he crooned. 'But I thought that you were giving it to me . . .' I stammered. 'Sure, it's yours, but we share it, yes?' he said, sliding into bed alongside me. I said, 'No, no, I don't want that . . . that wasn't . . . I didn't think that's what you wanted.' He said, 'What do you mean? I'm giving you a beautiful first-class cabin, and you think it's just like that?' 'Well, yes. I did,' I said, firmly. Less pleasantly, he said, 'No. If you want the cabin, I have to share it with you.'

I got out of the bed, repacked all my things and returned to my lowly cabin in the middle of the night. I didn't feel scared; I didn't think he was going to rape me; I knew all I had to do was start screaming and there would be people right next door – he would have got into trouble. I was seventeen: it had never occurred to me that there would be a price to pay! How naive of me: I felt angry and embarrassed at my stupidity; I told nobody, I just thought 'What a fucking creep.' After that, I avoided him, and he avoided me, and that was that. I was in steerage for the rest of the voyage.

The boat docked at Haifa. The arrivals hall was chaotic, packed and boiling. The heat hit you, as if you'd walked into a wall – it almost knocked you over. I looked up at the notice over the entrance arch: 'If you will it, it is no dream' – a quotation from Theodor Herzl, the founder of political Zionism. That's what he said about the state of Israel in 1880; it was eventually realised in 1948. It took a long time for Zionism to achieve this result.

I was excited to be in Israel, eager to discover what escapades lay in store for me at my *kibbutz*, and eagerly boarded the train for the Negev. When I got there, they said, 'Welcome. So, you are going to wash and dry the dishes for five hundred people.' That was my job. I thought, 'Fuck that!' I hadn't travelled across the world to be doing dishes for my whole stay; I wanted a job in the open air. I told them that, and I was transferred to the fields, picking oranges.

It was invigorating but hard work. I was intoxicated by the energy of the *kibbutz*, at finding myself surrounded by fascinating, tall and handsome young people. They are an extraordinarily good-looking nation. I loved to see the girls in their army uniforms – they were *gorgeous*. It was a place where new things were happening, where the sea was being transformed into drinking water and used to irrigate the land. The desert was blooming.

A lot of young Jews from England went out to be on a *kibbutz* and make new things happen. That wasn't me: I was not a pioneer. I'd always assumed that Jews didn't really do any kind of practical, manual work, because Mummy said, 'If you want a job done, get a man in to do it.' Daddy could no more put up a shelf than fly, so we had proper workmen in to do jobs around our house. I wouldn't dream of digging the garden or doing woodwork or anything like that. It's not what we do. Other young Jews spent a year in Israel, helping to build a nation. I hadn't come to build Israel; I just wanted to experience this thriving new country for a few months. I thought of it as an alternative summer holiday.

I didn't meet any Palestinians nor Arab-Israelis, but at that time I didn't have a consciousness. As my politics developed, I fell out of love with Israel – and I didn't go again, for a long time.

Cambridge

I went up to Cambridge in October 1960 and that's when my life started. That was the moment I knew I would have the chance to become *myself*. I knew it was going to open a door of endless possibilities. And it did. It was at Cambridge that I became *who I am*.

I was determined to make an impression, not least sartorially. I decided to smoke a pipe. I wore a circular blue fur hat and swore all the time. That certainly got me noticed, although looking back I see how silly and exhibitionistic I must have seemed.

My parents drove me to Cambridge in our Daimler Conquest Century saloon. Daddy bought this wonderful car second-hand from Organs Garage in North Oxford. It was his pride and I felt it was a perfect car to transport me to my new life. Liz and I were at Newnham together, which was and is an all-female college. It was founded in 1871 by a group of radicals – philosophers, campaigners, scientists, writers – who came together to create a Cambridge college that organised 'lectures for ladies'. They built their own library in 1897, because at that time the women students couldn't use the university libraries. (It wasn't until 1948 that Cambridge allowed women to receive degrees.)

Newnham is divided into four halls; Liz and I were in Old Hall, which was the oldest part of the college, and is the most elegant. For three years I lived there in beauty and fellowship, some lust, a little learning, and sowed the seeds of my career.

The friends I made at college remain dear to this day. I had no brothers and sisters but suddenly I felt part of a family, of a community – a much-used word these days, but so it was. We undergraduates lived together on site, each in our own room, and we breakfasted together. Breakfast makes a community. You arrive fresh (or not) from sleep, you share your night thoughts, discuss the day's events, lectures in the offing, love and the lack of it. Plus, there was always a proper cooked breakfast, and the scrambled eggs were excellent. I'm told I used to come down to the breakfast table each day and announce, 'I have just had a wonderful bowel movement.' This is (alas) possible: every morning Daddy asked me if I'd moved my bowels. I was merely continuing that tradition.

Going to Cambridge meant I was finally allowed to own a bicycle. Mine had a little basket on the front for my books and shopping, and a bell to warn people of my approach. As I am very short, I couldn't reach the ground by merely lowering my feet from the pedals; at every traffic light, I was obliged to dismount fully – a nuisance. Now that I'm a driver, I view cyclists with dislike – there are too many on London roads and they are aggressive. But in Cambridge, sixty years ago, it was a pleasant way to get about.

At night we used to sit in each other's rooms, drinking hot chocolate or tea and talking. I think I talked a lot. The confidences we exchanged cemented our closeness.

The top floor of Old Hall above the gateway was our eyrie; there were four rooms and the kitchen – called the Common Stock. That's where I kept my food.

When people came for tea and cakes, mine were always better than anyone else's. I'm a good hostess – learnt from Mummy – and

I'd prepare my speciality, which was fried mushroom stalks. I'd discovered you could buy mushroom stalks more cheaply than mushrooms in the market. And very often I'd have smoked salmon and cream cheese. I've always felt that smoked salmon was an essential ingredient of any social occasion. But it must, like a woman, be MOIST!

The star of our year was blonde, caustic, brilliant Susan Andrews. She died five years ago from Alzheimer's – Liz Hodgkin, Annie Whitehead, me and a few others scattered her ashes in the River Lee. There were two other Jewish girls – Liz Miller from Hull: very elegant and beautiful, a gentle soul; and Laura Kaufman, reading Law: intense and nervous, unsatisfied, with a perfect, chiselled face. Her family background was unhappy; I wasn't surprised when I visited her dark Mayfair home and met her tight-mouthed mother, so different from mine, but in Old Hall Laura laughed a lot. And there was glamorous Jill Corner, from Darlington, reading Modern Languages: glowing dark eyes and a soft North East accent; all the boys adored her. She was Catholic, plagued with stomach problems, often fainting but always lovingly surrounded with admirers, a loyal friend even now. And my closest friend, Sophy Gairdner, from a magical Cambridge family of four sisters: calm, thoughtful, compassionate. Sophy is still part of my life. My Newnham friends became my family. I cannot imagine being without them. I honour and cherish what they have given to me and continue to give.

First-year students to Cambridge, as with most universities, are invited to attend the Freshers' Fair, where the different societies display their wares. Each society had a table with their leaflets, programmes and badges, and the president of the society sits there to answer questions and encourage the freshers to join. Mummy always went to the Ideal Home Exhibition – it was similar and equally mouthwatering. I knew I would join the Jewish Society and as many drama clubs as possible, but the Cambridge University Social Services Organisation (CUSSO) was a delightful surprise: their leaflets explained that they visited prisons.

My OHS obituary in the Form magazine had predicted I would become a probation officer rather than an actress. My delight in criminals had started as a schoolgirl; one of my hobbies had been to go to the Oxford County Court sessions and listen to the cases, sitting in the public gallery. I saw and heard the details of crime close up, and joining the social services organisation was a continuation of that. I sometimes wonder if the appeal of the criminal community might stem from the DNA input of my felonious grandfather.

I went to visit Broadmoor (an institution for the criminally insane) with CUSSO; I've never forgotten it. We were taken around the jail to meet the inmates, and we were left alone with them. I can remember this very vividly, because many of the incarcerated at Broadmoor looked as mad as snakes. Sorry if that offends some of you, but it is so. They looked vicious and deranged and of course I knew that they were nearly all murderers. Our group was taken to the carpentry workshop, full of saws, drills and screwdrivers – useful tools for murder. And I was so interested in talking to the inmates that I got left behind: everybody else continued the tour, and I was left chatting to the men making cupboards and shelves and toys. I suddenly realised that I was on my own in a room full of sharp objects and mental patients; for the first time, I became scared.

I remember thinking: 'I must not show that I'm terrified. That would be very rude.' So I said, 'Oh, blimey, I am so sorry. It's been fascinating talking to you, but I've got left behind. I'd better hurry up and join the others.' And I left.

Naturally, at the Freshers' Fair, I joined the drama societies: the Mummers and the CUADC – the Cambridge University Amateur Dramatic Club, which has its own theatre called the ADC.

It was then that I started to act regularly and, I suppose, determined that I would become an actress. You had to audition to join the ADC, and the piece I chose was Lady Bracknell's interview with Cecily Cardew. On stage, I wore trousers tucked into hockey socks because it was so cold – perhaps unsuitable garb for Lady B, but I must have made the right choice because Christabel Keith-Roach (bless her) saw my audition and immediately said, 'We'll have her. She's good.' So, I joined the Amateur Dramatic Club and worked a lot with all the college drama societies, including Queens and Trinity Hall (every college, apart from Newnham, had its own drama group), doing Shakespeare and Marlowe and many obscure modern plays too.

Acting became the focus of my Cambridge world. That, and my crush on my moral tutor, Lesley Cook, on which more below. Oh, and sucking people off.

I didn't have sexual intercourse at Cambridge. Some did; I didn't. It was partly because my parents told me that I mustn't, and also, of course, because I didn't know then that I was gay. (We called it 'queer'.) But I had the usual hormones of a young woman, so I was tearing around rather frustrated. It was imperative to have a boyfriend – there was a competitive element in it. Other people were pairing off, kissing and rubbing and 'necking' as it was called, and I didn't know what to do with myself. And so I just sucked people off.

My prowess at oral sex was well known in Cambridge. I felt it was one of my best things – certainly the sexual activity I'd had most experience of performing. It didn't matter to me whose penis was in my mouth, it was all grist to the mill; I knew I was giving pleasure, which was what delighted me. One day, in my second year, I was cycling along the cobbles and I stopped for the traffic lights. I looked to my right; alongside me there was an open-topped car driven by a handsome American soldier. I cannot explain my impulse but I called over to him, 'Would you like to follow me to my college and I will suck you off?' The young man blinked but he followed me; I parked my bike, he parked his car, followed me to my room, and I performed as promised. Afterwards, he seemed pleased and said, 'What do you say I come back next week and bring some friends?'

I related this at breakfast the following morning, and everyone seemed quite taken aback by my boldness, but I thought I was a good girl – a bad girl would have had full intercourse. I hadn't let him anywhere near my vagina, after all. He was a pleasant chap, from Texas.

My friends' favourite story of my misdemeanours happened in the Newnham bike shed. One evening, late after rehearsals, I was in the bike shed sucking someone off. And Lesley Cook, my moral tutor, was parking her bike and she saw me. She didn't see the bloke as he was in the shadows, but she saw me bending down over something and said, 'Goodnight, Miriam.'

'Goo' 'ight, 'iss 'ook,' came my polite reply, my usual, clear diction muddied as my mouth was full of cock.

I didn't just suck off random strangers, however. In fact, I now had a boyfriend. The first was a decent guy in his third year called Ted. One of my Old Hall friends had been asked to bring another girl along on a blind date. I joined her and her chap: Ted was with them. The third-year males really were men, as they had done National Service; this had ended in 1960, so our male contemporaries had come straight from school and seemed boys in comparison. Ted was clearly a man, an engineer – truly, I remember little more than that about him. I didn't love him but our sexual fumbles were fun and it meant I had a boyfriend. The second was David Bree, also studying engineering; he was the lighting man at the ADC Theatre. He said he fell for me from his lighting box high in the eaves. Once I came on stage, he didn't look at anyone else. I was in a nursery production of *The Sport of My Mad Mother.* He didn't see all the things that I think of when I think of myself: he didn't think I was fat; he saw someone he really fancied. He thought: 'That girl's got oomph.' He was from Norfolk and he invited me, several times, to stay with his parents. They had boats on the Broads and we went sailing – very *Swallows and Amazons.* David and I spent a year as an 'item'. It was easy to meet as we were both at the ADC most of the time, rehearsing: me on the stage, David in the lighting box.

I was cast as the Third Witch in the Marlowe Society's production of *Macbeth,* directed by Trevor Nunn. The make-up involved sticking false beards on our faces, but it turned out that I was allergic to the spirit gum and my usually excellent complexion bubbled up into a swollen pus-filled expanse. I kept to my room for fear of running into Lesley Cook. Thankfully, by the first night, the boils had disappeared.

After the Cambridge run, the production travelled to the Theatre Royal, Newcastle. At the first night party, an extremely drunken affair, I met Jack Shepherd. We were to act together ten years later in *The Girls of Slender Means* and then (less successfully) in *The White Devil.*

Once in Newcastle, David and I had unfettered time together. We spent hours in bed, enjoying the varieties of positions in our sexual repertoire. David has a remarkable mouth – generous lips – and his kissing technique was excellent. We also had our first major row: when he wouldn't let me bring fish and chips into the theatre. At the time I couldn't believe he would come between me and my food, but our fight taught me an unbreakable rule of the theatre.

I had joined the Jewish Society because my parents wanted me to, and I did, in fact, have a Jewish boyfriend too, called Michael. He was studying Law, and in my second year he invited me to the Pitt Club Ball. The Pitt Club was the Cambridge equivalent of the Bullingdon Club in Oxford, full of snotty, ex-public-school boys. Michael had been to public school; he was a tall, chunky Sephardi, belonging to a good family. He spoke well and might have been considered 'a catch' from the social point of view. But he also had very bad breath. There was no groin excitement on my part. I knew that my parents would have loved him, but it was never going to happen. The Pitt Club, however, attracted me; I was my mother's daughter after all. I was curious to see for myself just how snobbish it was. So I accepted his invitation.

That year of 1962, I actually went to three May Balls – the Pitt Club Ball with Michael; the Kings May Ball, the grandest of all, with Saam Dastoor (now Sam Dastor); and then to Caius, with David. That was quite a good tally for a girl who didn't sleep with any of them. Saam was particularly gorgeous. He read English and wanted to be an actor. He had fine dark eyes, a slender figure and a superb speaking voice. The only drawback from an acting point of view – he looked Indian. He was a Parsee and wore his Nehru suit – white and high-necked. We stayed up all night and went down the river to Grantchester in the early morning for breakfast. Sam is still my friend; he constantly refers to his 'disastrous career' and feels English racism deprived him of the roles his talents merited. He's quite right. He played the Fool opposite Paul Scofield's Lear, but he should have been Leading Man at the RSC and the National. Even more frustrating was not being cast as Gandhi in the film. He would have acted Sir King Bensley off the screen.

Liz, naturally, joined the Labour Club and CND. The shadow of a nuclear war weighed heavily on all our imaginations. I remember the Cuban crisis of April 1961 when the US invaded the Bay of Pigs. It was spring term in my first year away from home. We were all terrified, that weekend in particular, when the political commentators really thought that an atomic armageddon was about to be unleashed. Our considered reaction to the horror? We queued up for the Newnham phone box to call our parents. That was the measure of our political consciousness. Liz said of those days: 'We were certain that the world was going to end in a nuclear holocaust. And when it didn't, nothing has seemed quite so bad ever since.'

We undergraduates were not left to deal with our terrors alone, however, as each college had a moral tutor, *in loco parentis*, whose role was to support us. The aforementioned Lesley Cook was the moral tutor of Old Hall. She was a dashing woman with vibrant, strawberry-blonde hair, and was very tall and athletic: she sailed, she rode – her Dalmatian, Rubble, bounding along behind. I thought about her most of my time in Cambridge – I desired her fiercely. To this day I still do not know whether Lesley Cook was of my persuasion. I suspect that she probably was, and I did tell her repeatedly that I loved her. The avowal of my passion must have been awkward for her because she was a moral person; sleeping with a student would have been unthinkable. My way of reaching her was to bring her bags of fudge from the Copper Kettle, the much-loved tea shop on King's Parade. At midnight, I would knock on her study door when I saw there was a light under it. She would let me in and I would give her the fudge, then I'd sit on the floor, and talk and listen. She dazzled me. She was an economist; her specialist subject was cement. Cement was not particularly dazzling to me, but we managed to range beyond it. We would talk about the world, politics, Cambridge, sailing, drama – everything. I was never happier than gazing up at her, trying to engage and amuse her. I think she liked me but, alas, never more than that.

Towards the end of that first year, one of the third years, Susan Earp, killed herself. Her friends had all been going to a party; she had told them that she didn't want to go and stayed behind. When they went to fetch her for breakfast the next morning, her door was locked and they smelt gas. They broke the door down and found her lying there, dead. One of the girls gave a scream that resounded through the whole building: I've never forgotten that sound. I knew immediately that such a howl of despair and shock could only mean that somebody had died. That day, I remember standing at the bottom of the stairwell as the coffin was being carried down the winding Old Hall stairs. That is when it hit me that she was really dead, a few feet away from me in that coffin, and I felt guilty – because I had known she had been unhappy. We *all* knew: when she came down to breakfast, we could see from her expression that this was a soul in torment, but we wouldn't have dreamt of speaking to her because she was third year and we were first year.

I decided that I must never let an unhappiness go unremarked or uncomforted again, and if I saw anybody unhappy, I would talk to them. From that time, I instituted coffee gatherings when people in the third year would talk to people in the first and second years. We deliberately cut across those barriers.

Lesley Cook felt responsible for Susan's suicide. She told me: 'I feel I have let her down, and let the university down and her parents and the college.' She was not responsible, but she felt guilty because Old Hall was in her charge. Not long after, she left Cambridge to go to Sussex University and another tutor replaced her.

The last time I saw Lesley Cook was puzzling. It was years later when I came to Brighton Theatre Royal with *The Killing of Sister George*. To my delight she wrote, inviting me to stay with her on Saturday night. I accepted with alacrity and drove there after my two shows. She seemed extremely pleased to see me. We had a light supper and then she said, 'I'm sure you're very tired. I want you to have my room, I'll sleep in my spare room.' Of course, I tried to argue, but she insisted.

As I was getting undressed, she came into the bedroom in her underwear and said, 'Sorry to barge in. I've left my nightie in here.' She looked gorgeous, still a woman in her prime. I gawped at her, stammered, 'Oh, of course.' There was the slightest of pauses – and she left. Should I have launched myself at her? I wanted to but I didn't. I didn't sleep a wink that night. Breakfast was very agreeable and I left. It's one of the might-have-been moments in my life. We stayed in touch; she died some years ago. She was very dear to me.

I never felt alone or lonely at Cambridge. While I was surrounded by my friends, Mummy and Daddy also loved coming to see me there. So much so, that Ruth Cohen, my principal at Newnham, remarked: 'Your parents are here so often, Miriam, I could swear they're keeping terms.'

As you see, quite clearly, I have not separated myself from my parents, and I probably never will, but I must admit that I was a little bit embarrassed by their frequent presence. Daddy got quite friendly with Ruth Cohen; I think he once asked her something incredibly personal about her knickers. I've tried to forget what it was.

In my second year at Newnham, my close friend and supervision partner Sophy Gairdner and I had a joint twenty-first birthday party on the banks of the Grantchester River. Nearly two hundred people came and it was a roaring success. It went on from lunch to late. All the food had to be carried across the meadows from the car to the riverbank. People arrived by car, on foot and in boats. The Gairdners brought masses of drink; Mummy had done the catering, but in the haste to get to Cambridge early, she left 600 meatballs behind in Oxford by mistake. Daddy drove all the way back to Oxford to fetch them. That's how much they loved me.

After the party, I stayed at Countess Elisabeth von Rietberg's house in Adams Road. She was a generous, rather lonely divorcée, who seemed to enjoy spending time with students. In the morning, the headline in the Sunday papers was 'Marilyn Monroe found dead'.

Adventures in Academia

When I first arrived at Cambridge, my Exhibition to Newnham College was for Anglo-Saxon. About three weeks into my first term, I realised that Anglo-Saxon was not a language anybody spoke. I thought, 'What am I doing here? What the hell am I doing reading Anglo Saxon? That's bollocks. I want to communicate with people.' I don't even know why I'd plumped for it in the first place. I think I imagined it was special and different, whereas English seemed a rather predictable subject, but I was wrong. I went to see Dorothy Whitelock. I asked if I could change. Professor Whitelock was very understanding. The college authorities even allowed me to keep my Exhibition – and my long superior gown, the outward manifestation of my award.

So I switched course and I never regretted changing. I was, however, surprised by the level of academic vituperation that the academics had for each other. I was always a Leavisite: Dr Frank Leavis and his wife, Queenie Leavis (who was Jewish, by the way), embodied the intellectual fulcrum of Cambridge for me, but they were loathed by most of their colleagues.

Lady Lee, the wife of the Master of Corpus Christi and mother of my great friend Susan, gave a party for the Faculty; and when the Leavises walked into the room, everyone else walked out. It was a demonstration of hostility and contempt the like of which I've never heard. That was the sort of thing that could happen at

Cambridge, especially in the English department, which was riven with bitterness, recrimination and back-stabbing.

I don't know why people felt such animosity to Dr Leavis, although he *was* caustic. He would make cutting remarks about the Master of St Catherine's College, Brigadier Tom Henn, who was very much an army man. He'd seen active duty during the war, and used to give his lectures with a swagger stick under his arm. He would point it at the blackboard and say, 'Today we're on the Symbolists,' and strike the board with a resounding thwack. He and Leavis sniped at each other in their lectures. Leavis was wittier: the hall was always packed when he gave his lectures. He spoke with a curious, slightly dying cadence to his sentences – the opposite of theatrical, but in its very opposition to theatricality, it was *unbelievably* dramatic. He fascinated me. It was when I was listening to Dr Leavis that I felt I was drinking in knowledge, that I was with the best people, that I had fulfilled my mother's dream.

It was a heady time; I loved the Leavises: I think they knew it, because they were always extremely nice to me. Queenie gave me a photograph of them together, captioned 'Creative Quarrelling'. Dr Leavis had been her tutor. They had met when he was a young academic and she was his student, and they fell in love and got married. Of course, her family was against the union because he wasn't Jewish, and his family were against it because she was. They were used to opposition from the very beginning, therefore, and were never defeated by it.

My new supervisor, Jean Gooder, head of English at Newnham, who is still alive, said that when I came up for my entrance exam, the marks I got were Alpha Gamma, which are unusual marks, because they're both the top *and* the bottom mark. I think it means they weren't quite sure whether I was going to be very clever or very stupid. I am never quite sure myself!

Jean Gooder was a Leavisite too, so she managed to get Queenie to tutor our year: not everybody had that pleasure. We used to go to their house in Bulstrode Gardens, and she would not only teach us, but she also cooked for us: at the end of every term, there was always a wonderful array of goodies to eat at teatime. As well as being a renowned academic, Queenie Leavis was also a Jewish housewife and, accordingly, the most fantastic baker. She fed us scones and strudel and cheesecake.

All in all, the Leavises had a profound effect on me. They taught me that literature has a crucial moral dimension, and I believe that too. I wasn't just a theatrical butterfly: I did concentrate on certain aspects of my work, but I have to admit I didn't spend hours in the university library, because, more often than not, I was rehearsing: in my three years at Newnham, I took part in twenty productions. But I'm a more serious person than people give me credit for – I'm not just a funny little bundle. In fact, quite recently Jean Gooder sent me Queenie's critique of me as a student and I was gratified to discover it was extremely positive.

I remained in touch with the Leavises. Frank Leavis was never made a Professor at Cambridge. He was never elected to a higher status than Reader at the university, because there was such combined opposition to him. He had to fight every step of the way. But to his students, he was, and is, a hero. Dr Leavis was, above all, a superb teacher. He opened the delights of English literature to me and thereby enriched my life. At his final lecture, the hall was packed, people standing in rows when all the seats had been filled. His slight figure, gown billowing, came out. He gave the lecture, and then paused. 'I've come to the end,' he said, with his characteristic dying cadence. 'And this is the End.' Not a dry eye in the house.

I always felt that Cambridge belonged to me – to me, personally: it was *my* Cambridge. Cambridge gave me everything that I have. It gave me knowledge, friends, emotional excitement; it was an extraordinary time – exactly as it should have been. And in a professional sense, it was the study of Dickens that I undertook whilst there that would prove vital to my career, leading to the show I wrote with Sonia Fraser, *Dickens' Women*.

I feel emotional about Cambridge and Newnham. Whenever I return to the city I'm in tears, because I see around every corner the ghosts of the people I knew, the ghost of myself riding down Sidgwick Avenue on my bicycle. It was a time when I was fully alive, when I became fully myself – it gave me the person I am.

Footlights

My Cambridge days were not a time of unadulterated joy, however. I lost my smile a little when I performed in the Footlights review of 1962, which was called *Double Take*. I didn't like the Footlights boys, and they *really* didn't like me. They made that obvious. At that time, and indeed the whole time I was at Cambridge, a woman could not be a member of the Footlights Club: girls were not welcome; we attended as guests. The first female member of the Footlights was Germaine Greer in 1964, the year after I left the university.

It's a club with a fine reputation and powerful professional influence in the world of light entertainment. Many great comedians started at Footlights: Stephen Fry, Peter Cook, John Cleese, David Frost, Hugh Laurie, Eric Idle, all the Goodies. Every summer term a revue is produced and goes to the Edinburgh Fringe, and often to Broadway and further afield. Throughout the year, 'Smokers' are held: informal concerts where students try out their material and hope to be noticed for possible inclusion in the revue. It is intensely competitive.

When I was asked to audition for the revue, I was delighted if apprehensive. Mummy was overjoyed. She phoned the *Oxford Mail* and gave an interview to them about my brilliance. That didn't make me popular with the lads! I wasn't sure what my role could be. I can't sing or dance, I wasn't beautiful, but I knew I could be funny. The trouble was, they didn't really want 'the girl' to be funny – and that's all

I knew how to be. The publicity photo was of me emerging from a gents' loo with a finger to my lips. Good photo, silly idea.

I was the only girl in the show. I was a pert little madam and I thought I was as good as they were – and they didn't. They thought I was a jumped-up, pushy, over-confident, fat little Jew. But I was funny, and they didn't like it. If you think about it, their *Monty Python* programmes didn't feature funny women, only the occasional dolly bird. And I certainly wasn't that.

Their attitudes towards women stemmed from the minor public schools most of them had attended. They weren't used to dealing with strong, opinionated women. This was before feminism: women were not meant to be funny; they were meant to be decorative. These chaps wanted to sleep with women, not compete with them. I was neither decorative nor bedworthy, and they found me unbearable. The problem was exacerbated by my excellent notices, which were resented. It was actually tangible – the level of competition sharpened. They acknowledged each other's cleverness, but only just, and there was considerable class antagonism. David Frost was looked down on, for example, because he was merely a middle-class lad from Gillingham, and they were not happy when Clive James arrived during the Sixties. His brilliance was unstoppable, but they disparaged his Australian roots – a shortcoming that allowed Clive to be the object of their disdain. But it was like water off a duck's back with Clive; he had no respect for any of them. And they quickly changed their minds about his acceptability.

Cambridge was a competitive place; in Footlights, that became toxic. It was the first time in my life that I experienced that sort of competition. During the entire run of that 1962 revue directed by

Trevor Nunn, they treated me as if I were invisible and did not speak to me at all. I was sent to Coventry: someone had decided I was not to be spoken to offstage. I would go on to do my bits, and then the minute I stood in the wings, I was ignored: silence and cold stares. Initially, I had no idea why. It hurt a lot. When I say 'they', I refer to that most distinguished group of John Cleese, Graham Chapman, Bill Oddie, Humphrey Barclay (who became the Head of Light Entertainment for ITV), Tony Hendra and Tim Brooke-Taylor. Only two cast members continued to talk to me: Robert Atkins and Nigel Brown.

I'd not met studied cruelty like that before. I was nineteen and it was painful. I used to go back to my Newnham room and weep, but I got over it . . . sort of.

In truth, my dislike of that whole, largely male, world of comedy has never left me. I feel awkward, admitting to such bitterness sixty years later – it seems absurd, it shouldn't matter; I should have got over it. But I haven't. The treatment I received by those boys at Footlights was diminishing, pointed and vicious. On reflection, it is they who diminished themselves. I admire the Monty Python creation and I think they were men of genius but they were not gentlemen. Cleese, Oddie and Graham Chapman were total shits – and they have never apologised bar Tim Brooke-Taylor. All the perpetrators went into light entertainment and I went into drama so, thankfully, our paths were to seldom cross.

The crowning nastiness of that whole ghastly experience was that I wasn't invited to the traditional end of production cast party. I was furious. I went to the then president of Footlights, a pleasant chap called Chris Stuart-Clark. (The Monty Python team used his name later for one of the characters in a programme they wrote.) I told Chris that I hadn't been invited. He seemed surprised but said it was probably 'an oversight'.

'No, it isn't an oversight. It's completely deliberate. But I would like an invitation.' I got one and I went to the party. Oddly, I can't remember a single thing about the party, except for my determination to attend. When I see a wrong, I will confront it; I strongly believe in sticking up for what is right. Injustice offends me, deeply.

And, nearly sixty years later, I haven't forgotten.

Saved by the Beeb

I turned up to my Finals in a green ball gown carrying an apple – I was determined to put a brave face on failing my exams. But I left Cambridge with a 2:2 Bachelor of Arts in English (there's a reason it's called the actor's degree).

I like to think I missed out on my 2:1, or my first even, because I did so much acting. By my second year at university, I knew that I wanted to be an actress. I had not been sure of it before, but by then I was resolved.

When I was in the Footlights, everybody said, 'You must get people down.' I had no idea what they meant, but learned that I had to ask agents and producers and directors of the BBC to come and watch the show – 'That's how you will get work.' The Footlights, even then, was a known repository for future talent. So I sent a letter to a radio producer at the BBC, John Bridges. He came down and watched the show, and afterwards, kindly told me that he thought I was talented. He gave me his card and said, 'When the time comes, will you write to me?'

And so, I wrote to John Bridges and said, 'I've left Cambridge, and I really would like to join the BBC Drama Repertory Company. Could you help me?' The company was so sought-after that you had to wait a long time to get an audition. It wasn't until some months later that I actually got the call.

By then my TV career had already begun, in what would later be seen as my trademark shocking style. In 1963, along with my teammates Liz Hodgkin, Jinty Muir and Susan Lee, I represented Newnham College in the debut series of Granada TV's *University Challenge*. We travelled up to Manchester by train, a happy group. But Liz, Jinty and Susan were all completely oblivious to the man masturbating opposite us. My masterstroke was to offer him a peppermint, whereupon he promptly detumesced. I should have kept one for myself. When during the show I couldn't remember something that was on the tip of my tongue, in frustration I swore loudly and we lost the point. It was beeped out of the actual transmission, but I believe I was the first person to swear on national television. I was certainly the first woman to do so. (This predates theatre critic Kenneth Tynan, then the literary manager of the National Theatre, infamously using the F-word during a satirical discussion TV show called *BBC-3*, which is the usual example cited.) The tapes no longer exist sadly. We won our first round, but were knocked out in the second by University College – despite the best efforts of those dear girls. I met Bamber Gascoigne again last year and he acknowledged that my 'FUCK IT!' has resounded in his memory for almost sixty years now.

Before I left Cambridge, Tony Palmer had proudly announced that he had set up a tour of Europe with three plays: *Romeo and Juliet*, *The Importance of Being Earnest*, and a play of *Zuleika Dobson*. I was going to be the star of the tour. I was to play the nurse in *Romeo and Juliet*, Lady Bracknell in *The Importance of Being Earnest* and something else in *Zuleika Dobson*. I felt on the threshold of a great adventure. I was so excited I was finding it hard to sleep. Then, suddenly, about a week before we were due to start, Tony announced: 'I'm sorry. I haven't been able to get the money going. It's off.' It felt like the end of everything. What was going to be a thrilling time travelling around

Prisoner D1321: my great-grandfather Simon Sandmann (note the shifting spelling) who served seven years in Parkhurst.

The Margolyes family, Glasgow, 1908: Daddy extremely serious in his straw boater.

Mummy and Daddy's Bayswater wedding with pages and bridesmaids modelled on *Little Lord Fauntleroy*, 26 June 1930.

A rare picture of Mummy and Daddy relaxing on the beach.

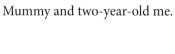

Mummy and two-year-old me.

Channelling my inner Calamity
Jane on Margate Sands.

The three of us heading out for an afternoon stroll.

My first notice: the *Oxford Mail* ran a piece on my winning an elocution competition, aged 9.

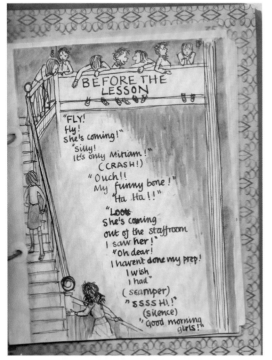

Somehow I was always late and in trouble: cartoon from our 1956 form magazine, drawn by Biddy Peppin.

OHS Upper Fifth, 1957: I can still name every girl.
I'm second from the right in the bottom row.

Hamlet in 1959: a sketch …
by Biddy Peppin.

… and the real thing (Claudius's beard less
convincing): me and Margaret Oldfield.

Watching the battle: Nina Katkov and Elizabeth Parnell, the warriors.

My seventeenth birthday party at 409 Banbury Road, Oxford.

Mobbed by the locals of
Trafalgar Square with
Anna Truelove in 1959.

Daddy, Mummy, Whisky and me.
That bench is still in my garden.

With David Bree at the
Caius May Ball, 1962.

In *Blood Wedding*, directed by Anthony Everitt, just one of the twenty productions I was in at Cambridge.

E. HODGKIN SUSAN LEE JINTY MUIR M. MARGOLYES

NEWNHAM, CAMBRIDGE

University Challenge, 1963: I think from my expression I had just been the first woman to swear on live TV.

Europe doing these plays simply evaporated. Tony is now a famous television director, and I still see him occasionally; largely, these days, at the funerals of our mutual friends. I'm friendly enough, and I think he quite likes me; secretly, though, I've never stopped feeling resentment towards him, for the two years of my life that were lost to acting as a result.

———

Having graduated, I didn't know what to do with myself. I was doing nothing, wasting time, so I went back home to Oxford. Later that year, our fortress family fell apart when Daddy made a pass at our au pair, Boyte, a winsome Norwegian. Nothing happened – in fact, Boyte complained to Mummy, which is how she found out, but it broke Mummy's heart. Her 'good man' was good no longer. Mummy told me, although he had begged her not to and, like Mummy, I could never forgive Daddy. It cemented my view of men as flawed and incomplete beings, incapable of sexual control. Nothing in my life since has led me to change my mind.

There was nothing in my future. I didn't get auditions easily because I hadn't been to drama school, but while I was waiting for my antici-pated glorious career to take flight, I had to do *something*. So I got a job selling encyclopaedias from door to door. I hated it – not the encyclopaedias – but because I had to manipulate people into buying the *Children's Britannica* by making them paranoid about their children's future education, implying that only a bad parent wouldn't sign up. It went against everything I believed in. And when the atmosphere at home became unbearable, I decided to move to London.

It was a strange time in many ways. I would take the tube from Plaistow (where I was living in West Ham vicarage with a very nice family called the Griffins), into the West End to see all sorts of theatre productions, which I loved. I found a new job in market research, which involved asking people questions about which contraceptive method they used. I was working for a respected company called Norland, which had offices in Soho Square. My designated area was Henley-on-Thames. I had to approach people on the street. The company gave me a card on which were listed six or seven different methods of contraception, and I'd give it to people and say, 'Now, which one do you use? Is it number one? Number seven?' but they never gave a number – they'd always just say very directly, 'Oh, my husband withdraws.' It was fun; it was a licence to ask questions. I was getting paid to be a sticky-beak and nose into people's intimate sex lives.

———

After two years of selling encyclopaedias and probing passers-by about their contraception strategies, I wrote again to John Bridges at BBC Radio. He arranged an audition for me with the BBC Drama Repertory Company. It involved a piece of narration, and then something with characters in it, to show versatility. I decided on an unscripted railway journey in which I played all the characters in the compartment. That was when all those little dramas I had created, walking up and down Banbury Road as a schoolgirl, finally came to fruition.

I arrived at Broadcasting House in Portland Place, London W1A 1AA (I can never forget that postcode) and John came to fetch me from reception. I was taken up and introduced to Norman Wright, a staff producer, whose job it was that week to take the auditions. I told them what I was going to do, saying: 'I am now going to give you an example of my astonishing versatility.' No hiding my light under a bushel! Then I was shown into the studio, and John and Norman went into a separate little room to listen to me on headphones.

I was excited, because it was a proper audition. I settled myself at the microphone. I started with my improvisation set in the railway carriage. I hadn't scripted it; I'd just made a list of the accents that I wanted to show them, and then had a conversation between all the characters, making it up as I went along.

Many years later, they told me that it was the most astonishing audition they'd ever heard because I switched between so many voices – male, female, Scottish, Yorkshire, Brummie, Cockney, all the regions, all the ages, French, German, Aussie, etc.

After a week, a letter arrived: 'You did a very good audition and we are sure that we are going to be able to offer you some work in the future.' True to their word, in early autumn 1963, I got my very first radio job.

It was in an 'Afternoon Theatre' play called *Defeating Mrs Dresden*. It went out at 3 p.m. on the Home Service in November that year. I played the 'Hotel Proprietress', so not exactly a major role, but I found it terribly exciting.

Norman was directing, but when he said, 'Right, Miriam, you'll take a flick for that, and then on page seven you'll take a flick for that . . .' I had no idea what he was talking about. 'What does that mean? What is a "flick"?'

Kevin Flood, one of the other actors, whispered: 'See that little light that's on a stand by the microphone? Well, that light is called a "flick", and when that goes green, that's when you have to start talking.' It was my very first lesson in radio.

After that I got a part in *Howards End* which was produced by William Glen-Doepel, and then followed parts in lots more plays, until in 1965 they offered me a full-time engagement for a year. There were a lot more then than there are now, and so from that point on I would be taking part in four or five radio drama productions each week.

There were about forty members of the Rep, and it was considered a fine job to have landed. You got to work with people like Paul Scofield and Claire Bloom, Coral Browne, John Osborne and Jill Bennett, Sir Donald Wolfit, Patricia Routledge and Wilfred Pickles. Wilfred Pickles was famous for going around England interviewing ordinary people in his show *Have a Go* (with Mabel at the table and Harry Hudson at the piano) but he was a good actor as well.[*]

You did anything you were asked. If they wanted narration, you did narration. If they wanted character work, you did character work. You did announcements. You did anything and everything that you were asked to do. We didn't play leading roles (that came later): we played the 'other parts', and because I was versatile, I was useful and had lots of work. And so my career began in radio, which was not at all what I had expected. And it looks as if it will end in radio, too!

---

[*] He played Tom Courtenay's father in the 1963 film *Billy Liar*, and Hayley Mills's uncle in *The Family Way* (1966).

It was in the BBC Rep that I met my friend, Patricia Gallimore, a.k.a Pat Archer, wife of Tony in BBC Radio 4's *The Archers*, and we remain really close. In the 1970s I went on holiday with her to Gozo, near Malta. One of our friends in the BBC owned a house there and we rented it. When we were leaving to fly back to London, we needed to get the ferry over to Malta and the airport. We had rented a car while we were staying in Gozo, and so I dropped her at the harbour, told her to take all our bags and board the ferry, and I'd return the car to the rental place. When I came back to the ferry, it was just easing out of the harbour! I pelted down the quayside, my bosoms hitting me on the chin, to try and jump onto it at the very last minute. I was running and running, but it was too late and I missed it. Pat was on the deck shouting, 'Miriam, what are we going to do?'

I had to get to Valletta because I was carrying the plane tickets. No wonder Pat looked so anxious. I stood there, looking desperately around the harbour, where there were, of course, a lot of rowing boats and fishermen, who naturally had sat and watched the whole farcical scene unfold. I went up to one of the fishermen and I said, 'I missed the ferry, is there any chance you could row me to Valletta?' And this old chap said, 'Sure, sure, get in.'

I jumped down into his boat. It was quite a big drop down to sea-level from the mooring place. When I landed in the little wooden vessel it very nearly upended with the force of my significant bulk. Once it, and I, had regained equilibrium, I sat in the stern and he started to row.

It was quite a long way over to Valletta by rowing boat, and so we chatted to pass the time. He was a nice, old fellow in dungarees and he spoke good, albeit heavily accented, English. He said, 'You see this island?' I said, 'Oh, yes, I haven't been there.' He said, 'That is Comino. Nobody live there. We go to Comino, you and me, now.' I said, 'No, darling, I can't. I've got a plane to catch. Really, I've got to get there because my friend is on the ferry with all our stuff and I have the plane tickets.' But he was insistent, 'No, no, we go,' he said. 'We go!' I replied, 'No, we *can't* go! I've got to get that plane.' Then I saw that he had taken his penis out of his dungarees and he was enthusiastically masturbating. I thought, 'Blimey, what am I going to do? I don't want to get raped. Not on the sea.' So, I got up, went over to him and tossed him off.

He was fine after that; he calmed down. The penis was popped back inside the dungarees and then on he rowed, all the way across. When we finally arrived, he helped me up and I asked him how much I owed. He smiled. 'No charge, Miss.' Bless him, what a gent!

Later, when I was telling this story to a friend and said that I had to toss him off, she replied, appalled, 'You mean you threw him overboard?' I said, 'No! I didn't throw him overboard – I tossed him off!' She got it, eventually.

———

Radio, for me, is the most perfect performance medium. It's the most concentrated: there's nothing else to do but get the voice right. And you don't have to learn the lines! But the creative process remains the same. Acting for radio is no different from acting for the stage, or any other medium, really; it's an exercise in imaginative travel. You journey from yourself into this other person that you have crafted. You are using some of the bricks of your own humanity and personality, and slowly stepping over into another persona which you are inventing, based on the text that you're given and the backstory that you might imagine for yourself. It's always about creating the character with truth – that's the job, whatever medium you're working in.

Radio drama taught me that you should always *talk to an audience as if it's one person*. Working in radio teaches you to focus totally on the person you're talking to. It was superb training. In my early radio days, you could stand on either side of the mike and look into the eyes of the actor opposite. But, later, microphones developed and we actors found ourselves on the same side of the mike. The sound might have been better, but the connection between us was much harder to achieve.

Turning the pages of the script was another skill to be mastered. It had to be done completely silently: a bunny dip away from the microphone, holding one corner of the page between thumb and finger, then turning back, having turned the page as you turned away. Modern paper makes it almost impossible to achieve a silent page turn.

The radio artists I worked with through the years were probably the most skilled in the world. I'd grown up with their voices as a child, and for me they were celebrities. Marjorie Westbury was the queen of Radio in her day. She played Paul Temple's wife, Steve, in the famous detective series. She was small and dumpy like me, but had a clear, warm sound and knew how to use it. She made such an impression on one of her listeners that she was left £42,000 in their will.

So far, this hasn't happened to me.

The other great ladies of my radio days were June Tobin, absurdly sexy and great fun; Grizelda Hervey, always smoking with a husky voice (no wonder) – her Irene in *The Forsyte Saga* was one of the greatest performances I ever heard. Mary Wimbush, who was loved – especially by Tony Jackson, a gifted young actor, who won the Carleton Hobbs radio prize at RADA and had a long affair with her, despite her being very much his senior. They're all dead now, but their voices live on. The recordings in the BBC archives hold magic; the Corporation should digitise them all and give us the chance to listen again to the great voices of the past.

The engineers and studio managers also taught me the skills of the medium; explaining that I shouldn't talk straight into the microphone, but speak slightly across it. That way, the voice is still present, but not *threatening* the mike – you won't 'pop' and distort the sound. I discovered for myself that a smile is helpful for warming the tone of the voice. I don't know why, but the lift at the corners of the mouth gives a 'shine' to your sound; there is an energy of some kind, a warmth and pleasure, which communicates across the microphone.

When working for radio, of course, you must also be keenly conscious of time. Announcers require that particular facility when they know the 'pips' are approaching, heralding the news. Once, when a live radio production of *Hamlet* seemed in danger of bumping into the 'pips', a resourceful announcer softly interrupted Hamlet's fight with Laertes with: 'And there we must leave Elsinore . . .'

I was lucky to work for many renowned radio directors in the studios of Broadcasting House. David Thomson, for example, an endearing eccentric who had came into drama from the Features department. In 1968, he directed me as the 'Old Gal', an upper-class woman in her nineties, in *A Breath of Fresh Air*, a play set during the First World War. I still think it's one of the best things I ever did.

I enjoyed working with Reggie Smith (also from the Features department) whose productions may have suffered from the rollicking lunch hours we spent in the George Tavern; Betty Davies, tall and Welsh and sexy, who always wore hats, and lived to be a hundred; and Audrey Cameron, Scottish and quite waspish. And the late, great John Tydeman, of course, the immensely influential director who became head of BBC Radio Drama. He directed me 'down the line' reading Sue Townsend's *The Queen and I* in which I played every member of the Royal Family sitting in a studio in Los Angeles, while John was in London. That was made into a disc and went platinum. John was at Cambridge with me and became a great friend. We were both homosexual and fell in love with Australians.

Enyd Williams started as a studio manager and became one of the BBC's finest directors. She persuaded me to record *Dickens' Women* in the Paris Studio in Lower Regent Street for Radio 4. I didn't believe it could work, but her sensitive understanding of the piece made it one of my most successful broadcasts. Enyd taught me so much, for example: 'When you take a breath, don't let's hear it, Miriam. You have to snatch your breath, but softly and quietly.' I notice some newsreaders breathe heavily. They need Enyd to teach them.

Radio is a civilised medium; you have only your voice to use but, of course, when you're acting a part, the whole body comes into play. A voice is a person: if you're just doing a voice, you've left the humanity out – you're only doing half the job.

Our producers in the 1960s were remarkable. The real oddballs had come to the Drama department from Features. Former actors David Thomson and Reggie (R. D.) Smith were huge characters. Martin Esslin, a refugee from Nazism, was intellectual, precise but with a great sense of humour; Ronnie Mason was always smoking, full of mischief.

I remember when B10, the flagship studio, opened in the basement of Broadcasting House. It looked like a moon landscape, with a choice of acoustics, staircases which led nowhere and masses of sound effect doors, full of different bells, knockers and planks. They were covered with the wittiest graffiti, which should have been preserved like Banksy's work. Patricia Gallimore remembered one that ran: 'Miriam Margolyes thinks Clement Freud is a School of Thought. Clement Freud thinks Miriam Margolyes is a School of Porpoises.' Others were far more scurrilous and while we were waiting for our green light we used to read the doors – suppressing our sniggers.

Radio is a particular world and I belong there. The great, glory days have gone – that was in the fifties and sixties, before television became the medium of choice. I was in the last generation brought up entirely on radio: every night I listened to *Children's Hour* with Derek McCulloch, to *It's That Man Again* with Tommy Handley, Deryck Guyler, Jack Train, Joan Harben and Dorothy Summers. I heard *Dick Barton*, *The Brains Trust*, Gilbert Harding, and *The Barlows of Beddington*. *Toytown* with Ralph de Rohan and Norman Shelley.

These voices are part of my youth and it is a source of high delight to me to think I follow in their footsteps, in their *voicesteps*.

Swinging London

D espite my BBC contract, I wasn't earning much, but it was a proper salary at last, and Mummy decided it was time for me to move out of Plaistow. She hated Plaistow; she felt happy, in one way, to have arrived in Oxford, and my returning to a place she felt she'd escaped from was a blow – an entirely class-based attitude. She said, 'Well, you can't live there *now*, darling. It's time to move to somewhere else.'

I wanted somewhere within reasonable distance of Broadcasting House, on the Central Line and perhaps near Hyde Park. I stayed in rooms in Lancaster Gate, in Portland Road, Notting Hill and viewed many flats in Rachman-land. (Peter Rachman was the unscrupulous slum landlord who took over West London and exploited his tenants outrageously.) After some looking, I found my flat in Gloucester Terrace, a beautiful street of early Victorian, white, five-storeyed houses resembling the terraces of Brighton, but in the heart of London. Mummy always called it Bayswater, but it was Paddington, really.

The house was owned by a Jewish lampshade-maker called Mr Sagar, and his wife, Sibyl; they lived in the basement and were both hunched, as if the house above pressed them down, like two little moles that seldom came up from downstairs into the light. They resembled people from a Dickens novel: Sybil was cadaverous, with a deep voice; they had no children and seemed to lead entirely solitary lives, but were educated and artistic. I wish now I'd asked them more about themselves and why they became lampshade-makers and what their backgrounds were. They were intelligent and entirely benevolent, but in those days I didn't see that – I laughed at them and thought they were 'odd', instead of celebrating their individuality. They had a tough cleaning lady, Mrs Morgan, who took many years to get to like me.

My flat was on the ground floor. My bedroom at the back of the house had a flat roof above it, and in the summer I could go out there and talk and drink with friends. I decided to have a flatmate and found a 'nice Jewish girl', Rosalind Stoll, who has remained a dear friend. The rental was twelve guineas a week, which was £12/12s. Imagine living in central London now for twelve guineas a week!

I was never part of Swinging London. If I had been part of the West End set, going out in Soho at night, that would have been thrilling and fun, but I was always someone who read books and went to the theatre. I knew the whole scene was going on, but I never had anything to do with it – I didn't like fashion and I didn't like the Beatles or the Rolling Stones, and I didn't like pop music. I disapproved of it. I also hated the mods and rockers and the violence and Teddy boys: Swinging London left me cold. Apart from Dusty Springfield, that is. Even then, she was my girl. Such an astonishing talent and such a tragic life, all because she came from a Catholic background. She was gay at a time when you couldn't be.

However, I relished the loosening up of the sixties towards gay people. The Sexual Offences Act of 1967 decriminalised homosexual acts between two men over twenty-one years of age *in private* in England and Wales. In 1965, I had joined a group called the Gay Yids and wore my Gay Yids badge when I went to the BBC. People found it rather shocking. I quite liked that, because I thought that being gay was something that could make me more interesting. For me, it was a plus, a feather in my cap. I held Gay Yid parties at the flat and it was during one of them that Saul Radomsky, the great South African theatre designer, met Israeli chef, Oded Schwartz. I loved being a matchmaker for real.

Heterosexual swinging London seemed much less fun. It was harder to help people. One night, I was walking home to Gloucester Terrace from the theatre when I saw a woman lying in the gutter, sobbing her heart out. My sympathies immediately aroused, I went over and asked her if something was wrong. She sat up on the pavement and wailed, 'He threw me in the gutter! He threw me in the gutter!' She was quite a pretty woman in her thirties and she was crying, her hair in a mess and her eye make-up smeared all down her face. I said, 'Look, it's late now and I think you should go home. This is my card. I live in Paddington. Come and see me around eleven tomorrow morning. Let's have a chat about this because I'm sure it's not as bad as you say.'

The next morning I looked up her boyfriend in the phone book. I didn't think about it, I just rang him and said, 'Hello. You don't know me, but I met a friend of yours last night who was in a very miserable state. I don't exactly know the background of the story, but you really can't treat women like that, you know. It's not right.'

His reply was eye-opening: 'Oh, I know who you've been talking to but you don't know the full story. I met her in a gambling club. She was the pretty girl dealing out the cards, and I fell for her and we had an affair. I'm a married man, and I know that I shouldn't have done it. I just lost my head and I fell for her, and she fell for me, and she got obsessed. One night she climbed up the drainpipe at the front of my house, and my wife and I were in bed, and she banged on the window and gave my wife a rotten fright. She's lost her marbles, this girl. She's gone so bonkers that I had to take out an injunction to stop her from coming round. She won't leave me alone. I used to love her, but I can't stand her now. I don't want her anywhere near me.'

Just then, there was a ring at the doorbell and I thought, 'Oh Jesus! It's her! What have I got myself into?' I took a deep breath and opened the door, and there she was, looking perfectly calm and normal. I brought her in and made us both cups of coffee.

I really thought I was helping. I thought that she deserved to know the truth. So, speaking tentatively, I said, 'Well, you know, people fall out of love – it happens.' She wasn't having any of that. 'No, no, he's in love with me, I know it. He hasn't fallen out of love; I know it. It's just that everybody tries to make him get rid of me.'

'Listen, you're a pretty girl. Wouldn't you be better off forgetting about him and finding someone else, starting a new life?'

'No, no, I don't want that,' she cried.

I decided to bite the bullet. 'Look, darling, I've spoken to him.'

She went nuts. Her eyes widened, and she started to wail and thrash about, as if I'd pressed a button: 'What, you've spoken to him? What did he say? What did he say?'

'I think, to be quite honest, that it's really over,' I said, gently.

Then the dam broke. Her pain and neurotic rage burst its banks and drowned her. She ran round and round the kitchen, screaming. Then she snatched my bread knife from the counter. She came close to me, the knife held high, her voice at scream level, her eyes mad and wide, threatening: 'Don't you say that to me! Don't you dare say that to me!'

Well, now I was scared. I realised this woman was off her head and dangerous and I had to get out of there. I ran to the kitchen door which had a lock on it. I put the snib down and got out of the door in a desperate panic. My phone was just outside the kitchen door: I phoned a friend: 'Michael, please come NOW. I've got a lunatic in the flat and I'm scared.' He promised to come straightaway but didn't turn up for another two hours. That was Michael all over!

After a bit, I couldn't hear anything when I pressed my ear to the door. Very carefully, I opened it. There she was, crouched and sobbing, the knife on the table. I said, 'Look, I've made a mistake. I thought I could be helpful, and I've made it worse. So, I'm asking you, please, please, just go home. Try to forgive me. I meant to do well by you but I haven't.' She didn't say anything; she just took her handbag and left. I leant against the door, breathless with relief.

Most people, if they see a woman crying in the gutter, make sure that she's not injured, and then they go on their way. I tend to rush towards the situation and tackle it head-on. I can't help it. I am fuelled by curiosity and thinking that I can somehow be a shining light, a good Samaritan and help. But in this instance I made things much, *much* worse. It was a real lesson. And it was yet more evidence that Swinging London wasn't nearly as much fun as everybody said.

The Importance of Voice

My world has always been about speech. Voice is vitally important to me. My professional life is often based on understanding and replicating voices: identifying the subtle nuances of geogra-
phy, time and class; searching for a character's background, and then
mining that rich seam to create them, using speech as my starting
point.

Listening to the radio as a child, I remember hearing Dylan Thomas
intoning in his sonorous, South Walian voice, pulling me into his
world; the particularity of his vision excited me; he was a magician. That's why I chose his reading of an excerpt from 'A Visit to
Grandpa's' when I was on the radio show *Desert Island Discs*. Kirsty
Young told me I'd chosen more speaking records than anyone in the
history of the programme.

Growing up, and well beyond that, BBC voices were almost univer-
sally RP (received pronunciation), different from the beloved imper-
fections of the voices of my family. In my parents' push to choose the
best education they could for me, a big part of that education was
ensuring that I shouldn't speak like Mummy – or like Daddy, who
never lost his Glasgow accent.

There is an Oxford High School voice; I have it, as did most of the
middle-class girls who went to my school. But accents separate people:
used as clues to a person's background they enable and reinforce snobbery. I thus acquired an accent that was different to my mother's: I

could hear the difference and that sharpened my awareness of class, and separation. I'm sad because I can't hear my mother's voice in my head any more. Hers wasn't a stereotypical 'Jewish' accent; it was powerful, and well-produced, but there was an unpolished South London inflection to it, slightly different from Cockney. Mummy wanted me to sound 'posh'; my voice was an important tool for social mobility, and so she sent me to elocution lessons.

One of my father's patients was an elocution teacher called Miss Mary Plowman, who taught at the High School. I went weekly for private lessons to her flat in Iffley Road. She was an eccentric but lovable woman, who had whiskers and always (like my mother) wore a cape. She suffered from narcolepsy and would fall asleep quite suddenly in the middle of a diphthong. She taught me about diphthongs and triphthongs and iambic pentameters and diaphragmatic-intercostal breathing and the value of vowels and consonants. In my occasional master classes to drama students, I quote Miss Plowman: 'Remember, vowels carry the emotion in a word – consonants carry the sense.' Dame Maggie Smith, another of the High School's illustrious former pupils, was also taught by her.

I enjoyed Miss Plowman's lessons; she made me conscious of 'lips, tongue and teeth'. And breathing, was of course, VITAL. 'Oddi-orri-oddi-orri' she would make me repeat very fast. 'Breath is the material of which voice is made.' She entered me for the Guildhall School of Music & Drama exams. I became the youngest person in the country to have the letters 'LGSMD' after my name.

I don't entirely approve of the concept of elocution. We should judge people according to the purity of their *morals*: the purity of their vowels is neither here nor there. And it's a pity to iron out the rich variety of accents available in the British Isles. We shouldn't all sound the same. Therefore, in some ways I regret that my vowels are pure – because they are: I doubt you'll hear a purer vowel in Equity. That purity was due to Mary Plowman – she was my vowel creator. However, when I want to approach a stranger, to ask the time or to use their loo, I always use the Scottish accent inherited from my father, rather than my own. Scottish has a pleasant and trustworthy sound, and it relaxes people.

After I'd had a few lessons, Mummy entered me for poetry competitions at music and arts festivals – competitive events in places around the country: York, Leamington, Coventry, Warwick, Banbury – all over England. I don't know if such festivals still exist. Mummy would teach me the set poem and I would recite it before the judges. I was always placed in the top three. I have a collection of medals from those times, stored in a drawer. Almost every weekend, we were off somewhere in the Standard Eight to another festival.

There was one drawback, however: the school did not approve. Mummy was called to see Miss Stack, who felt that the festivals were not helpful to my homework. She was wrong: the poems I learnt and the experience of performing in public was extremely useful. I've never lost my nerves, and I'm still often physically sick before going on stage, but at least I do it.

My voice was also useful in another way. Whilst working at the BBC Drama Repertory Company, I became aware that some of my colleagues were making lots of money doing commercial voice-overs for television, advertising various big-name brands of goods. Patrick Allen was the first leading voice artist. Patrick was an actor, with a distinguished career in British films, and he was blessed with a rich, commanding, quite posh voice that enabled him to enjoy a flourishing second career as the self-styled 'grandfather of the voice-over'.

In the seventies, this was a booming growth industry, yet there were fewer voice-over opportunities in TV commercials for women. Generally speaking, people *believed* a male voice: the man was the 'expert'; in fact, male voices accounted for 93 per cent of all commercials. I asked my fellow actors how they'd got into it (I knew it was an extremely lucrative area of the business). Somewhat ungenerously, they would say, 'It's difficult. Almost impossible.' The people who were in the know wanted to keep it to themselves. Mummy always said, 'The world is big enough for everyone' – but then she'd no experience of commercials!

Marise Hepworth, one of my colleagues on the Rep, who was a successful voice artist, told me to get in touch with Wendy Noel, who worked at the Bryan Drew agency in Shaftesbury Avenue and specialised in representing voice-over artists. Patrick Allen was one of hers. If you got on to Wendy Noel's books, apparently, you were made. I sent Wendy a tape and she wrote back and said, 'Well, you're good, but I've got a full stable at present, so I can't really offer you anything. But if I get a gap, I'll get in touch.'

Eventually, many years later, she did.

Sexy Sonia

I have been in showbusiness for over half a century and in that time I've done all kinds of jobs: many of which I remain immensely proud of to this day, and others that, well, were somewhat less glamorous . . .

In the early seventies, while I waited for the much-anticipated phone call from Wendy Noel, imagining my carefully trained RP tones ringing out of radios and television sets everywhere and persuading people to drink a particular brand of tea, eat a certain kind of chocolate bar or even smoke a cigar (more stories on all those to follow), I got a call from Marise Hepworth.

My very first voice job was not what I had expected at all.

'I'm doing some recordings for the Ann Summers sex shop. Would you like to do one?' Marise said.

'Well, how much do they pay?'

'You get £300 in cash. No repeat fees.'

I said, 'I don't deal in cash.' (I've followed my father's advice and have always been ferociously careful. All my income is declared, so I've never been in trouble with the Inland Revenue.) But at that time, £300 was a tempting amount. 'How do I get on to it?'

'Go to the Ann Summers shop, make an appointment, and the guy who runs it will sort you out with an audition.'

I wasn't entirely comfortable about the pornography aspect – Daddy already thought being an actress was akin to prostitution. I rang the shop and asked: 'This is voice only, isn't it? We're definitely not on camera, are we?'

The woman reassured me that it was a porn audiotape – a take-home wanker's kit, basically.

I duly went along to the shop on Tottenham Court Road. The chap at the till sent me to the back of the shop. I pushed my way through slightly greasy, pink and white, fringed plastic curtains, along a murky corridor, and arrived in a cavernous warehouse space, set right back behind the street. It was pitch-black in there and rather eerie, because there were no windows. The shelves were piled high with sex toys of every imaginable description: scrotum twisters, ticklers, handcuffs, nipple clamps and dildos. I'd never seen anything like it. I don't go in for all that lark. I prefer natural to electrical goods.

I introduced myself to the man, and he said, 'Oh, yes. Miriam Margolyes. Well, Miriam, I've written the script. Here it is, and the microphone is over there.'

I said, 'You want me to do it *here*? In the warehouse?'

'That's fine. I just need to know that you can handle it. We'll do the real thing in the studio.'

I gulped slightly and started to read out his appalling script, which was full of heavy breathing, squeals, vocal intercourse and more. I realise for all my dirty talk, I'm quite prudish, and I found it rather unpleasant having to pretend to achieve orgasm in front of this creepy bloke. However, it was a job, I gave it my all, and my moans and squeaks echoed back convincingly from the walls of this urban dungeon.

'Yeah, that was good,' the warehouse fellow said. 'When are you free?'

When I said I was quite free for the next week or so, he gave me a date, and told me to report to Molinare studios in Foubert's Place, just off Carnaby Street (which still exists, but it doesn't do that kind of thing any more).

I turned up at the appointed hour to find that the engineer, David Hodge, was someone I'd worked with before. He was one of the very top sound engineers and I would go on to choose him later to record my show reel. (The sex tape wasn't on it.)

He seemed a bit taken aback to find that I was the voice on this job, so I was all brisk and businesslike: 'Yes, I'm not sure how we're going to do it, but I'll just do the best I can.'

The script had no redeeming features: no characterisation, and it didn't even have a story. It was the account of schoolgirl called Sonia meeting a man and then engaging in a prolonged fucking session, all described in graphic detail. Not many words, but so much panting and gasping and squelching. Simulating orgasms (and there were a lot of orgasms) involved a significant amount of heavy breathing, and I had a bad headache by the end. Truly, one climax is much like another, but I was having to delve into my subconscious to achieve the variety I felt was expected. And at least if you have real sex, you have some fulfilment at the end – my only fulfilment was the three hundred quid. But I wasn't complaining: that was a big pay cheque for those days.

When it was all finished and on sale, naturally my commercial instincts came to the fore: I wanted to find out how it was doing. It was called *Sexy Sonia: Leaves from My Schoolgirl Diary*. I went into Ann Summers (the shop was full of browsing men all deliberately avoiding eye contact) and said loudly to the chap behind the counter, 'Oh, hello,

I wonder if you could help me. I'm "Sexy Sonia" and I wondered how I was selling.'

Some of the customers' heads turned but the salesman froze. 'Shhhhh!' he whispered. He didn't want the customers to connect me with the tape; I assume he thought that if the punters saw me, they probably wouldn't buy it.

I said, 'Oh, sorry, I just want to know . . . how is my tape doing? Is it selling?'

I was delighted to discover that *Sexy Sonia: Leaves from My Schoolgirl Diary* was a nice little earner. Not that it made any difference to me financially, because it was a buyout – in other words they give you your flat fee of £300 and off you go. So, I didn't get any royalties or repeat fees, but it was a matter of pride to know that my voice was stimulating ejaculation all over the United Kingdom.

I just did two sexy tapes; nevertheless, I have been tarred with the brush of pornography ever since. I used to have a copy of *Sexy Sonia*, but sadly I don't know what's happened to it . . . If anyone finds a copy in a charity shop, do let me know.

Women Are Better than Men: Discuss

I have twice fallen in love with males. There was Anton, of course. I do remember feeling groiny about him. Then much, much later, I fell for a professor of journalism when I was in Shanghai. I told him that he was probably the only man that I'd ever really fancied. I think he was, in equal measure, both appalled and surprised. But nothing came of it. Nothing at all. Then there were the boyfriends in Cambridge, and all those older men in Oxford, but we didn't copulate in the way that normal people do – only mouth or wrist jobs. It wasn't sex, it was kindness.

Such experiences were invariably speedy; with men you need to seize the day. Take this story which amuses me even now, possibly because of the coupling/uncoupling of both train and me. I was on a train in Germany in the early sixties and noticed an attractive man sitting opposite me. The train slowed down: I looked hard at him and he returned my gaze. Then he got to his feet, looked at me again and I followed him out into the corridor and down to the loo in the next carriage. We locked the door and began (without words – my German is poor) a vigorous sexual session. This did not include penetration but enthusiastic hand jobs, and on my part, considerable mouth work. After he came, I suddenly realised what the metallic noise I could hear in the background was. In our coupling we hadn't realised that the train had *uncoupled* itself from our carriage. In a flash I was running back up the tracks after my departing luggage. My encounter had been absorbing, but not worth abandoning my suitcase for! I managed to grab the last door of the last carriage and drag myself on. I still wonder what happened to him, left in the middle of nowhere with his trousers around his ankles.

I kissed Bob Monkhouse once. Forgive the non sequitur. It was in a BBC television play, *Enter Solly Gold*, by Bernard Kops. I was playing a small part and Bob Monkhouse had the leading role. In one scene, he had to kiss me. It was the best kiss I think I've ever had: slow, searching, not slurpy. I thought, 'If I was straight, I would go for Bob.' He was interested in people – wise, kind, funny, generous, all the things you hope a star will be. Most people saw him as just a comedian, but he was much more than that. His eldest son suffered from cerebral palsy and Bob campaigned for disabled charities all his life and, famously after his death, in an advertisement to promote awareness of prostate cancer, the disease which killed him. He is one of my heroes and I'm glad to acknowledge him in this book.

In total contrast I name Terry Scott, who was the nastiest person I've ever worked with. How the divine June Whitfield put up with him, I cannot imagine. He was horrid to the chorus girls, tried to grope and kiss them, and if they wouldn't play, he rubbished them publicly. Of course, he would have behaved himself with June.

I haven't spent much time thinking about men, really. My world has been largely female-centred, and I'm perfectly happy with that; I don't feel I've missed out. Women's souls are fascinating and compelling, not so with men. Of course, I retain some life-long male friends and they are precious; but there is no groin excitement when I'm with most men (nor they with me!), and as I'm not sexually interested either in their bodies or in their souls, for me they become peripheral beings. I am not hostile, but if they attempt to bully or scorn me, I will instantly retaliate, usually verbally. I realise I'm generalising but from my experience I find that the range of thought and conversation in most men is limited. They're not interested in feelings. Many men react with horror and fear when a woman starts crying. From this harsh judgement I exempt actors and homosexuals. Perhaps because gay people have been oppressed and scorned themselves, and still are in many places, they have an awareness of the dark side of life and a corresponding capacity to laugh, spread joy and express love. The gay world can be silly and trivial and excluding, but I'm glad I'm gay; I relish and appreciate my camp friends, I admire their style and panache, their energy and bravery,

I wouldn't want to be straight for the world. In the dreadful AIDS time in the eighties, I lost thirty-four friends; beautiful, talented, funny, warm gay boys – I mourn them, it was a terrible loss. What the boys do in bed I've never understood. I can hardly bear the thought of anal sex. I've never been fucked up the bum and I'm happy to die wondering (as Mummy might say). But I won't castigate anyone for their sexual practices, unless they're cruel or violent.

⌒

I formally became a lesbian in the summer of 1966. At school, I'd had crushes on girls and they were all-consuming. My father knew the father of one of my 'pashes,' and had talked about it with him in an amused way; they never realised that it was sexual. Men don't take lesbianism seriously, unless they want to watch. That's not a service I have ever provided. But my school 'cracks' generated passion so intense that I felt cut in two, almost fragmented by it. I was obsessed with the objects of my affection. I would follow them and moon over them. (When I say moon, I don't mean that I would expose myself. I've only done that to Warren Beatty, and he completely deserved it. The expression of shocked surprise frozen on his face still tickles me even now – more of this later.) But up until my mid-twenties, I'd never put two and two together. So, when it did finally dawn on me that I must be a lesbian, it came as a bit of a bombshell.

Early in 1966, I got picked up on the tube in London. There was this girl: multicoloured trousers, short black hair, intense eyes. I became conscious of her gaze, looking at me in a direct way, unwavering and decidedly inviting. When I got off at Lancaster Gate, she got off too, and somehow or other, and I'm really not quite sure how, we ended up back at my flat and there it began. We didn't sleep together – but it was exciting. She was Norwegian; later, when Heather and I had met and I was telling her about it, she called her 'Norwegian Wood', which apparently is a Beatles song about a mysterious girl who turns up, sparks passion and then vanishes for ever. This encounter stirred me up. Even when I went to synagogue, all I could think about was sex, and how much I wanted to have love affairs with other women. Let us say, I was ready.

My old Cambridge friend, Carey Harrison, had become a director at the Phoenix Theatre, Leicester. He invited me to join the company and take part in his first play, *Dante Kaputt*, but I was to start my time there with the well-known potboiler *The Cat and the Canary*.

I arrived mid-season: the other company members had already got to know each other, so I was on my own. The stage manager was a surly girl with bleach-blonde hair in corduroys called Marion. We hit it off instantly. After rehearsals one April evening, Marion and I walked home together and I invited her in. We sat on the sofa and had a cup of hot chocolate and a talk. I think she was lonely too. Then I began to feel that feeling . . . a hot moistness in *that* department. There was a pause and Marion moved closer to me – and kissed me. I responded, my heart racing. Her second kiss was rather different, more aggressive – she pushed her tongue into my mouth. I pulled away and asked, 'Is this sex?' I couldn't believe it. And that was in 1966. 'Is this sex?' I remember quite distinctly that I asked her. It was a genuine question, because it was so new to me.

Marion smiled. 'Yes,' she said. Well, it sure was.

I'd never felt as aroused as I did during that time in Leicester with Marion. I think everybody but me guessed she was a lesbian, but she was extremely reserved. And she definitely wasn't in love with me. I was there, I was handy – so to speak – but for me, the moment was intense because it was unique; it was the first time in my life when emotion and sex were coupled. Of course, I fell in love with her.

I knew that I was not 'the one', but Marion and I embarked on a relationship nevertheless. All went swimmingly against the backdrop of *The Cat and the Canary* until another woman appeared on the scene.

Anne Kristen was a fine actress, best known perhaps for her role as Olive Rowe in *Coronation Street*. She was bisexual, and she and Marion took one look at each other and that was it. I didn't have to ask, I just sensed it, and I was hurt. And maddened. I wanted Marion to explain it to me. Were we 'over'? She hadn't come to sleep with me for some days. I decided to confront her first thing one morning – I had a key to her room, but she wasn't there. It was obvious where she was. I went straight to Anne's hotel.

I said to the man on the front desk, 'I need to give a message to Anne Kristen. I'm from the theatre, it's very urgent.'

He said it was a bit early to disturb a hotel guest in their room – it was only 8.30 a.m., but I was adamant. 'No, it's extremely important that I talk to her. I need to see her now.' Reluctantly, he told me her room number.

I went up and hammered on the door: 'I know you're both in there and if you don't let me in, I will make a shocking row and you will be discovered.' They knew it wasn't an idle threat. Anne opened the door. And there was Marion, lying in Anne's bed. I was incandescent with rage and jealousy. I jumped on the bed and slapped and punched them both. 'Don't hurt her,' Anne begged. That maddened me further and I deliberately stamped hard on Marion's reading glasses. When my frenzy was spent, I left and went straight back to Marion's room, and scrawled on the mirror, 'LESBIAN CUNT' in red lipstick. Although I was nominally a grown-up, my reactions were those of a teenager on acid.

I had never experienced rejection like this before – the anguish and fury and jealousy. I didn't think I would ever feel as intensely again. I went back to my digs and, all alone, watched England win the World Cup. While the whole country went wild with joy, I felt like my heart had literally broken. Later I was summoned to talk to Clive Perry, the artistic director. He said coldly, 'I'm sorry, we won't be requiring your services next season.' He didn't mention the reason but I knew I was being sacked for violence. And justifiably so. I was lucky not to have been arrested. And that would have meant a lesbian drama in the

Leicester Mercury. The last time one of my family was in that paper was in 1877, when great-grandfather Simon went to prison for fraud.

Of course, it was alarming for Anne, who kept out of my way; we never discussed it. Years later I worked with her husband in Scotland, the fine actor, Iain Cuthbertson. I don't think he ever knew: I hope not. And in the way of theatre, which is a merry-go-round, with everyone coming across each other again at least once, when Anne met me again and propositioned me, I refused. But when I eventually got to know her, long after the Leicester Lesbian moment, I found I liked and admired her and when she died I truly felt sad. How strange life is.

I don't know why I fancied Marion ... because she was there? Because she fancied me? Because she made the first move? That kiss was the thing that set it off. I had never felt confident enough to make the first move. Somebody once said to me, 'You're a flirt, you are.' That's probably true, but I suspect it's more about wanting to evoke a reaction, rather than get into bed with someone. Women are more subtle: we don't trap people up against filing cabinets; such behaviour seems peculiarly male, but there may be exceptions.

The encounter with Norwegian Wood made me realise that my sexual preference was obvious to other gay women, even if it hadn't entirely been obvious to me. I was ecstatic. Now I had a sexual identity. Now I could say, 'I am a lesbian.' Everything fell into place. And it was fun. I still think it's a terrific thing to be, which is good, because it's not going to change.

But may I say strongly that being a lesbian is not enough – it's not all there is; it's simply another adjective to describe a person. And when people say, 'Oh, you must meet X, she's a lesbian too,' I groan with irritation. I don't want to live in a *lesbian* world. I want to live in

The World, with everyone else. I would never deny my sexuality – indeed I am often accused of trumpeting it far too stridently and often – but please don't shut me or anyone else in a lesbian cage. Some gay women only want to be with gay women. I don't. I pick the people in my life because of who they are, not because of who they sleep with. Let's open the closet and take our place in the world.

Heather

I didn't have a mature, loving relationship until I was twenty-seven. But once I found her, I knew. She and I have been a pair, in love and in life, for fifty-three years.

Heather is my polar opposite. She is reticent, incredibly private and reserved. I know this is her worst nightmare: to be exposed and publicly known in a book. I have never given her full name in interviews and I've asked her permission to write about her here. It's all right for me to be exposed: I quite enjoy the idea of exploring my innermost self and handing it out in little parcels. But she doesn't.

We sat down, and I said, 'You know I'm going to have to mention you, don't you? You are the central person in my life. How can I not speak about you? That would be absurd.' And she said, 'Yes, I see that. I wish it weren't necessary, but I can see that it is.' I've made sure that I don't overstep what she would want. But celebrating the love of your life is important.

Let me tell you about how I met Heather.

It was all thanks to one of my dearest school friends, Katerina Clark. When Katy went back to Australia to ANU – Australian National University – and I went to Cambridge, we continued to write to each other. During the five years after I'd left Cambridge, Katy was at Yale doing her master's degree. Two scholarships were given annually to Australian women graduates: Katy had one, and Heather was the other recipient. (Katerina and Heather were both from Canberra, so when they went to Yale, naturally they became friends.)

I wrote to Katy and told her my big news about being gay; she replied, 'Oh! My best friend here is a lesbian . . . you should meet.'

In the summer of 1968, Katy said that she was coming to London for a research trip, and her friend, this lesbian called Heather, would be coming with her. I replied suggesting we meet up. I thought it might be quite exciting, but Katy told me: 'Don't tell Heather that you know she's a lesbian, because she wouldn't like me betraying her confidence.'

It was arranged that she, Heather and I would go with a couple of other Australians to see *The Charge of the Light Brigade*, the film about the Crimean War, directed by Tony Richardson. They picked me up in a VW to go to the film; being the fattest, I sat in the front and showed off noisily all the way there, talking about cock-sucking and farting.

Behind me, I glimpsed this creature with white-blonde hair, which I find devastatingly attractive, and I just *knew*. I can remember it as if it were yesterday – the absolute knowledge that this was the woman that I had always sought and longed for. And she, of course, was in blind ignorance of how her life was about to change: I knew that this was for ever, but she didn't, she didn't have a clue.

When we got to the cinema, I insisted on sitting next to her. I didn't look at the film at all, which Heather found disconcerting and odd: for the entire movie I turned my whole gaze on her. I drank her in, and she was discomforted by this, as you can imagine. I'm not sure Katy enjoyed the film much either; she was worrying I would let slip what she'd told me.

Years later, I saw the film. The violence of the war, guns, noise and stiff-upper-lipped Englishmen were all a long way from the passionate emotions I had been harbouring.

Afterwards, I said to Katy, 'Bring Heather to lunch on Thursday, and don't tell her that you've told me that she's gay.' Of course, we didn't say gay then, the word was *queer* – and we were queer. Katy said, 'Miriam, I can't not tell her.' Katy's got that thing, you see – integrity – that gets in the way sometimes. Nevertheless, she promised she wouldn't tell her, and she didn't. I then said, 'Just say you've got an appointment at two o'clock and you have to go, and you leave us two alone.'

Katy was never comfortable with even the whitest of lies, but she agreed and so, on the Thursday, they arrived. We sat down to eat. Suddenly, in the middle of lunch, Katy leapt up and said, 'Oh, God! Is that the time? I'm really sorry but I've got to go.'

I saw her out, and at the front door she turned and sternly said, 'Now, don't you say *anything* because she's going to be really . . .' and I said, 'No, of course I won't!'

Perhaps it was knowing that Heather was gay that gave me the courage to make my move. After I had bundled Katy out the door, and returned to the kitchen, Heather said something like, 'God! Why on earth did Katy go off like that? I would have gone with her.'

I said, 'But I didn't want you to go with her, I wanted you to stay.' There was a pause. I said, 'I'm queer, and I think you are too . . . aren't you?' She started to shake. I got up from the table, went around behind her chair and stood and stroked her head. A masterstroke, if I may say so. I have good massaging hands and I think that calmed her down.

Heather and I started our relationship that very night – and it never stopped. She phoned Jan Adams where she'd been staying, and explained that she wasn't coming home. I heard her say, 'I like Miriam.' Next to getting into Cambridge, that was the best moment of my life.

It was a feeling of connection on a level completely different to anything I had experienced before.

My emotions, my attention *and* my sexuality were totally focused on Heather. She engaged my interest and always has. She's powerful and enigmatic. She is also reserved, and feeling her respond to me and realising that I could awaken *her* affection and sexuality was an intoxicating experience.

We didn't get out of bed for a week.

Later, Heather told me that she had said to herself at lunch that day: 'Miriam can't be queer. She's so noisy!' For Heather, the whole concept of being gay was shrouded in secrecy. She couldn't imagine that anybody could say, 'I fancy you. I'm gay. Let's fuck.'

My parents were two opposites attracting: Heather and I are the same. Those early patterns are important – they form the paradigm for your future relationships. I am a clone of my mother, whereas my partner resembles my father – she's a thoughtful person, a quiet, unde-monstrative scholar. Although theirs was a passionate relationship in which they were often at odds, my parents adored each other.

Being in a relationship with someone for fifty-three years is a big achievement. It's difficult to look at someone objectively when you love them. And I love Heather. I get angry with her and she gets very angry with me, but I recognise her complete integrity. Nearly every-body has flaws of honesty; Heather has none. It doesn't make her an easy person to be with, but there is a complete decency about her, which is refreshing and precious and rare.

Heather is an academic and a scholar: an Indonesianist. To begin with, she was working in Malaysia at Kuala Lumpur University, then she got a job at the Free University of Amsterdam, and she's been in

Holland ever since. She would come to London, of course, and I would go over to her seventeenth-century house on the Prinsengracht. We used to keep a little day boat on the canal outside the house. It had an outboard motor engine, which you started by sharply pulling a string, like a lawnmower, and off this little boat went. I loved that, but, eventually, because we didn't use it enough, we gave it away.

This last winter, all the Amsterdam canals froze over. It doesn't happen often nowadays – one winter, about twenty-five years ago, all the canals were completely frozen, and everybody was out skating, racing by, laughing, their breath in clouds. We watched them for hours, sitting at the high glass windows overlooking the canal: it was like looking at a painting in the Rijksmuseum.

After one of Heather's research visits abroad, she caught a respiratory virus. It developed into the illness called chronic fatigue syndrome and has never left her. At one time in the nineties, it got so bad she couldn't walk or stand, and I had to feed her. Many thousands of people never recover and doctors don't yet know what causes it. Indeed, for many years it wasn't recognised as an illness. Dr Ramsay was the only doctor who got it right. He told Heather she would never recover. She never has. It meant she had to work part-time at the Free University in Amsterdam, but her half-time is equal to anyone else's full-time. Despite all the odds, she has continued to teach, consult and write; her latest book, *Seaways and Gatekeepers*, is a work of majestic scholarship about the trade routes of South East Asia from the seventeenth century until today. I am deeply proud of her.

She has been a huge influence on my life. People ask, 'What is the secret of your relationship?' I reply it is love and trust, and telling the truth. Never let the sun set on a quarrel. And communication – that is paramount: you must talk to your partner. We don't live together, either – we have always led separate lives, which is probably why we've lasted this long. She likes to work and I do, too. The day after she completed her latest book, she began the next. She said, 'What would I do if I didn't work? Who would I be?'

Normally, we see each other about eight times a year, but I speak to her every day on the phone, sometimes more than once. We have never lived together for long periods, except when we had holidays. Our houses in Italy and Australia have filled our lives in the way others have children.

Our farmhouse in Tuscany is where we really come together. It has meant that when we do have that time, I am always happy to say hello, and sad to say goodbye. And that's still the case. I will try as long as I can to have these two lives. Life's like cheesecake: you want to have as much as you can.

We often talk about whether to live together. We've been talking about it more and more recently. Heather's better in the kitchen than me and she doesn't mind my farting in bed (that's how I knew I had a keeper). We don't know if it would work; we'd just have to find out. I think it would, because we really do love each other. At this age, I don't so much feel physical lust – I mean, sex is not important to me any more, although, of course, there was a time when it was *absolutely everything* – but I feel mental lust for Heather. I love her more and more. My happiest moments, really, are just lying in bed with her and gazing at the ceiling and talking about anything and everything. That's my biggest joy.

It may be that we will only actually finally get to achieve that when we're both in an old people's home together. I always had the idea that we would build our own and gather all our friends there, and that's what I'd still like to do. There would be a library and a garden and memories shared. And animals. And a swimming pool, with easy steps down. I'm starting to plan.

We used to travel together. It was because of Heather I became an Australian and travelled there first in 1980. She would explain Asia to me and our visits to Indonesia and Thailand and Malaysia revealed that continent in a way no one else could have. I doubt we'll do much travelling now, but the blessing of my life has been to find the person who opened the world to me and was prepared to share my world too; she has always been my fiercest critic. 'Keeping the options open' is our mantra now; my home will always be where she is. Life is sweeter shared.

Coming Out

My parents controlled my thought processes, or at least Mummy did, and so, even though I was a grown woman of twenty-seven years and I knew I had found the woman for my life, I didn't immediately shout it from the rooftops. I didn't tell most of my friends, or even my fellow housemates, about Heather at first.

It might seem that I've always been stridently 'out'. Not so. I don't know how long it took me to feel confident about being openly gay in *every* circumstance. I felt safe on the sixth floor at the BBC in the Radio Drama department. I can remember working with Paul Scofield, Patricia Routledge and Fenella Fielding in Noël Coward's *Present Laughter* in 1974, and I brought my copy of *Gay News* into the studio. I came back from lunch once and found Dame Patricia reading it, a look of distaste on her face.

In 1968, at the heady start of our relationship, when Heather stayed at my flat, I was very much *not* 'out'. Once, Billy Todd (that's the Hon. Hilary Todd, daughter of Lord Todd of Christ's College, Cambridge), who lived in the middle flat, came downstairs into the hall where Heather and I were talking and I shoved Heather behind the front door, because I was so embarrassed about anyone seeing her. She was extremely offended – well, she was furious. And my response was less than charming: 'Sorry, but you look so much like a lesbian.' She says she can still feel the imprint of the door handle on her tummy where, in my panic to hide her, I'd slammed it back so firmly that she was pinioned right up against the wall.

Once I relaxed, I introduced her to the rest of the house. It so happened that the people above me were a gay male couple, who don't wish to be named, and then above them, there was Hilary Todd and Valerie Sarruf and Erica Eames, who were *not* gay, and above them there was another gay couple, Alistair Durie and Colin Del Paul, who in their nineties are still living happily together in Bath. So, it was a house of much gaiety. One day, when Heather and I were making love rather enthusiastically, I fell out of bed. I made quite a noise. I was very worried about what Mr Sagar below us in the basement would think was going on. Would the ceiling survive? He came up and knocked on the bedroom door and said, 'Is everything all right, Miriam?' I told him I was fine. 'Oh, good,' he said, and went back downstairs. I'm perfectly certain he knew what was going on. But, as most of the house was pullulating with homosexuals, it was clear he and Sibyl didn't mind.

It was only after I had slept with Heather that I told my mother that I was gay. I went home to Oxford one weekend and told Mummy, who immediately told my father. I don't think they really believed it. They were not sophisticated. They didn't understand how I could possibly love another woman in *that* way; it had no reality for them – it was nonsense, it was a perversion. They couldn't regard it as an emotion worthy of mature consideration. My parents knew that it was *possible*, but they didn't think it was possible for *their* Miriam. Miriam wasn't going to be like that because Miriam was perfect, and to be a lesbian was *imperfection*, and so it simply couldn't be entertained for one moment. It also meant that I would never have a nice Jewish husband, and therefore they would never have grandchildren. I think that was part of their sorrow, or disbelief.

Mummy really couldn't handle it. She was an extraordinary, incredibly capable woman who loved theatre, opera and music; a many-sided individual, but closed-minded about homosexuality where her daughter was concerned: it was shameful – people weren't supposed to do that sort of thing. It wasn't *proper*. She and my father insisted I come into the drawing room and swear on the Torah that I would never have relations with a woman again. I did as they asked, but I broke my promise. I stayed with Heather because I loved her, because my whole soul cleaved to her: it would have been impossible to stop. And because, somewhere along the line, I knew they were making an unreasonable request.

A few days later, Mummy had her first stroke. I always believed that my coming out in some way caused it. Her second, devastating stroke came three months later. This started the long period of her appalling illness, and the blackest time of my life. The only good thing was that I had Heather.

I still regret that I told my parents. It caused the person that I loved most in the world a pain she could not bear. I didn't do it to hurt her, but it was a horrendous time and I was very unhappy. I knew I couldn't change what I was; I shouldn't have told them.

I told them because my relationship with my mother was completely loving and open – we had no secrets from each other, we had always said everything – but I should have been aware that that was something I *could not* say. I wasn't angry with my parents for not accepting what or who I was, because they came from a world that could not adapt. It was their tragedy, but it didn't become my tragedy. I'm lucky that I wasn't more damaged by their reaction: I'm remarkably unbitter. But I am inexpressibly sad that my mother didn't live to see any of my successes, to know that I'd got wonderful notices and won awards and acclaim, or to be there when I received my OBE from Prince Charles.

In retrospect, I think that the stroke was an accident waiting to happen and perhaps my telling her exacerbated it. Maybe also it was the realisation that she couldn't contain me any more. She was *very* controlling and she trusted no one. She held me so powerfully within her fortress, that if she hadn't had a stroke, I might never have been able to form a relationship with Heather. In some ways it was fortuitous because I feel sure if my mother had been at full strength, she would have so hated knowing that I was in love with Heather, she would have done her best to end it.

I realise now that telling people things that they can't deal with is an indulgence. I believe that if people want to reveal their sexuality they should, but the matter should not be forced. Some people cannot accept their loved ones being homosexual. And if they can't accept it they shouldn't have to. It's indulgent of those of us who are gay to say you've *got* to know this, you've *got* to share this. I don't think that's right. Of course, it's better if people can be open with the people they love and talk about it with their family – it's always better if everybody can truly be who they are meant to be – but my insistence on opening up hurt the people I loved most in the world.

My friend Ian McKellen and I have a constant difference of opinion on this matter. He feels that you should come out as an encouragement to others and be true to yourself. And I say, it depends who you're coming out to. It hurt my parents too much and it didn't please me particularly, so I think it was an error.

My beloved agent in America, the late Susan Smith, was terrified that I would come out publicly there. She said, 'We don't understand that sort of thing in Hollywood; don't do it, just keep your own counsel.' She really didn't want me to be gay. She said, 'I don't mind, I don't care, you can be whatever you want, but don't be *out* in Hollywood. *Sei schtum*. Don't speak about it.' So, I didn't talk about being gay when I went for interviews, but among my friends I didn't hide it. While I agreed with Susan that my sexual life was my own business, I don't see why anyone's sexuality should be of any concern to the suits in Hollywood. It really shouldn't matter if you are gay or straight: people should just get over themselves. When I got my OBE, it was for services to drama. It wasn't for services to sex or to lesbianism. On the other hand . . .!

———

The night my mother had her stroke was the only time I ever saw Daddy cry. She walked all over the house in a kind of state of dementia and then, in the morning, she couldn't move. He stood at the end of the bed, and the tears fell out of his eyes. She went to hospital then, but afterwards she came back to the house and Daddy looked after her until she died, seven and a half years later.

Daddy couldn't have been more loving and caring. The stroke took away Mummy's speech and paralysed her down one side. Daddy had to do everything for her: feeding, bathing, dressing, and getting her to the lavatory. He put her to bed and got her up again the next morning, and he would cook and clean and wash. I would come down from London once a week to do the shopping, and often Heather would come with me. She found the whole situation very distressing, so she would busy herself emptying the cupboards and washing them out and scrubbing all the floors until the house shone, while I stayed with Mummy, trying to cheer her.

Daddy looked after my mother on his own, without any help. It was hard and relentless; there was no charity like Crossroads to provide respite care and, after the seventh year, when Daddy was in his eighties, he couldn't cope. Mummy was taken to the dementia unit in Littlemore Hospital. Daddy would visit her every day and I would go when I came down from London. I used to sit with her, and hold her hand and hug her. I weep as I remember the horror of it, to see my mother like that, unable to speak or move. I remember that her hair was all straggly and she kept saying over and over again, 'Flora, Flora.' That was her mother's name, and I knew then that she wanted to die. She wanted to be with her parents. She adored them in the way that I adored her and Daddy. It was the bleakest time of my life.

Once Mummy went into Littlemore, I was aware that she would die very soon, but it was Heather who answered the inevitable phone call. It was 30 August, 1974. I was at an Equity meeting when I was told there was a call.

Heather said, 'Miriam, I've got something very sad to tell you.'

I knew. 'Is it Mummy?'

Heather said, 'Yes, she died.'

My immediate thought was, 'Thank God. Thank God, she's dead.' I wish I hadn't thought that, but I must tell the truth. I felt grief, but also relief; the agony was over; for Mummy and Daddy and for me. In these pages I've described Mummy as she was – so full of life and energy and love. She will always be there in my heart.

I believe Mummy's illness and death had a positive impact on me: I saw the dark side of life. Before her stroke, I'd seen only the sunny side.

But the personal experience of tragedy opened my eyes and gave me a compassion I had lacked until then. I realised then that life could get up and bite you – and now Covid has got up and bitten us all. I know that kindness and gentleness are the most valuable commodities. Now, more than ever, they demand distribution.

Life on the Road: *Fiddler on the Roof*

In 1970 I was cast as Yente the matchmaker in the UK tour of *Fiddler on the Roof*. That was my first *big* job. My salary was £50 pounds a week. Actually, it wasn't much more than I earned at the BBC, but I wanted to be an actress using both my voice *and* my body.

Fiddler on the Roof is a musical about Tevye, a poor milkman, his acerbic wife Golde and their five daughters: Tzeitel, Hodel, Chava, Shprintze and Bielke. Tevye wants to marry the daughters off and turns to my character, Yente, the matchmaker, to find them suitable – ideally wealthy – husbands. The matchmaker is both a gossip and a philosopher, like all Jewish women – it's a good part, with opportunities for comedy.

I'd seen the London production at Her Majesty's Theatre, Haymarket. It had been running very successfully for three years and I loved it. Topol and Miriam Karlin played the leads. Many years later I made a film with Topol (*Left Luggage* with Isabella Rossellini) and served on the Equity Council with Miriam. She was a truly magnificent person – a terrific actress with powerful political convictions. I honour her memory. But back to 1970.

I was asked to audition for the role of Yente, and it was a part I was born to play, but she has a song, and I can't sing. The fact that I cannot carry a tune has been a blight on my career because I *look* as if I can sing: I've got the breasts for singing; I've got the face for singing; I've got the pipes . . . for spoken word, yes, but not for singing, alas. Unlike

Mummy, who had perfect pitch, I am tone-deaf. I feel sure I would have had leading roles on the musical comedy stage if I'd been able to hold a tune, but there it is. You have to make the best of what you've got; and for this production, I could become Yente, but the song had to be cut.

We were what's called the Number One Touring Company and the contract was for a year, going to Manchester, Bristol, Nottingham, Birmingham, Liverpool, Newcastle, Glasgow, Aberdeen, Edinburgh and Leeds, which for a young person is huge fun. Such tours don't happen much any more – they're too expensive. We were a big company – about forty of us – including dancers, plus the orchestra on top. This makes for a significant financial undertaking.

We rehearsed in London at Her Majesty's Theatre for five weeks. Our director was not Harold Robbins, who'd directed it on Broadway, alas, but Tommy Elliott, who was the company manager of the show in London. His job was to copy exactly the London production; he was grumpy and devoid of artistic flair. He shouted nastily at Mollie Hare, our oldest company member, whenever she didn't get something right. The choreographer was Irene Claire, very good and patient with people like me, who weren't good dancers. I thought that I was much better than Cynthia Grenville, who was playing Yente in London – how ridiculous to cast a non-Jewish actress in this most Jewish of parts. But then again she did sing well.

During rehearsals the cast got to know one another, working out who we liked and who we didn't. Then we were off on tour.

We played Manchester for two months, then to each city for two or three weeks. The whole troupe went everywhere en masse by train, and I immediately palled up with my understudy, a witty Australian called Andonia Katsaros, also a lesbian. She had been famous in TV in Australia for *The Mavis Bramston Show*. At the time, I didn't know I would also make a career in Australia. She and her partner, Maureen, are still my chums. It was a great adventure, meeting up on the station platform at Euston, getting our stuff together in a babble of chaotic excitement and giggles. And a wonderful opportunity to see the great cities of England and Scotland, which we did on our days off. Some people travelled with their spouses. Chris Saul brought his wife, Diana Eden, a blonde actress from Darlington, with a deep voice and a wicked wit. She has remained an important friend to this day. Enid Blackman brought her chap, Nick, whom she later married. Julio Trebilcock from Chile brought his wife and little baby. And Andonia brought Maureen.

We opened at the Palace Theatre in Manchester on 13 April 1970. Of course, the unknown factor about touring is the accommodation, and who you're going to share with. For the Manchester run, five of us rented a house in a quiet little country village called Handforth (which is now apparently where all the footballers from Manchester United live). I shared with Sean Hewitt, Kim Braden who was Chava, one of the three eldest daughters, and Rita Merkelis who played Tzeitel; Rita is Lithuanian-Canadian and married to Johnny Lynn, a clever chap who wrote *Yes, Minister* and is the nephew of Abba Eban, the Israeli politician. I had been at Cambridge with him, and knew him from Footlights, where he was a gifted percussionist; I didn't like him then, and I don't like either of them now. I had a little kitten on the tour; I begged Rita to keep our dressing-room door shut, and she never did. Typical! Luckily the kitten survived and eventually came back to London with me. Rita had an inflated idea of her own importance and was very snooty with the company. In Manchester one day, at the swimming pool, I said to her, 'Rita, if you look down your nose much more, you'll go blind!' They live in Beverley Hills now; Rita left the business and became a psychotherapist; I believe she has a flourishing practice.

Sean Hewitt was an exceptional Canadian actor playing Motel the tailor. He was mercurial, pixie-like in stature, with a ferocious temper and a superb singing voice. He became my closest friend on tour; a most adorable man who stayed in my life until he died in 2020.

In the Handforth house was also a repellent girl called Isobel Stuart, who played another of Tevye's daughters, Hodel; actually, she was a fucking nutcase. Her stage name had been Sylvia Jewison, but she changed it; no one quite knows why. She travelled with her cat (nothing wrong with that) but she and I had a major fight – and I mean an actual physical fight. I was clearing out the fridge at the end of our tenancy and I threw away some yoghurt cartons that belonged to Isobel. She lost her temper and hurled a knife at me. I don't think she meant to hurt me – she was probably slightly deranged. She certainly had anger management problems but then, so did I. The truth is that while we were playing a loving family on the stage, we were at daggers drawn in Handforth. After the incident with the knife, I complained about Isobel to Equity– which is *not* what you're supposed to do. You're supposed to manage the dispute within the company, but it wasn't managed by anyone and I was outraged. I don't know what happened to her. All I can remember now is that she had an affair with a trumpeter in the orchestra and I never shared with her again. Our poor company manager, Roy Astley, found us all quite a trial.

Madhav Sharma played Perchik in Manchester and then abruptly left the company. He was in deeply in love with a girl in the London chorus; the relationship was foundering through absence and when he naughtily took a night off to visit her, he was sacked. But we suspected there was an additional reason to let him go. Madhav had a mellifluous speaking voice (still has), with rich tones, clear diction, and a keen intelligence. But he couldn't quite grasp the notes of Perchik's song. 'Now I have Everything' isn't easy. I'm tone-deaf, and I liked him a lot, but it had to be acknowledged he had everything but the last note – it was nearly always flat. Not *always*; our leading man, Lex, was a great supporter of Madhav's and championed his cause, but to no avail. And so, after Manchester, his understudy Christopher Saul took over.

There were couplings on the road. Our Scottish stage manager, Bill Hutchinson, was nuts about Kim Braden; Donald Proudfoot did ask me for a kiss. Apparently, my lesbian predilection was not generally known; it must have been before I broadcast the fact, although Heather was safely installed at Gloucester Terrace. I think she joined me once. But the main sexual activity took place among the gay boys in the company (it was just before AIDS took so many in our profession). Most of our male dancers were gay. I loved them all – great characters, with the sense of fun and campery I still relish. The chief of police was played by handsome, white-haired Trevor Griffiths. He looked imposing in his uniform when he came onstage to enforce the exodus from Anatevka, rather less so when he was sitting in his dressing-room, knitting!

Lex Goudsmit, our leading man, had come from the London production; he took over from Topol in London and was by far the best Tevye I ever saw. He totally inhabited the character, had a superb singing voice, and a sense of fun with both power and gravitas in his performance. He was a delightful human being. His wife came too, and the company loved them both.

Our Golda for six months of the tour was Thelma Ruby. She was a wonderful company mother, intensely professional but she loved a good laugh. She travelled with her wire-haired dachshund Candy and we went on a dog-mating expedition together, another extension of my role as the Matchmaker. The male dog in question was called Guy: Thelma wanted to teach Candy to sing 'I'm in love with a wonderful Guy.' She remembers my being very anxious that Candy was *enjoying* the experience. (Did you know that the dog has a bone in its penis? Unlike man . . .)

The show was hard work: we performed eight times a week. There were two matinees, one either on Thursday or Wednesday, and one on Saturday – but I was young and full of energy. I liked to get to the theatre about two hours before curtain up; it takes me a while to get into character. The best way I can describe that process is that slowly you divorce yourself from what's going on around you; you think about the show and you think about moments that you weren't so happy with and how they can be improved. It's a continuous process of getting into focus as the run progresses.

The other cast members were housed in different accommodations around the area, and after the performance we'd usually end up heading off in different groups for dinner and drinks – most actors don't like to eat a big meal before a show, so we tended to eat quite late. It was nearly always Indian, Italian or fish and chips, rather than going back to our lodgings and having to cook something from scratch at about midnight! On Sundays, when we had a full, blissful day off, we would often find a special pub or fine restaurant and go off in a group.

It was during the run at the Nottingham Theatre Royal that *both* my understudy and I very nearly missed a Monday night performance. If the main actor is a no-show, well, it's not ideal but the show goes on with the understudy; but for *neither* of us to turn up would have spelt disaster. At the time Heather was on a research trip to England and was living in my flat in Gloucester Terrace. I tried to get back nearly every weekend to see her on the Saturday night after the second show, and if the leg of the tour was within reach of London, I could stay until the Monday morning. My understudy, Andonia, had a Mini estate, and she would always give me a lift, but one day when we were driving back on the Monday afternoon to Nottingham, the Mini broke down on the motorway. Andonia wanted to stay with her vehicle; I had no idea how I was going to get to the theatre and, of course, she was my understudy, so one of us *had* to get back. Nothing for it – I had to hitch a ride. I flagged down a passing car and pleaded with the driver, 'Now, listen, you've *got* to take me to the stage door of the Theatre Royal. I'm an actress and I'm appearing tonight in *Fiddler on the Roof* and we have fifty minutes to curtain up.' And that wonderful man took me right to the door.

Apart from Manchester, where we had our Handforth bolthole, and Glasgow where I stayed with my father's family, I was mostly in rented rooms. Back then, each theatre provided a list of approved theatrical digs – of course, the list of 'theatrical landladies' is a repository of real characters who have formed an intrinsic part of theatrical lore.

All the established theatrical digs had a well-thumbed visitors' book; it was fascinating to see who had just been staying there, or had lodged there in the distant past. The visitors' book also became famous as an efficient and discreet way for lodging actors to pass on information to the next incumbents – famously, 'Quoth the Raven' was code for the warning: 'Don't set foot here again', because the full line from Edgar Allan Poe's 'The Raven' reads, 'Quoth the Raven, "Nevermore."' Apparently, the letters 'LO' or 'LDO' would be a cheering sight for the male visitors, alerting them to the possibility that the 'landlady obliges', or 'the landlady's daughter obliges'! I never came across those types of coded messages in any of the places I stayed in, but I enjoyed getting to know my landladies – if only purely in the strictly non-biblical sense.

My landlady in Leeds, for example, was an adorable Jewish lady called Sadie Shooman. Sadie was the secretary to Dame Fanny Waterman, the founder and director of the Leeds International Piano Competition.* Sadie made wonderful chicken soup and chopped liver. Another of my landladies, Shirley Rubinstein, was married to the playwright, Alan Plater. She loved theatre, enjoyed talking about it and we remained friends until she died. Possibly the most famous theatrical landlady was Mrs Mackay. I didn't actually stay with her, but Mollie Hare, the oldest member of our company did. On an earlier occasion, Mollie's sister, Doris Hare – a well-known musical comedy actress – was staying with her, and Mrs Mackay knocked on Doris's door and came in. She said 'Good morning' to Doris. Doris said, 'Good morning' in return. Then Mrs Mackay went over to draw the curtains, turned to Doris and said, 'Well, your mother's dead.' Mrs

---

* Since that stay in Leeds, I've always wanted to meet Dame Fanny Waterman, and just last year, soon after her one hundredth birthday, I achieved my ambition, thanks to my dear friend, the late Dr Richard Shephard, who used to be the director of music of York Minster.

Mackay had taken the phone call and was meant to break the news gently to her. Let us say she lacked finesse. On a more upbeat note, Derek Nimmo told the story of when he was performing in Bolton during rationing, his mother delivered some delicious steak and asparagus to his landlady as a treat for him one day. When he arrived back at his digs, the landlady proudly told him she had cooked his steak, and 'put the bluebells in some water'. Another of my favourite landlady stories is one that Lionel Blair's gifted sister, Joyce, told me. Joyce was one of my best friends in Santa Monica. Lionel arrived in new digs somewhere up north. He went to the loo, and when he had done his business, he tried to pull the chain but no flush was forthcoming. He was pulling and pulling and pulling when his landlady, hearing the unsuccessful pulls, called up to him, 'Mr Blair! Mr Blair, you have to *surprise* it!'

For Christmas, we were at the King's Theatre in Glasgow. We had a full Christmas season there, which was for about two months, so I stayed with Auntie Eva and Uncle Harold in Pollokshields. After that we were in Aberdeen for January, then on the second-last stop of the tour we played at the King's Theatre in Edinburgh. The stage was on a revolve – it had a mechanism which meant that it slowly rotated a full 360 degrees – and that was how the scenes changed. We were all on stage in Anatevka when it started its stately turn – and then suddenly lurched to a halt. Several cast members fell off. The mechanism had jammed and we were stuck on stage mid-scene, so they had to stop the show for about half an hour. Those who had kept their balance had to sheepishly go off into the wings and wait for the mechanism to be fixed.

Leeds was the last stop. By the end of a full year on the road we were all extremely tired. It was Passover, and I had taken over the role of the Jewish mother of the company when Thelma Ruby left. As such, I decided that it was my job to find somewhere for me and my fellow Jews in the company to go for our *Seder* night, the special supper that we all have at Passover. I asked the theatre management to put an advertisement in the local *Jewish Echo*.

A woman rang up. 'Oh, hello, I saw your advertisement about finding people to play host to members of your company for Passover. I would like to offer a *Seder* night meal to Barry Martin.' Barry had taken over from Lex and was now the star of the show playing Tevye. I said to her, 'I'm so sorry, Barry has relatives in Leeds, so he will be going there for supper. However, I have got a young lady in the company, she's a violinist in the orchestra, and it's the first time she's been away from home. So, it would be really kind if you could offer her your hospitality.' 'Oh, no, I'm sorry. I only want Barry Martin.' 'I didn't realise your hospitality was so selective,' I replied, and put the phone down.

A few weeks later, when I gave a talk to the local Jewish ladies' coffee morning, I told the story. Of course, everybody knew who she was. They were suitably shocked. Some people thought I shouldn't have said anything, but she had behaved badly. If I think somebody has done something wrong, I will expose it. In her case, it was a positive pleasure to do it.

Quite a few of the Fiddler cast have stayed in touch, although it's fifty years since the show closed. Some have died, particularly the male dancers. John Chester was our Fiddler until one night he was on the roof and got drunk and fell off, and got the sack, God rest his soul. He was a sweet boy. And then there was Rex Stallings, playing one of the grooms. Rex and I kept in touch and when he died in California I was living nearby. His ex-wife asked me if I would bring his ashes back home to London. It was a strange, sad feeling to be sitting on a plane, holding in this little box all that remained of my tall, handsome friend.

During the tour I had been learning to drive. I took my first test in Birmingham, and I failed: I remember my knickers fell off as I opened the driver's door. It wasn't a ploy to distract the examiner: the elastic gave out. Then I took another test in Liverpool and passed. Right away I bought a brand-new car – a white Volkswagen Beetle. It cost £850. Now I could leave a party when I wanted, no more waiting around for lifts. This was true liberation.

Going on the Stage:
A Masterclass of Sorts

Strangely enough, it was a film rather than a play that made me think that acting might be the profession for me. I was sixteen when I first saw *Les Enfants du Paradis* at the Scala Cinema in Walton Street, Oxford. It intoxicated me.

Made in the early 1940s, while France was under German occupation, the film deals with love and rejection and the passionate rivalries between different nineteenth-century theatre companies. Jean-Louis Barrault plays a mime hopelessly in love with the actress, Arletty; we see behind his mask and sense the pain of rejection he's feeling – a most extraordinary piece of acting, with not a word spoken. The film is not so much about individuals as the world they inhabit; it leaves you with a great sadness at the end, a melancholy, that's very much in keeping with my own nature.

What I found thrilling was the way it portrayed theatre: it made me realise that this was a place where art happened: it wasn't peripheral, superficial nonsense. It was about the development of the soul: people spent their whole lives in the theatre and relished it and grew in it. And I wanted to be a part of that world.

I love an audience. If I hadn't been a professional actress, I would have been a terrible show-off. Many would say I am! To have a live audience of hundreds and hundreds of people, all looking at you – that to me is heaven. I love contact. I love action and reaction. It's how I know I'm alive. I cherish my audiences and I'm grateful for them.

My father was baffled by it. He said, 'Oh, I don't know how you do that. It would frighten me to death. Who would do such a thing?' The thing is, standing on the stage doesn't frighten me to death, it frightens me to *life*!

But Mummy understood. She had studied singing and dancing and had wanted to be an actress. She almost had been – she was one of twelve finalists in the Golden Voice Competition of 1936, which then was the equivalent of *Britain's Got Talent*. But a 'nice Jewish girl' didn't go on the stage – certainly not in the twenties and thirties – so her passion became a hobby. She used to entertain around Oxford for charity, and for me in our front room. When I decided on a career in acting, she was delighted that I had chosen the path she longed to take and that she could perform vicariously through me.

———

What makes a good actor? I think it's a talent, or should I say a person-ality disposition, that you're born with. However, I think you can improve and refine your gift through attention to detail, careful obser-vation, a love of people and a desire to communicate. How much of it is training, how much of it is innate? A mixture of both. I have no formal training: I didn't go to drama school, mainly because I was already twenty-two when I left Cambridge and I didn't want to remain a student for another three years. I read quite a bit about theatrical technique but mainly I have learnt on the job and through observing others.

That's why I admire Eileen Atkins so much, because her flawless technique doesn't get in the way of *truth*. She performs economically according to that old dictum 'Less is more', which infuriates me because although I know it is right, I always want to do more. I am an over-actress. And technique must be the spark that ignites the performance; truth is *inside*, but technique is the match that you strike to allow that truth to glow. I avoid analysing my own technique because I'm frightened that it's a small, weak thing and that if it hits the light and the sun shines on it, it might completely fragment and disappear, so I tend to let my instinct guide me and hope for the best.

When I read a text, I use the bricks of my own personality to fashion a character. It's the text that gives you the mortar, the other elements of what you're creating and what you have at the back of your mind's eye. When I get a play script, I want to see if the character has changed at all during the course of the piece. Is there an arc to the character? Or, if not, does she *move* in any way from beginning to end? If there is no movement, I have to try to put it there, because it's boring to know everything about a character from the minute they step onto the stage. The actor or actress must surprise the audience in order to engage them and to entertain them. That's what I look for in the writing. But the surprise must be organic, from within. Imposing it won't work.

The great actress Edith Evans used to say, 'Before I go on stage, I say to myself, "I am beautiful. And I have a secret."' That was her method, but that's not for me. First of all, I certainly don't think I'm beautiful. As for 'I have a secret' ... well, I don't have any secrets – that's my strength. But it certainly seemed to work for Dame Edith.

I try rather to discover what it is that opens the door to a character for me, and it's always different things – maybe a single line of my script, or something that another character in the play says. I see every rehearsal as an opportunity both to offer and to glean something new from my fellow actors – as long as you are receptive to that dialogue and you open yourself to the moment, the process of finding your way into a character becomes a continual foreplay. Every inch of your skin has got to be sensitive to the moment, and if you're lucky, the moment comes – but it can go again just as quickly. It is a flash, and you can't control it and you can't compel it – you just have to be available. That's the most important thing: *you make yourself available for the moment*. When it happens, it happens and it is exciting when, suddenly, you can forget *yourself*. That's what occurs in the best moments when you're on stage – you're not *you* any more: you're the person you're playing.

I've worked with some fine actors in my time and one of the greatest is Vanessa Redgrave. What I particularly admire is how she is able to combine extraordinary technical ability with complete truth. She doesn't act; she just is. That's rare. And she startles you. When I was working with her in 1988 in Tennessee Williams's *Orpheus Descending*, we rehearsed in a church in Chelsea. One day she was magical: everything seemed to gel and even the light around her danced. It was an extraordinary experience and we all felt blessed to have observed truly great acting – but there was only us, there was no audience. She was always good after that, but I don't think she ever quite caught that light, that sparkle, that was in the rehearsal room at that parish church again. It was pure blinding magic.

I think that you *see* how you want to appear on the stage. And I don't mean physically: what I mean, rather, is that somehow you 'see' what you want to do with your character, how you want her to be. What is her reality? You glimpse it, distantly, and as you rehearse, and with the help of your colleagues and your director, and the costume department and the make-up artist, and so on, gradually, it all feeds into your 'being'. Then the creation, your character's being, starts slowly and imperceptibly to take root, and to be there for you to step into on the first night, or whenever the first audience appears.

That's why I hate it when people ask to watch a rehearsal. Sometimes directors say, 'Oh, I've asked a few people to come in to see how we're going.' I can't bear it, because a performance is a fragile butterfly of a thing – and it has to be coaxed and nourished and soothed. Exposure too early is scary and frightening, because an actor's nature is to perform – that is what we do. And that's how we think of ourselves – we are the performers and you are the audience. When we see an audience, we will perform, but if we're not ready to deliver our performance, then something phony, invented and inorganic is risked being laid onto the fragile structure that is slowly coming into being. (I'm talking about acting for the stage here, of course, and theatre is where I feel at home, and where I feel I know what I'm doing. Acting for film is another beast altogether.)

My stage fright has only increased as I've got older. The expectations of the audience have become so much higher and I don't want to let them down. I now have a bucket in the wings because I am so often sick before I go on stage. I'm not alone in this regard: Maggie Smith told me in Australia, when she was performing the Alan Bennett monologues in Sydney, how terribly nervous she gets, to the point of vomiting.

When Stephen Fry ran away after everything went wrong with *Cell Mates*, I knew just how he was feeling. I tried to tell him that all would be well and that he shouldn't be so hard on himself. I know that feeling of despair, of feeling trapped, that horrible panic, and I know that he suffers with an even deeper kind of depression. I worried that he might kill himself. This calls forth the entirely sensible question: why do we do it to ourselves? And keep doing it? The thing is that once you're on stage, you're on, and when it works there is no feeling like it; to inhabit your part and to hear the audience gasp and know that they are catching their breath because of *you*.

The dread of forgetting one's lines, I think, is the basis of all anxiety in the theatre, and it has been for me. As I get older, it feels ever more perilous – even thinking about it now makes me feel nervous.

In 1979, I was in the Snoo Wilson play *Flaming Bodies* at the ICA with Julie Walters. I had an eight-page monologue and I just couldn't remember it. My panic built up during rehearsals and by the afternoon of our first night, I was in a state of terror. I told Julie that I knew I couldn't do it and I wasn't going to go on. She tried her best to soothe me: 'Don't worry, Miriam. You'll remember it. It'll be all right on the night. You'll be fine.'

'No, I fucking won't,' I wailed. 'It's hopeless!' And I ran out of the ICA, hailed a black cab on the Mall and jumped into it. Julie was hot on my heels and she jumped straight in after me. We then spent the next few hours driving around London as the taxi-meter clicked up and she desperately tried to talk me round. Poor Julie, it was early in her career and she must have been in flat despair. But I was adamant: I'd had days to think about it and I knew I couldn't remember my monologue. On we drove until eventually we got the cabbie to stop somewhere and we went for a cup of tea. I didn't do the performance that first night – but I did it on the second night and it was fine: I remembered that bloody monologue after all and survived to tell the tale. I believe Julie forgave me; I hope so.

To learn my lines, I often go off and lock myself away for a week or two and do nothing except learn and properly get to know the text, and I see no one and do nothing apart from that script. Then I hire someone for another week to run through it again and again with me until it is written deep into my brain. I then remember it until the end of the last night of the show – then it's wiped clean.

Forgetting one's lines is only one of the potential pitfalls of performing on stage. When I was in Sir Peter Hall's 1993 production of *She Stoops to Conquer*, I played Mrs Hardcastle with Donald Sinden as Mr Hardcastle and David Essex as Tony Lumpkin. Everybody adored David Essex. He had perfect manners and a melting smile. Like Leonardo DiCaprio, he was safe with me but not with anyone else. We laughed from morning to night. Donald was another wonderful colleague. He very much enjoyed my dirty stories and had a way with audiences. For example, one night somebody in the audience had a hacking cough. They kept coughing and coughing and coughing, and finally Donald stopped the performance. He went to the front of the stage, leaving Squire Hardcastle behind, and said in his ordinary voice (except that it wasn't an ordinary voice at all, but a magical one of strength and masculinity), 'I say, that's a bad cough you've got there. Has anybody near you got a throat pastille, or something?' Somebody passed the man a cough sweet, and Donald said, 'Have a good suck on that, that'll help you.' Donald was a delightful colleague. At the curtain call one night, a particularly unresponsive audience – real puddings all evening, suddenly erupted into a standing ovation. Donald muttered to me: 'Too late.'[*]

It was after one performance of *She Stoops* that Princess Margaret came backstage. She was tiny and cool but had enjoyed the show and congratulated us. Carl Toms, who was a friend of hers, had designed the show. I knew he had been ill and, without thinking, I asked if she would pass on to him our loving best wishes. For a split second, her eyes narrowed and she stiffened: she was deciding whether I had been guilty of massive impertinence. But she saw from my concerned face that I only wanted to send Carl good wishes. She relaxed and said, 'Yes, I will. I enjoyed your performance, rushing *acraws* the stage, backwards and forwards, backwards and forwards.' And she smiled. The danger was over.

I have only once broken character. I was doing *Dickens' Women* at the Hampstead Theatre Club and a lady in the audience had an epileptic fit. At first, I didn't know what it was: it was a continuing snorting and growling sound. I thought, 'Do I stop? What should I do?' The audience was becoming restive and clearly anxious. Finally, I decided I must stop the show. I held up my hand, came to the front of the stage and said something I never thought I would say: 'Is there a doctor in the house?' And, of course, because it was Hampstead, nearly *everybody* stood up. The numerous doctors in the house attended to the lady, the show resumed and, I'm pleased to say, she fully recovered.

Mobile phones ringing and buzzing and beeping are another hazard. It's disgraceful that people are allowed to bring them into the

---

[*] Sheridan Morley described me in the *New York Times* as 'rattling and quivering around [Donald Sinden] like a vast plum pudding filled with firecrackers'.

auditorium in the first place; they should be obliged to hand them into the cloakroom. When I was playing Madame Morrible in *Wicked*, I could see clearly when people in the audience were using their mobile phones. In the interval I would report it to the ushers, and ask them to find that person in the second row, or the upper circle, or wherever, and remove the offending article. People don't seem to understand that if they are using their mobile they can be seen – you can see the light on the phone from the stage and it's obvious if someone is photo-graphing. It's rude and horribly distracting. As actors, we are trying to create a little world for those on stage, and for the audience in the theatre. We have a pact not to tear down the walls of the little room that we've built for each other.

The noisy munching of sweeties and incessant chitchat of some audi-ence members is another bugbear. Once I was in the audience of a show in New York. I don't remember which show it was, but there were people talking and volubly snacking on a shared box of Maltesers. They talked and rattled and crunched all the way through the show. In the interval, I couldn't help it: I burst out and said to them, 'You are barbarians!' They looked at me, and I said, 'You've been talking and chattering right the way through the show, spoiling it for everyone else. Have you no manners? Did your mother never tell you how to behave in a theatre?' One of the men said, 'What the fuck are you talking about? Get out of here, I'm a member . . .' I cut him off. 'Shut up! Somebody else is talking, not you. I don't want to hear you talk, your talk is stupid. Behave your-self!' And they did shut up after that.

We've forgotten how to behave in a theatre. Maybe some people talk all the way through whatever they are watching in their own home and they don't realise how much it impinges on others when they do it in public. That excitement of being in a space with other people all experiencing the same moment, that is the magic of theatre. And talking kills the magic.

One of the funniest things that ever happened to me on stage was in 1966 during the Leicester Repertory production of *The Widowing of Mrs Holroyd* by D. H. Lawrence. The play is an examination of the humiliations in a marriage. The husband, a miner, is fed up with his wife for always behaving as though she is somehow better than him. One night, he goes to the pub and brings two tarts home with him and they're all a bit tiddly. I was playing one of the tarts and in the scene the husband is arguing with his wife while the two tarts are drunkenly looking on. My direction was to sit down on a chair and act sozzled.

We had our dress rehearsal, all was well. However, in the period between the dress rehearsal and the first performance a few hours later, the chippies – the carpenters of the theatre – had attached castors to the bottoms of the legs of the armchair in which I was to sit. But no one had told me that. So, when I plonked myself down heavily, as if totally plastered, the chair seemed to be moving downstage. It was a raked, sloping stage: I assumed it was the power of my acting, that I had so perfectly embodied the drunken tart, I was simply imagining my rolling progress – but no! I really *was* moving! The chair (and I) slid slowly but inexorably down to the edge of the stage. Then it rolled off, tipping me on top of an unfortunate punter in the front row. Amazingly, I wasn't hurt – the punter luckily also largely survived – but neither of us could speak we were laughing so much. Eventually, I somehow managed to get back on stage, someone hoicked the chair up as well, and the show went on.

Such malfunctions can happen to the great as well. In 1967, I saw

Laurence Olivier in Strindberg's *The Dance of Death*. A dramatic, serious piece – and a great actor. That night, a door in the scenery would not open, so Sir Laurence made his exit through the fireplace. When he re-entered through the door, he was carrying a large sword. That's the way things are done in the theatre.

Let me share with you one last theatrical malfunction. In 1963, as a student, I played Mary Cavan Tyrone in *Long Day's Journey into Night* by Eugene O'Neill at the ADC Theatre, Cambridge. The abiding memory of my performance was on the first night, the opening of the third act.

Stage directions: 'Dusk is gathering in the living room, an early dusk due to the fog which has rolled in from the Sound and is like a white curtain drawn down outside the windows.' In order to achieve this effect, the stage management had been working very hard in the wings during the interval, using the fog machine. They were surprisingly efficient.

When the curtain rose, I was onstage with Cathleen, the servant girl. But I couldn't see her. She couldn't see me and the audience couldn't see either of us – though I could hear the front row was coughing hard. Mary's first line is: 'That foghorn! Isn't it awful, Cathleen?' In my anxiety, I said instead, 'The fog is thick tonight, Cathleen.' There was a roar of laughter from the audience which lasted a good minute, accompanied by clapping and foot-stamping. I just about managed to keep from 'corpsing'. It's a searing, brilliant play, but that was a moment of sublime comedy.

The Joys of Being an Understudy:
The Threepenny Opera

Everyone has landmark productions in their careers; *The Threepenny Opera* by Bertolt Brecht with music by Kurt Weill was certainly one of mine. Weill's widow, Lotte Lenya came to see the show; alas, she never came to our dressing room. I was not in any way a star despite having the terrific Kate Feast as my agent.

The last theatre piece I'd done was *Fiddler on the Roof*, the previous year; a few TV roles had followed. But this was the Prince of Wales Theatre in the West End; a famous director, Tony Richardson in charge; with huge stars like Vanessa Redgrave (Polly Peachum) and Barbara Windsor (Lucy Brown) and Annie Ross (Ginny Jenny, a whore) and Hermione Baddeley (Mrs Peachum) in the leads. I was delighted. Among a big cast were also Joe Melia who played Macheath – 'Mack the Knife' – and Arthur Mullard as 'Crook Finger' Jake. My main role, Nelly, was called simply 'Whore' but I also took on an understudy role for the first and only time. I understudied Barbara Windsor (or 'Ba', as we all called her).

It was hard work for us all: a show of the size and complexity of *The Threepenny Opera* would normally have two months of rehearsals, but we opened on 10 February 1972 after only a month. The show later transferred to the Piccadilly Theatre on 10 April.

Tony Richardson staged *The Threepenny Opera* as if in a fairground, with a real carousel, painted in dark and light silver, in the centre of the stage, designed by Patrick Robertson. The theatre had a revolving stage and Nelly was one of four prostitutes (I have played a lot of whores in my time) who sat on this merry-go-round which, as the reviewer for the *Stage* noted, was 'at once gay and charming and strange and forbidding'.* The three other whores were formidable personalities: Patricia Quinn, who is now Lady Stephens, widow of Sir Robert; Diana Quick; and Stella Courtney, an older actress who smoked continuously.

We four tarts shared a dressing room and had a wonderful time, gossiping and going off after the show to Gerry's Club, run by Annie Ross's husband, Sean Lynch. I never went in for all that partying and the Soho scene, but Annie knew all the late-night spots around Soho and the West End, and we all followed her. They drank for hours. I just ate. Annie was where the action was; she was part of that world, and I enjoyed tagging along. She took us to the Buckstone Club, an after-hours dining and drinking club in a basement behind the stage door of the Haymarket Theatre on Suffolk Street in St James's, where Ronnie Barker met Ronnie Corbett. I had never been anywhere like that. Famous jazz musicians who'd probably been playing at Ronnie Scott's and actors in all the West End shows came and caroused, and I mixed with the glamorous people; that was a taste of the highlife, but it's not my natural habitat. Sometimes Annie would sing; I knew her records from the Lambert, Hendricks & Ross days; but when she did 'scat' singing . . . that was my favourite.

Annie was surprisingly nervous about acting and had a respect for Vanessa and her classical theatre work. She never hid her vulnerability

---

* R. B. Marriott, The *Stage*, 17 February 1972.

and perhaps never realised how magnetic she was as Jenny Diver. Hearing her sing was one of the joys of that production. We remained friends until she died in New York aged eighty-nine.

As Jenny Diver, Annie was the star tart and Diana, Pat, Stella and I were her supporting blousy girls. Eleanor Fazan was the choreographer. She was patience itself, as well as creating some unusual dance numbers. I'm a terrible dancer, but Diana and Pat were irritatingly brilliant. Stella died in 1985 but Pat and Diana are still in my life. Pat later became famous as Magenta in Richard O'Brien's *The Rocky Horror Show*; and the marvellous Diana Quick was superb in *Brideshead Revisited* and wrote a brilliant book, *A Tug on the Thread*, about her discovery of family connections to the British Raj. To my eyes, they were both frighteningly sophisticated; they smoked pot and went to clubs and knew about jazz and fashion. I had never even seen marijuana before and I was deeply impressed and rather shocked; it was just something I'd never done. I was quite po-faced with them about it, until they made it quite clear that I was a pathetic idiot and I didn't have to smoke if I didn't want to, but they were going to. I don't think it made the slightest difference to their work. Stella, who was sixty to our twenty-somethings, was rather appalled too but she smoked like a chimney and didn't complain. For the record, I still know nothing about marijuana or any drug, and don't want to. My drugs are chopped liver and cheesecake – probably equally damaging, but they taste better.

Vanessa Redgrave and Ba got on like a house on fire. That surprised me because they came from very different backgrounds. They were also miles apart politically. Nobody else in *The Threepenny Opera* company was the slightest bit interested in Vanessa's politics, nor the ideals of the Workers Revolutionary Party – most certainly *not* Ba, who was an ardent Edward Heath fan. By then, I was a convinced socialist; it was around this time that I joined the WRP and leafleted people and signed petitions and actually went to the Blackwater Estuary summer camp (but that's a story for another chapter). In fact, the whole cast was England in microcosm: Joe Melia, whom I deeply disliked but at the same time admired for his acting, was the son of Italian immigrants. He went to Downing College, Cambridge, but never spoke about that to me. All he wanted to talk about was football. At that time, and foolishly, I scorned football (now I am a strong Arsenal supporter). One night we were all on stage, waiting to begin the show in our places behind the 'Iron' (the front stage curtain). Joe was bemoaning an Arsenal defeat the previous night. I laughed scornfully; Joe snarled at me, 'You silly cunt!' and I slapped his face. Curtain up! I cannot substantiate the widely held belief among the cast that he slept with both Vanessa and Annie (I never dared ask either of them), but Ba definitely wasn't an admirer.

Victor Maddern was another cheeky chappie; a terrific character actor in British films and a sweet guy. He had a mushroom farm and every week brought punnets of mushrooms for the cast and left them at the stage door for us to take home. Arthur Mullard, another definitely working-class actor, I got to know better later, when we did voice-overs. Every night after the show he went back to his council flat in Islington, although he died a millionaire. Famously cockney, he was once asked by a commercials director if he could change his accent to be more upper-class. Silly request. He was always begging me to suck him off. The excuse I gave was because he had never changed his jumper, not once in the entire run and I just didn't fancy being that close to old wool. I read later that he'd abused his daughter and his wife had committed suicide. We knew nothing of that then but the news made me shiver.

Henry Woolf was the other Jew in the cast. Short like me, and massively intelligent, it turned out he was Harold Pinter's best friend. One day he said, 'You would do anything to live life on your own terms'. I was shocked by his perspicacity. He was a good actor, a brilliant critic, but left the business and became an academic in Saskatchewan.

I became particularly fond of Hermione Baddeley; she would hold court in her dressing room, before and after the show, sharing memories of her life in theatre, always pouring out gin for me, wine for the others. Hermione had been nominated for an Oscar for *Room at the Top*; her older sister, Angela, played Mrs Bridges in *Upstairs, Downstairs*. I liked her; perhaps because she was a (closet) lesbian; her girlfriend Lady Joan Ashton-Smith hosted our first night party, in her stylish all-white flat, designed by Sibyl Colefax. At that party I met David Bailey, the photographer. He was short, cockney, with a sharp grin and the air of someone who deliberately refused to show respect for anyone. He said to me, 'You're an interesting bird. Come to my studio, I'll photograph you.'

I wish I had.

I used to walk home after the show, past all the prostitutes who gathered outside the stage door in Denman Street. I became friendly with one of them, a pretty Irishwoman, and used to talk to her every night. I asked her, 'Why are you doing this work?' She explained, 'Ah, well, I've got a little boy and I want to look after him. This way, I can send him to a good school and he'll have a proper upbringing and a good education. I do it for him. It doesn't matter to me one way or the other.' I said, 'Do you do whatever they ask?' She said, 'Well, I just don't like them kissing me. I won't let them kiss me. That's one thing I don't allow. But they can do whatever else they like.' I enjoyed talking to this lady, hearing news about her son – but I never connected my encounters with this real-life prostitute with my role in the show. She was light years away from my Nelly!

Barbara Windsor was fabulous. Of course, she's famous for her *Carry On* films, but before that she had been part of Joan Littlewood's company at Stratford East and loved theatre. She announced at our first conversation: 'Miriam, I'm a star.' And pointed to the gold star affixed to her dressing-room door. I asked her about the Krays, whom she had known when they ran London crime. 'They were gentlemen,' she said. 'When I came into the room, they stood up.' She knew she was special but she worked hard and took her work seriously. She gave an interview to the *Observer* during our rehearsals. I love this extract: '"Well, dear," said Miss Windsor, "I've always voted Conservative, if that's what you mean. Most actors do."' She said that apart from Jennie Lee, Labour governments were bad for the profession: they stuck the prices up. '"Of course, we all know Vanessa's a raving socialist, but she's a lovely girl, so you just don't mention E. Heath in her company." "Brecht?" "No, dear, I don't know him. We used to call Joan Littlewood 'Mother Courage'. 'Barb,' she'd say, 'you must do me a bit of Brecht one day. It would be nice for you.'"'

I'd never been an understudy before, but I learnt my lines dutifully and they made a costume for me, as I was much fatter than Ba. Our understudy rehearsals were run by Keith Hack, whom I'd known at Cambridge. He used to rehearse us in the Stalls Bar at the back of the auditorium.

One day, as I turned up at the stage door on the Saturday before the matinee, relaxed and happy, the stage manager grabbed me and said, 'Miriam, you're on.' I thought he was joking. I said, 'Stop it. Don't do that to me.' He said, 'No, really, Miriam, you are. You have to go *now* and get your costume sorted. Barbara has a sore throat. She's off till Monday, so you'll have two shows to do.'

I wanted to die. I was terrified. I did know the part, but I nearly shat myself. Then I thought, 'Come on, you're a professional.' I stopped shaking and started thinking fast. I said, 'Right, I had better run through the music.' They offered me Ba's dressing room with the star on the door, but I wanted my own surroundings. Vanessa came to my dressing room as I was getting dressed and said, 'Miriam, what would you like me to do? I'm here to help; just tell me anything you need.' I asked her if we could run through the songs (never my strong suit), and we did. She was and is the loveliest person, a superb colleague, a generous company member. I raced through the songs and checked the costume still fitted, all the time muttering the lines to myself as my dresser buttoned me in.

Standing in the wings just before the curtain went up, I heard that awful groan when the front-of-house manager announced that Barbara was indisposed and her understudy would take on the role. I thought, 'Fuck it. I've got to show them. They've paid! I've got to give them something.' And I did – I don't know how I did it, but I did whatever I had to do.

The audience is always told that an understudy is making their first appearance in a role. At the curtain call, Vanessa led me forward to take my own bow. She also brought a bottle of champagne to my dressing room at the end of the evening. Vanessa is like that; she takes people for meals, she cooks – she's a proper mother of a company. It's true that her politics frighten some people – not me. I know she's not an antisemite, that she has a heart of gold and a shrewd head. Ba loved Vanessa: 'I know she talks posh and all that, but she's really nice!'

I did the show for the two performances. On the following Monday, when Barbara came back, she came to my dressing room and said, 'I heard you was really good the other night, Miriam. I better watch myself with you. I'm not going off again and no mistake.' And she never did.

Through the years I met Ba again – we were both friends of Kenneth Williams – and she was always warm and loving to me. She had an innocence and a vitality which was irresistible and when she died recently, I wept. I felt, along with the rest of England, that I had lost a friend. Her husband, Scott Mitchell, truly loved her and took care of her. At last, she found the man she deserved.

———

Looking back, I don't think it was a very good show. I phoned my friend in Canada, Robert Cushman, who is a critic and was at Cambridge with me. I knew he'd tell me honestly; he did. But the show sold well, it was enormous fun to be in; and at last, I was a working actress in the West End.

When a Play Goes Wrong:
The White Devil

Sometimes a production goes wrong and nothing can fix it. In interviews, if I'm ever asked about my worst-ever professional experience, without any hesitation or deviation, I say: John Webster's *The White Devil* at the Old Vic with Glenda Jackson in 1976.

It started promisingly. When my agent told me about the job, I leapt at it. This was a rarely performed classic from one of the greats of Jacobean drama; there was a staggering cast and we would be playing at the Old Vic. The Old Vic is a theatre steeped in theatrical history, especially for classical productions. It housed the National Theatre for twelve years until the concrete structure on the South Bank had been built. Our production was the first to take over the Old Vic after its departure.

The White Devil (or, to give it its full original title), *The White Divel; or, The Tragedy of Paulo Giordano Ursini, Duke of Brachiano. With The Life and Death of Vittoria Corombona the famous Venetian Curtizan*, is a difficult and strange revenge tragedy, which was first published and performed in 1612. I knew the play from Cambridge but had completely forgotten it. Webster's best known work is *The Duchess of Malfi*; but both plays are violent and complicated. With actors like Glenda Jackson, Jonathan Pryce, Jack Shepherd, Madge Ryan, James Villiers, Patrick Magee and Frances de la Tour, I was joining a cast to die for, and so in the beginning I was thrilled.

194

I was playing Zanche the Moor (later I would come to call her 'Zanche the Less'), servant to Glenda Jackson's Vittoria Corombona. I steal money from Vittoria and betray her brother Flamineo to my new lover and things go downhill from there. I was the black devil to her white. I regret to admit that I was 'blacked up' for this role, the second time I'd done so; ten years previously, I was Mammy Pleasant in *The Cat and the Canary* at Leicester Rep.[*]

Mammy Pleasant's accent wasn't in my repertoire and rather than listen to a tape (the usual actor's route), I decided to accost a West Indian lady in Leicester market. I went up to a friendly-looking woman at a vegetable stall and said 'Excuse me.' She looked up, 'Yes?'

'I'm an actress and I'm playing a West Indian part in the next play at the Mercury Theatre. Would you be kind enough to give me some lessons in your accent?'

She raised her eyebrows, 'What accent?'

That was tricky. 'Well,' I said, 'I want to sound Jamaican. Are you Jamaican?'

'Yes, I am Jamaican.'

'Would you let me bring the text to your house? It would just be an hour or so. I'll pay you.'

'Pay me for TALKING?! No. Just come.' And I spent a couple of hours with her, learning to sound like a voodoo queen. The line that still rings through my head is: 'I see spirits all around you.'

Back to *The White Devil.* The director was Michael Lindsay-Hogg,

---

[*] Almost as bad as blacking up, in a film called *Stand Up, Virgin Soldiers,* I played Ethel, the Chinese whore, and for that part I had my eyelids pulled towards my temples with a kind of sticky transparent tape so that it supposedly made me look Chinese (more on this later). It's very embarrassing to have to admit that, but I did.

the illegitimate son of Orson Welles. Michael is a charming man, and now we are friends on Facebook after all these years, but Michael thought that it was enough to get a fabulous cast together: he didn't have a vision for the play. He'd come from television, directing *Ready Steady Go!* where improvisation was key. Perhaps he thought that when these actors stepped onto the stage, the performance would generate itself. He is definitely a non-interventionist director. Well, it's not like that in theatre. You can't just throw people onto a stage and expect them to make it work. Sure enough, it proved a catastrophe of unparalleled horror from slow start to ignominious finish.

I've talked to other cast members about our experience. Not all hated it as I did. Tom Chadbon had a wonderful time; and it's important for me to say so, because my own misery obscured my vision of the wider truth. Adam Godley, aged eleven, played Giovanni, the child prince. He shared the role with Jonathan Scott-Taylor (following Equity rules about child performers). It was his first job and he stole the notices. He remembers Patrick Magee giving him racing tips and treating him like a grown-up. He loved talking to the old stage door-keeper and once missed an entrance because of it. Glenda fixed him with a steely glare: 'Don't worry, but don't EVER do it again!' He never did, and went on to become a distinguished actor, to be seen again on Broadway in *The Lehman Trilogy*.

The rehearsal room at the Old Vic is right at the top of the building. It has a glass roof and 1976 was the hottest summer on record. Everyone boiled, we poured with sweat all day; the physical discomfort was intense; somehow that spilled over into the rehearsal process. (Adam remembers Glenda buying everyone ice creams and lollies to counteract the extreme heat we were suffering. Maybe she missed me out on her run to the ice cream van.) There was bad feeling from the beginning. The mood was unpleasant and rivalry and discord amongst the cast members sporadically bubbled over in little moments of irritation and nastiness. Jonathan Pryce was particularly combative and scornful if anyone made mistakes. He patrolled the set like a shark, eating up errors from other cast members, although Tom Chadbon remembers Jonathan being larky and fun, enjoying one of the longest corpses (which, in the business, means laughing so much on stage that you can't speak your lines) he'd ever experienced.

The cast contained many strong and gifted actors but there was a collision of acting styles. Some had come from the Bill Gaskill Royal Court tradition; others from the Peter Hall Royal Shakespeare Company way of doing things. I also sensed a rivalry among the younger men vying for Glenda's attention. Jonathan Pryce and Jack Shepherd were openly contemptuous of James Villiers, a gentleman of the Old School, with perfect manners and a plummy, posh speaking voice. James refused to battle for a place on the stage; he felt it would be beneath him to push himself forward. He fell for Glenda in a big way; he was always susceptible to female charms and couldn't resist buying her a pair of flared jeans one day. His then wife, Patricia Donovan, was my dresser.

It didn't help that I was nervous of Glenda Jackson, a star actress with a formidable reputation. My impression was that she liked people to be frightened of her. At the best of times, Glenda has little patience and no humility. She doesn't suffer fools gladly. I admit I behaved foolishly and I was certainly made to suffer later as a result. She was horrid to me. I didn't like her but I acknowledge her considerable gifts – she has given great performances. Occasionally she hits those heights, but she didn't in *The White Devil*. I believe she knew that she was rubbish, which made her even nastier. Although it wasn't just her – everybody involved behaved badly.

The White Devil contains incest and murder and cruelty expressed in magnificent poetry, and Michael was all at sea. His production wandered between various epochs – it was neither a costume drama, nor was it a contemporary reimagining. There was no focus or particularity to it, because although we were dressed in modern clothes and smoking cigarettes, we carried old-fashioned pistols *and* Jacobean swords. Even getting onto the stage was hard: there was a revolving door stage left resembling a New York hotel entrance. It's easy to get stuck in a revolving door, especially when carrying a sword. It seems for some time, in other productions, Michael had wanted to use revolving doors; now he took his chance.

It's never a good idea to take a production out of its location or period: a play is set in a time and place for a reason. Occasionally it can work: Baz Luhrmann's film of *Romeo + Juliet* is an example, but this was a mishmash – a hideous hodgepodge of absurdity. And we knew it. I remember Patrick Magee getting so infuriated at just how awful it was, that he slammed his hand into the brick wall of the rehearsal room, tearing it badly on a nail, and ending up having to go to hospital.

The rehearsals rapidly became acrimonious. There was no generosity, no sense of collaboration or of comradeship in the cast, just competition and rancour: they were fights, they weren't rehearsals. Every day was like that. Nobody wanted to come into work. Glenda may have thought she was giving a good performance, but no one else did. She and I had a falling out; I cannot remember what it was about: I called her a cow, and she called me an amateur. I think she won that one!

It became ever clearer that we were in the middle of disaster. On the day of the opening night, Glenda called an impromptu meeting with the girls – all the women's dressing rooms were on one side of the stage and the male dressing rooms were on the other. Once we were gathered in Glenda's dressing room, she said, 'Look, I don't want to open the show tonight. I don't think it's ready and if we open when it's not ready, we're not doing ourselves a favour. Do you all agree?' We did. Glenda then went to see Michael, who called a full company meeting. All the women were keen to delay, all the men wanted to go ahead. Jack Shepherd summed up the male view: 'This putting it off is not a good idea. I want to get it under my belt.' His part was huge, as Flamineo drives the plot and he saw the attempted postponement as a female conspiracy. He was anxious to do the play, psychologically ready to tackle it. It was put to a vote; and Michael, determined not to upset Glenda, made the casting vote ruling to cancel.

I was the Equity deputy (equivalent to shop steward) on the production, so Michael told me to go to Andy Phillips, the lighting designer and one of the producers (who happened to be Glenda's boyfriend) and tell him about the company vote; the wheels were set in motion for the cancellation of the performance. Boards were placed outside the theatre and the press was informed.

We were all devastated: not just about the first night, but at the open division in the company, which the voting procedure had exacerbated. A small, disconsolate group of women went to La Barca, a local Italian restaurant, to have supper. When Jack Shepherd walked in and saw me, he said loudly, 'You cunt!' The whole restaurant went silent. I was shocked, not by the word but by the venom in his voice. At the time, I was terribly upset. I'd always liked Jack; we'd had previous great success in *The Girls of Slender Means*. Now I realise it came from his frustration and misery at having the moment of final resolution removed, as he saw it, unfairly. It was a 'coitus interruptus'. And you know how nasty men can be when *that* happens.

The next night we opened. During the curtain call as we were taking our bows, André Previn, who was in the audience, got up and shouted, 'Rubbish!'

In a change to Webster's original text, I was allowed to live at the end of the play (Edward Bond's idea) but it was harder by far to face the other kind of 'dying'. It is agony to go on stage every night and know that your work is poor.

Unsurprisingly, we got terrible notices and consequently the audiences stayed away. The whole production had been set up to test the waters for a new permanent company, along the lines of the RSC, doing classical and modern plays to a high standard. It was the flagship venture for Bullfinch Productions. But with the theatre more than half empty every evening, it was clear that the law of the box office had spoken and the show would have to come off. Bullfinch Productions decided they must keep the show running to save face and offered the cast a 30 per cent wage cut. A percentage wage cut favours the higher-paid members of the company – when you're only earning £50 a week, as I was, a 30 per cent cut is a substantial amount. Glenda was earning £350 a week, so it was considerably less of a financial blow for her.

There are strict rules about wage cuts, because they change contracts already signed with the employee. Equity called the crucial meeting where the wage cut would be discussed and voted upon. Only Equity members of the company were allowed to attend. I made a passionate speech against the proposal: 'You can't ask people to take wage cuts. After all, we still have to pay our rent and pay our electricity bills in full, and you don't say to the electricity company, "Can you make a thirty per cent cut to my bill?" Actors are being made expendable. And it's wrong.'

It turned out that Glenda had concealed that she was actually a member of the production company, Bullfinch Productions. She had been involved in setting up the show and employing cast members. Therefore, she had no right to attend the company meeting. But she did, and knew exactly how everyone had voted, although Equity told us that the management would never know who voted against a pay cut. A book was presented for us to sign and express our choice – to accept or not. It was one of the few occasions when I was deeply ashamed of my Union.

The rule is usually that one dissenting vote negates the acceptance of a wage cut. The 'secret' information was given to the management; only two people voted against– myself and Frances de la Tour. James Villiers didn't like the situation and said so, but needed the money and so he signed. He made a point of apologising to Frankie. I'm sure everyone signed for similar reasons: we all had rent to pay and bills to meet.

Frankie and I were sacked.

It should never have been known that we had voted a certain way. Equity should not have let that happen. I'm a passionate trade unionist; I was on the Equity council for many years, but at that moment, my union let us down badly, and I will never forget it. Frankie and I collected our things and walked out, and everybody said their awkward goodbyes.

The show limped along for another six weeks and then closed. My dresser, James Villiers's wife, Patricia Donovan, played my part; Fidelis Morgan played Frankie's part. I'd had a rumbunctious affair with Fidelis which had started in the dressing room, when she sat on my knee to do my make-up. I'm afraid we now seldom speak to each other.

Getting into Character: *Endgame*

The best moment for an actor is the phone call that tells you you've got the job. For me, the second-best is the first read-through, when you get to meet everybody. We all gather round a table in a big room with the director, and in chairs behind us are the technical crew: costume, hair, make-up and so on. I like to make an impact on these occasions. So, when they go around the table and everybody says who they are, I say, 'Miriam Margolyes, eighty-year-old Jewish lesbian.' That usually raises a smile. I'm sure some people think, 'Gosh, she's brave!' And the people who have heard it before groan, 'Oh, God!' But I think everyone is nervous and a laugh helps to dissipate the fears.

At that first gathering, you have to draw a careful line between delivering a performance – because you haven't found your performance yet, so you shouldn't be delivering – and giving an indication of what your performance *might* be. I relish those occasions and, once we start, I'm not nervous at all because I don't have to worry about losing my lines: I've got the text in front of me. I also know that I've been cast for a reason and, in the first read-through, the challenge is *to show* that reason and to be alive to what the cast is offering – it's a joint voyage of discovery.

The director's role is vital but there are surprisingly few good directors. It is both their vision of the play and their ability to unlock an actor's talent to achieve their full potential that marks a great director. In 1978, Max Stafford-Clark directed Julie Covington in Caryl

Churchill's great play, *Cloud 9*. Julie was having great difficulty with a long and crucial speech in the second act. She spent hours on it, and knew it wasn't right. And then Max said, 'Just sing it, Julie. Don't speak it. Sing it.' He knew that she was a singer, the original Evita. And it worked. She sang the whole speech and forever after that the speech flew and was illuminating and a high point of the play. I detest the man but I acknowledge his brilliance. The show was a great success, one of the Royal Court's triumphs.

Why do I detest Max? In 1978, I too was in *Cloud 9* at the Royal Court. The Joint Stock company, which Max had co-founded, had a particular rehearsal technique. The writer would sit in, while various improvisations were performed. The play was about sexual politics (among other things) and the cast was selected for their sexuality as well as their talent. I was the lesbian in the company, Tony Sher and Jim Hooper were the gay men and everyone else was straight. Max decreed that we should have a 'truth' session: one by one, members of the company would sit in the middle of the circle and answer questions posed by the other company members; the questions were deeply personal, often sexual, often unsettling. Max would sit in, taking notes. He insisted these sessions must be totally confidential. Heather came to answer questions, and so did Julie Covington's mother.

In 2007, Max published a book, *Taking Stock*, a detailed account of the plays he'd directed. In the chapter on *Cloud 9* he used the notes he'd made at the time, quoting great chunks from the supposedly 'confidential' sessions he'd attended. He concentrated on my remarks which were, as usual, totally uncensored and revealing. He sent me the proofs, but only *after* I wrote him a letter of sympathy following his severe stroke. I phoned the publisher, Nick Hern, and demanded these passages be removed. It shocked me then – as it does now – that Max felt entitled to use deeply personal information obtained in a professional context to sell his book, choosing to ignore completely the code of confidentiality he had himself established. He is a fine director, but his personal morals stink.

In 2009 I was cast in Samuel Beckett's *Endgame* directed by Simon McBurney (of Théâtre de Complicité) at the Duchess Theatre in London. It's a one-act play with just four characters, and I was the only woman. Mark Rylance was Hamm; I was playing Nell, Hamm's mother; and Tom Hickey, an Irish actor, was playing Nagg, husband of Nell and father of Hamm. Richard Briers was going to play Clov, Hamm's servant. I don't know why, but Richard dropped out after the first rehearsal and Simon McBurney took over the role.

Our first meeting for the read-through was enormously cordial, but I felt uneasy. Mark Rylance is one of the greatest actors in the world. He's not 'grand'; he is approachable, loves a laugh, listens attentively and is generous with praise. I was nervous of working with him, I knew he would spot my ignorance and ineptitude. But he made me feel at ease because he shared his own anxiety. And when you feel that you're fellow-travellers, the panic subsides and the creation can begin. Simon too, has that gift of instant democracy. It is a blessing.

The problem was that I had always thought Beckett was a waste of time and I didn't have a clue what he was on about. For a start, for most of this play I would be wedged in a dustbin. I really wanted to work with Simon and Mark, however, so when I was offered the role of Nell, I accepted like a shot – and then I panicked. I didn't have a clue about how to play this part. I sat there at the read-through in dread. In the end, I just came out with it: I told Simon that I felt completely at sea – I couldn't understand where we were; how and why were we in dustbins? (I still haven't fathomed that one, admittedly.) I said that he was going to have to tell me how to play my role, and, luckily for me, he did. I was also a bit nervous about the Irishness of my character. I'm good at accents, but a bad Irish accent is an embarrassment. So, rather than launch into full 'Oirish', I decided that I would simply have a suggestion of Irishness. It was carefully done, measured out, so it was perfectly obvious that I wasn't Irish, but at least nobody had occasion to accuse me of a bogus brogue.

It was unlike any other rehearsal process I've ever experienced. For the first week or more, we didn't attend to the text at all: we just played physical games. I had been brought up in a different way – you start and finish with The Text; but Simon had us playing football, and catch. In fact, I had seldom been so physical out of bed, and I was the one who barely moved: I kept saying I'd go in goal.

We also spent a lot of time improvising and playing status games, where Mark, Tom and I would take turns coming into the room, and we had to show our status: who's up and who's down, who's the boss and who's the poor underling. If it's used skilfully, that kind of exercise can be enlightening and, happily, on this occasion, with Simon's direction, it was. It can also, however, be a total waste of time. For example, if a director says, 'Be an ostrich', or 'Be more brown,' (that was actually said to me) I know it's not going to work. I belong to a more conventional school of acting; I'm with Sir Noël Coward, who said, 'Learn your lines and don't bump into the furniture.'

But more than anything, rehearsals come to life when we connect with the other people on stage; something happens when you work together and it's *good* – the performance grows, it flowers. The moment of creation should be honourably shared, when no one is trying to be more important or take the eye, because we make the moment *together*. I don't understand why Laurence Olivier said to his fellow performers: 'Don't look at me.' How do you work with someone if you can't look at them? As I said, on stage, every glance, every moment, is telling me something and I must be ready to receive it.

I have worked with actors who tend towards a less generous, less democratic approach to the art, or the work, or whatever one calls the job that we do. They keep moving while someone else is talking. Start knitting in the middle of someone else's speech, noisily open a letter, or start sweeping. Quite wrong: if it's someone else's moment, you have to allow it; you have to pass the baton, and unfortunately some actors don't like doing that. A good director enforces baton-handovers.

Simon is a precise director, and his standards are high. He had a way about him that made me want to try harder to please him. He knew everyone's part better than we knew them ourselves. He gave me the single best piece of direction that I have ever had. In the dustbin, Nell is recounting her memories, talking about herself as a young girl and Simon said, 'As you're going back into your memory, just stroke your hair.' And as I was talking, I gently stroked my hair, in that tender way that you might if you were conjuring up some deep, long-forgotten memory of your youth. Suddenly, as I touched my hair, it happened: I saw myself in the mirror, Nell as a young girl, and all at once I embodied that look that you give yourself, suffused with the pleasure of seeing your reflection when you're young and gorgeous. It was that simple gesture, a preening moment of a young woman in her excitement, remembering . . . 'Oh, I was so beautiful!' then, she, the character, was somehow back in that moment of time.

When people talked to me afterwards, everybody spoke about the moment when I touched my hair. That was Simon's gift to me – he opened the door. It was clever of him, because the instant I did that, it was as if I had turned on a switch and the part itself then fell into place. He might have said the same thing to some actors and they would have just stroked their hair, but I knew what he meant: I *saw* what he wanted me to convey in that moment. I remember it to this day.

I wouldn't say it was the hardest role I've ever taken on because, to be truthful, I think every role I'm about to do is the hardest one I've ever done. But this was particularly difficult. Within our production we showed *everything*. It was a happy and completely terrifying experience – testing and intellectually trying. Beckett doesn't write like other writers. He has a different vision of the world. It takes a while to see it.

My part was the smallest part in the play, and sometimes I was quite relieved about that, but for the moments that Tom Hickey, who was in the other dustbin, and I were together on stage, I felt that we were an old married couple, that we *did* have a history together. Tom gave me that feeling; he was one of the 'sharers' and so generous in his praise. I'd say, 'I don't know what the fuck I'm doing.' And Tom would tell me, 'It's great. Just keep doing what you're doing!' He gave me confidence.

Tom died in Dublin in May 2021; I mourn his passing with all my heart.

PG Tips and the Caramel Bunny

My voice-over work took off in 1974. I'll always remember it, because it started on the afternoon of Mummy's funeral. At the graveside I could hear somebody wailing. I thought to myself, 'God! How absurd to be carrying on like that! This is a private moment. Why on earth would anyone do that?' Then I realised; it was I who was screaming.

We came back from the cemetery. We were in the sitting room at home and now I had to be the hostess, politely handing out tea and Jewish biscuits to all the mourners. Suddenly, the phone rang, and I picked it up, because when the phone rings, that's what you do; it hadn't occurred to me to take it off the hook.

A crisp, female voice said, 'Hello, is that Miriam?' It was Wendy Noel, enunciating clearly down the phone. She had been an actress once, and then became a voice agent, working for Bryan Drew. She said, 'I've got room for you in my stable now and I've got a booking for you on Thursday next week.' She told me the time and said I'd have to be at a certain studio to do the voice-over. 'Is that all right? Can you do that?'

And I said, 'Oh, yes. Thank you. I'll be there.' She told me to write it all down, and not to forget. I was in grief but as I put the phone down, I thought, 'If only Mummy could know I've got the best voice-over agent in London.' It was a major door opening because Wendy was the queen of the voice agents and all the advertising executives trusted her – if Wendy Noel suggested one of her voice artists, well, you got the job.

Not for a second did I think of saying I wasn't feeling up to the work. It was my profession. I wanted to say yes. I wrote down all the details, and I turned up on the day for my first gig. Punctuality is a key factor in voice-over success. Where seconds count, you can't afford to arrive late. I never did.

I started slowly, but from that first job came more and more until, eventually, by the middle of the eighties, I was the top-earning female voice-over artist in the country – and it was extremely lucrative work. At the top of my tree, I was doing about eight a day, rushing up and down Soho, my pager affixed to my jumper.

In those happy days of voicing commercials, Soho was the hub of the capital's advertising and film world. The top sound studios were mainly based there. The sound recording revolution was started by Stefan Sargent and his business partner, Robert Parker. They were the pioneers in commercial *radio* advertising. TV advertising had been going for ages, of course. Now I was a regular at Molinare where they trained many of the top engineers. Soon other studios came into the expanding voice industry. There was the John Wood Studios and Angell Sound, run by Nick Angell. It was in Angell Sound I first met French and Saunders. I listened to their work, improvising a radio commercial and knew, beyond doubt, that they would become stars. Their timing was superb and they knew each other so well, their work was instinctive.

At the John Wood Studios in Broadwick Street, I became friends with John himself. He taught me a great deal about how to make commercials believable, how to save seconds when needed. He had built technically superb studios but more than anything, he created a family atmosphere. All the engineers were lovely blokes, while glamorous Maureen Lyons at the front desk knew how to make clients feel special.

John reminded me of the first session I ever did with him: I was running through the script in my little sound booth and he heard a big bang. 'What was that noise, Miriam?' he asked. 'Sorry, John,' I said. 'I just put my tits on the table.' Well . . . it broke the ice, if not the table!

Often, there would be several other actors in the voice-over booth; sadly, the days of large casts in voice-overs have gone now. Many came via the BBC, because we knew how to use a microphone.

When bookings started to increase, and my friends were as busy as I was, a group of us clubbed together to rent a little flat in Broadwick Street. Sharing the flat were me, Tony Jackson, Ray Brooks (who was mainly a television actor); Martin Jarvis; John Baddeley; David Tate (best known for his work in the original radio series of *The Hitchhiker's Guide to the Galaxy*); Patrick Allen, who was probably the most well known; and Geoffrey Matthews, another gifted pal from radio.

On any one day, there was a lot of time hanging about in between jobs, and having the flat meant instead of having to go backwards and forwards from Soho to home, we could wait there. It was Tony Jackson's idea. He was a working-class boy from Birmingham, with black hair, black eyes, massive sexual energy and he was a terrific voice-over artist with intelligence and artistic flair. As one of the major male-voice success stories in the early seventies, Tony was making about £50,000 per annum; that was a lot of money then. If he hadn't taken to drink, he would have been a big star but, sadly, died too young.

It was a small world and we were much envied by other actors because everybody knew that we were making money and having fun. We weren't all in the flat at the same time, of course, because sometimes someone would have a job in theatre, or film, but we chipped in and paid our share regardless. I suspect some of the men may have used the bedroom for an afternoon fuck. It was tremendous fun to be with my fellow actors and so convenient; I used to have a swim at Marshall Street Baths, and then did my shopping at Berwick Street Market. There were lots of little restaurants and places to go. One of my favourite shops was Andrew Edmunds in Lexington Street. Every time I got a good job, I bought a nineteenth-century political cartoon from Andrew. Rowlandson, Gillray and Heath were my favourites. The spur to purchase came from the size of the ladies depicted. They are all remarkably fat, stout, portly, roly-poly, substantial, heavyset, weighty, blubbery – you get the picture? Well, so did I. It isn't the politics that grabs me, it's the fecundity. They are the classical equivalent of the seaside postcard, breasts and appetites barely contained, the full panoply of Georgian excess in glorious colour.

We were getting so many bookings that Wendy Noel made us have little pagers, and she would page us the details of the next job. We sat and chatted in the flat waiting for our pagers to buzz; every buzz meant money. We would have tea, coffee and pastries from Cranks, the famous vegetarian restaurant next door to the swimming pool. We'd bring in all the food and laugh and wait for the money to roll in. It was an amazing time.

As with radio, there is an art to commercial voice-over work. When you're creating with your voice alone, the focus has to be absolutely tight. I always ask the director to specify age and class. If you can centre your character accurately in a class category, it will be authentic. Then comes the geographical region. I always like to offer several readings to give them a choice. I believe I was easy to work with; I enjoyed a joke and loved to shock – I would change my tights in John Wood's foyer if Maureen would look out for me. Sometimes, if annoyed with stupid directors, I'd pull up my jumper and frighten them with my bra. But when I was in the booth and working, I was totally focused. The skill is in the timing, which was usually thirty seconds – the duration of most TV commercials. I was famous for my accuracy. I could shave four seconds off if required.

Of course, commercials aren't live, so the engineers can help you a lot. My tips for doing voice-overs, are not to speak directly into the mike and to breathe quietly (although with advertisements, the sound engineers can cut out the breath so that it doesn't get in the way). I always made friends with my sound engineers. They are as skilled as I am and their expertise can help me in so many ways. They can clip your take to make it fit the time, they can make you sound amazing. We are a team, the engineer and the voice.

I have always relished the detail needed in voice work for commercials, because you only have your voice to create a whole world. You have to pick out the words in the script which sell, and you have to colour them, lean on them, elongate them, or make them suddenly stand out in a certain way: words like 'free', or 'you', or 'love' – these are words that have bubbles of excitement in them. You use that emphasis and nuance when you're delivering your text. I was also renowned for being ruthless with the scripts; if I thought that the grammar was bad, I would say so: 'I'm sorry, I'm not saying this. It's incorrect – can we alter it, please?' Those advertising chaps always said yes.

I liked working with the creatives and directors, but every now and again, somebody thought that they would show off a bit and give you a bad time. There's a famous tape of Orson Welles losing his temper at an inane session director who was mucking him about: the product was Findus frozen peas. Only once did I not complete the recording session. I said to the director, 'I'm sorry, you're asking me to do something that is undoable, and, frankly, not worth doing.' And then I walked out of the booth.

When there were a few of us working together on a voice-over, it was in a larger studio, and each of us had a mike; or sometimes you had one for all of you, and you had to be sensitive and withdraw – or 'recede' as it's called – i.e. you back away from the mike in order to let your colleague have it. But, more and more, it's just me on my own these days. I go into a little separate booth, put on my headphones, they close the soundproof door so I'm sealed away from the world, and I begin. It's lonely, but you can keep the pencils.

From about 1978 all the way through to the mid-eighties, I recorded a good number of the famous PG Tips adverts with the chimpanzees. I was Dolly, who had a charlady voice, while Ada, the other chimp (whose real name was Choppers), was Stanley Baxter. Nowadays you couldn't do it because they used real chimpanzees from Twycross Zoo, who were dressed up and filmed drinking tea and so on. In one of our ads, Dolly was at the sink up to her elbows in suds, when she says, 'I'm fed up with this washing up. My Phil always calls me his little dishwasher.' Then Stanley, playing Ada, replies, 'What do you call him, then?' and I reply, 'Bone idle!' At the end of each commercial, Dolly would have a swig of Brooke Bond's PG Tips, and say, 'It's the taste.' I loved doing it and we were working with all the award-winning advertising chaps. Alan Copp, the producer, for example, was also responsible for the famous dried mashed potato SMASH advertising campaign, and the director, Bernie Stringle, was *the* top TV commercial director at that time.

Often it was just me, Stanley Baxter and Bernie Stringle together in the studio. It was difficult doing lip sync for a chimp, because the mouth of a chimp doesn't move in the same way as a human mouth. They had somehow made the chimps' mouths go up and down, open and close, open and close, and we had to synchronise our voices to that. So, we had to make sure that the words opened and closed, exactly in time with their mouths. Normally, how it works – and this is the same for doing lip sync for a chimp, or dubbing a foreign language film – is that they run the bit of film which you are to voice, and something called a 'wipe' goes across the screen. It's like a finger, and when this finger hits a certain point, in the middle of the screen, that's your cue to start to say your lines. But Bernie didn't depend on that: the moment you had to start to speak, he used to touch you on the shoulder. He told me once how an anxious actor had worried about getting the sync right. Bernie had said, 'Don't worry, I'll give you a tap on your shoulder when you need to start.' The moment came, Bernie tapped his shoulder – and the actor fainted dead away.

We also had the beeps: three beeps – *beep, beep, beep: start.* That's how you knew when to begin, because otherwise it's quite tricky.

It was great fun and the adverts were extremely popular – probably *the* most popular and successful TV commercials ever made, until the BT ones with Maureen Lipman. In those days we were good friends and she recommended me for a part in the 'ology' series with Beattie, playing another Jewish housewife.

Footlights Smoker in 1964 with (from left) David Gooderson, John Cameron, Eric Idle, Susan Hanson and Graeme Garden. Don't believe the smile.

Gerald Scarfe's unique costume designs for *Ubu Roi* in 1963. I always knew I was a cunt.

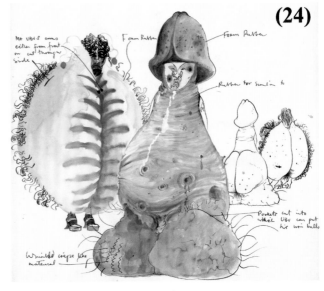

(24)

A voodoo queen with Helen Weir in *The Cat and the Canary* in 1966.

The Threepenny Opera in 1972: Stella Courtney, Annie Ross, me and Patricia Quinn as the whores (top right). Vanessa Redgrave and Barbara Windsor (below right). I was also Ba's understudy.

Heather, Katy and me
in Clapham, 1973.

The famous naked Valentine from
The Girls of Slender Means, 1975:
me, Mary Tamm, Patricia Hodge
and Jane Cussons.

The White Devil with Jack Shepherd and Glenda Jackson, 1976.

Blackadder: in 1983 as the Spanish Infanta, never knowingly underplayed, and (below) in 1985, Lady Whiteadder eats a turnip closely watched by Rowan Atkinson and Tony Robinson. Is Baldrick corpsing?

As Gertrude Stein with
Natasha Morgan as Alice in
1985. Enough said.

In *Little Dorrit*, 1988.

'If it weren't for the nerve a little sip of liquor gives me':
as Mrs Gamp in *Dickens' Women*, 1991.

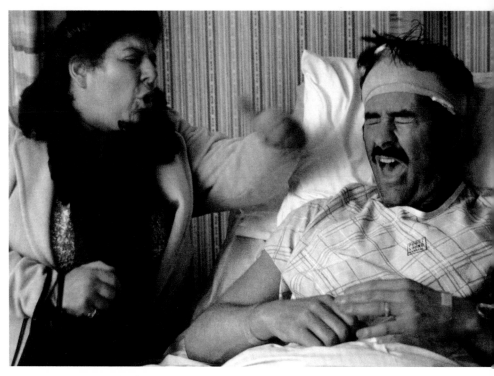

I went to Kevin Kline's hotel room to practise this slap for *I Love You to Death*, 1990.

With Tomas Milian as my
unreconstructed husband
in *Frannie's Turn*, 1992.

With Donald Sinden in *She Stoops to Conquer* in 1993.

With Daniel Day-Lewis, Winona Ryder and seven Pomeranians in
The Age of Innocence in 1993.

With Joanna Lumley as spiteful aunts Spiker (her) and Sponge (me) in *James and the Giant Peach*, 1996.

I never thought I'd play a sheepdog: *Babe*, 1995.

As well as regions and class, I can do sexy. Although I don't have a sexy voice normally, I can imbue it – to me, a sexy voice is an exhausted voice, of somebody who's had so many orgasms they've hardly got the strength to speak. So, I would breathe through my lines and I got known for being sexy. Although, of course, as a person, sex is not the thing I project. I project energy. I don't project cunt, but exhausted cunt I can offer, vocally, when required.

That's how I got the job to do the Manikin cigar advert, which was a *very* sexy ad. The director of those ads was a wonderful character called Terence Donovan, who was also a famous photographer, noted for his iconic fashion photography in publications like *Town* and *Nova* magazine in the sixties. (He also had a building firm and would later become *my* builder when I was doing up my house in Clapham.) I loved him. He was a great big fellow from a poor background in Stepney. His father, Daniel, was a lorry driver and Constance Violet, his mother, was a cook. Even when he became famous, he never changed from being a down-to-earth, friendly, unassuming, pragmatic, entrepreneurial East End lad.

Terence had branched out into film direction and television commercials in the seventies, and I was the voice for the beautiful, sexy girl with a sublime body, played by Carole Augustine, a young British model and actress (who had made a brief appearance in *Confessions of a Window Cleaner*). She tragically died soon after in 1975 of a drug overdose, aged twenty-one. In the ad she stood beside a tropical waterfall, all in white, revealing a gorgeous tanned midriff and cleavage. She was dipping a tobacco leaf in the water of a rock pool and stretching it lasciviously across her lips, and I had to say, '*I come to show why Manikin flavour plenty enjoyable. I need water, see?*

Water make leaf stretch. Wrap cigar well. Mouth enjoy flavour, yes? Manikin flavour special.'

I did a whole string of these ads, several with Carole – presumably all the different films shot on that one same trip to Antigua – with the lines: *'Manikin bring you best tobacco. Tobacco plant tall. Manikin wrapped only with tobacco picked from middle. Middle leaf best, make manikin cigar special.'*

For the next campaign, there was a new stunning beauty in her place, but I still voiced the ads in the same sultry tones: *'Manikin tobacco fermented . . . Make cigar smooth and mellow, so Manikin flavour pleasing to man. Manikin flavour special.'* All ending with the words *'Sheer enjoyment'* sung to the familiar tune. It was one of the most successful advertising campaigns of all time; look it up on YouTube.

Another of my classics was the Cadbury's Caramel Bunny ads, which ran in the 1980s and 1990s. I don't know where that voice came from, but to some extent I was channelling Sexy Sonia, to which I added an Oxfordshire spin and a hint of creamy West Country sumptuousness for good measure; it seemed to suit the voluptuous bunny's sensually languorous demeanour.

It was a lovely experience taking part in all these big advertising campaigns, and some people never wanted anything else. But I did. I wanted to be doing more with my acting career.

Bryan Drew was my agent for everything, both for voices and for what I would term 'proper' acting work, on stage or film. I was getting the voice jobs all right, thanks to Wendy Noel. But then Wendy retired and *all* I seemed to be getting was voice work. I really wanted to act, to be a proper actress playing all sorts of parts and I thought, 'Well, maybe if I suck Bryan off, I'll get better work.' I went to his office one day and did exactly that. I thought of it then as a 'career incentive'. I remember saying, 'How do you think it's all shaping up, Bryan? Because I don't seem to be doing much except voice-overs.' It must have been me that offered, because I don't think I would have been top of Bryan's list for mouth sex. He was a nice man, even if he was a bit lazy. Maybe the conversation stalled and it seemed a good moment. I said, 'Would you like me to suck you off?' And he must have said yes, because I did. But it didn't bring me any more work. Put that one down to experience.

Soon after, I left Bryan Drew; it left a nasty taste, I suppose.

To Dub or Not to Dub

The BBC provided the perfect training and diving board into the world of voice-overs. My voice, thanks to all those years of elocution and radio acting, is my not so secret weapon, but even I was surprised at the lengthy list (stretching across several pages!) of all the parts I've played. The Cadbury's Caramel Bunny and PG Tips' chimp are just the tip of the iceberg, as my voice is there embedded in literally hundreds of TV series and films, many of which I've now forgotten. Dubbed voices are never credited, and this anonymous artistry and skill are known only to those of us who stood in darkened studios years ago and tried to recreate, as best we could, the passion and flair of the original performance.

My favourite adventures in audio all started with 'Sexy Sonia', of course, after which I decided that, really, I preferred a script with words, rather than panting and moaning. After the dubbed version of a Japanese series called *The Water Margin* (I played all the female roles except Princess Titicaca, who was my old Cambridge friend Elizabeth Proud) became a surprise hit in 1976, I was booked again to perform most of the supporting female characters in another dubbed Japanese action TV series, *Monkey*, in 1978. We were a voice cast of about seven: there was Burt Kwouk; along with Andrew Sachs, of Manuel in *Fawlty Towers* fame; David Collings; Maria Warburg; Peter Woodthorpe; and Gareth Armstrong. When I went to Australia, that was one of the things that most impressed the technical crews that I worked with: the camera and lighting and all the gaffers and so on. They would say, 'You did *Monkey*! Bloody hell! I used to watch that every day when I came back from school. That was my favourite programme!' They were all just thrilled with it, but the tragedy is that I don't remember it at all.

When you're dubbing, you don't watch the whole thing; only the scene that you are voicing. You go into a darkened room with a huge screen, like a cinema, and you stand there, maybe five or six of you behind your own individual mike. They play the loop, and we look at it, though I always prefer to listen to the guide track, and then you record your lines. I'm always so intent on getting the wipe, and starting exactly on cue when the wipe goes across, that I don't really have time to think about the film itself. I just do my job, and then we go to the next scene.

I don't really approve of dubbing. I believe in subtitles. I never go to a dubbed film: they always sound dead to me, because they don't have the acoustic of the original action. Although they do try to reproduce it, and a great deal of time is spent doing that, in my opinion it never works. I don't like animation either, and I would never go and watch a cartoon movie in the cinema. I want the real thing. So, because I wasn't interested in *Monkey* or the story, I took no account of it, and that's why I don't remember it.

Perhaps foolishly, I've never seen the films I've voiced. I prefer not to. It's noticeable that I am often asked to be an animal; I've been a snake, an owl and a glow-worm, but maybe that's because I've made many animated films for children. I've also been various kinds of monsters: some requiring masses of make-up; in others, my own face was deemed frightful enough.

My favourite voice of all was the mother dog, Fly, in *Babe*, the film of Dick King-Smith's 1983 novel *The Sheep-Pig*. (The film in a sense changed my life, but more on that later.) *Babe* came out in 1995, but I was working on it for several years. When the producer, George Miller, rang up and asked if I could come out and record in Australia and that he would fly me out first class, I thought he was joking. His call came as I was in studio, narrating an extremely sad documentary about the Holocaust. He said, 'I want you to meet the dog. You'll enjoy it.' I thought, 'You're not kidding.' I wasn't going to tell him that I didn't need to meet the dog; I could easily have done the recording just as well in a studio in London.

So they flew me out to Australia; I was introduced to the dog and we got on quite well. The film set was in a little rural village called Robertson, about eighty miles south of Sydney, in the lush green Southern Highlands of New South Wales. It's more like Dorset there than Dorset. Then I was driven back to the studio in North Sydney.

Chris Noonan, the director of *Babe*, was meticulous and demanding, making me do take after take. But his attention to detail created *Babe*, and he helped me to create Fly.

Chris co-wrote the film with George Miller, and yet George never really acknowledged Chris Noonan's part in creating *Babe*; whenever prizes were won – and *Babe* received 7 Oscar nominations[*] – it was George who would go and collect the prize, not Chris, and I felt that was unfair. I'd also like to pay tribute to Christine Cavanaugh, the voice of Babe, who died in 2014. I never met her, but I think her work is sublime.

---

[*] *Babe* ultimately won the award for special effects. Other awards include the 1996 Golden Globe award for Best Picture.

Australians, for the most part, are not tremendously demonstrative, but Chris was *extremely* quiet, gently mannered and reserved, and so for a long time I didn't know if I was giving him what he wanted. Then gradually he opened up a bit, then I knew that I was delivering. We spent eight or ten hours each day in the studio, just the two of us together, and I had to go over it and over it ad infinitum, until Chris was satisfied.

On my first recording of Fly's role, I did it in a Scottish accent – because Fly was a Scottish border collie and I like to be literal – and it was perfect. But then the big cheeses at Universal, the film company, said they didn't understand a word Fly was saying. Americans just can't deal with accents. I had just given Fly's voice a tinge of Scotland, but the suits said, 'No, we want it mid-Atlantic.'

So, they flew me back again, all-expenses paid and first class, naturally – and I obliged with the Fly you hear now. It's good, but Scottish Fly was truer.

The narration by the African American actor Roscoe Lee Browne starts, 'This is the tale of an unprejudiced heart . . .' When you hear those words in that inimitable rich, commanding and dignified voice, you think, 'Ah, this is a serious film.' *Babe* is a film about prejudice and about inclusiveness. I loved it, and I still love it.

Banged Up in Bow Street

It was a Thursday, the day of the State Opening of Parliament. I wanted to deliver a voice-over tape to my agent. I parked the car on a busy Shaftesbury Avenue and ran upstairs to deliver the tape; I took, honestly, no more than a minute. When I returned to the car, there was a motorcycle policeman in jackboots, writing a parking ticket.

'How *dare* you do that? I was only up there a minute!' He slapped the parking ticket under my windscreen wiper. 'Well, you've parked on a double yellow line,' he replied. I lost my temper. I snatched the ticket off the windscreen, tore it into little pieces and threw them in the air. 'You've got a dick *that* small!' I shouted, indicating a very small member with my index finger and thumb. The policeman's mood darkened. 'Right. Now I'm doing you for parking on a double yellow line – *and* for littering.' He was writing more in his notebook. I was enraged. 'Go on, then! Arrest me! I don't care what you do,' I bellowed. 'Miss, I'm going to have to take you to a police station,' he said. 'I *demand* to be taken to a police station!' I retorted.

The policeman radioed for back-up. Because of the State Opening of Parliament, there was a fleet of police cars in the area. Seconds later, three panda cars flashing blue lights screamed up behind me. Six more policemen climbed out and joined us. They shoved their arms under my armpits and half-lifted, half-frog-marched me across the road, my little legs wriggling in the air.

By this time, quite a crowd of curious onlookers had gathered. I shouted out, 'You see what happens in England?' And I was pushed into the backseat of a police car.

I was taken to Bow Street police station and led to the holding area. I was still so angry, I wasn't even frightened. The arresting officer took me to the station sergeant's desk, told him the nature of my offence and the sergeant took down my name and address and booked me in. Then the officer said, 'We're going to empty your handbag.' He opened it, turned it upside down, gave it a shake, and the contents fell out onto the custody desk. Item by item, he picked everything up and inspected it; then he picked up something wrapped in silver paper. 'Aha! Well, well, well. What have we got here, Miss Margolyes?' he said, triumphantly. Clearly, suspecting drugs.

'Well, officer, if you open it and look closely, you'll see it's a packet of Trebor peppermints.' The police officer looked a little deflated. My middle-class confidence needled him. He thought, 'I'll show that cocky bitch.' (Yes, I am imagining that's what he thought, because of his next words.) 'Well, nevertheless, you will have to be examined.' I looked at him. 'Oh, really, why is that?' 'Well, we don't know who you are,' came the reply. 'But I told you my name.' 'Yeah, but you can't prove it, can you?' 'What are you talking about? I'm an actress on television!'

'Well,' he said. 'I've never seen you.'

There was nothing much I could say to that. My suggestion that we call my agent, who would gladly verify my identity, was met with: 'I don't have time for that, love, sorry. We're very busy. This is a busy station.'

The station sergeant took me into a private examination room and told me to wait as he was going to call 'the matron', and locked the door behind him. I guessed that the matron would give me an intimate physical examination to look for drugs so, while I was waiting, I took off all my clothes. I was completely naked. When the matron walked in, she took one look at me, and said, 'You been here before?' 'I most certainly have not!' I retorted. 'Well, how did you know to take your clothes off?' 'Because I knew very well that you were going to give me an examination. And I'm not going to be examined in my clothes,' I told her. 'I'm an actress. I'm used to taking off my clothes.'

She asked me to lie on an examination table, and proceeded to carry out a vaginal examination. And she also poked up my arse. Obviously, she came away empty-handed. I put my clothes back on.

They thought being fingered in the vagina would distress me. How wrong they were! I thought all my Christmases had come at once.

When the station sergeant returned, I asked again to make my telephone call, but I was told that I couldn't. I said, 'I know my rights: I'm allowed to make a telephone call.' 'Oh, no, you're not,' he said. 'We're very busy. We can't give you a telephone at the moment, so I'm putting you in a remand cell.'

I asked him how long he was going to hold me. He said, 'I don't know. Could be quite a long time . . . it might be overnight.' 'You can't be serious!' 'I'm sorry about that, miss, but that's the way it is. Anyway, you better come with me, and we'll pop you in a cell.'

The prison officers were on strike which meant the remand cells were full, because those on remand couldn't be processed into the jail. There was a three-week backlog. Despite this, as I followed him down a long corridor of occupied cells, he eventually located an empty one, and locked me up. In the cell there was a high, small, single-barred window, a long, narrow bench from wall to wall topped with a dirty mattress, and a lavatory with no seat in the corner.

I thought, 'I've got to keep calm, I've got to stay sensible and not get scared.' I could hear people talking in the cells down the corridor. To steady myself, I started to recite Wordsworth's poem, 'On Westminster Bridge':

> Earth has not any thing to show more fair:
> Dull would he be of soul who could pass by
> A sight so touching in its majesty:
> This City now doth, like a garment, wear
> The beauty of the morning; silent, bare, [. . .]

Then I heard someone say, 'Blimey, there's a woman in there.'

I put my head to the bars. I couldn't see anything, but I said, 'Hello, is somebody there?' A man's voice replied, 'Yeah, what are you doing here?' I said, 'I was caught parking on a double yellow line.' He then said, 'Blimey, I didn't know they could put you in for that.' I asked him what he was in for, and he said, 'Burglary.'

'Did you do it?' I asked.

There was a long pause and he said, 'No comment.'

We talked for a bit. He said, 'You know, I've been three weeks in this fucking cell. And there's no hot water. We haven't washed. It's not right.' Well, it wasn't right. I told him, 'If I ever get out of here, I will do something about it. And if you give me your phone number, I'll phone your wife and tell her that you're all right.' He said, 'Would you do that? I'll write my number down.' Then he said, 'Do you want a book to read?'

'Well, yes, I suppose I do. I might be here a long time,' I replied, gratefully.

'I'll get the chap to give it to you.' He called the policeman, who was patrolling up and down outside in the corridor, and asked him to pass me his book. It was a book of jokes! He'd written his wife's telephone number on the title page.

Time was ticking on by now, and I was growing desperate. I said to the patrolling policeman, 'Look, I've got a voice-over at four o'clock, I've got to get out.'

He said, 'What do you mean by "voice-over"?' I explained: 'Well, I'm an actress, and I have a job to do in Soho.' And he said, 'You're not going to get out for *that*!' 'It's my livelihood,' I insisted. 'Well, I don't know whether I'll be able to sort that for you,' he said. 'But I'll bring you lunch.'

I was brought a meal – some godawful pudding and an unrecognisable main – all slopped onto one plate. Revolting. I went back to chatting to the men down the corridor, which passed the time.

Eventually, the station sergeant came, unlocked my cell and took me to the desk. He charged me with parking on a double yellow line, littering and causing a breach of the peace – I imagine that was because I said the motorcycle policeman had a small dick. I think that was the thing that really irritated him.

He discharged me on bail, with instructions to attend Bow Street Magistrates Court the following morning.

I made it to the voice-over, only slightly late. Everybody was terribly amused by my tale, but when I got home, thinking about my impending court appearance, I was quite shaken, mainly worried that my father would find out.

I went to court the next morning. I was told to sit in a separate waiting area with a bunch of people who'd also been arrested the day before. Most were drunks, all either Irish or Scots. At least I could work on the accents. When it was my turn, I stood before the magistrate as the arresting officer read out my three charges. The magistrate asked how I wanted to plead: I said, 'Guilty.' He asked if I had anything to add in my defence. I said, 'I'm very sorry. I know I shouldn't have said the police officer had a small dick, but I was cross. I was only away from my car for a minute; I thought that to give me a ticket was an over-reaction. However, I accept that I shouldn't have got angry; I shouldn't have said that; I shouldn't have torn up the parking ticket and thrown it on the ground. But I don't think I should have been given a vaginal examination.'

There was an audible intake of breath from those assembled. Taken aback, the magistrate said, 'What do you mean?'

'Well, the officer thought my peppermints were heroin or something,' I explained. 'And I was given a vaginal examination because he thought that I'd stuck some drugs up myself, which I had not!'

The magistrate listened, and said, 'Is it a first offence?' I said, 'Of course it's a first offence!' Then he said, 'I'm going to fine you £25 for causing litter because you tore up the notice, and you shouldn't have done that. All other charges dismissed.'

———

I often wonder what happened to the nice man in the next cell. As promised, I did ring his wife, who was pleased to hear he was all right.

The whole affair was a revelation to me. My spirit was unbowed by it, because I just thought the police were silly to lock me up for all those hours and to pursue charges. But I was protected by all the things my parents had fought so hard to provide me with: the confidence of my class, education and social status. It clearly demonstrated how different life is for people without my advantages.

Money Talks

When people say to me, 'Oh, I never talk about money, religion or politics,' I say, 'What the fuck do you talk about, then? Those are the things that matter!' Money is one of life's essentials and there's no point pretending that it isn't. It matters how you earn money, what you do with it, and how you spend it.

I was always brought up to have a healthy respect for money, and not to waste it. My parents personified two different reactions to having been brought up in poverty. Daddy was naturally stingy – turning off the lights everywhere; Mummy was naturally generous. She liked to give; Daddy didn't. He did give, in the end, but he never made any payments gladly – and he had to be prompted, even for synagogue dues. When we were getting out of a taxi, for example, Mummy would always say, 'Come on, Joe, give the driver a tip!'

He used to ask me, 'How much are you earning now?' Usually, in the early days, the response would be, 'Oh dear, oh dear.' Later, as I got wealthy, he'd respond with pleasant surprise: 'Oh! Really?'

I've always tried to keep a balanced attitude, erring on the side of generosity where possible, because I think meanness is horrible. Like my mother, I've been canny with my investments. It was never expensive clothes and cars with me – it was always houses. I didn't have any children (a lifetime's investment in themselves); that meant I could afford to buy property. Twice I've bought houses with other people. I advise young people to pool their resources with those they trust, and buy at auction, having had a surveyor's report. And have an agreement drawn up, with three important headings: Usage, Maintenance and Disposal. This will lower the chances of a breakdown in communication.

One of the main things that Heather and I have done together is buy houses and restore them. You can't do things like that when you have children. You either have to have houses or children. Unless you're *exceedingly* wealthy. People have always said, 'Oh, you must be sensationally rich to have all those houses!' Actually, no: I've never made exorbitant amounts of money, but I have always bought cheaply – and wisely.

The first house was a 300-year-old farmhouse with eighteen olive trees in Tuscany, which we bought in 1973 for 12,500 Italian lira. For our second holiday together (our first was on the Isle of Skye; I was desperate to get into Heather's bunk on the overnight sleeper but it proved impossible: they're not generous, width-wise), Heather and I went to Rome. My mother's favourite au pair, Francesca, had become an air hostess and she invited Heather and me to stay in her apartment while she was away flying for a couple of weeks. It was in a lively part of the city and we had the place to ourselves. Rome was gorgeous; we walked everywhere, never tiring of the buildings, the statues, the noise, the life of the city. The Vatican offended me; I stood there, thinking how wrong it was that so much money should be spent on all that gilt and lavish decoration, while there were so many poor Catholics in the world. I rejected the Holy City but I *loved* everything else about Italy and the Italians.

I came into a bit of money when Mummy died. I said to Heather and our friend Peter Lavery: 'Let's go and buy a house.' She thought it was insane but fun, and while Peter couldn't join our Tuscan house-hunting trip, he was in – sight unseen. I'd researched Tuscan places for sale and we took the night train to Italy. We stayed in a cheap hotel in Siena and took buses to the surrounding villages. Once established in the village cafe, we asked people if they knew of a good property. We had several exciting rides in the back of Fiat 500s, and eventually found the farmhouse of our dreams. We met an American architect, William Broadhead. I gave him power of attorney, so he could complete the *contratto*. He was in charge of all restoration and La Casella, Montisi, has been the joy of our lives ever since. William died two years ago; he was one of the most honourable men I've ever known, and his perfect taste and honesty made such a difference to our lives.

Then, I was on a roll . . . I was happily living in my rented flat in Gloucester Terrace when, one day, Peter told me that he'd seen a nice house just around the corner from where he was living in Clapham, and suggested that I should have a look at it. I said, 'Well, I'm not living south of the river!' (I have a silly habit of making knee-jerk and somewhat dogmatic statements which are rapidly proved wrong. For example, 'I am not going to have a German car'; the first car I had was a Volkswagen Beetle.) I went to see this house in Clapham and I loved it immediately and I bought it. You see, I can change my mind.

It's a Victorian semi-detached house, built in 1856, with a big bay window and steps up to the front door. In those days it wasn't smart at all; it was rather run-down, but I loved its big, spacious rooms and garden. I had asked Jan Taylor's husband (I'd done a puppet show with her) to come along and view the house with me. He was in property, and he said, 'It's a good house, Miriam.' The asking price was £21,500 (for a four-storey house), which he said was not bad. I decided to buy it. I went to the estate agent in Streatham and put in an offer. The agent said, 'I ought to tell you, that a chap is coming to see it with his surveyor this afternoon, and he's told me that if the surveyor's report is OK, he's going to pay the full asking price.'

'Well, in that case, I'm going to buy it *now*,' I replied. The estate agent was a bit taken aback and said, 'But you haven't had a survey done!' I said, 'I don't care. I can tell it's OK, because my mother used to buy houses.' I knew the things that you look for, cracks and all that, and it looked sound to me. He said, 'But you haven't checked!' I told him that I was buying it. Luckily, Halifax gave me a mortgage, and the sale went through. I gave him the 10 per cent deposit cheque there and then.

The house was in quite a bad state: the basement (where I'm living now) had been condemned by Lambeth Council, but I didn't have the money to do it up. I installed five or six friends in the house, all happily paying £2 a week. Every Friday, I would go and collect the rent in cash, which I put into a pot to save up for the building work.

In the basement flat next door were Mr and Mrs Smith, a couple who'd lived there since the war. One day, when I was collecting the rent, Mrs Smith was in her garden. She called out, 'Mirian [she never could say 'Miriam'], I want to talk to you, come over here.' I went over to her side of the wall, 'Listen, this is a nice road. We don't have rubbish on this street, Mirian.' 'No. I'm well aware of that,' I replied. 'Well, those friends of yours . . .' and she paused for effect.

'Well, let me tell you something,' she said, 'cos I don't think you know this! The other day I was out doing the weeding 'ere in the front garden, and I 'appened to look across into your front windows there

– the big bay window up there.' She pointed up at my house. 'You'd never guess what I saw . . . well, it was them two in there [pause], stark naked [pause], eatin' *marmalade*.' I gasped with horror, as I realised that that was expected. I don't know if it was straight out of the jar, but Mrs Smith must have had a *very* good look to know it was marmalade and not jam. 'Well, we can't have that in this street. I mean, people in the nood? I don't want to see nothing like that again,' she concluded, folding her arms in outrage. 'I quite agree, Mrs Smith. I'm so sorry, and I will tell them about it,' I said, reassuringly.

I told my friends, 'Please don't eat marmalade naked in the front window, because Mrs Smith doesn't like it.' And they never did it again.

After two years I'd saved up enough money, and everybody moved out so I could get the place fixed up. At the time, I was doing a lot of voice-overs. One day, in the studio voicing the Manikin cigar ad, I was talking to Terry Donovan. 'I've bought a house but it's in a rough old state. I'm going to need a lot of building work.'

'Oh, I'm a builder,' Terry said.

'What do you mean, you're a builder? You're a famous photographer and a director of commercials!'

'I've got a firm with all me old mates,' he said. 'I'll do your place up for you. We're good, we are.'

It was a funny linking of the two worlds. Terry had a Rolls-Royce, so he gave me a lift over to Clapham in his Roller, which now, of course, are commonplace in the street, but they weren't then. Terry had a good look over the property and he said, 'Yeah, it's a nice house. You done well there, Miriam. I'll sort it out for you, no worry'. He added, 'I'll get my man Slim to come over. Slim does all the estimates for me.'

A few days later, Slim turned up. He was devastatingly handsome, charismatic, a gorgeous bit of rough, probably a crim. If I'd been straight I'd have sucked him off like a shot. Slim carefully inspected the house from top to bottom and agreed that it needed a lot of work. New staircase, complete central heating and rewiring and replumbing. He named a figure and we shook hands on it there and then. Terry and his team did a fantastic job – they were honourable, decent, hard-working and reasonable.

I kept in touch with Slim over the years. Once, when I hadn't been paid for a voice-over job and was owed several thousand pounds, I asked Slim if he would come round to see this advertising chap with me and encourage him to cough up.

He said, 'Yeah, that's meat and drink to me. That's easy.'

So, flanked by Slim, I marched into the man's Soho office.

'Hello, Adrian,' I said.

'Oh, Miriam, how lovely to see you.'

'Well, I don't know if it's *that* lovely to see *you*. I'm a bit pissed off because you haven't paid me yet.'

'Don't worry, I'll send you a cheque, Miriam. I'm sorry it's taken so long, sometimes these things get a bit delayed,' he said. 'I'll do it, honestly. I'll send you a cheque, it'll be coming soon.'

'Do you know what? It's going to come even sooner than that. It's actually going to come now, right now,' I said, rather masterfully.

'I can't do it absolutely right now because—' He stopped.

'Oh, yes, you can. Do you know how I know you can? Because Slim here . . .' I turned to Slim, and continued: 'He wants you to give it to me now, don't you, Slim?'

'Oh, yeah, if you owe somebody money, you have to pay it, don't ya?' Slim said, menacingly.

It had an instant effect. Slim was obviously not someone to mess with and my debtor was visibly rattled.

'Right. OK, then,' he said, nervously, as he got up and fetched his cheque book, hurriedly writing out my cheque.

It was quite useful knowing Slim, but that was the only time I had to call upon him to put the screws on. Slim didn't even do anything – he just stood there, and I knew that would be enough. So, Clapham was house number two.

Then, in 1977, I bought the Gun Emplacement, a cottage by the sea in St Margaret's Bay, Kent. My mother had left me two, small farm-workers' cottages, side by side in a little village called Minster-in-Thanet, three miles from Birchington-on-Sea. She had bought them in the fifties to rent to holiday makers, but when Mummy died, I decided to let them out to students at the University of Kent. Within eight months, I had a letter from the Council to say that they were having great difficulty with blockages in the septic tank: my student tenants, it transpired, were using newspapers to wipe their bottoms, and not lavatory paper. If this practice continued, the Council informed me, I would be liable for the cost of unblocking any subsequent obstructions. That was a headache I did not need: having to tell tenants how to wipe their bottoms was not something I thought a woman of my talent and experience should have to do. I put the cottages on the market and sold them within a week. With the money, I thought I must buy another place in the country. I didn't know quite how to go about it, so I enlisted the help of Peter Ashenden, a retired surveyor who lived on a houseboat on the river at Sandwich.

'I want to buy a house, near the sea, totally unreconstructed but it must be quiet; I don't want any neighbours,' I said.

Within a week, Peter had found me the Gun Emplacement. It wasn't on the market yet, but he had popped into the local estate agent and they told him they'd just received the instruction to sell it. Heather and I drove up to St Margaret's Bay and Peter showed us around. It was perfect: the sea view was exactly what I wanted, and there were no other houses nearby. It was an ugly, little, flat-roofed bunker, a one-storey concrete structure with a chimney, but its selling point was the unique location: in unspoiled countryside, perched on Lighthouse Down, overlooking the white cliffs of Dover with fabulous uninterrupted views across the Channel to Calais. We rushed all around it (that's something, I realise, that Heather and I do: when we see a house we like, we run; we run all around it and up and down), and I bought it right there on the spot for £10,500.

It was constructed by the Army in 1910; Sir Peter Ustinov had been billeted there during the Second World War and he later bought the house from the Ministry of Defence as a writing retreat in 1946. I've had the Gun Emplacement as a seaside home for more than forty years; because of its wartime history, when I'm in residence there, I like to be addressed as 'Bombardier Margolyes'.

Two years ago, and of course unbeknownst to me, a Merseyside gang of drug smugglers rented it from me. They were using it as the secret helicopter drop-off point for millions of pounds-worth of cocaine; they had Dutch pilots who would fly in over the North Sea, and drop the drugs onto the flat roof of the house or in the garden. The gang escaped to Thailand before the police had cottoned on to their ruse. The arms of the law are long, however, and they were eventually arrested over there and flown back for trial.

The first I knew about it was when I was phoned by a policeman. He said, 'Do you own the Gun Emplacement?' I said, 'Yes.' I had to tell him that I'd rented the place out in all innocence, and certainly was not a member of the drugs gang. I don't like drugs at all: I wouldn't know if a gram of cocaine got up and bit me, so I was upset – but it was also quite thrilling, like something out of a Bond movie. Their trial was reported in the *Daily Mail* ('The White Sniffs of Dover' was the headline). Everyone on Twitter thought that I must be part of the gang, and I was renamed Miriam Escobar.

Too Fat to Go to Bed With

Actresses are often obsessed by the way they look and I'm no different. I love my face; I'm disgusted by my body. I loathe it. If I could migrate my whole personality and my face onto another body, I would be delighted. My weight has been a constant in my life – a negative constant. I bitterly regret it, but I haven't done enough to change it; it's still a nuisance and medically unwise, and yet, here I am, still fat: somehow over my eighty years I've managed to eat my way to 94 kilos. And now, to add insult to injury, lengthwise, I'm shrinking – I have lost an inch in height and am now 4ft 10ins.

I fully understand that most people would say: 'Get over yourself and stop overeating.' But it's not so simple. I worry about it all the time. Whenever I shop for food I think, 'I mustn't have that.' It's a constant battle. It's a hard, miserable fate being fat. And there are loads of fat people who would agree with me. They might not want to be perfect, but they don't want to be fat, either. And they're right.

A lot of people say, 'Oh, if you were skinny, Miriam, you wouldn't be the same.' And, no, I wouldn't be the same but, maybe, that's what I'd like. I sometimes feel it would be so nice to be the sharp, nasty but devastatingly sexy, skinny person for a change. In my late twenties, a lovely voice-over actress called Norma Mitchell said to me, 'Miriam, if you weren't fat, I would jump into bed with you in a minute.' I know she meant it in a nice way. 'Not much I can do about that,' I thought.

I've never forgotten it; in fact, I nearly called this book 'Too Fat to Go to Bed With.'

Moderation has been something that I have shunned and run away from, so mine is an appetite untrammelled. Greed is the flaw in my make-up. A modicum of discipline, a reining in is needed, a breaking of these desires and needs and longings. It makes me think less of myself, so when people make fun of me, inside I'm shouting along with them. I see what they mean and even though I think it's wrong to 'fat-shame' people, I almost want to do it to myself, because I think I deserve it.

In this way, as in so many, I resemble my mother. Despite all her style and passion for fine things, Mummy was too fat and she knew it. She was an excellent cook and her suppers and lunches were legendary. No one else I have ever known has made tomato and onion sandwiches, lightly sprinkled with salt and pepper, with such care and attention to detail. I can almost smell now her chicken soup served hot as soup must be, with matzo balls, or vermicelli, lots of carrots, onion, celery, and the feet, heart and gizzards of the bird, and my favourite, the neck – all to be sucked dry. Every Thursday she'd make delicious fish by dipping it in egg and matzo flour and frying it in olive oil. I used to love watching her, but all that rich, fried Jewish food wasn't good for her, as it isn't for anybody. She loved all the wrong food, cooked it well, and rewarded herself with it, for the things she didn't have.

Daddy and I were always trying to stop her from having too many potatoes. When I was about thirteen or fourteen, we were having lunch one day – roast chicken. Mummy reached to take a second helping and I said, 'Mummy, please don't, it's bad for you.' She declared she hadn't had *that* much, and so surely she could have some more. And she spooned more potatoes onto her plate, greedily shoving one into her mouth. Suddenly I snapped. I stood up from the table, pushed all the plates so that they crashed to the floor and I ran down Banbury Road – which is a very long road – all the way down to St Giles' Church at the bottom. I collapsed on a grave in the churchyard and I cried and cried and cried. Eventually I walked home, but I sat in the churchyard for hours. I remember that day so vividly: the intensity of my feelings, my anxiety about Mummy, and my disgust at her needing to have more potatoes.

She had once been a slender little thing, an amateur dancer, and often showed me her ballet routines, and how to use my arms gracefully, like the chorus in *Les Sylphides*. But once she stopped dancing, the weight piled on. Her belly hung down, her breasts drooped, and it affected her heart. Her weight ruined all our lives – just as mine does now.

My mother was ambitious, for all of us. And in her lifetime, none of her ambitions came to fruition. So there was perhaps an anger behind her appetite. After she had her stroke in 1968, she could only say, 'I can't afford a carriage' – a line from the song 'Daisy, Daisy' and 'Pouf, I want . . .' – this last, over and over again. She thought she was speaking sense and her frustration grew as we indicated we didn't know what she meant.

One day I was shopping with her in Oxford. There was something she wanted me to buy, some item of shopping that she was desperate for, but, of course, she couldn't tell me what it was. So I was wheeling her chair up and down the supermarket aisle and pointing at various items, hoping that this might jog her mind and make her able to communicate with me.

'Mummy, look, is it that?' I said, pointing at a box of cornflakes, or something.

'I can't afford a carriage,' she said.

'Is it that?' I asked again.

'I can't afford a carriage.'

She was so distressed and desperate that I felt the best thing to do was to park her wheelchair in one of the aisles and go and finish the shopping myself, and that's what I did. After a few minutes, this great cry came from the aisle where I'd parked her. Her brain had for one moment relented and allowed her to find, for this one time, the thing that she was searching for and with all her strength she roared out to me, 'JAM!' It was both the funniest and the saddest thing I ever heard.

I see the same lack of self-control, or self-respect perhaps, in me now – the very same thing! Thank God, I've never had a drink or drugs problem. I've always been uninterested in that, but whatever I've wanted, I've wanted with an insane passion.

As a child, I was never skinny, but I was active. I first started putting on weight when I was about eight or nine, and by the time I was eleven, I had a 36-inch bust. As an adolescent, my ever-increasing girth made me miserable. At the school dances, I was a conspicuous wall-flower. Fat and short, staring angrily at the spotty Magdalen College and St Edward's schoolboys, who were the only available males, I hugged the radiators all night while my friends waltzed around with their beaux. In my fury and pain at the public indignity, I went up to the domestic science room and hurled eggs at the windows. The sight of the yolks sliding down the glass gave me some relief. It's a humiliation that you don't forget, and even early in life you learn the pain of rejection because your body isn't wanted.

As a teenager, being fat made me quite aggressive on occasion, because I won't be bullied, but it also made me develop my sense of humour: you can't go around furious and miserable all the time, so you have to make people laugh. At lunch, when I was at school, friends remember me gleefully announcing, 'A moment on the lips, forever on the hips!' as I took a second helping of stodgy, calorie-laden, school-dinner pudding. I remember a less amusing incident involving my immoderate appetite, however. One day I took four helpings of chocolate semolina, and I couldn't finish it, and the teachers made me sit and look at it all afternoon because I was greedy. I remember the shame, hot tears pricking at my eyes as I stared queasily at the congealing pudding, so I suppose I did care. I just didn't care enough to stop eating.

Happily, my teenage years behind me, I went to university and there I realised that I had a spark of something that was more valuable than beauty: I had energy, and energy is always attractive. Nevertheless, due to my shape, I have never achieved elegance. I look at myself and I feel envious of people who have 'normal', slim bodies, and I get annoyed that I can't get ready-to-wear clothes; I have always hated shopping for clothes. Those terrifying words 'I don't think we've got anything in your size' were like stabs in my heart. It's been the story of my life.

When I started appearing on stage and in film and television, I spent a lot of time in corsets because I was often cast in period drama. Like Dawn French, I've always been described as a 'roly-poly' actress, although even now when I read that, a rage rises in me. Everybody that I do an interview with has to cope with the fact that I'm overweight. They know it because when I walk into the room, it's the first thing they see – a fat person. It's wrong and it's unfair, but it's a fact that people are judged on their looks and on their shape. It's how people are conditioned into seeing people, and I have a round shape. Roundness is my fate.

I have never been asked to lose weight for a part, but I have always wanted to be slimmer, so I have often gone on diets and tried various slimming treatments over the years. I first went to Tyringham Hall in Newport Pagnell back in the seventies, which was an erstwhile naturopathic health farm in a Grade I listed stately home designed by Sir John Soane. It was an upmarket sort of place, frequented by quite a few fellow thespians and 'celebrities', notably Julie Christie, Rula Lenska and Roy Hudd. The treatments were carefully tailored to each individual client, and I was put on a fairly draconian regime, where I fasted for three weeks at a time.

One winter, I had checked myself into Tyringham Hall and it was snowing heavily. They had various water treatments including ice-cold power showers, glacial plunge pools, cold-towel wraps and a sauna. I had read that in Scandinavia, after their sauna, people would go outside and cover themselves in snow. So, once I'd heated myself up to a boil, I ran out buck-naked from the sauna and rolled about on the snow-covered lawns. Suitably invigorated and tingling pink all over, I got up – only to see that a party of visitors was being shown around by Sidney Rose-Neil, the director of Tyringham, who, rather curtly, said to me, 'Can I see you later?' I went to his office and he said, 'I quite understand that you wanted to experience the sauna, but please don't go cavorting in the snow again, because the sight of a naked Miriam Margolyes is not something all our visitors may appreciate.' I took that on the chin(s), because sometimes the sight of my unclothed flesh frightens even me.

Fasting for three weeks sounds physically impossible but I had some raw foods and lots of liquids, like green juices and water. I would feel raging hunger for about three days, then it passed; I wasn't thinking about food and it worked – I did lose many pounds. The trouble is, alas, that I would put it back on again when I went back to ordinary life.

Later, when I was preparing for my *Dickens' Women* world tour in 2012, I knew I would need to be super fit; a one-woman show is immensely exhausting. I decided to spend six weeks at an Ayurvedic centre in Jaipur, called Chakrapani Ayurveda Clinic. There they prescribed and administered an oil enema every day: they pumped some oil up my arse and, after about half an hour, I'd go to the loo quite copiously. I suppose it shifts everything that's caked around your intestines. I would absolutely recommend an Ayurvedic session in one of those places – it's a severe regimen, but marvellously cleansing and it does somehow kick-start weight loss. I've never done meditation though, and I don't go in for those smart spas where you go and get your eyebrows threaded.

In 2020, I did a programme about it: *Miriam's Big Fat Adventure* for BBC Two, a two-parter looking at the obesity crisis and the body-positive movement, and exploring my own relationship with my weight. After a lifetime of worrying about it, I wanted to come to terms with my body. I wanted to work out why I am, and always have been, overweight. Could I change? And I'm not the only one: the whole country weighs more than it ever did. I was on a mission to understand why we do it to ourselves, what it's doing to us, and how other people cope with it.

It was a surprising experience because I met some gorgeous, empowered women of the body-positive movement, dancing about and having a wonderful time, and I realised that non-skinny people could be entirely at ease and happy in their own skin. I had never really believed that until I met those people, and I admired them and wished I could be like that. Making the programme helped me to be much more compassionate towards myself. I've been fat all my life; there it is. I have an endomorphic frame. You just have to face who you are and deal with it, and for the most part I do.

My First Time on
Broadway was . . . *Wicked*

In September 2006, I opened in *Wicked* at the Apollo Victoria Theatre in London as the first British Madame Morrible. At the audition, they'd said, 'You know that Madame Morrible has a couple of songs?' 'Well, I'm sorry but this Madame Morrible won't have any songs, because I can't sing,' I replied. Then they said, 'Can't you do what Rex Harrison did in *My Fair Lady*?' I said, 'Well, I suppose I could try.' So that, in fact, is what I did. I just recited the lyrics in time to the music in that classic *Sprechgesang* delivery.

In 2008, after a sell-out, Olivier-award nomination run in London, I was asked to play the role on Broadway. When I arrived at the rehearsals at the Gershwin Theatre in New York, the musical director, Stephen Oremus, whom I'd worked with in London, said, 'Miriam, Stephen Schwartz [the composer] would really like to hear you sing Madame Morrible's song.' And I said, 'Well, I'd love to hear me sing it too, but I can't sing, that is the only trouble.' Stephen said, 'I don't believe that, Miriam. I think you *can* sing – you've just *told* yourself that you can't. And I want you to come with me and just kick it around. You'll get there. I know you will. Just be brave. Let's go for it!' I agreed, so we went to the rehearsal room. Stephen sat at the piano, and we practised and practised and practised and practised and practised. And at the end of it, he put down the piano lid and said, 'You know what, Miriam? You're right. You can't sing.'

So, I continued doing my Rex Harrison version for five months on Broadway. Every night the theatre was packed to the gunnels. It was quite an experience to step out there, thinking, 'I'm actually on Broadway.' I loved standing in the wings, watching the dancers, the lights flickering on their beautiful bodies. They were larky and fun – as the oldest person in the cast, to be on such good terms with all those gorgeous, talented young people was a joy. I'm still in touch with many of them and there's a standing invitation for them to stay with me if they come to London.

The company was very welcoming when I arrived: it's a bit daunting to join a fully formed company, and I was taking over from a terrific actress – Carol Kane – who originated the role of Morrible. But they took me to their hearts and couldn't have been friendlier. They wanted to know what I'd been paid in London. Now, I love talking money, because the more information performers have, the more powerful they are. And so when they asked me what my London salary had been, I willingly told them. I wish I could remember the exact sum now, I think it was £3,500 per week.

A few days later, I got a call from David Stone, the producer of *Wicked.* It started as a friendly phone conversation but very quickly turned nasty. He said, 'The company has been complaining about you: I hear you've been bragging to them about your London salary.' I couldn't believe my ears! 'Bragging? Not at all! They asked me, naturally, for a comparison, and I told them the truth, as I always do.' There was a pause, then, 'Do you want to destroy me?' David Stone asked. I was baffled. How could I, a small-part actress, destroy the most powerful producer on Broadway? He continued: 'You know, of course, the new salary negotiations are underway? You're deliberately trying to destroy me.' Nothing I said could shake his assumption. I put the phone down. I sent him a huge bottle of vintage whiskey – no response. We never spoke again until I left the show five months later. The show is still a huge hit all over the world. It deserves to be. David is a successful producer of immense wealth. But I wouldn't swap my reputation for his, any day.

I'd never seen myself as performing in musicals: I wanted to *act*, to be in a *play* on Broadway, but it never happened. The closest I got was to BAM, the Brooklyn Academy of Music, in Peter Hall's production of *The Importance of Being Earnest*, playing Miss Prism to Lynn Redgrave's Lady Bracknell, in 2006.[*]

I knew exactly how to play Miss Prism; she may be a Victorian spinster governess of impeccable morals, but she is *boiling* with sexuality. Her romantic soul is in a frenzy of love and longing for Reverend Chasuble. She may not look it, but she is still moist.

Terry Rigby was my Chasuble. An excellent actor, but he didn't like me at all, and refused to accept that we were a parallel romantic couple to the other young lovers. It was hard to play with him, so it wasn't a happy experience, but Lynn was magical – superb as Bracknell, a loving company leader – and bravely fighting the cancer which would kill her five years later. We all loved Lynn and trusted her completely.

I looked up the reviews just now as I write this, which is the first time I've ever read them. I strongly believe reviews should *not* be read during the run of a show. Good reviews can make you smug, bad reviews depress; and if a company member is singled out, it can cause

---

[*] The cast was Terence Rigby, Bianca Amato, Charlotte Parry, Robert Petkoff, James Waterston, Geddeth Smith, James Stephens, Greg Felden, Margaret Daly and Diane Landers.

jealousy. I give strict instructions never to mention or discuss reviews in my hearing while the show is running. But it was a long time ago, and since mine were good, I reproduce them here!

'Manoeuvring her stout form like a miniature battleship, Miriam Margolyes is formidable and robustly funny as Cecily's gently censorious governess, the fatefully forgetful Miss Prism.' That was from *The New York Times*. From *TheaterMania*: 'Giving Redgrave a run for the money is Margolyes, whose Prism moves about with the slow splendor of an ocean liner going out to sea. Miss Prism often repeats the warning "You reap what you sow," and what Margolyes reaps is great appreciation for her performance.'

To be compared to one ship is unfortunate, but to be compared to two looks like carelessness. I think I'll sign out as Rear-Admiral Margolyes.

Call Me Gert and Leave Out the Rude Part

In 1982, my cousin Esta Charkham asked me to read a script her friend Silvio Narizzano had given her. The script was written by Win Wells, about Gertrude Stein – the literary lioness of the twenties and thirties – and her lover Alice B. Toklas. It was called *Gertrude Stein and a Companion* and it was to change my life.

Lesbians are quite fashionable now, but it wasn't always so. I slightly preferred it when it was brave to be a lesbian – now it's a bit old hat. But Gertrude and Alice are icons to us dykes. They were witty, successful geniuses; they had a long, loving relationship; they survived Vichy France throughout the war although they were Jewish; and they were both strong, fascinating and remarkable women, whose contribution to twentieth-century literature was profound. The play told their story.

Win wanted to hear it read, so a reading was performed at his flat – for a free lunch I'll do anything. At that point the play, which explores the forty-year relationship between Stein and Alice B. Toklas, was three hours long and written for eight characters.

Cut to a couple of years later, in 1984. I was looking around for a new project when I remembered Win's play. Gertrude was a brilliant part for me, and I decided it had to be done. Since my radio repertory days, Sonia Fraser had been a good friend. I respected her opinion, especially since she had become a director, and I'd done two successful productions for her. I loved working with Sonia: she knew how to get the best out of me. I showed her the text. She suggested we cut it down to a cast of two and pruned the original script to an economical 100 minutes.

Although Win Wells is credited as the author, it is Sonia who is responsible for the text that's now performed all over the world. The reason Sonia never insisted on her work being acknowledged was that Win was dying of cancer when we started rehearsals, and neither of us wanted to cause him any disquiet. Sonia herself died in 2013. I miss her every day; no one gave me such brilliant direction and such loving support.

———

The final script provided a challenge, because each of the two actresses – my Gertrude and whoever played my Alice – had to play several parts. Among other characters, I would play Ernest Hemingway; my co-performer would play Gertrude's brother and Alice's first lover.

Sonia had cast Lesley Joseph in the role of Alice B. Toklas. Lesley is famous now for *Birds of a Feather*, but few realise she is a superb serious actress – and she was the image of Alice B. But then she got pregnant. If there's one thing Alice B. cannot be, it's pregnant! So, only a couple of days before we were leaving for the Edinburgh Festival, we found Natasha Morgan. She was much more beautiful than the real Alice, but spiritually she fitted the role.

Natasha was brilliant, but she was difficult. (She won't like my saying that, but it was true.) I find it interesting how you can work opposite, indeed play the *lover* of somebody you dislike, and yet show love on stage. Natasha infuriated me, but when I became Gertrude the moment of theatre was so powerful it overrode any personal animosity I might have felt.

I booked the Richard Demarco theatre in the Canongate Lodge off the Royal Mile and some accommodation in the city. Sue Ayres designed a brilliant set. Sonia hired Peter Jarvis to accompany us on saxophone and clarinet and he wrote some superb music. It was going to happen.

Before I took on the role, I wanted to see the portrait that Pablo Picasso had painted of Stein, which was kept in her Left Bank apartment in the Rue de Fleurus in Paris until she died. Gertrude had bequeathed it to the Metropolitan Museum in New York.

I found the gallery catalogue: '*Portrait of Gertrude Stein* by Pablo Picasso painted 1905 to 1906, oil on canvas, accession number 47106, on view in gallery number 911.'

I went to the reception desk.

Receptionist: 'I'm sorry, ma'am, the Gertrude Stein portrait is not on display today.'

Me: 'What? You can't be serious. I've come from England to see this picture.'

Receptionist: 'Ma'am, I'm sorry, the gallery's closed for refurbishment.'

Me: 'I'm not accepting that. I'm an actress. I'm just about to play the part of Gertrude Stein. Call the curator!'

Receptionist: 'You want me to call the curator?'

Me: 'Yes, please.'

Receptionist: 'Yes, ma'am, just a second, please. Hello, Mrs Cohen, this is front desk here. There's a young lady who wants to see the Gertrude Stein portrait. Yeah, I told her it's not on display, but she's an actress. She's kind of overexcited. Would you be able to come out and talk with her? Thank you. You're in luck! Mrs. Cohen will be right out. She will meet you by the totem pole.'

Me: 'What totem pole?'

Receptionist: 'Ma'am, the totem pole. It's right over there. It's at least thirty feet high. You can't miss it.'

Me: 'Oh, sorry. Thank you.'

I went and stood by the looming totem pole. In a few moments, Mrs Cohen came out. She gave me a long look and said, 'Good morning, I understand you want to see the Gertrude Stein portrait. Follow me.' I followed her through the museum from one end to the other, along corridors, through galleries. We came to the elevator. We got in and went down, down, down, all the way to the sub-basement, where they store the pictures not on display. And, again, we walked from one end of the gallery to the other.

I turned a corner and there, leaning against the wall, was Gertrude Stein. She was looking straight at me. The power of the painting is immense; the pose was one I was to adopt for the play: leaning forward, hands on her knees, with a thoughtful gaze – that's how the show opened. You could not escape the eyes, there was a kindness in them I hadn't expected. I shall never forget the experience of seeing her there, 'looking as if she were alive', as Robert Browning said in his poem, 'My Last Duchess'.

Now I was ready to be Gertrude.

———

As anyone who's been to the Edinburgh Fringe will attest, it's no picnic. The competition is immense, the fight to put up posters bitter and sometimes violent. The theatre wasn't ready when we arrived; actually, it was not even *built*. Scaffolding poles were on the floor; the posters we had sent weeks before were lying in the office, undistributed. So we all had to go fly-posting, desperately seeking publicity, chatting to strangers, handing out the flyers.

Sonia checked the booking in the Fringe Office. 'What're the bookings like for *Gertrude Stein and a Companion*?' she asked.

'Oh, you've sold six,' the lady said encouragingly.

'For the first night?' Sonia asked.

'No, for the entire run!'

The first night was half-empty, but the next day our fantastic reviews came out. From then on, it was a triumphant sell-out, winning a Fringe First Award, then a transfer in January to the Bush Theatre in London and another transfer in April to the Hampstead Theatre; both theatres sold every seat for every performance.

The Sydney Festival then invited Sonia and me to do the show for the tenth anniversary festival in 1986, again to sell-out audiences and glorious critical acclaim. Sonia won the Green Room Award for Best Direction. We opened in Sydney at the Belvoir St Theatre. That's where I first met Geoffrey Rush, who's become a good friend. (I played Peter Sellers's mother – Geoffrey played Peter – in *The Life and Death of Peter Sellers* in 2004.) We then opened in Melbourne after the Sydney run, and had a similar triumph at the Universal Theatre, Fitzroy.

Buoyed by the play's reception Down Under, Sonia and I decided to take *Gertrude Stein and a Companion* to America, during the summer and early autumn of 1986, on a campus tour where we played only to university audiences. We had hoped to play in professional theatres, but two women, who should have known better, stopped us.

Lucille Lortel in New York and Blanche Marvin in London had snatched Sonia's script idea and presented their own mangled version of the play at the Lucille Lortel Theatre in New York in January 1986. The only good thing to come out of their machinations was that I hired an excellent lawyer, the late David Latham, to protect our campus tour – yes, they tried to shut that down as well, even attempting to bring in Actors' Equity to stop us. (Years later, Sonia's daughter, Rachael, joined David's firm and went on to become a distinguished entertainment lawyer herself.) Ms Lortel died in 1999; if Ms Marvin is still alive, I hope she will never attempt to send me Christmas cards again, for two reasons: we're both Jewish, and I loathe her. The Colorado College was our first American destination. The idea was that we would teach a semester in theatre studies (Women in English Theatre) and perform *Gertrude Stein and a Companion* at the end.

I enjoyed teaching, but Colorado College seemed to be full of rich, stupid kids on drugs. I found that irritating, so I opened by laying down the law. I said, 'Now, in class you will not be necking with each other. You will be paying attention to me and to Natasha when we are speaking, and you will write an essay and hand it in without this nonsense of computers.' (I'm a computer person now, but I wasn't then.) They accepted my strictures, and I was quite popular in the end. Those young Americans were completely different from their English counterparts. How privileged they were, all with wealthy parents; like Australians physically, but they lacked the toughness of the Australian youth. They were flabby, both mentally and physically – big and blue-eyed, but soft and lazy. I had no time for laziness, then or now. I won't have it.

At the end of term, we were in rehearsals for the first show. There is a scene where we're walking around the Luxembourg Gardens in

Paris, and Alice B. Toklas is holding a little basket with Tuscan herbs in. Natasha suddenly announced: 'I can't do this. I can't work here. I'm sorry, I'm not doing the show.' I said, 'Why, what's up?' Natasha said, 'These herbs – they're not Italian!' I said, 'Darling, we're in America. They can't get Italian herbs. These are the herbs that she would have had in America.' She said, 'No. I've got to be absolutely authentic in my work. I can't stand this!' She stormed off, and we had the devil of a job to get her to come back. In the end she did agree to perform, but only after I had to practically go on my knees and beg for her return.

The last performance with Natasha was in Kingston, Ontario, at the university there. It had been a bumpy ride, but the work was good.

In 1987, Sonia and I decided to take the show on a tour of Australia, opening in Sydney, then back to the Universal Theatre in Melbourne in December. As an English actress, it was unbelievably difficult to get permission to do theatre work in Australia; I had to find an Australian Alice B. Toklas. Luckily, my friend Chris Westwood said that she knew the perfect person.

I arrived at Sydney Airport to meet my mail-order bride. I looked up . . . and up. And there she was, Pamela Rabe – my perfect Alice.

Pamela is nearly 6ft tall – Alice B. Toklas was about 4ft 10ins – but it didn't matter. In her acting, Pamela encapsulated the brilliance and the charm of the character.

We instantly had a terrific working relationship; what a relief, after all Natasha's tantrums. Pamela went on to win best actress of the year.

A few years later, I returned to America to play Gertrude again. Every year, in Michigan, there is a huge lesbian festival called the Michigan Womyn's Music Festival. The festival organiser had rung me and said, 'Miriam, we'd love to invite you to join our festival. It's just for five days, and women come from all over the world to the Land.'

'What's the Land?' I enquired.

'A wealthy lesbian lawyer owns a large property in Cedar Rapids and she welcomes our festival there for those five days. This year, as usual, we are expecting thousands of lesbians and we would be honoured if you would provide the entertainment. It's often music, but this year, for the first time, we thought we might have a play.'

'Golly,' I said, 'that's quite a tall order, but all right, I'm in.' I called Pam and she agreed to fly over and perform the shows.

———

Pamela and I were met at Grand Rapids airport by a sweet young girl, all braids and hippyness. She said, 'Hi! I'm River.' That was the first warning bell. Then she said, 'Oh, WOW! It's just so great that you two are here.' She explained that the land on which the festival was held was 'womyn's' land: no men were allowed on it.

River then drove us to the Land, which was a nice big meadow. It was her job to show us to our accommodation. I looked across the Land, which was a sea of tents. It looked like a Woodstock for dykes. River said, 'We have such a great tent for you, Miriam. Follow me.' 'Tent?' I shrieked. 'Tent? Look, I don't want to be difficult, River, but I don't sleep in tents. Mummy always said that Jewish girls don't sleep on the ground. [I have no idea if that's true.] Is there any other kind of accommodation that we could possibly have?' River replied, hesitantly: 'Well, you could have a log cabin, I guess . . .' 'That's the one! Thank you,' I cried.

River led the way across the Land; we followed sweatily, weaving our way carefully through the legions of treacherous tent pegs. Eventually, we arrived at our lovely log cabins – by a mosquito-infested lake.

It was the middle of August, and it was hot – and I mean 40°C in the shade hot. Unfortunately, there was an illness going around the Land: norovirus, an extremely unpleasant stomach bug that causes vomiting and violent diarrhoea. We didn't get it, but apparently everybody else had a dose. So it was boiling hot, and the Port-a-Janes (note: not Port-a-Johns – the American name for Portaloos) were brimming with diarrhoea. The only time that men were allowed on the Land was when they came to empty the loos. At this, a great cry went up from all the womyn: 'MEN ON THE LAND! MEN ON THE LAND!' What with the norovirus and the heat, this sole male function was now a frequent necessity.

The next day was assigned for our shows. The matinee was to take place at 2 p.m. in their open-air theatre. And I must stress again that this was the middle of August, and it was boiling hot. They picked us up and took us to the theatre. I put on my velvet, long-sleeved, floor-length Gertrude Stein costume. I went out on stage; I took my pose in the Gertrude Stein chair and looked out to the audience. And that's when I became aware I was being watched by 4,000 nipples, give or take a few (most people had two): sitting expectantly were over 2,000 enormous, and I mean ENORMOUS, lesbians, each and every one stark naked! (I don't know what it is about lesbians, but we're not known for svelteness. We're quite a chubby brigade.) There was A LOT of flesh on view. It was completely overwhelming, but my main concern was, of course, Pamela, because she was due on stage in a few seconds and there was no way I could warn her.

On her cue, Pamela appeared, tall, beautiful, statuesque. I saw her look down at the audience, and from side to side. I knew I mustn't look directly at her, because if our eyes met that would be the end of everything. But I couldn't resist taking a peek out of the corner of my eye when I heard her come on. For a couple of seconds, she was transfixed – not with horror or disgust – but with huge surprise. Then, like the trooper she is, she gathered herself together and went on with the show. We somehow controlled ourselves – we never looked at each other, not once, because I knew that would be curtains – and we performed.

The lesbians clapped and clapped and clapped. Well, of course, they loved it. I mean, we don't often get to see our own stories up on stage. It was right up their alley, you could say. And at the end they gave us a standing ovation. Quite an eye-watering experience.

After the applause had finished, we got off the stage and collapsed into each other's arms. We were quite hysterical. Pam said, 'Miriam, I love you very much but, please, NEVER bring me to a place like this ever again!'

I'm as big a feminist as anyone, but now I always say, when you see 'women' spelt with a 'y', run like hell!

In Therapy

I went into therapy because I wasn't always faithful. Adultery is a silly, tiresome thing and I'm sorry that it happened. But it did, and I have to admit it. The problem for Heather and me has always been that we have lived separate lives. Being apart so much, and being in show business – which encourages speedy intimacy – can give rise to infidelity.

I had an affair with a woman I met on the campus tour of *Gertrude Stein and a Companion*. She was a professor. I've said before I won't fuck anyone without a PhD. She was my landlady and she seduced me. It was quite exciting, but she was peculiar: she liked to be hit. I'd never come across that before. Sexually, I'm straight as a die. In the early days, Heather would tease me about that. When we first got together, I said, 'I'm not really experienced at this.' She said, 'Don't you have any chains?' Somewhat aghast, I said, 'No!' And Heather laughed and laughed. What I'm saying is that I don't come to bed armed with electrical goods. Or indeed anything.

The Californian professor told me in a deep voice, 'The repertoire of love is wide.' When I didn't say anything, she enquired, 'Have you ever experienced pain in the course of love?' Of course, I said, 'No!' because I hadn't. Indeed, if anybody tried to hurt me (never mind the repertoire of love), I'd biff them from here to Doncaster. She then waxed lyrical about how magical and fantastic it was. I had no idea what she meant.

'Do you want me to hit you?' I ventured.

She answered, yes: she would like me to hit her – with a hairbrush. I got out of bed, went to the dressing table and picked one up. 'This one?' I asked. 'Yeah, why not. I want you to *hurt* me.' She turned over and exposed her buttocks. I raised the hairbrush high and gave them a good whack. She screamed: '*Not that hard!*' Well, I didn't know – did I? I'll *never* make a good dominatrix.

It was a damaging relationship, and not just where the professor's tender buttocks were concerned. Heather found out and she was angry, shocked and disgusted. We then separated for six months: the worst six months of my life. The loss of Heather fragmented me; I couldn't bear it. I asked friends to help. Hodge suggested I needed a therapist to put me back together. Roly Curram found me Margaret.

If you get the wrong person, it can tear you apart. I was lucky: I got Margaret Branch.

When I phoned to make the appointment for my first session, Margaret said, 'Now, I have to find out whether I like you, because if I like you, I may be able to help, but if I don't like you, there's no point in your coming.' She explained that I had to pay for two rounds of therapy in advance. She preferred cash. 'I like it in brownies.' She meant ten pound notes.

After our conversation, she decided that she did like me and would try to help. Margaret and her partner Camilla lived in a top-floor flat on Hamilton Terrace, St John's Wood. She used to say, 'Knock on any door in "the Wood" and you'll find a therapist. "The Wood" is full of therapists' – and it is. When I first met Margaret, she was in her early seventies, a bird-like little woman, staccato in her speech patterns. Camilla was twenty years older, had a sepulchral voice and would answer the door and usher customers in. Margaret told me that when Camilla went wandering one day, a very nice young man brought her home. He turned out to be Boy George.

Margaret had a lot of clients, or 'customers', which is what she called us; if we were in show business, she called us 'talented toddlers'. She said that I had an emotional age of about four and if I was exceptionally lucky, she'd help to get me to twelve. 'But that would be a triumph,' she added. It was a long journey; we became extremely close. She often said, 'Miriam, don't be glib! Don't be glib! DON'T BE GLIB!' She used to say important things three times. If I got worked up about something, she'd say, 'Now, Miriam, you're splashing your yellow wellies in the puddles again.' And always, after I'd handed her the 'brownies', she'd sit in her chair opposite me and stare into my eyes. 'What about you, what about you, what about YOU?' she would enquire fiercely. And so the session would begin.

Margaret said that I must be objective about my parents. To make any criticism of Mummy feels like treachery, but I must acknowledge she had terrible moments. I don't think it was bipolar disorder – she was never calm enough to be depressed – but she was tumultuous, and it seemed there was a blow-up almost every month. She didn't give any advance warning; you had to gauge her moods, and they were ferocious. She would give my father a terrible time. Their marriage was a loving and intense one, but it was marred by shocking quarrels. Daddy simply became quiet; he didn't speak; he just stood passively, enduring the full force of her unbridled rage. Those were the times I hated him. I wanted him to stand up to her and be more assertive, but he never was. He just accepted it – I used to run into another room and put my hands over my ears, because I couldn't stand to hear her shout at him, and see his weakness.

I know that a few of my friends didn't like Mummy at all. They thought that she was controlling, possibly a rather dangerous kind of woman. Margaret helped me to accept that, in some ways, she may have been. But when you love people, you have to accept them in their totality. Mummy was flawed, but she was also magnificent. Margaret showed me the flaws, and showed me the flaws in myself.

She also asked Heather to come and meet her one day. I was surprised when Heather agreed but, over the months of therapy, I had been growing as a person; Heather thought it was worth it and she found Margaret impressive.

After roughly two years, Margaret said to me, 'I think I've done enough for you now, Miriam. Your emotional age is now twelve.' She ended the regular weekly visits, but suggested 'top-ups' – refresher sessions, when I felt I needed them. 'Now you're a friend, we can talk as friends,' she said. 'It's different.' And so we did talk as friends.

It was at one of the times when I visited her as a friend that Margaret said, 'I want to tell you something, and I don't want you to speak about it until after I'm dead.' She told me that another of her customers had been Jacqueline Du Pré, the renowned British cellist. She asked if I had heard of her, which, of course, I had. Jacqueline was one of the greatest cellists of all time; her great gift was like a meteor flashing across the music world, which crashed to the ground when she was stricken with multiple sclerosis aged twenty-eight; a horrible, slow, debilitating decline. When you have a great gift like that, I can't think of anything more terrible than not being able to use it.

'We were friends for many, many years,' Margaret said. 'Jacqueline said to me, "Margaret, if I wanted to kill myself, would you help me?" And I said, "Of course I would." Because I would.' One day, Jacqueline had telephoned her. She'd said, 'Margaret, remember what I said? What I asked you, and you said you would . . .? I want to do it today.'

Jacqueline's husband, the pianist and conductor Daniel Barenboim had left her; he had a new relationship in Paris and had a child and had more or less abandoned her. I think he just couldn't bear to see what had happened to Jacqueline; how the disease had transformed the beautiful, gifted young woman he had married into someone crippled, shaking and helpless.

Margaret told me, 'Jacqueline said, "I've given my staff the day off. I want you to come over." I went to her house as she asked – I had a key, and I took along a syringe and the liquid. I let myself into the house. I went up to her room where she was in bed and we talked for a bit. Then I said, "Are you absolutely sure that you want me to do this?" And Jacqueline said, "Yes. I am. And I can only trust you to do it for me." I was a trained nurse during the war, I knew what to do . . . If you want to help someone to die, or to murder someone, without a trace,' Margaret said, 'you inject them above their hairline.' I always remember her saying that. She continued, 'So, of course, I kissed her, and I injected her. Then I looked around, checked that there was no trace of my presence, and I let myself out of the house. Just hours later, of course, Jacqueline's close friends sat with her as she died, and nobody ever knew it was me.'

I felt honoured that Margaret should tell me, but I found it shocking; the most sobering thing I've ever heard. I suppose she felt that she didn't want that knowledge to go with her to her grave without *anybody* knowing what Jacqueline had asked of her. And yet, although she was obviously deeply affected by it, Margaret related it to me entirely matter-of-factly. She believed that it was the highest mark of love for Jacqueline that she could show, to release her from the horrors of her illness. Perhaps telling me was the ultimate proof of our friendship, because, obviously, if she had been found out, she could have been charged with murder. I hope by telling this now, I have kept my promise to Margaret.

Margaret told me that she had known Gertrude Stein and Alice B. Toklas in Paris but she decided not to attend my show at the Hampstead Theatre Club. 'I wish I'd gone. I should have gone but I thought you'd never get them right.' She always regretted it.

I am forever grateful for her wisdom, her insight and her friendship. The prospect of losing Heather nearly broke me. When I came to Margaret I was in bits, but she put me back together again. I am quite sure I would have lost Heather if I hadn't gone into therapy. I realised then that I can't live without her and I never gambled with my happiness again. Sometimes I jokingly say that I think I'm perfect. Well, I'm not, but for a talented twelve-year-old, I'm not far off.

Only Connect

One morning, at the beginning of term at Oxford High School, I saw a strange, new girl in the playground. She had a quality of deep solitariness. She had blonde hair and a long, pale face like a Viking and was standing there all alone, her arms by her sides. Nobody was talking to her, so I went up to her and I said, 'Will you be my friend?' She looked at me, somewhat nervously – with reason – and said, 'Yes.'

My offer of friendship was borne out of two things: a genuine sense of compassion because she was on her own, and a violent curiosity to know who she was. To this day these remain my two motivating factors, and they have served me well. From that moment on, Katerina (Katy) Clark and I were friends. It was through her I found Heather: my friends have enriched and deepened my life immeasurably and in so many ways. Daddy, on the other hand, was somewhat caustic about friendship. When I asked him why he didn't have any friends he snorted, 'Friends?! Friends are people who drag you down.' How wrong he was.

I was popular at school. But I was also frightened of not being popular. I would always ask people if they liked me. A sign of insecurity, and yet at home with my parents I was surrounded with love, so I don't know why I was so anxious about it. Perhaps it's because I was an only child that, all my life, my friendships have been my lifeline. From the age of eleven I had four lists: 'Love and Hate', 'Sometimes Love', 'Sometimes Hate', and 'Sometimes Love and Sometimes Hate'. It was a moveable thing, because my relationships were volatile.

Liz Hodgkin, Katy Clark, Catherine Pasternak Slater and Anna Truelove are just a few of the many strong friends that I've kept from school. Seventy years on, I can name every single girl in a form photograph taken at Oxford High. There's nothing more valuable than friends who *really* know you and still like you. I take friendship seriously: there are responsibilities and commitments involved. For this reason, I'm the driving force in our school reunion group: I feel responsible for keeping us all in touch, sending updates and information about our get-togethers. When one of our number dies, I tell everyone the funeral details.

I've always wanted to get close to people and understand them – at times, perhaps, to extremes. I remember at Cambridge, my friend, the late Susan Andrews, once shouting at me, 'For God's sake, Miriam, just give me some *space!*' Initially, I thought she meant that I was standing too close to her, but she explained that I crowded her soul. I got in the way, I now see that. I was always asking questions: 'Why do you like that piece of music? What makes it important to you?' I've always wanted to *know* people. It's curiosity partly, because I can't imagine that people are different from me, and yet I can't imagine anyone being the same. This paradox is at the heart of all our intercommunication: 'Are you like me?' 'Why are you not like me?' 'Could you be like me?'

I usually pick up a new friend or two on a production, which is why my phone contains a list of 11,833 names. Take Patricia Hodge, for example. Hodge has an icy, aristocratic hauteur about her, but she loves filthy jokes. We met in 1974, when we were both in *The Girls of Slender Means* for the BBC. The cast of the show, together with the director, Moira Armstrong, became a team. We behaved like schoolgirls from St Trinian's. There's a scene where we girls had to escape through a narrow window and the only way to get through was to take off all our clothes. I complained to the camera crew that it wasn't fair that we didn't even know their names while they had seen every last bit of us. They rose to the challenge. They arranged for Don Smith to snap them all naked, bits covered by large placards with their names on. Each girl was presented with their own copy of this revealing photo in a brown envelope. We had to have the last laugh. I asked Don to quickly take a nude picture of us for Camera Crew 14. It was 13 February so we made it their Valentine. The picture is in this book.

We have always met for reunions over the years and, at ninety years old, Moira is still very much part of all our lives. She is a cherished phenomenon of the golden days of television. And when our beloved Mary Tamm died in 2012, thirty-eight years after we first met, all the 'Girls' attended her funeral. I write this two days after our latest reunion which was held at my house. Everyone brought something wonderful to eat as they know I can't cook. As we talked and laughed for hours, the years fell away.

Hodge has been there when I've needed her, particularly when I've got into scrapes. A confidence shared with Hodge would never go any further. She's much more private than I am – I'd trust her with my life. When I had my disastrous affair in America and Heather left me, it was she who suggested therapy, which, in turn, led to meeting Margaret Branch.

And the best thing is that friendship is contagious. Once someone is your friend, they bring new friends into your life. In Bali in 1983 I got close to my guest-house cleaner, Mahardiker. He was a temple dancer when not looking after guests. He had a natural physical grace;

carrying up my breakfast on a tray, he would check his appearance in the mirror on the stairs – just a quick look to ensure his 'line' was clean. One day he said, 'Sister, [he always called me Sister] what is your religion?' Somewhat surprised, I said, 'Well, I'm Jewish, but I don't really believe in God.' He smiled and said, 'We have another Jewis [this was how he spoke] in the guest house. You must meet.' And so he introduced me to a young, shy, Australian, Robert Green. He became my greatest chum and eventually my lawyer; his family in Australia became my family; his mother Beryl became my close friend and through her I met Robin Amadio who then introduced me to Andrew McKinnon, who brought *Dickens' Women* to Australia and changed my life. Mahardiker died of AIDS some years ago. He was a beautiful (if naughty) man.

I want to make people happy; I've always tried to smile and say positive, complimentary things. In the theatre, that is sometimes difficult. There is an art in going backstage after seeing a performance. Certain formula responses can mask disappointment at a production without destroying the person. Famous ones are, 'What about YOU!' delivered with a big smile and a hug, along with, 'You really stood out tonight.' With close friends, I say, 'I thought you were marvellous. Shall we talk about it tomorrow?' because, occasionally, you can say something useful, but *not* straight after a show. I always mention if I can't hear what people are saying, or if their hair hides their face, because that's something that can be immediately rectified. We all should try to make people feel good: if you can't say something nice, then shut up and don't say anything at all. Of course, sometimes I can't help saying horrible things about people I don't like, but it's not, on the whole, to their faces.

We are all scared. We are all secretly shaking with fright inside, uncertain of what we should be doing, saying and thinking; anxious about what our lives are going to be. I believe that if you can allay those fears, if you can soothe people, and hug them, and make them feel it's going to be all right, you're doing a public service. Often most of us are too busy, or worried, or tired, or just can't be bothered to take on the difficulties that another person is going through. But if you can, it makes the most enormous difference to try to understand the other person, to try to feel their pain, and to see the world through their eyes. This is at the heart of acting.

People are hungry for affirmation, for validation, for a sense that they matter: to know that their presence on earth is of importance to *somebody*. When I was making *Miriam's Big Fat American Adventure*, I visited a well-run women's prison in Virginia. I met two young recidivist offenders – drug addicts who'd been convicted of thieving. I talked to them for quite a long time; I told them the truth: that they were both beautiful and intelligent, and that they could and must do more with their lives than spend them in prison. 'I know that you've got a contribution to make,' I said.

These two young women told me that nobody had ever talked to them as if they were human, or as if there was any potential there for a better life. I found that remarkable and sad. I don't know if it made a difference to their fate after they were released: drugs were the way of life there; they were addicts and it would have been very hard for them to break away from their social environment – but they were incredibly grateful that I had spent time with them, looked into their eyes and talked to them about themselves. Many people need that, and that's why I still think that my early obituary was right, I would have made a good probation officer. I like to think of myself sitting behind a desk, looking into a criminal's eyes, and making him see that there was a future beyond prison.

My friends aren't bound to me by blood or obligation, but through affection, experience, shared interests and kindness. One of the greatest pleasures of writing this book has been double-checking memories, gossip and naughtinesses with my friends – and finding out so many more. This book could have never taken shape without them and it has made me miss them all the more keenly – especially those who are no longer here. I grieve for them afresh. I'd like to name those who have died before me, to thank them and honour their memories.

My dear friend, Sonia Fraser, director, acting coach, confidante. Together we wrote *Dickens' Women*, toured the world and shared our thoughts. I miss her terribly. My friend Liane Aukin, who died in 2016. Director, actress, thinker. She bought a house near mine, in Kent. Liane was beautiful, articulate, argumentative and a wonderful cook. We would talk for hours. Carol Gillies, my friend from Newnham, who became an actress; we shared a dressing room in *Orpheus Descending*. How we laughed. John Shrapnel, my lovely chum from Cambridge, fine actor. Mark Lushington, best talker I ever heard. Kay Daniels, Australian academic, cleverest, wittiest, Heather's first love. Beloved Roger Hammond, brother of my Newnham friend Hilary, loyal, enthusiastic, very funny, a gifted actor. Richard Shephard, composer, Director of Music at York Minster, urbane and elegant, such a generous appreciator, died of motor neurone disease too soon,

I miss him dreadfully. Robin Park, Scottish, a singer who lived in Amsterdam, so funny, a gentle man. John Tydeman, my BBC radio drama mentor, a Titan and yet very tender. Peter Sokole, a gifted viola player, struck down by COVID. Laura Kaufman, my Newnham friend. Joan and Ken Harrison, Heather's cousins in Australia in their nineties, an inspiration on how to grow old, and so good to us. Ruth Alboretti in Montisi, Irish, wise and such a wonderful hostess. And most recently, Jack Palladino, brilliant private detective, Heather's brother-in-law, murdered by thieves in San Francisco – he photographed them on the camera they tried to steal.

Everyone I've known leaves footprints on my life. Thank you.

Friends bring out the best in me, and that's what I cherish: they make me feel that I am worth knowing. Maybe it's a good idea, as Shakespeare said, to bind your friends to you with hoops of steel. They certainly are my armour and my fortress.

Blood Will Tell

Early in my career, I got the chance to audition for *Crossroads*, a now defunct soap opera set in a hotel in the Midlands, which was very popular and used to go out on ITV every day. It was hardly distinguished television but it was a solid job, so I didn't care.

I took the train up to Birmingham for the audition and arrived at Pebble Mill Studios. A woman in reception with a clipboard greeted me. She said, 'Right, then. So you're the three o'clock, are you? That's Miriam Mar . . . oh, that's new.' (Like many others, she had difficulty with my last name.) 'Well, just take your script, love, and go in the waiting room and I'll call you when we're ready. All right?' I did as she asked.

I was just about to sit down when I felt that ominous trickle. Fifty per cent of my readers will know what I'm talking about, and the other fifty per cent won't have a clue – my period had started. I found the ladies' room. In those days, and I'm talking about fifty years ago, there used to be a big brown box fastened to the wall called Southall's Sanitary Towels. It was a vending machine and you put your money in the slot, usually a two-pence piece, and pulled open the drawer to retrieve the little carton containing the sanitary towel. I had my money ready, so I put it in the slot and pulled open the drawer – and it snapped back with my finger in it. I could not get it out! I was pulling and pulling and I was in agony. Finally, the drawer snapped open again and I was able to extract my finger, bleeding, lacerated and extremely painful. I ran it under the cold tap, I got the sanitary towel, fixed myself up, and finally I went back to the waiting room.

After a few minutes the lady with the clipboard came out and said, 'Right, that's Miriam Mar . . . oh, dear . . . Miriam . . . Oh! I can't deal with that. Miriam, they're ready for you now. It's in there.' I took my script and I went into the room where they were waiting to audition me.

At an audition there's usually about four or five people sitting stony-faced behind a desk. I stood in front of them and I was just about to begin the reading when I saw that the script pages were covered in blood. They were sopping, just seeping with it. I looked up at the people sitting at the desk. Their mouths were hanging open and they looked a bit green. I said, 'Oh I'm terribly sorry, you see, my period started.'

Well, that was altogether too much information. Now they looked as if they might throw up. I hastened to explain: 'No, no, it's not . . . umm . . . IT'S MY FINGER!' and I quickly gathered my wits, launched into the audition piece – and, period or no period, I got the part.

The role was for a rather unpleasant woman, who wore a head-scarf and was perpetually grumpy. The actress playing her daughter was Jackie Holborough. Some years later, Jackie went to prison for being involved in a conspiracy to kidnap a tobacco king in South Africa. She also founded the feminist theatre group Clean Break. I liked Jackie, we palled up in *Crossroads*. If she reads this, I hope she gets in touch. I remember having a bit of a tussle with Noele Gordon, the star of *Crossroads*. There was a green room where we rested between takes. I sat in an armchair, Noele came in. 'That's MY chair,' she barked. 'Oh, sorry,' I said, 'I didn't see your name on it.' We reckoned she only had the job because she was sleeping with the boss of the channel.

Two Spikes Would Be an Extravagance!

Some are born comic, some achieve comedy, while some have comedy thrust upon them. I am definitely in the third camp. There's something about my face and my body which makes people laugh. I've always known that. It's professionally useful, socially perhaps a bit limiting, but I'm asked to dinner parties because of it and I'm not going to moan about looking different. We all have to deal with the cards we've been dealt and make the best of it. And truly, I think I have. And I cannot deny that I have always enjoyed a good bit of slapstick and physical comedy – my farts are legendary amongst my friends.

My loudest and most public fart was probably with Graham Norton when we went to see Dolly Parton. Joe Mantello, who'd directed me in *Wicked* and Dolly in her musical *9 to 5*, had arranged tickets. Graham loves Dolly (who doesn't?) so I asked him along. The show was magical and Joe set up a meet-and-greet moment afterwards. I hadn't realised that we would be two in a queue of about 150 people waiting to see Dolly, shake her hand, have a photo and leave.

We started queuing quite merrily in the cavernous tunnel under Wembley Stadium, on the way to Dolly's dressing room. After forty-five minutes, it became slightly wearisome. And I could feel a fart gathering as the moments passed. I held it in for a *long* time. But there came that moment when I knew I'd reached the end of The Holding.

My fart, having gathered momentum during the wait, finally burst forth like a bullet from Big Bertha, the wartime gun. I promise you it came unaccompanied, but it was fierce because it had been constrained for too long. It exploded gloriously with such a gigantic boom, I fear the security guards thought it might have been a terrorist attack.

Of course, the architecture of the tunnel helped to prolong and amplify my wind break. The entire queue gasped and shook; Graham, a slight figure, trembled and nearly fell; I was in a paroxysm both of embarrassment and relief. It was a long fart, joyous and unafraid, it must have lasted about four seconds – that's long for a fart. Finally, it ended – there was complete silence. And then laughter rolled along the tunnel.

Thankfully it wasn't smelly, just deafening. Meeting Dolly eventually proved almost an anticlimax, it was so short and sweet. Queen Elizabeth I said to the Earl of Oxford, when he returned to court after his seven-year banishment following an inadvertent breaking of wind, 'My Lord, we had forgot the fart'. I don't think I ever will, not least because Graham reminds me of it frequently.

Let's scroll back to a sweeter smelling time in my comic career. I had assumed comedy wasn't for me after the nastiness of Footlights had revealed the boys' club that controlled it. I knew I wasn't likely to get any work from them. But then in 1968, I was asked to join a satirical BBC TV programme called *At the Eleventh Hour*. The cast included Roger McGough, Richard Neville (notorious from the Oz trial) and Ray Davies of The Kinks. I remember laughing a lot but sadly at none of the actual jokes. My best sketches were a series of five-minute monologues as 'Valerie's Mother' written by Esther Rantzen. She had based the character on her own mother. I wore a fur hat and a crimplene dress and used the voice and mannerisms I knew well from my visits to North London. Valerie's Mother was definitely larger than life: pushy, noisy and sometimes insensitive. When both Marty Feldman and Larry Adler took offence at my portrayal, calling it 'antisemitic', we were invited on to a TV news programme called *Talkback*, to debate whether my character was indeed a 'stereotype which encouraged a kind of potted thinking' about Jews. At the end of the debate the studio audience were asked to vote and in the words of no less an authority than the *Jewish Chronicle*: 'Less than 10 per cent thought that such characters helped to spread antisemitism – which is hardly surprising with people like Miriam Margolyes and Esther Rantzen responsible for it.' (Phew!)

At a wedding I went to at the time, a fellow guest started by praising my acting and then went on to say 'I do love that Valerie's Mother sketch you do on TV. But why do you have to put on that silly voice?' I had to bite my lip; she was speaking to me in identical tones but clearly didn't recognise herself. And that proved my vision of comedy to me. Comedy is life, built big perhaps, but always built true. Anthony Smith, our director, believed in the show, but sadly it was judged 'too rude' and it never even made it to the end of its first series. As Esther said, 'That's life!' And I've been doing comedy on and off ever since.

Radio comedy is kinder than TV but I had to go through the archives to recall these long-forgotten series: *Oh Get On With It* with Kenneth Williams and Lance Percival and *Things Could Be Worse* were both aired in 1976. I took part in one episode of *Just a Minute*, which I didn't enjoy at all because Clement Freud was so desperate to win.

The greatest radio comedy series in my opinion was *Round the Horne* in the late 1960s; there were 67 episodes and Kenneths Horne and Williams were the stars. Ever after, the BBC has tried to find a replacement – I don't think they ever have. But Kenneth Williams consequently became the master of radio and I was delighted to work with him and Ted Ray in *The Betty Witherspoon Show* in 1974. Ted was wonderful before lunch; afterwards his timing slipped a bit. He had been a great star and perhaps radio felt a little too small for him. Kenny became a dear friend. He was a complex personality, both enjoying his power to evoke laughter and yet filled with a deep melancholy nothing could assuage. He was the cleverest and funniest man I had ever met, fiercely opinionated about everything from the agonising dullness of his fellow *Carry On* actors to why *Doctor Zhivago* was 'a pain in the arse as a film'.

When I had supper with him and his mother, Louie, to whom he was devoted, he often told vivid stories about his friend Joe Orton, who had been murdered just down the road from where he lived. Orton had written the character of Inspector Truscott in his 1966 play *Loot* for him.

The hugely successful *Carry On* films that made him famous were packed with innuendo and smut. Yet when Kenny told me he was celibate, I believed him. He pretended to be very shocked when I talked about sex. 'OOOooooh Stooopp!' he would say with that famous snigger when it was plain that he was loving every salacious second.

I went to his surprise fiftieth birthday party which he hated. Some friends had thought it would be a good idea – how wrong they were!

He opened the door, thinking he was going to a quiet dinner and suddenly fifty people were shouting 'SURPRISE!' His face wobbled. He whispered to me, 'Oh God, Miriam, what a nightmare.' But he bravely and politely continued the pretence of loving it until he could make an escape.

When Kenny died in 1988, an open verdict was recorded by the coroner. But I think the bleak last words written in his diary the day before were a giveaway: 'Oh, what's the bloody point?' Kenny had the gift of shifting the clouds away for other people, but not for himself. I had recognised that pain in him from the beginning and so had Maggie Smith. She phoned me out of the blue – it was probably our first proper conversation – after seeing the tribute to Kenny I had done on a TV programme. 'You were the only one who saw his sadness,' she said. They were close friends, sharing the same dry, merciless wit and drawling delivery. When she later joked that her entire career had been an extended impression of him, I could almost hear Kenny bashfully responding 'Stoooppp it.'

I continued in radio comedy with *Marks in His Diary*, in 1979, directed by the young Griff Rhys Jones. It was his first proper job. That's where I met David Jason, a lovely man. Our star was Alfred Marks, who was one of the world's best joke-tellers. But the jokes took all day to tell, thus curtailing our rehearsal time to a frightening degree. Alfred had a joke for all occasions and insisted on sharing them with us. He should have had a show to himself, he didn't need us. His joke-telling is only outstripped by Barry Cryer. Now 86, he still rings me up every few months with a new joke. I adore Barry, he is a genius; I just wish I could remember the quips as he does.

In fact I only have two reliable jokes. When the lights failed at an *Evening Standard* Theatre Awards dinner a few years ago, I rushed to the microphone to fill the gap. Luckily my jokes stretched just long enough for the lights to come back on.

———

I also worked with another legendary comic Kenneth: Ken Dodd, on radio first and then on TV for years. His shows were divine, if nerve-wracking experiences. He liked to rewrite the script up to the last moment; often I had no idea how a sketch was going to end, when he would push a crumpled scrap of script into my hand as I approached the mike.

How you look doesn't matter on radio of course, but Ken was the last of the great music hall stars and his hair on stalks, his toothy grin and mad clothes (my favourite was a maroon maxi coat allegedly made out of 28 moggies) definitely enhanced his comedy on TV. He was very loyal and the radio cast – Jo Manning Wilson, Michael McClain and Talfryn Thomas – were all brought over to White City for the even more terrifying television recordings in front of live studio audiences. He pulled you in front of the camera, saying 'Tell this joke, Miriam', and until I saw it unwinding on the autocue I had no idea of the punchline.

Ken's work *seemed* spontaneous but was deeply calculated and crafted. Every joke and the reaction to it was scored and marked down offstage in the notebooks he kept his entire working life. He got into the *Guinness Book of Records* for the world's longest joke-telling session in the 1960s: 1,500 in three and a half hours (that's 7.14 jokes per minute). Every time he introduced himself – 'Good evening, my name is Kenneth Arthur Dodd, singer, photographic playboy and failed accountant' – he was sharing the joke of his own successful court battle. In 1989 Ken was accused of eighteen counts of tax evasion. But what HMRC hadn't realised was that no Liverpool jury was ever going to convict their favourite comic, one who still lived in the Merseyside home he'd grown up in, and the case was dismissed.

Comics are special; the dangers of the job perhaps unrealised by most people. It is terrifying to be responsible for audience laughter, so perhaps my dislike of 'comedy' stems mainly from fear. Comedy isn't just slapstick, of course, and I loved every second of being in Sue Limb's wonderful literary radio creations. In *The Wordsmiths of Gorsemere*, I played Stinking Iris, William Wordsmith's extremely chatty cleaning lady, in a somewhat unspecific north-eastern accent, Newcastle by way of Sunderland. Here she is, assuming the Wordsmith siblings are lovers: 'My lips is sealed. Ye cunning pair of lovebirds! No wonder your good man do look pale and peakie. I heard say as this free love do take it out o' ye.' In *Gloomsbury* which ran for five series, I was Vera Sackcloth-Vest, chatelaine of Sizzlinghurst, while Alison Steadman played Ginny Fox, Nigel Planer was Lytton Scratchy and John Sessions was everyone from Llewd George to an extremely deep-voiced Gertrude Klein. Jonathan Coy was Henry Mickleton, my long-suffering husband based, of course, on bisexual Harold Nicolson. Jamie Rix was our director. In the studio John used to fall into a deep sleep except when required to act, which he did ferociously and immediately. We all played several characters: one of the joys of this kind of radio comedy is that, if you're versatile enough, you can play with yourself (if you see what I mean) and be all the characters in a scene.

Alison was particularly flexible at flicking between aggressive lesbian Ginny Fox and Mrs Gosling the housekeeper. I would have played *Gloomsbury* for ever if allowed.

My other comedy moments have included playing 'Smelly Photocopying Lady' in *The Hitchhiker's Guide to the Galaxy*; the Mother in *The Comic Strip Presents* . . . whose chicken soup recipe is desired by the Devil to serve at soirees in hell, and Right Eyeball in *Family Guy*. My editor was wildly excited to discover I had been in *The Young Ones* but then disappointed to discover that I couldn't remember a thing about it. Sadly I still can't. Lovely Rik Mayall was in it; at the time I thought it was frightfully silly and couldn't quite understand the fuss. (My student days were more about F. R. Leavis and cock-sucking – though never together.) I've even asked Alexei Sayle and Nigel Planer to jog my memory but they can't remember anything about my being in it either. If anyone out there does, please do let us know.

In 1982, when I got the call to be a part of *Blackadder* working alongside Rowan Atkinson, Tony Robinson, Tim McInnerny, Brian Blessed and Elspet Gray, my interest was piqued. When I heard that I'd be playing the ugly Spanish Infanta, and I'd be working with Jim Broadbent as Don Speekingleesh, an interpreter, I felt I'd been given a present, not just a job.

Blackadder was broadcast in early summer 1983. It was written by Richard Curtis and Rowan Atkinson. In my episode, 'The Queen of Spain's Beard', the king (Brian Blessed) decides to cement an alliance between England and Spain, by marrying his second son Edmund

Blackadder to the Spanish Infanta. Edmund is excited at the prospect until, that is, my entrance as the Infanta – a short, plump, sexually rampant princess with a monobrow and a hint of hirsutism around the upper lip and chin. I often describe myself as an 'overactress', but I must say my appearance in *Blackadder* as the irrepressibly lascivious Spanish Infanta is one of the performances in my life which I can truly say is *not* understated. I delivered all my lines in voluble and babbling Spanish (which I don't speak), all the while licking my lips and making eyes at a terrified Rowan Atkinson, with his skinny little insect legs in black hose and that awful Henry V bowl-cut hairdo.

Jim Broadbent, in a long, fringed, black wig, doublet and tights, is brilliant as the Infanta's translator. He was delightful company, funny and clever (I was cast alongside him again on *Blackadder's Christmas Carol* when I was Queen Victoria to his Prince Albert). Brian Blessed thoroughly enjoyed his psychotic characterisation as Richard IV; on the set, he never knocked on a door, but just crashed straight through them, sending the set carpenters scurrying to build a replacement. The sound of his bellowing ripped through Television Centre. Well, some things never change, but he's a dear guy.

Although I didn't know many of the other regular cast members personally, I instantly liked Rowan Atkinson. The thing that fascinated me most was his nervousness. I don't know if he still is, but he was *extremely* anxious and shy and he used to get angry with himself for getting things wrong. His stammer is not evident now – but he definitely had a faltering delivery then, and it used to infuriate him. He was such a good actor: he was his own fiercest critic. He was never nasty to anybody else, but he just couldn't bear it when he made mistakes and would work himself into a frenzy. It was painful to see; his face would contort with rage at himself.

When I was in America, I went to the first night of his one-man show at the Brooks Atkinson Theatre on Broadway, *Rowan Atkinson at the Atkinson*. It was brilliant but I could feel that it wasn't going down well with the audience – people just couldn't understand his humour – and I knew he'd be terribly disappointed. After the first night party, everybody went to Sardi's restaurant on West 44th Street. Rowan was already well known for *Blackadder* – the place was packed. Then the reviews came out and they were bad. It was fascinating to see how all the people at the party just drifted away – one minute the room was full of babble and a great throng of merrymakers, the next minute there were only about six people left, and I was one of them. I can't remember who else stayed on, but it was a chilly experience because America does not like, cannot deal with, and is afraid of failure. Rowan was a failure that night. He has never been one since, but he was that night. I think it was the audience who failed him.

After a two and a half year break, *Blackadder* returned in early 1986. The second series was set in England during the reign of Queen Elizabeth I. I got the call to play a new character, Edmund Blackadder's aunt, Lady Whiteadder. Lady Whiteadder is one of my most memorable and much-loved characters – but *Blackadder II* almost didn't get commissioned. Although the first series had enjoyed something of a cult success, it had been outrageously expensive to make, so expensive that Michael Grade, the BBC's new network controller, had needed a fair amount of persuasion to give the new series the green light. But the terrifyingly charming producer John Lloyd wound him round his little finger – and the rest is history.

Blackadder II, however, was a much pared-back affair. The episodes were all shot in the studios at the BBC's Television Centre in Wood Lane, using minimal rickety cardboard and wooden sets, in front of a live audience. Ben Elton came on board as the new writer and he also doubled-up as a (very funny) warm-up guy. We didn't really rehearse our scenes any more than for anything else I've worked on – we did one rehearsal on camera, then we just went for it. The show was presented as it was and I don't think it changed much from beginning to end.

Working for television with a live studio audience is a curious thing, because the spectators help you to time the laughs, but it's *not* like acting for the stage: you have to act for the *cameras*. In fact, quite often the audience members watch it on a screen rather than actually being in front of the set itself, so while you are aware of their reaction, it's your performance captured on film which matters. Filming on a small set, the camera men stand quite close to the action, and can zoom in close to focus on your face; so often, the real comedy comes as much from the close-up shots of the cast's facial expressions (especially Rowan's, of course, whose facial gymnastics are legend) as the fast-paced flow of the characters' witty repartee. It's a dual experience in that respect, and you must rely on your director.

I relied on Mandie Fletcher, the clever young director with eight years' experience in theatre work, who had directed episodes of the BBC hit shows *Butterflies* and *The Fainthearted Feminist*, whom I hadn't known previously but I grew to really respect and like. She later said: 'I was put onto *Blackadder* as some kind of punishment by the Head of Comedy, I remember. I wasn't that experienced then, and arriving was like walking into a public school halfway through the second term in the middle of a pillow fight.[*] It reminded me rather of a much nicer version of Footlights so I knew just what she meant.

—

In *Blackadder II*, my episode is called 'Beer'. Over breakfast with Lord Percy, Edmund receives a letter announcing the imminent arrival of his aunt and uncle, Lord and Lady Whiteadder (my stony-faced screen husband was played by Daniel Thorndike, nephew of Dame Sybil and cousin of my lovely friend Diana Devlin), the two most fanatical Puritans in the whole of the kingdom. Thus ensues a catastrophic comedy of errors, with Edmund trying, unsuccessfully, to keep his insalubrious drinking pals and Lady Whiteadder apart. I loved every moment of it.

> **Lady Whiteadder:** Edmund! I trust you have invited no other guests?
>
> **Blackadder:** Oh, certainly not!
>
> **Lady Whiteadder:** Good! For where there are other guests, there are people to fornicate with!

We had a lot of fun on the set because Lady Whiteadder was such an amusing character. She gave me flashbacks to my caricatures of the more ridiculous teachers at school. While I'm capable of quite deft pieces of characterisation and *Blackadder* was a clever comedy and a clever

---

[*] Quoted in *The True History of the Black Adder*, by J. F. Roberts, Preface Publishing, 2012.

script, I will admit that my characters are broadly drawn – I may draw big, but I draw true. It's hard to be subtle booming out lines like: 'Wicked child!!! Drink is urine for the last leper in Hell!' I particularly relished repeatedly slapping Rowan and Tim each time I boomed, 'Wicked child!'

Lady Whiteadder resonated with people, particularly middle-aged men; I don't entirely know why, because she is – not exactly a hypocrite – but a raving Puritanical nutcase. Perhaps it's because she was so bawdy, without intending to be of course, especially when she's getting her lips round that phallic turnip that reminds her of her wedding night with such evident relish. That's the brilliance of Ben Elton's comic writing; he is able to push something to the edge, and over the edge – Lady Whiteadder is definitely over the edge. Blokes often quote bits of script at me, more often than not: they loom up and boom in my face: 'Wicked child!' Thankfully, they don't accompany that with Lady Whiteadder's double thwack . . .

I loved the boys – they were a sweet, funny bunch – and I'm still friendly with all of them, particularly Stephen Fry, of whom I'm extremely fond, and the late Patsy Byrne (who played Nursie), for whom I've often been mistaken. And, of course, I know Tony Robinson from our time together in Leicester in 1968; I've seen him again quite recently, because he was president of Equity and he was knighted which was a bit of a surprise – Tony was as flabbergasted as anybody.

The *Blackadder* atmosphere was totally different from the nail-biting competition of the Footlights. A generation or two later, there was a pleasure in each other's success and a generosity of spirit between the lads that I hadn't seen before. It was just as funny, funnier even, but without the personal edge. I prefer Harmony House – by which I mean I like people to get on – and my *Blackadder* pals were gentlemen and gentle men.

Not least because this time I was allowed the last word:

Blackadder: Right! Well, perhaps this time I might be allowed to continue, and perhaps finish, with any luck . . .

[Suddenly, from under Queen Elizabeth's dress, Lady Whiteadder emerges, grinning.]

Lady Whiteadder: 'Luck'? Hah hah hah! Way-hey! Get it?

[Everyone says, 'No . . .']

Lady Whiteadder: Oh, come on! 'Luck'! Sounds almost exactly like 'f—'.

It is a Far, Far Better Thing

I discovered Charles Dickens when I was eleven, reading *Oliver Twist*. I have loved the world Dickens demands you enter ever since. With hindsight, it's possible that his delight in the criminal world, his compassion for the poor and his sense of mischief (the Artful Dodger) meshed with my own emerging personality. 'Please, sir, I want some more.'

And I wanted more. After *Oliver Twist*, I went through all fifteen novels – Dickens created over 2000 characters. And there is a lot more – 14,000 letters (no, I haven't read all of them) and novellas, journalism, speeches. Words poured out of him. More than any other writer I can think of, Dickens distilled his life into his work. Though a genius, I can't help thinking that he was a complete bastard, or I should say rather that he was an *incomplete* bastard, because he wasn't *totally* shitty. Dickens was a wonderful friend; he was a good father; he was a good employer. But when he turned against you, he had a cruelty and viciousness that was almost unhinged. All this runs through his books.

Throughout his life he felt underprivileged. He overcompensated by being a dandy. With his big, flouncy neckties and the flourishes of his hands, when he went to America some people thought this foppish figure terribly vulgar. His signature was absurdly pretentious; rather like that of Queen Elizabeth I's, or any twelve-year-old's, wandering all over the page. In that respect he's as grotesque, humorous, tragic and as manifold as any of his creations. The man interested me as much as the writer. Unsurprisingly, I chose Dickens as my special subject at Cambridge.

If I was damaged by my mother, it was because she made me over-confident rather than the opposite, because she believed in me so totally and gave me so much love. Dickens's mother, however, never made him feel that he was important. Most men get over it, but Dickens didn't; he never got over anything that happened to him. His attitude towards women always remained ambivalent. I find his preference for a certain type of pre-pubescent heroine, whom he invariably describes as 'little', or 'slight', 'tiny', 'small' or 'slender' – and all aged seventeen – more than a bit iffy. I am not little – and I am quite sure he would not have liked *me*.

But Dickens is the poet of the extraordinary; he pushes reality to extremes. I don't think there are many other actresses who are as temperamentally suited to interpreting his work as I am. As I said, I'm an over-actress; I'm at home in extremes: that's my weakness *and* my strength. Dickens is my element.

In the late eighties, I was lucky enough to win the role of Flora Finching in Christine Edzard's film, *Little Dorrit*. Flora was based on Dickens's first love, Maria Beadnell. Maria led him on and then spurned him; he took his revenge by creating Flora, when twenty-five years later Maria came back into his life, hoping to re-inflame his love. Alongside the pity and disgust Dickens felt for Maria, so physically altered: 'toothless, fat, old and ugly', he also allowed her pathos to come through in the character. That is his artistry.

The film had an enormous effect on my life. I had the chance to interpret a character using all my knowledge of that novel, and I was working with a brilliant cast: Derek Jacobi, Joan Greenwood, Alec

Guinness, Patricia Hayes, Max Wall and Cyril Cusack (the complete cast numbered 242 actors – extras not included) in a unique environment which stimulated all of us to give our best work. And when I won an LA Critics' Circle Award for Best Supporting Actress (with Geneviève Bujold) it brought me to America – but that's for later in my story.

Christine Edzard is an extraordinary woman, one of the best directors I've ever worked with, and I must take this opportunity to hail her achievements and those of her company, Sands Films, and especially her indefatigable colleague, Olivier Stockman, my favourite Belgian. The interview for the part took place in the ramshackle warren of the old warehouse by the Thames in Rotherhithe that is the home of Sands Films. Christine is exceptionally quiet; and that day she hardly spoke. This always frightens me, so I kept talking, frenetically, without pausing – just as Flora Finching would have done.

She gave me the part and, in the film, the lines I speak are exactly as Dickens wrote them; Christine had the wisdom and the confidence not to change Flora's stream-of-consciousness speeches. But there is also a sadness beneath the comedy of Flora Finching. As a fat person, I know what she went through; Flora wanted to be desirable still, and thought she *was*. On the outside, there is all the coquettish pantomime; inside there is the desperate, longing woman.

Every scene was filmed inside the studios. Delightful dressing-rooms were created in the old warehouse; every morning there was a vase of flowers in everyone's room. Cast and crew ate lunch and supper together in the canteen prepared by Molly, an expert chef; we became the *Little Dorrit* family. Hair and make-up were brilliantly done by ex-BBC Pam Meager. Harry Ellam sewed the embroidery for the costumes, based entirely on original pictures. He called it 'painting with threads' and did his exquisite work on countless shawls, waistcoats, purses, braces, flounces, collars, ribbons, and even the slippers worn by Sir Alec Guinness. Marion Weise was my dresser. Every day she had to lace me into my corset. She'd never done it before and her face, the first time I had to strip off, was a picture. She did recover eventually. There has never been a production like it: Christine was nominated for a screenplay Oscar; Derek Jacobi and Alec Guinness won awards for their brilliant work – and so did I!

It wasn't the first time I'd played a Dickens character: I had been Mrs Corney (who becomes Mrs Bumble) in the 1985 twelve-part BBC dramatisation of *Oliver Twist*. But it was the critical acclaim for my portrayal of Flora Finching that made me think it was the right time to try to put my ideas on Dickens into *theatrical* shape.

Sonia Fraser and I went to see Frank Dunlop, who was then running the Edinburgh Festival, with the idea for a one-woman show telling the story of Dickens's life through his characters. This was certainly the most respectable production I'd ever proposed to Edinburgh Festival. The first time I had appeared at the Festival was in *Ubu Roi* at the Traverse in 1963, directed by Gordon McDougall. I played Ma Ubu. I remember the costumes were designed by Gerald Scarfe in the shape of the male and female genital organs. So I really *was* a cunt, and wore the costume! It caused a great fuss at City Hall – the usual uproar from the Edinburgh aldermen trying to protect their citizens from filth.

I made lists of the female characters I wanted to play: there had to be Miss Havisham from *Great Expectations*, of course; and drunken midwife Sarah Gamp from *Martin Chuzzlewit*. But I also included the lesbian Miss Wade, from *Little Dorrit*, a figure of twisted power and pathos; Miss Mowcher, the dwarf manicurist from *David Copperfield*; Mrs Corney, the workhouse matron from *Oliver Twist*; and Dickens's tenderest portrait, Miss Flite from *Bleak House*, a crazy little old lady – a ward of the court and victim of the interminable lawsuit Jarndyce v. Jarndyce – who goes every single day to the High Court of Chancery, awaiting a judgement on her inheritance. There was also a trio of blokes: the beadle Mr Bumble from *Oliver Twist*; Towlinson from *Dombey and Son*; and Pip from *Great Expectations*. In total, I played twenty-three Dickens characters.

Then Sonia and I started to piece the script together, linking the characters with the figures from Dickens's life who had inspired them, with lots of cutting and pasting, and printing. Remember, we didn't have a computer then. We also talked to Claire Tomalin, who was writing her biography of Dickens. Claire was incredibly generous and talked openly and without reserve, not withholding any of her insights for her own book. We also spoke to the great Dickensian scholar and professor of Victorian literature at Birkbeck, Michael Slater, whose book *Dickens and Women* provided so much meat for our play. Michael gave me hours of his time and vast knowledge. We've become close friends and never stop talking Dickens.

It was clear that Dickens's relations with women informed his work: the damage caused by his mother; his unsuccessful first great passion, Maria Beadnell; his Scottish wife Catherine Hogarth, whom he married in 1836, and with whom he fell out of love; Mary Hogarth, his seventeen-year-old sister-in-law, who died in his arms. His sorrow at losing Mary was so great that he wanted to be buried with her ashes; and finally, in 1857, his meeting with Ellen Ternan, his last love, who was to be his mistress until his death.

Michael doubted that Dickens's relationship with Ellen Ternan was consummated; he is convinced she never allowed him to sleep with her. I said, 'Michael, I can't agree with you. Of *course* they slept together!' It is unproven that Ellen may have had a child who died, but *of course* they had sex. It took us nine months to finish the script. We worked all hours – sometimes, I was so overwhelmed and exhausted that I would fall asleep on the floor: that's always my escape when I'm frightened of something, but that's how we did it. It was a true collaboration; without Sonia, it could never have happened.

I had never wanted to do a one-woman show; it's lonely and frightening being on stage alone, never hearing another voice. So when the time came to take our show to the Edinburgh Festival, I asked David Timson to play Dickens and Mr Bumble, and to sing the haunting contemporary songs Michael Haslam had found. And Sonia engaged Helen Crayford to play the piano.

The show was originally called *Wooman, Lovely Wooman, What a Sex You Are!*, which is a quote from the ballet master Mr Turveydrop in *Bleak House*. We performed at the old university medical lecture theatre in Teviot Place. We had no idea whether the show would work until I said the last lines – and there was utter silence in the theatre. I stood there in the dark and I thought, 'Oh my God – they don't like it.' Suddenly, there was an explosion of applause that came roaring out from the auditorium and people were on their feet, stamping. It was a moment of unalloyed triumph. There was just me on the dark stage, then the lights went up and I could see Sonia in the wings, joy across her face. It was an extraordinary moment. That was when we knew we had a show. It sold out immediately and later we were asked to transfer to the Bush Theatre in Shepherd's Bush and then to the Hampstead Theatre Club in Swiss Cottage.

In 1990, Sonia and I took the show to America. David didn't want to come with us because he had just got married so we had to find a replacement. Norman Lear – who had me on a retainer (more of which later) – wanted to show me off to the Hollywood community in readiness for the upcoming sitcom he'd planned; so he put up the money. I asked my friend Susan Loewenberg, who ran LA Theatre Works, to help, as Norman knew everything about television but not much about theatre. We did a try-out performance. Unfortunately, our replacement for David hadn't learned his lines. Norman wasn't impressed. 'It's a bit heavy, isn't it?' he said. Then he had a bright idea. 'I know. Why don't you get a ladder in the interval? Go onstage, climb the ladder and tell some Jewish jokes.' He thought that might lighten the mood. Honestly!

Susan Smith, my beloved American agent, had a better idea: 'Ditch the guy, he's hopeless, doesn't know the lines, waste of time. Do it yourself, all alone, as a one-woman show. You'll be terrific.' The idea scared the living daylights out of me, but I took her advice. We changed the text a bit, I learnt the lines and when we opened at the lovely Tiffany Theater on Sunset, I played all the parts including Mr Bumble. The proposal scene was such a hit, people swore there were two actors on stage. Our little one-woman show has had a long life. I went to London first, back to the Bush Theatre, then to Hampstead and then to the Duke of York's Theatre in the West End with one of the best sets (by Kendra Ullyart) I've ever seen, based on a giant reproduction of Dickens's books. Our show was nominated for an Olivier Award, in the Best Entertainment category.

In 1993, the British Council invited us to tour India with Jonathan Rutherford on piano and a terrific production manager, Mark Pawsey. Whatever the drama, Mark could deal with it. Even when our luggage and the travelling set disappeared in Bombay, he was calm. Around India we went, it was a tale of ten cities: Delhi, Chennai, Bangalore, Visakhapatnam, Agra, Patna, Lucknow, Bombay (Mumbai), Allahabad and Hyderabad. In Patna, the set and costumes again didn't arrive; they had got stuck on a train. So I performed in the open air on a sandy floor in my own clothes, without lighting and it was one of the best shows I've ever done. The Indian audience was intelligent and responsive. They know and love their Dickens, and the Q and A sessions were a delight. At one in Delhi, I wanted to give the blind members of the audience a chance to 'feel me' so they would know more about the show and the texture of my Victorian trouser suit. I took one blind patron's hands and placed them on my chest. He quickly pulled his hands away – 'Oh, you are fat!' he exclaimed. I may have smashed his dream.

In Kolkata (Calcutta) we arrived on the same day as Mother Teresa. I hoped I'd be able to meet her and our driver assured me I would. He would take me to her ashram at 4 a.m. when she prayed at the service and met those, like me, who wanted to talk to her. I got up early the next morning and was driven to her ashram. A nun welcomed me and guided me to a huge hall, with many worshippers. It was a Catholic service; my driver urged me to take Communion, but I felt that would be wrong. After the service, we lined up to meet Mother Teresa. It resembled a Papal audience; she was all in white, very small and brown, with an intense gaze. When she looked at me, I felt she saw into my soul; it was a disquieting experience. 'How is it in England?' she asked me. And then we dispersed. She had such tremendous authority you could be in no doubt that you had met someone very special.

In the year of Dickens's bicentenary, 2012, I was determined to revive the show – almost twenty-four years after its Edinburgh Festival debut. In the middle of 2011, Richard Jordan, who had seen the show when he was sixteen, took over with remarkable speed and I embarked on a ten-month tour. Starting in Australia and New Zealand, I returned for the Edinburgh Festival, then after the British run I went to Canada and America.

I had some narrow escapes on tour: I got furious with delays in the airport in Florida, and when being herded about interminably, I shouted angrily at the security officer: 'How big's your dick?' My group shrank with horror: he looked up, smiled slightly and said, 'Well, I prefer mine percolated.' I just let it go. Another drama was losing the antique stool I used for Miss Mowcher, when returning from our presentation at the Lincoln Center. I'd brought the stool with me from London – it was my grandmother's, and very precious. The Lincoln Center took great care of it; it was stored in a safe overnight and two security officers carried it to and from the stage. Afterwards, I was rushing back to catch the plane to London for a Harry Potter film shoot and left the stool in the taxi. I was in hysterics: Richard Jordan remembers my phoning him seventeen times and when he asked me to describe the New York cab, I said, 'It was yellow.' Amazingly, I got it back, thanks to the lovely taxi driver.

The world tour took in forty cities in England, America, Canada, Australasia. Andrew McKinnon, the distinguished Australian impresario, took over the Antipodean leg of the tour, and with a wonderful pianist, John Martin, who is a precious friend, we had seasons in Sydney and Melbourne and went all over Australia. Andrew introduced me to Bob Hawke. He and his wife, Blanche, who is also a real corker, invited Heather and me to a dinner party at their Northbridge home. It was the occasion of Bob's rapprochement with Paul Keating, with whom he'd been on bad terms for some years. A nice-looking man was sitting opposite me. When I asked him what he did, he said, 'I'm the premier of South Australia.' It was Mike Rann. I felt I was at the centre of Government.

After dinner, Bob and Paul Keating went downstairs to talk. When you were in Bob's presence, it felt as though the air fizzed around him. He made me think of *David Copperfield*: 'We must meet reverses boldly and not suffer them to frighten us. We must learn to act the play out. We must live misfortune down.' Dickens would have loved him. If only there were politicians now to match his greatness – they're such puny men these days.

We took our play all over the world, people admired it; my love of Dickens has made me much more famous as an actress, we even published the book. But then Sonia got sick and died, tragically before her time, in 2013. And while I remain passionately proud of *Dickens' Women*, I haven't the heart to do it again, without her.

Taking America by Storm

When I went to Los Angeles in 1988, it was on a whim. Just like Charles Dickens's trip to America in 1842, I was taking a chance: 'If not now, when?' I'd received a Los Angeles Critics' Circle Award for *Little Dorrit*. This was the prod I needed. I was in my late forties and I thought to myself, 'They're prepared to give *me*, a completely unknown English woman, an award and they've never heard of me? There will never be a better moment. I'm off!'

I had never thought of working in America; it was the glittering centre of the entertainment industry, way out of my reach. Many actors go 'on spec' – few succeed. But if you can piggy-back on an award, you have a better chance of standing out from the crowd of hopefuls.

I made a systematic plan. I wrote to Menahem Golan, the Israeli film producer and director whose company, the Cannon Group, had distributed *Little Dorrit* in the States. I made him a proposition: if Menahem Golan would pay for me to have three nights in a top-rate hotel in New York, I would pay all other expenses. 'I won't ask for any travel money,' I wrote, 'and I will find a publicist.' Naturally he agreed. I went straight to my beloved friend, Hodge. She knows her clothes.

She took me to a shop called Wardrobe in Marylebone, where the smart proprietor, Susie, grasped the challenge and kitted me out in an array of stylish garments for the fuller figure. I remember she said, 'Black stockings, *always* wear black stockings.' I bought a trouser suit, a smart overcoat and several tops. Hodge found me a make-up artist and hairdresser, and I had myself 'zhuzhed' up. That was the first part of the plan sorted.

A week later, looking presentable, I landed in Newark (far better than JFK for Manhattan), and took a yellow cab straight to the Plaza Hotel where Menahem Golan's company had booked me in. At that time, the Plaza was a super luxury hotel – one night there cost as much as my flight over (I, of course, had flown economy class).

Using my friend Stella Wilson's contact, I immediately hired a publicist, and within a matter of hours she got me on to NBC's *Today Show*, which was America's most-watched, daily morning news programme. I was interviewed by Katie Couric; she was delightful and made me feel that she was interested in what I had to say, and I felt quite at home. Johnny Carson in Los Angeles saw that appearance, and invited me onto his NBC prime-time *The Tonight Show*. That was big! It meant that my personality was marketable in America.

I flew to Los Angeles, where they put me up in a hotel in Burbank. I was nervous at the thought of the TV show, but I behaved naturally, with a certain amount of naughtiness. America is a prudish country; they don't like smut. I don't think they even laugh at the word 'knickers'. It's hard to do business with people like that.

Mr Carson was not a warm man: he was more interested in himself than in me. But he saw that the studio audience liked me and that was useful. I did my voices. The Scottish-Jewish one (basically, Grandma Margolyes's accent) went down very well. People rang in from all over America. Everyone who spoke like Grandma is now dead, so it revived memories. The transmission went so well that he asked me to come back. In fact, subsequently I've been on *The Tonight Show* several times, not only with Johnny Carson, but later twice with Jay Leno. Jay was lovely and open, and a listener. He took me to his home to see his car collection.

After that first *Tonight Show*, I decided I needed an American agent. At the time, I didn't have a green card, and it was difficult to get a visa for theatre work, whereas it was much easier to get one for films. My British agent, Lindy King, suggested various film agents in LA to me. I went to see them all: two women and four men.

It's an odd relationship, that of artist and agent; sometimes closer than marriage, but ultimately it has to be based on a shrewd assessment of the worth of each to the other. They all wanted me to join them; that's the only time in my life I had such an experience. They wooed me. Lindy's pick (how right she was, and has always been) was Susan Smith. Susan thought I was fresh and funny – she said it was like the Queen talking Yiddish. Thus began my foray into Hollywood. Susan was one of the most extraordinary and important people of my life, and whatever I write about her cannot convey the wonder and ferocity and sheer class this woman showed. Her language was bluer than mine, her politics were liberal, her cooking and hospitality legendary.

Susan had a New York flavour; she was plain, with a ferocious intelligence and a way with words. She was that rare bird: a Hollywood agent of taste. As Charles Dance said, she could smell bullshit a mile off and would have none of it. Susan was a discerning appreciator of talent – and you didn't have to be beautiful: she championed actors and actresses that she felt were interesting and different. So much in Hollywood is about externals, but not for Susan. She wanted to see inside the actor. And once she took you on, she was a passionate, loyal supporter. She cooked for you, designed your apartment, chose your lover. No holds barred. But if you fell from her favour, WALLOP! It was over.

I remember our first meeting. I was terribly nervous, but she sat me down, looked hard at me, barked questions for about thirty minutes, and then said, 'OK, I want you to join.' No messing about. If I got a job, she phoned with the words: 'Good news for the Jews.' We just hit it off. I was probably the fattest person that she'd ever had on her books. She had an impressive stable of clients; to be alongside Hollywood stars such as Kathy Bates, Charles Dance, Brian Dennehy and Greta Scacchi was an accolade in itself. She loved talent – quirky, off-the-wall, no matter. She encapsulated the pursuit of excellence. Her word was her bond; is that what they call 'old school'? Pity such honour has vanished from our business. But she had a respect for money and was a ferocious negotiator – boy, could she land a deal. I loved her to bits and I think of her with the greatest affection, gratitude and respect.

Almost immediately, Susan Smith introduced me to Norman Lear, the American television writer and producer who created or developed many of the big sitcoms of the seventies, including *All in the Family* (the American spin-off of *Till Death Us Do Part*), *Sanford and Son*, *Good Times* and *Maude*. It was a fortuitous and highly profitable meeting: Norman put me on a retainer of $350,000; that was for a year – and I didn't have to do a thing. I just had to *be*. I couldn't quite believe it.

The most onerous demand Norman made of me was to be introduced to his stable of writers, among whom, I remember, were Marta Kauffman and David Crane, the creators of *Friends*. That was the way comedy worked in LA: a group of writers was corralled into a room from nine to five and just wrote or tried to write; it was competitive and nerve-racking. I hate comedy: I don't like anything that's called 'comedy'. Let's just go with LIFE, eh? Norman would gather all these comedy writers in a room and I would go along and talk to them. They were then supposed to think up a character for me. Marta and Dave suggested a series based on the ghastly hotelier Leona Helmsley, who went to prison for fraud. I would have enjoyed that role, but it never happened. I think they were intending to make a TV movie with Anne Bancroft instead of me. She's dead now so it's still possible . . .

Once I had that great wad of money from Norman, the first thing was to find a permanent place to live. When I first arrived in LA, I stayed with Wendy Murray, an old friend whom I met in the health farm in Newport Pagnell, who had become a personal assistant for various film people. And my old friend, the great director Waris Hussein, gave me his West Hollywood apartment for months, and refused any rent. What a sweet generous man he is; I've never forgotten that kindness. Now, however, I had the money to get myself a swish apartment and I found the perfect place on iconic palm-lined Ocean Avenue in Santa Monica.

My apartment was on the twelfth floor, and my balcony overlooked the beach, Malibu, the Santa Monica mountains and, most importantly, the ocean. I loved watching the sun set over the Pacific. There were two bedrooms, a huge central living room with a sliding wall of glass onto the balcony, and there was even a swimming pool in the building. The pool was too small for me, however, so I joined the Palisades YMCA pool in Temescal Canyon, and the locker room of that lovely pool became my social centre. The other swimmers were my friends; I'm still in touch with Cassidy, who ran the place. She and her girlfriend Michelle were forgiving of my hopeless swimming ability. I did my forty laps every morning, stripped naked in the locker room and that's where we had the best chats. All the women were bright, friendly and funny; I miss them.

Back at the apartment at Santa Monica Bay Towers I felt like a film star; I believe Julie Andrews now lives in the same building. It was across the road from the Fairmont Miramar, where Bill Clinton always stayed when he came to LA. On one of the presidential visits, snipers were deployed on the roof of our building: one afternoon, I looked up from my balcony to see a man with a sub-machine gun up there, lying in wait. Terrified, I said, 'What's going on?' To which he replied, 'Oh, don't worry about it. We're just here for the President.'

LA is not my favourite place in the States; I much prefer San Francisco. LA is a strange mix of the exotic and the naff. It's not a city: it's a collection of neurotic neighbourhoods. But it does give you the opportunity of reinvention. They say you can be whatever you want to be there; I embraced that freedom wholeheartedly, but I had no intention of adopting any of the Californian lifestyles or fads: I don't believe in all their New Age nonsense. I might have dyed my hair once or twice for parts when I was in LA, but I never had any plastic surgery or tooth-whitening. I tried to steer a course between the Yiddisher Momma and the Venice Beach Girl – between Shelley Winters and Jane Fonda. I would say, on the whole, Shelley Winters won.

One of the joys of my time in California were the suppers Eric Harrison organised in his Gloria Avenue bungalow in Van Nuys. Eric was a retired wardrobe master born in Derbyshire, who came to America with *Soldiers in Skirts*, a drag show first devised during the Second World War for the troops. Then he'd been a dresser on Broadway to Sir John Gielgud when he came to America. Eric was very large in height and width, he had a broad Derbyshire accent, he was a brilliant cook and demonstrated a boundless generosity. He'd become friendly with many great names in entertainment and every few weeks he'd throw a dinner party. His little house was crammed with British memorabilia: it was a hymn to the Old Country. The table was set with gold plates, Crown Derby and Wedgwood, and fancy Sheffield cutlery. On the walls were theatre posters and autographed photographs of stars from old shows, all lovingly inscribed to Eric. Those lucky enough to be invited squeezed into our chairs, and were regaled with fabulous showbiz gossip of the most scurrilous and unmissable kind. The food was lavish, masses of cashew nuts, caviar, always smoked salmon, succulent lamb, great sides of beef, loads of vegetables, spectacular puddings, at least three; it was utterly delicious. I'd sit with husband and wife Vincent Price and Coral Browne; and Norman Lloyd (who died in May 2021 aged 106) and his wife Peggy; and Jeannie Carson (*Finian's Rainbow*) and her husband, Biff McGuire; and Patricia Morison, the original Broadway star of *Kiss Me Kate* and *The King and I*. Eric never sat with us: he hovered round the table, serving everyone (reminding us he'd been a steward on the *Queen Mary*) and adding stories of gay secret love in Hollywood.

It is to Waris Hussein that I owe the joy of Eric's suppers. He brought me along one day and thereafter I became a regular. Waris remembers Coral's story about Angela Lansbury, with whom he was working: 'Do you know why Angela always looks so surprised and bewildered,' she asked. 'Well, it's because she came into the bedroom on her wedding night and found the groom in her nightie!' I've no idea if that's true, but Coral certainly knew that Vinnie backed both teams. Never mind, they were deeply in love and that Hollywood marriage worked.

Please Do Not Wear Shorts

Santa Monica is the beachside suburb of Los Angeles, and when you're at the beach, you wear shorts. Everybody in LA wore shorts, so I did too – all the time. I don't think other people wore theirs to interviews though. I often had to drive down the motorway (I refused to call it the freeway) into Burbank to see the film people in the studios there and I wouldn't bother to change out of my beach attire: blue-and-white striped T-shirt, canvas shoes with little embroidered anchors on them, and my baggy shorts.

I admit shorts are not a flattering garment on anyone of my size and age, but it was left to my agent Susan to give it to me straight. I'd just got back from one of my meetings in Burbank and had barely got my foot inside the apartment when the telephone rang. It was Susan. The director I'd just met had obviously called her immediately I'd left to say, 'This Miriam Margolyes you sent to see us turned up in her shorts, Susan. That doesn't work for us.' Susan said, 'Miriam, you're my favourite client. Absolutely my favourite client!' Then she continued, 'I've just got one thing to say to you: don't wear shorts, Miriam, OK? In an interview, a meeting or an audition: please, just Do. Not. Wear. Shorts!'

I never did wear my shorts to interviews after that. I did what I was told and put on one of my smart new outfits. That was Susan all over; there was no filter, she told you the absolute truth unvarnished. She was also often terribly rude and abrasive, especially to her junior staff who were always leaving; she went through assistants like diarrhoea.

Susan was constantly sending me for auditions. Quite quickly I got a job on Lawrence Kasdan's 1990 black comedy movie *I Love You to Death*, starring Kevin Kline and Tracey Ullman, with William Hurt, River Phoenix, Joan Plowright and Keanu Reeves. I played Kevin Kline's mother. Norma Aleandro, the celebrated Argentinian actress, was originally cast in the role, but the part was for an ugly old bag; Norma Aleandro was a very beautiful woman, and one day at rehearsal she decided she didn't want to be an old bag. Susan sent the director a tape of my work and I landed the part. I didn't mind being an old bag.

Kevin Kline was delightful. He called me from his hotel shortly after he arrived and asked if I'd mind rehearsing the one scene we had together. In it, I had to slap his face. It's a funny scene and worth rehearsing but few stars would have bothered to take such pains to get it right. I went over to his hotel and we rehearsed. I seldom watch my own scenes, but I did watch that. We worked well together, and I was very good, so was Kevin.

River Phoenix was another cast member. What a lovely young man, very polite and gentle. He showed no signs of a drug habit and I was terribly sad when I heard he'd died from an overdose. William Hurt was quite the opposite: surly and self-involved. When I was introduced, I put out my hand to shake his. He simply turned away. I wasn't worth shaking hands with. What an arsehole.

The other two English actresses on the film were Tracey Ullman and Joan Plowright. I'd known Tracey years ago, when we shared a flat in Glasgow during the filming of *A Kick Up the Eighties* in 1981. It was clear from the start that Tracey was a gigantic talent. And Colin Gilbert and Tom Gutteridge had got together quite a starry cast: Rik Mayall and Ron Bain and Roger Sloman and Robbie Coltrane. And me. Tracey had a boyfriend, a nice electrician, but when Allan McKeown, a famous producer, came on the scene, they became a couple and got married. Tracey bought her ex-boyfriend a house; she was very generous to him.

Joan Plowright was worried about her husband, Sir Laurence Olivier, who was too ill to travel from England. I remembered meeting him outside the stage door of the New Theatre Oxford when I was at school. The power of his physicality brought a rush of moistness to my area. That's when I creamed in my knickers as I later told Graham Norton.

Of course, I didn't tell Joan that; it would have offended her, but I asked her about Sir Laurence. 'What was he like when you met?'

I'd taken her for supper to a good Malibu restaurant one Saturday night. She gazed out of the window at the ocean. She looked reflective and a little sad. 'He was . . . animal,' she said. There was a wealth of memory in that enigmatic sentence.

Larry Kasdan was fun and smart and very hospitable. He invited the whole cast for a party at his Beverley Hills house. We swam in the pool and laughed a lot. I felt I was really up there with the stars.

While I did a lot of voice-overs in LA, it was much harder to get work there than it had been in Soho. Everyone had to test, sometimes several times. I resented that; I expected to be given the job because I knew I could do it. I had ideas above my station.

At one casting session I recognised an elderly woman sitting opposite me and I thought, 'That's Carol Channing. What the fuck is she doing sitting in a casting pool with everyone else?' I went to the reception desk, and I said firmly, 'You have one of the greats of all time sitting here, completely unheralded. You will give her a separate room, a coffee and biscuits, and you will show her huge respect. She is a great lady. Her name is Carol Channing.' The receptionist said, 'Oh, my God, is *she* here? I hadn't realised.' And I said, 'Well, *realise now*.' I don't know about the coffee and biscuits, or even whether she got the job, but they took Carol Channing to a separate room after that. I did the right thing.

There's a lot of fear in LA. When you go for a casting session, you are herded into a waiting room full of other hopefuls; it's like a zoo – full of other actors; you have to sign a register and sit there, waiting to be called. You sit until someone summons you in for your audition. You stand in front of a desk full of people who look at you coldly. One of them barks, 'OK, what's your piece? What have you done before?' As a rule, they are not interested. They are extremely tough on actors; they don't care how scary it is.

I had one too many of such casting ordeals. I thought, 'I'm not going to be made to feel like a piece of dirt under their feet.'

The crunch came at an interview with Steven Spielberg, who is actually a most courteous and pleasant man. I brought with me copies of the brochure of my Tuscan farmhouse, and before they said anything to me, I said, 'Good afternoon. Thank you so much for inviting me to this audition. Before we start, may I show you my farmhouse near Siena, in case any of you would be interested in renting it?' I handed them each a brochure. 'I've had copies printed for you, so you may take them home to show your family, and put them in the office.'

I needed to feel confident, and once *I* took control of the interview, they weren't able to make me feel small. How could they make somebody who owned a house in Tuscany feel like a piece of dirt? They couldn't. They would look at the brochure, then they would open up

Juliet's Nurse takes a stroll with Romeo: *Romeo + Juliet*, 1996.

In *Harry Potter* with Maggie Smith and Richard Harris, 2002.
No wonder I was looking scared.

Getting my OBE in 2002.

'Lavender Bags': me, Maggie Smith and Judi Dench in 2006.

The Importance of Being Earnest with Terence Rigby, 2006. No love lost.

With Tom Hickey as Nell and Nagg, wife and husband, *Endgame* in 2009.

As Madame Morrible with Idina Menzel in *Wicked* (above); backstage after the *Royal Variety Performance* with Prince Charles in 2006 (below).

The Graham Norton Show: my unusual tattoo story cracks up Graham, will.i.am and Greg Davies (above); talking tits with Stanley Tucci and Jimmy Carr (middle).

Call the Midwife: as the benignly bossy Mother Mildred I shook things up at Nonnatus House.

Receiving my certificate of Australian citizenship from Julia Gillard in 2013.

With MK Turner in *Almost Australian*: two leading ladies on Arrernte Country.

The Real Marigold Hotel team photo in 2016.

Bucket in 2017: the joys of hitchhiking with Frog Stone.

Our splicing in 2014: Dave Pask, Denise Wordsworth, Heather Sutherland, me and Carol Macready.

I love this portrait … this much is true.

and we would have a conversation. They would say, 'Oh, my God, it's gorgeous. How long have you had that?' They saw me as a human being, not just somebody who desperately wanted a job. That's important, because when you're at a disadvantage, you can't do a good audition. I've always wanted to be taken seriously. *Don't dismiss me. You think I'm a little, roly-poly person? No: you'd better pay attention.* And it worked. I can't say that I ever actually rented the house to any of the casting people, but they were impressed.

I was still channelling Shelley Winters: when a casting director asked her what she'd done before, she leaned down into her bag and took out one Oscar, then the other Oscar and thumped them down on the desk. 'That's what I've done,' she said. I also love the story about the brilliant actress Athene Seyler. When a director asked her what she had done, she said: 'Do you mean *this morning*?' On another occasion when she was asked, 'What parts do you like playing?', she looked at them with a curled lip and said, 'Scornful parts!'

I'd advise young actors: 'Remember that when you go into an audition you have the right to be there. Your talent gives you the right to be there and don't let anyone put you down. Make them see you as a person. *Engage*. Make the first move: take control.'

Sometimes I went too far. There was one occasion that I particularly remember. The part was for the secretary of a detective, who was the lead role in the TV series. I was called in and as usual there was a panel of producers facing me. They told me a bit about the series and then asked if I knew who would be playing the lead role. 'No, I don't know,' I replied. 'Oh, it's James Woods.' I blinked. 'James Woods. Oh, I see. He's a bit of a cunt, isn't he?' You should have seen their faces. (Because he is!) I didn't get that part.

My Turn to Fail

The thing about living in LA is that everybody is afraid of Failure. And Fatness. And I was afraid of neither. They're so in thrall to success and celebrity that they're terrified it might not happen. You shouldn't fear failure. It's not something that we relish – no one wants to fail – but it may be something we have to endure in order to improve and succeed.

I was lucky; in LA, thanks to Norman Lear's extraordinarily generous retainer, every door was open to me. I'd never had so much money in my life and I didn't have to do anything for it. But eventually, the work had to start. The show that we finally landed was *Frannie's Turn*, created and written for me by Chuck Lorre. CBS picked it up and it was first aired in September 1992. Chuck was a former professional guitarist and songwriter turned scriptwriter; now he's one of the richest and most successful producers and writers in Hollywood, with hit shows including *The Big Bang Theory*, *Two and a Half Men*, *Grace Under Fire*, *Young Sheldon*, *Dharma & Greg* and the Cybill Shepherd series *Cybill*. I didn't like Chuck much; he was too desperately focused on succeeding and it was an angry focus; you were always conscious of his presence as a smouldering, choleric intensity which might erupt into rage at any moment.

The producers, Marcy Carsey and Tom Werner, were delightful, however. We first met at Art's Deli in Studio City. The LA delis were bliss for me, a Jewish girl brought up on chicken soup. Art's Deli was

312

the power-meeting place of choice for many Hollywood executives. But I knew most of the delis around. I ate my way in chopped liver from Zucky's and Izzy's and Fromin's in Santa Monica to Canter's (24-hour chicken soup and matzo balls) and Nate 'n Al's, and Junior's nearer to the studios. Marcy and Tom were unfailingly supportive and human. Despite the show's failure, they never made me feel it was my fault. (It wasn't!) I honour them still. A third producer, Caryn Mandabach, came to London and produces the wonderful show, *Peaky Blinders*. She's never asked me to be in it. Pity.

We shot our sitcom in one of the many huge, sand-coloured, concrete hangars on the CBS Burbank lot. In the studio next door, they shot *Roseanne*, the hit sitcom at the time, on which Chuck had been a writer and was also co-executive producer. People who worked on *Roseanne* were always escaping to our studio, telling us about how ghastly Roseanne Barr was, and how frightened everyone was of her. They all loved John Goodman, who played her husband. He visited too one day, a glorious chap. Our set was a happy, inclusive one, unlike theirs.

Chuck Lorre's work on *Roseanne* had impressed the producers and Norman gave him the opportunity to make his first sitcom – *Frannie's Turn*. He desperately needed it to succeed, so perhaps that's why his attention to every aspect and detail of the production seemed over-bearingly intense. Naturally, he came to every read-through, pre-shoot rehearsal, camera run-through and network run-through. The latter is a fearsome thing, a weekly rehearsal early in the production schedule, attended by all the big cheese executives. They write copious notes; anything which doesn't get a laugh gets cut and they demand instant rewrites. Then there's the live taping.

The series was my show: designed and built around my comedic talents and vocal versatility. I played an Irish-Italian seamstress called Frannie Escobar, a happy, gregarious woman muddling through a mid-life crisis: at work she has her arrogant couturier boss Armando to deal with; at home in Staten Island, Frannie has to contend with her cantankerous, old-school Cuban husband Joseph, his eccentric mother Rosa, a dimwit son Eddie, and a headstrong daughter Olivia, who seems destined to make the same bad choice in marriage as her mother. Frannie is a middle-aged woman finding herself, a late-blooming feminist. I felt it was a role any woman of a certain age could relate to; I knew what it was like to be plain and to be fat and to be overlooked. I lived with that all my life; in a sense, coming to America was the same transformational journey for me.

My routine during the run was unvarying. Round about 2 a.m., the new script would be pushed under my apartment door. Each version came in a different colour, and it was useless to learn the first offering, as pink, blue and yellow amendments would follow nightly – that was the worst part. Then the early morning swim followed by the long drive from Santa Monica to Burbank in traffic which was bumper-to-bumper the whole way. It was gruelling, we earned the money and I truly wouldn't want to spend my life in that world. Stress and tension were overwhelming, the gossip was poisonous, and yet I met dear people there too.

Frannie's Turn was taped in front of a live audience, who filed in shortly before we appeared. No deviation from the script was allowed. Each episode took about six hours to film; Chuck constantly sent in new lines to be learned, sometimes seconds before recording. If anything went wrong, or we paused, the tireless stand-up hired to maintain the energy of the studio audience would restart his stream of banter. I was worried that he was funnier than we were. Sometimes I joined in – I can't resist a live audience.

There's a terrible hierarchy in television, especially in America. They're so up the bums of celebrity over there that if you're the star, they'll do anything to keep you happy – but they treat any underlings and extras like dirt. On *Frannie's Turn* we often had extras; I would make a point of talking to every single person, laughing and joking with them, ushering them into the backstage kitchen for a sandwich or some M&Ms, and sitting with them at lunchtime. I always said, 'Hello. You're joining the mad scenes, are you? Where are you from? I'm from England.' I talked with everybody, not in a deep way, but so that they felt comfortable and confident, because if you're eaten up with nerves and fear, it prohibits the creative process. I've been there: I know what terror is.

Frannie's Turn premiered on 13 September 1992 – and ended barely four weeks later, on 10 October. It was meant to be thirteen episodes, but CBS, principally Jeffrey Katzenberg, cancelled it after five! I rang Jeff to try to change his mind. He wouldn't. The cancellation did seem somewhat random; other shows at that time were no better than ours; the show was gaining traction and we were finding a loyal audience as the series ended. Chuck Lorre was incandescent with rage. Some American TV sitcoms don't seem to reflect real life; *Frannie's Turn* did feel believable. It didn't gloss over things, it was about good people who were having a rough time and trying to work it out, but for some reason we were axed and other shows were signed up.

There was the usual round of pre-publicity interviews for the show. The CBS publicist in charge double-booked the *LA Times* (the most important interview) with another much less prestigious one. When I asked him to rearrange it, he just brushed me aside. I thought 'No mate, I'm not having that.' So I phoned his voicemail and left this message: 'This is Harry Margolis, Miriam's manager, the *LA Times* interview WILL go ahead. You WILL alter the schedule and if you don't, you're fired!' Amazingly he rushed to obey and I got the interview. He didn't find out till much later that the gruff, rude Harry was me. Don't mess with the Margolyes!

In my interviews the reporters kept saying to me, 'Don't you realise you're gonna be incredibly wealthy? You won't even know what to do with all the money you make!' I never believed them. I didn't think it would happen, so when it didn't, I wasn't cast down. I minded for my lovely cast, who were all adorable, especially Tomas Milian, who played my husband; he and I had a real rapport and kept in touch long after the show ended. I worked for Chuck one more time: in 2002, I played Chloe in an episode of *Dharma & Greg*. It was written by Dottie Dartland, who'd also written some of *Frannie's Turn*.

I have to say I wasn't very good But this quote from it makes me laugh:

Dharma: [reading a book about pregnancy] Set aside time each day to dialogue with your vagina.

Greg: Is that the new Harry Potter book?

My whole American adventure never truly entered into my soul; it was a superficial experience, so when my sitcom bombed, I wasn't consumed with feelings of catastrophe. However, I noticed that the day after *Frannie's Turn* was cancelled, everybody stopped calling: I did not receive a single phone call. Before I had been positively overrun with invitations, but the minute I became a failure, everybody ran a mile.

———

My agent, Susan Smith, could be caustic, and she told the unfiltered truth. Much later she said to me, 'Miriam, you've gone cold in Hollywood. When you came in, you were hot, and you're not hot now: you've gone off the boil.' I knew she was right. They always want the new, the different. I was highly regarded, but now I was a known quantity, therefore I was no longer remarkable nor passionately interesting to anyone. I could have told Susan that it was *her* job to make me hot again, but I didn't. I realised that the moment had come to leave America, but it was a hard decision. It was such an easy life; I had a five-star apartment overlooking the ocean and a car and friends I didn't want to leave behind. Special among them were writers Hal and Lilian (Lil) Hara. They'd escaped the McCarthyist purges in New York to start a new life under new identities. (Hal even became a jeweller: a very Margolyes thing to do.) They held an open house for passionate and articulate intellectuals of all stripes, who argued politics and ate Lil's amazing food with equal relish. When the truth about Stalin was revealed, both renounced Communism, dedicating the rest of their lives to working for true democracy in America. With the Haras I could leave behind the nonsense of Hollywood and competitive television, and talk about books, ideas and things that mattered. It was like having a Hodgkin family in LA. They kept me sane.

So I stayed for a few more years.

I don't quite know how I weathered that storm, what reserves I had within me, but maybe I had other priorities. I'm not interested in the trappings of celebrity. I like the money but nothing else. If I'd been building all my hopes on the sitcom working out, I might have crumbled, but happily I hadn't.

And other things happened quite quickly: I recorded the BBC radio version of Sue Townsend's *The Queen and I* in LA, for example. On its subsequent release on cassette, the audio recording proved a stunning success – in fact, it sold so well that it was between Elton John and Patsy Cline in the pop charts. I was gobsmacked.

A year after *Frannie's Turn* flopped, in 1993, I was in the 'comedy horror' film *Ed and His Dead Mother*, directed by Jonathan Wacks. I played Mabel Chiltern, a resurrected corpse and mother of Ed (played by glorious Steve Buscemi) who runs around killing people with a chainsaw. That's become a cult film and can be seen in the small hours, on minor TV channels. Then, barely a year after receiving my BAFTA for Best Supporting Actress in *The Age of Innocence*, in 1994, I was cast as the Nurse in Baz Luhrmann's 1996 Hollywood production of *Romeo + Juliet*.

That's show business.

Adventures in Cinema

I'm not a film actress. Acting on film is completely different to acting for the stage. On stage, it's all about talent. In films it's luck. On stage, we actors have some measure of control, but on screen, the director calls the shots. You can act away for all you're worth; but if you're not in shot, forget it.

My first major film role was as Elephant Ethel, a Chinese prostitute at the Golden Grape whorehouse in *Stand Up, Virgin Soldiers* (1977). (I did say that I've played a lot of tarts in my career!) The film's tagline was: 'England expects every man to do his duty.' The women don't even get a mention . . .! It was quite fun being in this film because my make-up made me quite unrecognisable. It was a substantial if politically incorrect stab at becoming Chinese. Ninety minutes in make-up, fish-scales at the side of my eyes to drag them upwards into an Asiatic slant, very heavy red lips and two wigs, one on top of the other. Tits corralled under my chins and the tightest of revealing costumes. When I came on set, I was greeted with piercing wolf whistles and howls of desire from the crew. When I left in the studio car to return home, I was unheralded and ignored. No one had a clue who I was.

My first brush with Hollywood, though, wasn't until 1980 when I was called to audition for Warren Beatty for a small part as the secretary of the Communist Party. I didn't even have a line but it wasn't a bad role. The film was *Reds*, and it was about the life and career of John Reed, the American journalist and communist activist. Mr Beatty who, according to his biographer, has had sex with 12,775 women (a number he disputes), insisted that he could only meet me in his trailer at lunchtime. I knocked at the door, he said, 'Come in.' He then looked at me up, down, up, quite slowly and said, 'Do you fuck?' 'Yes, but not you,' I replied. 'Why is that?' he asked. 'Because I am a lesbian,' I said. He grinned and said, 'Can I watch?' I replied, 'Pull yourself together and get on with the interview.'

I rather regretted what I'd said afterwards. For one thing it wasn't accurate. We lesbians don't do anything as simplistic as 'fuck', and for another thing it brought me down to his level. But he was trying to intimidate me and I wasn't going to be intimidated. And it worked: I got the job. I'm pleased that I've met him and he's in my life – he is Hollywood royalty, after all – but Warren remains a naughty boy who needs a smack.

Reds was his obsession: he co-wrote, produced and directed, whilst also starring in it. He wanted to control every aspect of the film. During the making of it, he would go around surprising people and filming them unawares. He would suddenly call out, 'Miriam!' and, as I turned around, startled, he would take a shot of me. He did it to everyone and they all hated it but only I was prepared to call him out on it: 'Warren, please. I don't like you doing that. We are actors; we should be able to simulate whatever it is that you want us to do.' He said, 'Well, I don't have time, and a lot of you can't do that.'

One thing I noticed: when on screen, he would mouth the lines of the other actor or actress acting alongside him. He had written the script, so of course he knew it all off by heart. I found it extremely distracting and irritating: 'Warren, in that scene, were you aware that you were mouthing the words of the other characters?' 'What do you mean?' he snapped. 'Well, you obviously know all the script and when the actors are speaking their lines, you're saying them too; we can see that your lips are moving.' He did *not* like my pointing that out at all. He looked at me with real rage and said between clenched teeth, 'Thank you.' No one else had had the balls to tell him and he was furious, but he knew it was true, so he accepted it from me though he clearly hated the fact that I'd shown him up. What a good thing I did; he'd have looked a right muffin if it had gone into cinemas like that.

I mooned at him once; he completely deserved it. I can't remember why, but probably because he made Diane Keaton do fifty takes of a shot she did perfectly well the first time. Mooning is a powerful tool; a bottom is not threatening; it's rude, amusing but unmistakeable. Diane had refused his marriage proposal and he took it out on her. She was completely delightful, totally without grandeur and joined us 'contract featured extras' (that's what the small parts were called) for supper one night, with friendliness and a sense of fun. She's one of my top 'faves'.

I was busy in 1989–1990, albeit in non-starring roles: I played a realtor (an estate agent) on *Pacific Heights*, an American yuppie psychological horror film directed by John Schlesinger, starring Melanie Griffith, Matthew Modine and Michael Keaton, shot in San Francisco and Palm Springs. In 1990, I was also, as said, a late replacement stand-in for Norma Aleandro in *I Love You to Death* and was delighted to fly back to London to work with Sands Films, Christine Edzard, Derek Jacobi and an amazing British cast on *The Fool*.

In 1991 I had fun with Demi Moore on *The Butcher's Wife*; I was thrilled when she shared with me the nugget that Bruce Willis farts in bed. Then I had the pleasure of working with Kenneth Branagh and

Emma Thompson in *Dead Again*, playing a mad medium. The film had a rocky start as the crew seemed to lack respect for Ken's directing and were noisy and uncooperative. It was his first foray into Hollywood and he was determined not to be messed about so, tightening his already thin lips, he sacked the lot of them. He meant business and wanted all to see that he was fully in charge. His shock tactic worked and the film was a success. Although my part was tiny, I was always treated with complete warmth and there was a real family atmosphere on set. Ken takes the work immensely seriously but loves camp jokes; referring to the male leads of his films as 'She' which is something Americans can find confusing.

We were far from the only Brits in Hollywood of course. In Henry Selick and Tim Burton's Disney production of Roald Dahl's *James and the Giant Peach* (1996) wonderful Joanna Lumley and I played the orphan James's sadistic and tyrannical aunts, sisters Spiker and Sponge. Joanna was the beautiful, thin, nasty one with a vicious tongue, and I was the fat, vain one, who delights in admiring herself in the mirror. The film was a combination of stop-motion animation and live action scenes. Henry wasn't used to working with live actors, only with puppets and in animation. He was forever asking us to perform impossible tasks, like running *backwards* uphill. One particular stunt I remember was when he asked me to fall downstairs onto my back, and let a tarantula walk across my face. I said to Henry: 'Darling, I'll give you one shot at this.' I insisted on a stunt double to do the fall downstairs, and I spoke to the spider wrangler beforehand: 'Is he sedated?' I asked. 'Oh, yes,' said the wrangler. 'But the poison sac is intact, or he won't move.' I lay on my back, the tarantula was carefully placed on my forehead, and the cameras rolled. His little, cold feet walked slowly across my face. I gave Henry his one shot. He got it and it's in the film.

Another stunt Joanna and I did together was being winched sixty feet up, strapped back to back with ropes, standing on a tiny round manhole cover, being spun centrifugally in the air and drenched with water. Our stunt captain was called Rocky. He was a sweet guy; he knew we were scared and said, 'The minute you want to come down, just shout "Rocky" and I'll have you brought down carefully.' I think we lasted fifteen seconds, then we both screamed 'ROCKEEE!' at the tops of our voices. And down we came. Never again.

Less fun was working with Arnold Schwarzenegger in the 1999 supernatural thriller *End of Days.*[*] What a pig of a man! Although he was relatively professional with me – because he didn't fancy me – he was awfully gropey with women he was interested in. He thought a lot of himself, but I wasn't surprised: he was a bodybuilder from Austria who had gone on to become a huge star.

In my whole acting career, this is the only fight I can remember – I was playing Mabel, Satan's sister, and I had to tussle with Arnold, a prospect I did not relish, but on the day he was professional – he taught me how to punch and scratch. My main and most lingering memory of being in that film, however, is of Schwarzenegger's bottom. My character was killed by having my throat sliced by a glass table at the end. The scene ended – and Schwarzenegger farted right in my face when I was down on the floor, trying not to move. It was such a

---

[*] Not surprisingly, *End of Days* was nominated for three Golden Raspberry Awards (Razzies) – Worst Actor, Supporting Actor and Director, but 'lost' to Adam Sandler (*Big Daddy*), Ahmed Best (*Star Wars Episode I: The Phantom Menace*) and Barry Sonnenfeld (*Wild Wild West*) respectively.

noxious cloud I shouted, 'Fuck you, Arnie!' I think he did it because I'd farted on set and he felt a tit for tat was due.

It was good to be back in England for my next film and *Ladies in Lavender* was a more fragrant experience, not least because I was now working with Charles Dance, Judi Dench and Maggie Smith rather than the Terminator. 'Lavender Bags', Maggie's nickname for the film, caught on and soon that was what everyone was calling it. It was Charlie's first directing job and he was outstanding, managing to get a tenderness out of Maggie that I had never seen from her before. Like Scorsese he was subtle and polite. One day he called me over for a discreet comment on my acting; but when I turned round and caught the rest of the cast looking at us, I couldn't resist calling out: 'Charles Dance has the biggest erection I've ever felt!' Whilst it's certainly true that I know more about cocks than cooking, I would like to stress that I have no knowledge of the Dance genitals, but he undoubtedly has big feet . . .

The two dames were playing sisters who both fall in love with a much younger man who washes up on their Cornish beach one day. They were the ladies; I was their housekeeper. It was an 'apron' role – and I give good apron. I made stargazy pie and beat carpets (Judi still remembers the ferocity of my thwacks) and peeled potatoes and occasionally gave the two sisters a homely piece of my mind. (Of course, I never do any housework in real life. I was ACTING!)

In the middle of shooting, a major investor pulled out and it was touch and go whether the film could continue. When word finally got out, I volunteered to suck off the money men if it would help. There were no takers. I don't think the dames were asked.

We three shared a sitting-out space. Judi knitted or crocheted,

Maggie did the crossword. They were always welcoming, but I felt intimidated, desperately reaching for increasingly unnecessary topics to keep the conversation going. My worst blunder was when I brightly said, 'Shall we talk about acting?' After a beat of disbelief, they lowered their knitting and crossword simultaneously and stared at me. 'Oh no, let's NOT!' said Maggie firmly. They have probably never thought about it again but the memory of that moment still makes my toes curl almost twenty years on.

Although Susan kept me busy working in all these movies, in film – then as now – I have to admit I lack screen technique. In fact, it wasn't until I worked with Annette Bening (Warren Beatty is very lucky to have ended up married to her) and Jeremy Irons on *Being Julia* (2004) that I began to get an insight into the art of acting for the camera. Jeremy Irons offered me some notes and rather than resenting it, 'Who the fuck do you think you are, telling me how to act?' I just thought, 'Oh, please, yes! Thank you!'*

I don't quite remember what Jeremy's exact words were, but it was about not doing too much too quickly, to reserve something different for each take. On set, you particularly shouldn't turn fast; for film work, you have to move more slowly so the camera can capture your movements and gestures. Another nugget was, 'Close-ups are everything. Always reserve your best stuff for the close-ups, because when the character is looking into the camera, or the camera is close, that's when your audience can see inside your soul, when they look into your eyes. And don't blink.' He encouraged me to think about my

---

* He and Sinéad own a castle in Cork. One day, I hope they'll invite me there. No harm in mentioning it.

advantages and build on them. I have big, expressive eyes and my face mirrors a lot, it expresses what I feel, and that can be useful. I tend to do things to excess, so it was a valuable insight to realise that it's not a bad idea to rein it in, to save it for later. Jeremy gave me good advice – people are always more interesting if they're hiding something.

I would love to be enigmatic. It hasn't happened. My need for constant attention is the seat of the overacting. It is really saying, 'Me, me, me, me! Don't look at the others: look at me. I'm more interesting!'

———

Let me tell you about working with Streisand. The first time I met Barbra was in the early eighties when she was casting her 1983 movie *Yentl*, an adaptation of Isaac Bashevis Singer's story about a Jewish girl who pretended to be a boy in order to study the Talmud. She had spent over a decade trying to get this film made, eventually producing, co-writing (with Jack Rosenthal), directing and starring in the film herself, which went on to earn three Oscar nominations.

I had to go out to Wembley where she was holding the casting. Barbra is a prima donna, but she has a right to be, so I was fascinated and excited to have the chance of meeting and maybe working with her. My agent told me that I was being seen for the part of a village woman, so I thought about how I wanted to appear to Barbra at our meeting. I decided to look the part. I came dressed in the sort of clothes one might wear to do the housework,* and laden with two well-worn shopping bags.

---

* My normal attire although I am allergic to housework.

I went into the casting room and there was this tiny little person sitting cross-legged on a sofa, a cap completely covering her hair so you saw just her luminous face. I plonked my shopping bags on the floor and then I sat down heavily, as if exhausted by life.

Barbra was extremely friendly. She said, 'How old are you?' I said forty-one. At that she exclaimed, 'Oh, you're forty-one! *I'm* forty-one!' I looked at her and said, 'Well, fucking hell, you look fantastic for forty-one. How incredible!' I meant it, and she was quite pleased. Then she asked me what I'd been doing, so I told her about filming *Reds* with Warren Beatty. She asked what that had been like, and I said, 'Well, he's an absolute bastard.' I told her about our meeting in his trailer and the 'Do you fuck?' story. Barbra loved all that gossip. I liked her; she was a huge star even then but she was approachable and fun, and I got the part.

Yentl was primarily shot in the small town of Žatec (northwest of Prague), which filled in for rural Poland in the early twentieth century. It was the first American production that had been filmed in the Czechoslovak Socialist Republic in almost a decade and when the plane touched down, there was a mass of expectant fans thronging the airport to catch sight of Barbra Streisand. Barbra is shy and nervous; she didn't want to exit the plane with all those people there. She said to me, 'You go.' I said, 'What do you mean?' She said, 'You go out, Miriam.' I said, 'You think they want to see me? Come on, Barbra, they want *you*! You're the one they're waiting for. Now, go out there and be Barbra Streisand.'

And she did: she stood up, took a deep breath and then she visibly *became* Barbra Streisand, the world-famous actress and singer. Thus transformed, head held high and face beaming, she walked down the steps from the plane and the crowd roared and cheered in welcome. It was fascinating to observe: before she went down those steps, she had to become another person – she had to become 'Barbra Streisand'. She couldn't be the Barbra Streisand that she was, because that wasn't enough. So, she gathered herself, she summoned up her film-star image to face the curious public. I think that her authentic, natural 'self' is quite small and shy, not wanting all this fuss, but she knows she *has* to do it, so she gets out there.

When I told this story to Heather, she said that in Indonesia people *consciously* present themselves in public, so they actually have a phrase in Dutch to convey that moment when people have to gather themselves up in readiness to perform: '*drempelvrees*' – 'fear of thresholds'. That's what Barbra was doing. We all do it to a certain extent, of course. Perhaps we don't *think* that we officially present ourselves in public; we think that we are carrying our persona inside and outside – but we don't. I know that I don't: I am a different person in public – I'm more upbeat, more fun, more outgoing than I really am in private.

Yentl was Barbra Streisand's pet project – it was an important work, dedicated to her beloved dead father. She was completely in charge of every aspect of the production; every detail had to be absolutely right, and she never relaxed. Consequently, she was tough on all involved. When she came on set, she looked around with a gimlet eye, checking that everything was just so. She was hands-on and sharp as a tack. I remember her arriving on set on one occasion, spotting a book that was upside down and instantly correcting it.

The next time I met Barbra was about ten years ago, on *The Guilt Trip* (2012) in which she starred with Seth Rogen. An offer arrived at my agent from the director: 'Could you come over? It's only a day's filming and we'll give you $1,000 and a first-class trip.' I asked my agent to reply as follows: 'Thank you so much for the offer. Make it $25,000 and I might come.' And they did. They were just trying it on. They flew me out first class and it was all extremely enjoyable. Barbra said, 'Oh, I remember *you*!' It was a long time ago and she's met a lot of people, so it was nice to be remembered, but she's not really interested in other people and, at the end, she left the set without saying goodbye to anybody. She read her lines from the autocue, which had been placed behind the person she was acting with. One of the other actresses wanted a photograph with her and she refused. And I thought, 'What a pity?' The only time I've spurned a member of the public was once when, desperate to go to the loo, a lady got in my way demanding a selfie. And I said, 'Get out of my way or I'll pee on your foot.' She moved aside with some alacrity, but I felt a bit mean.

Working with Scorsese:
The Age of Innocence

O ne director I longed to work with was Martin Scorsese. In 1993, Susan told me he was casting *The Age of Innocence*, Edith Wharton's study of manners and morality in 1870s New York, and that there might be a good part for me. I was thrilled. The interview would be held at his house in Manhattan.

I flew over to New York and, one morning, took a cab to his brownstone house on the Upper East Side. I was nervous but excited. I rang the bell, a maid answered and ushered me into a library, filled not with books but with tapes and videos of films – thousands of them.

Mr Scorsese came in and greeted me. He's a short man, with a kind smile and an intense gaze. He told me why he wanted to cast English actors in the film: the novel examines American society at a particular time when judgements were made about women, often cruelly. He wanted actors who could be authentically upper class, whose speech and bearing demanded respect and who carried themselves with confidence. He felt English actors were more at home depicting 'class' – we inherit it with our mother's milk.

My part, Mrs Manson Mingott, was an elderly lady of wealth and shrewdness, a loving grandmother, but a realist, keenly aware of the practicalities of life. (She is an upper-class version of the Nurse in *Romeo and Juliet* who knows the ways of the world and respects its rules. She is the voice of Society.) I asked Mr Scorsese why he was tackling a very different milieu from the ones we associate him with – the tough gangsters and mobsters of Little Italy. He replied, 'I'm interested in brutality, which can occur in the highest as well as in the lowest.' I felt we had connected and liked each other and I got the part.

Even before filming began, I found an unorthodox way to break the ice among cast and crew. I was the last person the crew saw during the make-up and costume tests, and I came at the end of a very long day. I could see at once how tired everyone was. I did what I often do to show my appreciation: I made a small speech. I said I was grateful that they'd all been so kind to stay so late, and that the best thing I could do to show my appreciation was 'to show you my breasts'. I lifted up my top, pulled up my bra and let them have it. Their faces were a picture. No one could be serious after that. It cheered them up no end. I think most crews are breast people.

I had read the book and I saw in my mind's eye how I wanted Mrs Mingott to be. When I asked Mr Scorsese, 'Shall I be more serious?' he said, 'Absolutely not. I want her to bubble.' She was a woman after my own heart. Upon recovering from a stroke, Mrs Mingott, rather than retire into ladylike convalescence, organises a party. 'People were expecting a funeral,' she says, with a hoot of laughter. 'We must *entertain* them.'

Fat as I am, I was *not* fat enough for Mrs Mingott. So they had to design a kind of bodysuit which I was then buttoned into. It was such fun putting it on that the dressers used to compete as to who would dress me, because we all died laughing. There were definite drawbacks, however, as it meant that I couldn't go to the loo. On the other hand, I have terrible nails. I'm nervous and I bite them, so they gave me false nails as Mrs Mingott, because she wouldn't be nervous, would she?

I think it was a distinguished film, better than it was given credit for at the time. When I was introduced to Michelle Pfeiffer for the first time I said 'Hello, Fatty' because she was so beautiful, I couldn't stand it. Bless her, she laughed. And I also got to work with Daniel Day-Lewis playing Newland Archer, scion of one of the most socially prestigious families in New York. I knew Daniel's mother, Jill Balcon, because we'd both had our wombs out in the same ward, on the same day, at King's College Hospital in 1974. She was the daughter of Sir Michael Balcon, she was Jewish and read poetry superbly, a delightful woman. I also liked Daniel a lot. It was fascinating to work with him as he really does hold his character off-screen and that can be disconcerting. The rumour is that when he played Christy Brown in *My Left Foot*, for example, he expected Fiona Shaw to wipe his bottom. Rest assured, she wasn't having any of that! He's a serious man, thoughtful, but he responds to female charms and Winona Ryder and Daniel were often intertwingled in the make-up trailer. He was quite shocked when I asked him if they were sleeping together. 'You can't ask questions like that, Miriam,' he said. Well, frankly, I didn't need to.

Much of the filming was on location in Troy and Albany in New York State, where they had found an old mansion that I would have happily moved into. Because we were depicting a family of some opulence and grandeur, we were treated to lessons by an etiquette specialist: table manners, handshakes, posture were all closely moni-tored. And the 'tony' ('high-toned') accents of the characters were taught us by the greatest dialect coach in America, Tim Monich. He schooled me in the drawling accent of the period; my performance owes a great deal to his insight. The word 'pearl' was a helpful start in finding the affectation of their speech. It was almost Southern in its elongation.

As always, the delights of filming lie in the other people you work with: Siân Phillips, Richard E. Grant, Stuart Wilson, Geraldine Chaplin, Mary Beth Hurt, Alec McCowan – what a glorious bunch.

I was anxious when filming started because I admire Mr Scorsese so much, but I needn't have worried. He turned out to be a gentle soul, driven by his love of film. He was intense, focused and nervous, totally fixed on the moment. And when he gave me notes, he *whispered*: he would take me to one side, away from the others so no one else could hear what he was telling me, and he would oh so quietly murmur his directions. It was as if he *distilled* something into my ear. He is discreet in that way. And it was always right and always helpful. Indeed, it was for this performance that I won my BAFTA for Best Supporting Actress.

However many times people scorn awards and say they're nonsense (as I have done myself), when you get one it's a gorgeous feeling. I was amazed I'd been nominated, as I'd certainly never expected it and had not mounted any sort of campaign – unlike Winona, who had written personally to every member of the Hollywood Foreign Press Association, who nominate the Golden Globe awards. I admit to being irritated because she'd been nominated as a Supporting Artist and therefore in competition with me, and she should have been put in the Leading Actress category. So, she got the Golden Globes *and* the Oscar as a Supporting Artist. The studio didn't nominate me for the Oscars, but I won a BAFTA and I'm terribly proud of it.

The ceremony was held at Drury Lane Theatre. I hired a smart ball-gown for the occasion and took Stella Wilson, my dear friend and publicist, to hold my hand. It was enormous fun. I knew I wouldn't win (Maggie Smith was another nominee), so I just enjoyed being there, seeing famous people. When my category came up, I thought I heard my name, but knew it was probably because I'd hoped so much to win. I didn't get up. Stella dug me in the ribs and said, 'Go *on*, Miriam, you've won!' I was in a daze as I tottered down the auditorium. Tony Hopkins, in an aisle seat, clutched my arm as I went past and said, 'I voted for you.' I got myself onto the stage and Sam Neill was there to present me with the surprisingly heavy trophy. I made a silly speech of which I've thankfully no memory; I was totally unprepared and wobbly with happiness. I'm sure it was thanks to the LA branch of BAFTA for voting for me en masse, but when Maggie Smith came up to me later and said, 'I'm delighted you won. You deserved to,' it was one of the crowning moments of my career. I only wished Mummy had been alive to see it, but Daddy was. He was proud of me enough for two.

Romeo + Juliet

Susan arranged the interview with Baz Luhrmann. The Nurse in *Romeo and Juliet* is Shakespeare's most Dickensian character: energetic and chaotic, funny and tragic all at once. She is the tragedy's alternative comic heart. While the studio wanted Kathy Bates, Susan and I both knew *this* was the part I was born to play.

But Baz threw me a real purler when he said, 'Look, Miriam, [Australians always begin their sentences with the word 'look'], I've got a particular vision for this film; it has to be set in a totally corrupt society; I want it to have the brutality and viciousness of a vendetta. That's what I want to show, so for my purposes, it's got to be South American. Do you think you could play the role in a Cuban accent?'

My jaw dropped, 'Cuban? What do you mean "Cuban"? She was written in Warwickshire!'

He said, 'Yes, but I want her Cuban. Can you do Cuban?'

I quickly said, 'Of course I can!' No actor is ever going to say they can't do something if they really want the part. And I really wanted the part, and it turned out Baz wanted *me*. And despite the studio's strongly expressed preference otherwise, he fought for me and won.

Of course, I didn't have a clue what a Cuban accent was like – Yorkshire I can do off the top of my head, but who knows Cuban, for God's sake? I went to the brilliant dialect coach Joan Washington (Richard E. Grant's wife by the way – he's a clever lad) and got my

335

Cuban accent up to speed. It was quite a gear-shift to say these lines – '*Now, afore God, I am so vexed, that every part about me quivers. Scurvy knave!*' – so that they sounded straight out of Havana, but Joan made it work.*

———

Baz was riding high on the success of *Strictly Ballroom*, his wonderful first picture. But this was a film on an entirely different scale: the budget was over $14 million. He immersed himself in the text of *Romeo and Juliet*. He shifted Shakespeare's play from Renaissance Italy to an imagined Verona Beach, full of drug gangs, drag queens and ruthless warlords. As the lovers from two rival business families, he cast Leonardo DiCaprio, a beautiful young actor then aged twenty-one, as Romeo, and Claire Danes as Juliet. Claire's great quality was her innocence. She wasn't, apparently, Baz's first choice, but her vulnerability was heart-rending.

Romeo + Juliet was a huge and important project that became an obsession. That's how Baz works. And he knew the play back to front. I remember his saying to me when we started: 'The play is a comedy until the death of Tybalt.' So he used the brilliant computer guys, who were given their own section in the studio, to shade the tones of the sky in different scenes, to reflect the changing, darkening mood as the play develops. Baz would often leave the set to go to the computers and be shown the various options available.

---

* I eventually got to play the Nurse in broad Warwickshire in Peter Hall's production of *Romeo and Juliet* in Los Angeles in 2001.

His partner in life and in the film was Catherine Martin – CM. She's one of the most remarkable designers I've ever known; quiet and unassuming, she's not a 'performer' in any way, but her ferocious imagination is able to call into being the most amazing sets and costumes. CM is Baz's parallel genius and, to his credit, he knows that.

We flew en masse to Mexico – many of the scenes were shot at the famous Churubusco Studios.

I fell in love with Mexico City. It's a fascinating, colourful and frenetic place, full of museums, art galleries, concert halls, and a vibrant culture of music and dance and art – and superb restaurants. Fossicking around flea markets, and junk and antique shops, is one of my favourite hobbies and Mexico City is a paradise from that point of view. Everyone on set fell head over heels for Leonardo DiCaprio, from Baz to Claire. I liked him tremendously and admired his work, but luckily I was immune to his groin charms. And I think he might have found that refreshing. He preferred me as a shopping companion. Like me Leo was into bling in a big way. We'd spend hours going through the markets together – I don't know that I've ever had such fun. Now, he's grown into a fine actor but, back then, he was just a handsome boy who didn't always wash; he was quite smelly in that very male way some young men are. Sometimes he wore a dress. I said to him: 'Leo, I think you're gay.' He burst out laughing and said, 'No, I'm not, Miriam. I'm really *not* gay.' I insisted, 'I think you'll find you are.' But I was wrong. He did it to be talked about – much as I did when I smoked my pipe at Cambridge.

Of course, he had far more money than anybody else, but he was always generous. He was a kid who wanted to have his young friends around, so he invited them to come and stay at the hotel at his expense. There was a whole group of boys and girls hanging out there, laughing and joking, and he was the leader of the gang. I remember Sara Gilbert (from the *Roseanne* show) coming to stay. Claire wasn't invited to join their shindigs however; I guessed she felt a bit left out, but always conducted herself with dignity. Her parents came to Mexico and stayed for the whole shoot to keep her company. They were delightful people.

Baz was completely committed to the project and determined to get every single thing that he'd asked for on his production. For example, he had ordered a huge glass tank of water to be built at the studio at vast expense. In the film, there are some beautiful shots of Romeo and Juliet looking through that tank. One day, while they were filming, it cracked and all the gallons of water poured out. Baz demanded that it be replaced just as it was. The big cheeses from 20th Century Fox had been getting increasingly agitated about the mounting bills, and they came down to the set from LA to remonstrate: 'We just can't run with this, Baz. This schedule is way over; you're going to have to moderate your requests.' But Baz was implacable: 'If you don't give me what I want for this essential scene, I'm walking.' From that point on, he had free rein. And he was right: that scene with the tank became iconic and is what people remember.

Claire Danes was only seventeen and, just by the way she looked at him, it was obvious to all of us that she really *was* in love with her Romeo, but Leonardo wasn't in love with her. She wasn't his type at all. He didn't know how to cope with her evident infatuation. He wasn't sensitive to her feelings, was dismissive of her and could be quite nasty in his keenness to get away, while Claire was utterly sincere, and so open. It was painful to see. When I was binge-watching *Homeland* later, I kept thinking about her as that lovesick young girl. She was so guileless. Recently, I was in a restaurant and she came up to me and said, 'I hope you don't mind my saying hello. We worked together on a film once, I don't know if you remember me? My name is Claire Danes.' It was the opposite of the arrogant behaviour of some stars, and so typical of her. I have seen Leonardo since too. We met up when he was in Australia making *The Great Gatsby* and had a great chat. Also, this time he smelt divine, I'm happy to report.

It could be scary in Mexico City. Our hairdresser Aldo – six foot four and camp as a row of tents – was held up at gunpoint, forced into a taxi then taken outside the city and threatened until he went back to his hotel safe and handed over everything he had. It was highly unusual to shoot a big budget Hollywood movie there for obvious reasons, but it definitely gave the film its strong, exotic flavour and an edge. I loved the people of Mexico. I particularly loved my driver. For *Romeo + Juliet* I was assigned my own car and chauffeur – I am not always afforded that luxury; it depends how big your part is. I always think drivers are among the most important people on the set, because they're the first ones you meet in the morning and their attitude to you can make a difference to your day. My driver, Gilberto Pulido Chavez, was heavenly. I loved him; I hope I see him again.

Everyone's favourite on set was Pete Postlethwaite, who played Father Lawrence.[*] It's a difficult part, long and rambling, and you're

---

[*] In Shakespeare's play, he's Friar Lawrence of course.

never quite sure where his morality is, but Pete was magnificent. He and Leonardo became great friends. Pete insisted on text study, which wasn't Leo's favourite thing but, through Pete's influence, he became a much better Romeo. They had a beautiful relationship. That's one of my most poignant memories of that experience. Pete died too young in 2011; I honour his memory.

I didn't know that it was going to be a great film, but it is. I never watch myself until the films are long over; then, perhaps only years and years later. It's partly self-preservation, because when you watch yourself, you're only conscious of the mistakes. Other people don't see those things; they see the whole scene – the whole film – of which you are but a part. When I watch things that I'm in, I only see myself – the untruths, the fluffs, the double chin. It's not an accurate response.

When I did eventually watch *Romeo + Juliet*, I felt unusually satisfied. Even Alec Guinness, who was hard to please, told me, 'I thought you gave a good performance.' Baz helped me a lot with the part; the Nurse's bawdy humour and garrulousness is easy to portray, but she is utterly devoted to Juliet; she was her wet nurse and their bond of trust runs very deep. The Nurse is also deeply *pragmatic*. She gives Juliet what she sees as solid advice: be practical – the families don't get on; forget Romeo, don't mess about with him – you can't do that; go for a nice boy . . . take Paris! Now he's a gorgeous fella – if you go with him you'll be fine. The Nurse doesn't have the sensitivity in her soul to see how passionately Juliet is involved, and so she doesn't recognise its importance.

The Nurse loves Juliet with all her heart, but in the end she lets her down.

Alas, alas! Help, help! my lady's dead!
O, well-a-day, that ever I was born!

And thus the play's most comic character turns the love story into a tragedy. Forget the leads, it is character actors who are the true engines of plot.

Would You Like to Go to Disney World?

I've done several big cartoon features – or 'animation features', as they like to call them now – for Disney and DreamWorks. I enjoy animation because of the detail and art involved in creating a character's voice.

Mulan was made in Orlando, Florida. Of course, I had to audition for the part (that of the Matchmaker) in California. You go to the Disney lot in Burbank, which is much cleaner than some of the studios. Every street on the lot is named after a Disney character – clearly Mickey Mouse is the foundation of their fortunes.

At the audition, you're shown several drawings of the character you're attempting to voice. I love that part of it: it's creative because you're digging into your repertoire, trying to find the sound which will match the picture. It can take hours, or you can hit on it very quickly.

I was flown down to Disney World Florida to record the Matchmaker. (It was not the first time in my career I had played a matchmaker.) The animation people are totally swept up into the Disney fantasy. And they were sure I'd love a tour of Disney World before we started recording. I'm not one for theme parks, and definitely not one for queuing. I couldn't believe the long lines of people so desperate to see a mock-up of the Eiffel Tower that they were prepared to queue for two hours or more.

I explained as politely as I could that there was nothing I'd like less. Puzzled, they said, 'But, wouldn't you like to see EPCOT? It's the Experimental Prototype Community of Tomorrow. It's a technical, interesting, knowledgeable place, like an encyclopaedia of the whole world.' 'How ghastly!' I replied tersely. They thought I was joking. They just couldn't believe I didn't want to go. But when they said we wouldn't need to queue because I'd be with them, and we could go straight to the front of the line, I decided to give it a whirl.

They hurled me into a phoney space ride, which I was informed would soon be leaving Earth. They were all trying to jolly me along, cajoling me: 'Oh, come in, Miriam. You're in a flying saucer!' I stood there in this 'flying saucer', swaying and jiggling. I'm not good on 'rides', and I quickly began to feel queasy. I explained to the lady astronaut who was in charge that I needed to get off. She tried to stay in character: 'Oh, I'm sorry, ma'am, the spaceship is on its course now; we can't deviate and we're already three miles above Earth.' I felt her grasp of reality was shaky. 'If you don't let me exit immediately, I'm afraid I'm going to be sick on your foot.' Cue an immediate emergency landing and I was able to get out.

I thought it was one of the most crass and untruthful places I'd ever been to. For example, they have scaled-down replicas of all the great wonders of the world, like the Leaning Tower of Pisa, the Palace of Versailles, the pyramids at Giza and so on. But the Leaning Tower of Pisa hardly leans at all; it's just ten foot tall. Then, next door to it, they have a restaurant, selling the food produce of the place that you're looking at: a pizza restaurant next door to the Tower of Pisa; a sushi restaurant next door to a model of Mount Fuji. Visitors go in their tens of thousands and then declare they've seen the Leaning Tower. No, of course they haven't! They've seen a *reproduction* of it in the most vulgar way. I really hated it. And I said I did. I'm afraid I voiced my profound scorn for Disney World.

I did get close to a real spaceship in Florida later, when a space shuttle returned to the Kennedy Center and we were invited to watch it land. At 4 a.m. we sat in the bleachers and this incredibly tiny little space module, so much smaller than I would have imagined, came down from the sky, and then just went bump, bump, bump along the ground right in front of us, coming to rest in the field. From it, four weary white-suited spacemen emerged, a little wobbly. The shuttle didn't look like a plane, or a rocket – in fact, it resembled a large hairdryer. I couldn't believe it had made such a momentous journey.

I did find that exciting. It was real and it beat EPCOT any day. For me, reality is the key. I'm not interested in the phoney. I don't want it in any part of my life. Disney World is a colossal waste of money. I think it's shameful – the fake, giant Mickey Mouses; the awful food; the endless queues; the shops full of overpriced junk that, of course, all the children must have so the parents end up bankrupt. Everything pumped up with sugar. The world can be a shit place sometimes.

Harry Potter

I've been a working actress for over fifty years so it is a decidedly odd feeling to know that, whatever else I do, however acclaimed or successful I am, I will go to my grave best-known for being Professor Sprout. I acted in those films twenty years ago, but I am still stopped in the street by kids and Harry Potter fans all the time.

My agent Lindy called to say that I was being considered for a part in the second of the series of films and she had scheduled an interview with the director and the producer. She was really excited about it. I was less so: I have never enjoyed, and am not interested in, fantasy or science fiction: as I said, I like reality; I like the here and now.

Lindy assured me that everybody was reading the books and this could well be the next Big Thing. She was right. It's always fascinating to be part of a movement and, of course, Harry Potter did become an extraordinary wave that swept the world.

I was told that I was being seen for Pomona Sprout, the Professor of Herbology and Head of Hufflepuff House, which at the time meant nothing to me, because I hadn't read the books – and I didn't have time to read them before the interview. I know it was naughty not to have read at least *Harry Potter and the Philosopher's Stone*, the first (and shortest) book of the series, before the interview, but I wasn't going to pretend I'd read every word; I was either right for the part, or I wasn't.

I went to meet David Heyman, the producer and founder of Heyday Films, and the director, Christopher Columbus. They were charming, friendly and made me feel very welcome. I confessed that I didn't know much about the series, but if they wanted somebody who could act a teacher, there was no question that I could play the part. 'I give good teacher,' I told them. (I didn't tell them that I don't particularly like children though. That would have been unnecessary.) They gave me a page of script to read; I didn't think that it was terribly distinguished writing, in some ways it was rather banal, actually, but I read it, and that was that.

A few days later, Lindy rang in great excitement to tell me that I'd got the part of Pomona Sprout in *Harry Potter and the Chamber of Secrets*. She was cock-a-hoop. I always want to know about the money. It was £60,000, with residual payments according to the American Screen Actors Guild agreement. This was important, because it carries medical insurance with it and, at my age, I was mindful of the cost of treatment if you didn't use the NHS.

Production started on 19 November 2001 – only three days after the general release of the first Harry Potter film, which had been a huge success. It was filmed mostly in the cavernous Warner Bros. Studios, Leavesden, a converted aircraft factory and airfield just outside Watford, where they had built all the colossal sets, from the impressive Great Hall that could seat more than four hundred children, to the Dickensian Diagon Alley, home to Gringotts Bank and Ollivanders wand shop, where Harry's wand chose *him*.

We also went on location to shoot scenes: to the cloisters of Gloucester Cathedral, and to Alnwick Castle in Northumberland, which is actually Hogwarts (and was also home to the 'Black Adder' himself, Edmund, Duke of Edinburgh). Location is fun. They put me, Maggie Smith, Richard Harris, Alan Rickman, Kenneth Branagh and Warwick Davis in the same lovely hotel. At the end of a long, often freezing-cold day's filming, Richard Harris liked to be welcomed by a roaring fire in an open grate, so the hotel staff had to keep it blazing all day because no one knew what time we might finish. And Maggie Smith got the room with the four-poster bed but she thoroughly deserved it. On the first morning, when I came down to breakfast, Richard Harris was having his toast and marmalade at another table with Maggie Smith. I said to him, brightly, 'Good morning,' and he growled, 'Fuck off.' I later found out that he had leukaemia, but I didn't know that then, and I was quite offended. I kept myself to myself after that, at least where Dumbledore was concerned.

My memory of the whole experience comes in flashes of scenes and moments. In one scene we had to play Quidditch; a bizarre experience, because it was all done on 'green screen'. We had to stand stock still by a pole against a green background. We each had a number, and when somebody called your number, you had to make a gesture of some kind, as if the elusive and darting Golden Snitch was right there at the end of your nose. I was decidedly non-committal about Quidditch, the sport didn't make my blood race at all. I remember determinedly swiping with my Quidditch stick at an imaginary Golden Snitch and becoming quite red in the face and sweaty with my exertions. Funnily enough, my next door neighbour is the president of the UK Quidditch Society. He's nuts about the game, but I can't get the hang of it at all.

The fun part of it, of course, was talking to the other actors when we weren't on camera. As the cast list was a roll call of the British acting elite, it was exciting to see who was on set each day, and to say hello to everyone and have a chance to catch up with old friends, like Julie Walters and David Bradley and Robbie Coltrane, at lunch. It was always a little scary to be working with Maggie Smith. I am very fond of her, but her reputation is justified; she is a great actress with a distinguished career, she loves to laugh and she's deliciously witty, funny and jokey, but there *is* that other side to her, which is biting. The stories are legendary. When one night Laurence Olivier criticised her vowel purity, she riposted the next evening looking pointedly at his black-face Othello make-up, enunciating with punishing clarity: 'How Now Brown Cow'; and when asked if she'd like to see Fiona Shaw as Richard II she said, 'I'd rather drink ink.' Luckily Maggie and I got on. Sometimes she would say, 'Oh, come and sit with me, Miriam, I'm bored.' I would go and sit with her and we would talk and laugh. She also had a much nicer trailer than I did.

I can't say if Maggie Smith, Richard Harris, Robbie Coltrane or Alan Rickman felt similarly underwhelmed by Harry Potter, but even if the main actors didn't consider these the greatest works of literature in the world, they took the work seriously. They're rattling good stories. Even if they didn't lift cinema into another sphere, they were unbelievably popular, which is something that we actors respect. The law of the box office is the *first* law of the movie industry.

Before we did our scenes together, I was introduced to the three youngsters – Daniel Radcliffe, Rupert Grint and Emma Watson – who at that time, right at the beginning of the film series, were *extremely* young. But they were three well-brought-up, beautifully behaved middle-class children. J. K. Rowling was determined that the films be shot in England, with English actors. I think she was right; there's a knowing, precocious quality about American child actors which I find unpleasant. Our trio were refreshingly unspoiled.

All the children on set were impeccably behaved and as I can't help my foul language, they decided that every time I said 'fuck', or some other 'bad word', I had to put ten pence into a swear jar, the proceeds of which would go to the World Wildlife Fund. I don't know how much the obscenity fund amounted to in the end, but it was an appreciable sum. Daniel claimed not to remember this when we met recently on *The Graham Norton Show*; I was probably careful around him, a nice Jewish boy, but with the other kids I didn't bother.

Even though I don't go dewy-eyed over children, I've always got on with them, perhaps because they think I'm more or less one of them: I'm short, so I don't tower over them like most grown-ups, and I'm also quite naughty, which they appreciate.

Our big scene together was in the greenhouse, where Professor Sprout is teaching her second years how to re-pot mandrake plants. Pomona is responsible for growing the mandrake crop to maturity, at which point their juice is used to revive petrified victims of the monstrous, serpentine Basilisks. Those screaming mandrakes were quite frightening because, even though all the sound effects were added afterwards, the animatronic plants moved in a lifelike fashion, and actually breathed *as if* emitting an ear-shattering scream. They were vile and scary and I cringed when I had to lift one out of its pot. The animatronics are controlled by off-camera engineers, who make them seem alive. The creatures were brilliantly realised in the Leavesden workshops. The basilisk was equally horrifying and huge. I remember thinking, 'Well, that's what cinema is all about now. It's not really about acting any more.'

The mandrake lesson scene took all day. It was quite tiring, so I tried to make the kids laugh. You must do if you're working with children; and realise that they are not going to be as focused as you are. You've got to discipline them too, so I was bossy and would tell them, 'Now shut up. You've got to be quiet, or we'll never get to the end of this shot.'

I was in Australia just before the filming started, and they contacted me to say that they needed me to come over for a costume fitting and they'd fly me back the same day. I told them that that would be tricky, as I was in the middle of rehearsals for a play in Melbourne, but they insisted. They booked a business class ticket for me; I flew in, a car met me at Heathrow and took me to Leavesden. I did the costume fitting, then flew back to Melbourne the same night. All in all, I came back to England for about eight hours: I didn't even spend a night there. It was exhausting, but that's what you do for films.

I gave a good performance as Pomona Sprout; I enjoyed it and I liked the people, and it made a great difference to my career. There's no question about that – it made me famous; more famous than I ever thought possible. Fans followed me in the street; people asked to have their photograph taken – selfies, as they call them – standing next to Professor Sprout. I still have to get photographs printed to sign and send out to my Harry Potter devotees. I even get recognised abroad – sometime after this, I went to Lithuania for another film role. I was at a ballet matinee, enjoying the show and, suddenly, I was mobbed by screaming schoolchildren! Usually when Jews are mobbed in Lithuania, it's to kill them, but this was because of Harry Potter.

I don't bother to reconcile the difference; it's just how it is. I'm proud to have been a character, if not a particularly important character, in an iconic series that will mean generations of children will know who I am; I am grateful for that. The only strange thing for me is being fixed as a certain character at a certain age, as Professor Sprout – or Lady Whiteadder – despite all the hundreds of other things I've done. But it could be worse: after all, in people's heads, poor Daniel Radcliffe is forever fixed as an eleven-year-old boy. And he's a very good adult actor.

I had to wait a long time before I rejoined the world of Harry Potter. Despite the fact that my character is in every book, I wasn't asked to reprise my role until the very last film: part two of the *Deathly Hallows*. It was lovely coming back to Leavesden, finding the trio grown up and gorgeous. I palled up again with Gemma Jones, an actress I admire greatly. The superb design work on the destroyed Hogwarts took my breath away. This time, the writing had a sombre tone; I thought it was more distinguished.

My contract was only for twelve days, but they said I'd completed all that was required after nine, and sent me home. Two nights later, the *Evening Standard* Theatre Awards dinner was held. Maggie Smith was with Norma Heyman, the mother of the Harry Potter producer. She waved me over to their table. 'Miriam, why aren't you on set? I'm sitting there, talking to myself, and you're supposed to be in the scene. Where *were* you?' she enquired forcefully. I explained that I had been let go. Maggie was cross. She turned to Norma: 'Norma, I can't work like that, talking into the air. Please tell David he must bring Miriam back so I've got someone to talk to.'

The next morning, they asked me to return to the set. I said of course I will, but it means a new contract, as you sent me home. They argued backwards and forwards. But I was right; they'd let me go, so I got my new contract and more money. Bless you, Maggie. It was entirely thanks to you, and I am very grateful.

Speaking of contracts brings up another Harry Potter story which I heard directly from Alan Rickman. He played Snape, and his charismatic presence on screen made him the most powerful character in the series. The final, very long, book, *Harry Potter and the Deathly Hallows* was being filmed in two parts. Warner Bros decided that both parts would be filmed together – and therefore he was only due one fee. His gifted agent, Paul Lyon-Maris, pointed out that if the films were separately released, Warner Bros would receive two incomes. Therefore, Alan Rickman should also get two fees for appearing in both parts. Warner Bros refused and said they would have to recast. Recast *Snape*? Alan smiled. 'Go ahead,' he said. The day before shooting was due to start on part two, they agreed to pay Alan both fees. You do wonder sometimes about the mental acuity of Hollywood moguls.

When I went to the premieres, if I'm honest – which I must be – I fell asleep. I've never, therefore, watched *any* of the Harry Potter films right through; even when I have glimpsed moments on television, I'm never absolutely sure what's happening – even in the ones I'm actually in! For that reason, I can honestly say that I've never seen a single Harry Potter film and I've still never read the books. J. K. Rowling is a terrific writer. I like her detective novels under the name Robert Galbraith, and I love the fact that she has become the richest woman in Britain through books. I'm sure that Harry Potter's world is a good world. But it's not my world. It's like this: I have to step gingerly over the gap between the Harry Potter world and mine, and hope that you'll understand that despite the fact that I'm head of Hufflepuff and you're in Gryffindor, I don't really want to talk about Harry Potter any more.

Down Under

Australia first came into my life as an eleven-year-old, when Katerina Clark started at my school. Her father, the historian Manning Clark, came to Oxford on a year's sabbatical and brought his family. Through Manning, I met his friend Barry Humphries. The Clarks and Barry Humphries symbolised Australia to me for a long time.

The next manifestation of Australia was revealed at Cambridge when I met Clive James and Germaine Greer. They were dazzling. I had never heard such caustic, confident criticism, such insolent wit, such coruscating verbal dexterity in my life. It was clear English snooty attitudes towards the Antipodes had to change. Transportation had been reversed: Australia had arrived to take over the UK.

Apparently, when Sir Noël Coward went to Australia to direct his musical *Sail Away* in Sydney in 1963, he was caught in the lift with two gushing old ladies. One of them said to him, 'Oh, Mr Coward, say something funny.' He looked at her coldly and replied, 'Australia.' He wouldn't get away with that now.

Clive and Germaine were mammoth personalities: opinionated, confident and untrammelled. They were not having any of the Great British Empire; they were not going to be cowed or made to feel small by Cambridge. They knew that they were bigger than all of it, and they were. Clive was a member of the Footlights: I liked him a lot. I didn't much like Germaine. I didn't see her often, because although she was at my college, she had quickly switched to the PhD programme. There was always a slight edge to our relationship. She was competitive and I got the impression that she didn't like me because *I* was the competition. She was quite spiky and still is: she likes a good scrap. As a Shakespearean scholar and a teacher of English, she is extraordinarily gifted. We've never become friends and I'm sorry for that; I would have relished it.

Clive and I knew each other up until the time he died. He was gravely ill, but still writing – and better than ever. When I wanted to perform his poem 'Japanese Maple' in *The Importance of Being Miriam* in 2015, and asked permission, he replied, 'With pleasure.' Many years earlier, Clive gave me my first good notice in 1974 when he was TV critic of the *Observer*, and it helped. He liked my work in *The Girls of Slender Means*. I like people who give me good notices – can't help it.

Australia always seemed to be a far-away country, filled with endless possibilities. It's much grittier than America: Australia is hard and sun-baked, threatening and on a grand scale, whereas America to me represented a kind of soft entertainment. After falling in love with Heather, it became clear that Australia was a country of impressive people, different from the English; tougher, unadorned and somehow – as Heather indicated – more honest. Some Australians think of England as the home country, and that they belong to England, but many other Australians feel that England has exploited Australia long enough and the time has come to pull the plug. Heather is definitely in that category – the 'blessed Commonwealth' was not at all the way she saw things. I realised that Australia could be quite a 'bolshy' place, a nation of people with unusual attitudes, possibly slightly uncouth. They had a different sheen from the English: Australians don't bother with superficial politeness. They dislike 'bullshit'. They provide more honest social encounters, although you can find the most absurd pretensions in the suburbs.

I made my first trip to Australia with Heather to meet her parents in 1980. She has a sister, Sandra, who had disappeared from the family. This was a source of sadness for Heather. There had been a rift: Sandra had been going to get married, but, at the last minute, she called it off because she'd fallen in love with somebody else. Heather remembered Sandra throwing the wedding cake out of the car window; it rolled down the road in front of them like an iced spare tyre. There was a huge row, Sandra didn't want to be in touch with her family, and so she left the continent and went to live in California. I was curious to see where Heather came from, who her people were.

My first greeting on landing in Australia was when the immigration clerk said to me, painfully slowly, 'Can . . . you . . . read?' I looked at her, and thought, 'What the fuck is this all about?' I said, 'Y-e-s,' quite slowly. She had in her hand some documents and, pointing to one of them, she said again, 'Can you read?' 'Yes,' I replied, again slowly. 'Can you read *this*?' I looked at the document and said, 'Yes!' Then I got a bit irritated and said, 'Look here, is there a problem? I've actually got a degree in English from Cambridge University!' The woman took a step back and said, 'Ahh, sorry, miss. You haven't signed your form. I thought you was an *ethnic*.' That was my welcome to Australia. And of course, she was right, I AM an 'ethnic'.

We went to stay with Heather's parents, in the entirely invented city of Canberra. It had been designed for civil servants to bring up their children in safety and comfort, by an American architect, Walter Burley Griffin. Heather's father, Traill, was the retired professor of mathematics at the military college of Duntroon (Australia's Sandhurst), a pleasant, cultivated man; her mother, Beatrice, always called Bea, was known as a 'party girl'. I didn't know then that she was an alcoholic. I saw no signs of it, but her habit had caused havoc in the family. They had no idea about our relationship. I had told my parents that I was a lesbian, but Heather's parents didn't have a clue – and this visit was definitely *not* a 'coming out' occasion. Heather had impressed on me that that was *not to happen*. Indeed, when her mother did find out, some years later, she was furious; she felt I'd seduced her daughter and taken her away. Consequently, relations between her and me were icy for a *very* long time. To Heather's mother and father, therefore, on this first visit to Australia, I was just Heather's 'friend'. I had my own room, and they were terribly nice to me.

I loved Australia. I felt at home immediately – I didn't have to think about it at all. The first thing that strikes you is the quality of the light: more blinding than you can imagine. It simply astonishes you. It's so bright that most people's eyes are crinkly from continually squinting against the glare of the sun. And then there's the mind-boggling vastness of the sky, bigger than any sky I'd ever seen.

After our stay in Canberra, we spent some time in Sydney with friends of Heather's. Sydney was glorious then; it hadn't become too crowded, dirty and busy like it is now. Recently, I was trying to cross the Harbour Bridge from the Eastern Suburbs to the North Shore. The psychological divide is similar to that in London between north and south. There are pockets of Jews right across Sydney, and I've got relatives on both sides of the bridge. My cousin, Ann Sarzin, a renowned cook, had invited me for supper on the North Shore; I was desperate to eat her famous fried fish but I couldn't get across the bridge. I waited in the traffic jam for two and half hours, and then I went home in despair. After that, I fell out of love with Sydney.

Back when I was young, Australia felt full of promise, excitement and confidence. It was all the positive things that you could imagine. The people looked beautiful; all the young Australians were physically gorgeous, blond and blue-eyed and slender and athletic. And Sydney was gay-friendly; that's an understatement. I'd never seen such outrageous campery, such glittering, gorgeous drag queens shopping in the streets around Kings Cross.

In Australia, I know that Man is young, and it is Nature that's old and powerful. You feel the power of the land in the red rocks, you marvel at the huge, twisted trees. When you're in Europe, by contrast, you feel that Man is ancient and has created timeless works of art and built great churches and cities, that Man has been around for a long time. Not in Australia; it's another dimension of existence, and it's had a profound effect on me.

I get angry now when I see unchecked racism in the current right-wing government. They are following the sad trends in the rest of the world. The socialist legacies of Gough Whitlam and Bob Hawke are being whittled away by greed and corruption.

I returned to Australia in 1984, when I brought *Gertrude Stein and a Companion* to the Sydney Festival and I realised this was a place I wanted to know much better.

In 1993, I bought a two-bedroomed, Federation semi in Bondi, a sweet little bungalow with pressed tin ceilings and a mantel over the fireplace, and then in 1998, after I worked on *Babe*, Heather and I and her sister, Sandra, built our dream home in Robertson, NSW, where the film was made. It's a country town, unspoiled and genuinely rural. We clubbed our finances together and hired an architect, Mark Jones.

Yarrawa Hill is our dream home. It's built on steel poles, with glass instead of bricks, and the material much used in Australia, Colorbond, which is painted corrugated steel and looks terrific. We furnished it with antique Indonesian furniture and had the best fun going to Indonesia and finding old things in warehouses and getting them shipped over. Heather and I have gone back and forth – until the 2019 pandemic locked us in and curtailed all movement.

On Australia Day in 2013, I became an Australian citizen. I stood, with about a hundred other people by the lake in Canberra, and heard my (then) prime minister – Julia Gillard – say, 'This is your new country. You will never want another. Welcome to citizenship. Welcome to Australia. Welcome home.' I blew a grateful kiss at the PM. It was a day of supreme happiness and real joy. It also made me realise how little I'd seen of the real Australia.

I wanted to travel outside my little bubble of people who think like me and sound like me and so, in 2019, as an overweight, unfit, but extremely gung-ho seventy-eight-year-old, I embarked on a 10,000km, two-month journey across the country to make a documentary, something I love doing.

For *Almost Australian* I clambered into a camper van and set off in search of the heart of this vast nation. I spoke to struggling farmers affected by drought; I met First Nation elders, indigenous activists, off-grid nomads and transgender Tiwi islanders, and spent time listening to the stories of refugees from Afghanistan and Myanmar. I tackled the Australian concept of 'mateship', visiting a trucker stop where I joined the blokes for a pint and the footie on TV; then on to

Alice Springs itself, reputedly the lesbian capital of the world. When I first went to the Alice, it was a hardy, pioneer kind of town. First Nation people lay in the street, drunk. They were invisible – people just stepped over them. And now it's lesbians all over the place! I also ventured out of my comfort zone: I got quite vocal at an Aussie Rules football match; I tried fiery new cuisines and even stronger drinks; my public dislike of children was challenged, when much to my shock I met a couple of kids I actually liked; and if that wasn't enough, I even went camping for the very first time and had to handwash my humungous navy-blue knickers, a spectacle that was gleefully captured by my cheeky cameraman.

I learned a lot in making that series, particularly about the troubled relationship between white Australians and First Nation people. Australia is a complicated country, with allegiances to England but strongly influenced by America, and it's not going in the direction that I want. The Australia that the visionary Labour prime minister Gough Whitlam envisaged is the Australia that I love. I was absolutely shattered when the Liberals won the 2019 federal election. I voted in London at the Australian Embassy; I was so sure that Labour would make it. It broke my heart when their defeat became clear.

I fear the country is in danger of becoming a colony of America, just like us. One only has to look at the rise of the right wing and the growing cruelty to migrants. When I first came to Australia in the 1980s, it wasn't like that. I'm also critical of the wholesale import of American trends and culture, most particularly on Australian TV – I want more Australian content. I want to see more of the highly gifted, home-grown Australian artists and actors: they're not being given a fair suck of the sauce bottle.

When *Almost Australian* was recently broadcast, I was interested in the reaction. Some of my observations on the documentary ruffled feathers Down Under, and rightly so. I'm quite aware of the uproar in Australia when I make any negative comment – Australians are sensitive to criticism, particularly from the English. Understandably people say, 'Who the fuck is she – she comes in, builds a house, enjoys it, then trashes the place?' But I want Australia to be better. And Australia is a country that can be improved. Unlike England, it's still got energy – it can go down a different, better path.

A New Habit

Every actress tries not to be typecast but I've played a lot of whores and matchmakers in my time. The nearest I'd got to the other side of things was in 1980, when I played an Egyptian gynaecologist in Mike Newell's first film, *The Awakening*, with Charlton Heston, a lovely big boy. They had to dig a trench for him when we were in the same shot. He was too tall! But I dropped the forceps on the floor when trying to deliver Jill Townsend's baby.

Undeterred, for years I had been a fan of *Call the Midwife*, the long-running BBC series adapted by Heidi Thomas from the memoirs of Jennifer Worth, about her days in the East End of London in the late fifties; the acting was of a high order, the stories were gripping and the attention to period detail formidable. It was exactly the kind of show I loved. I could see myself in it as a Jewish grandmother living in Poplar, a throwback to my immigrant roots. I knew my agent had mentioned me to them, to no avail. Every time I appeared on a TV talk show, I'd look straight at the camera and say, 'Please cast me in *Call the Midwife*.' Not a dickie bird.

Then one day, I went on the ITV programme *This Morning* and encouraged by the skilled and charming hosts, Phillip Schofield and Holly Willoughby, I made my plea again. I do like Holly and Phil. To my joy, my agent got an offer a few days later. But I was not to be a Jewish grandmother; quite the reverse!

To my amazement, I was to play Mother Mildred, a loquacious, energetic senior nun, who was bringing orphan babies to England from Hong Kong. I am not a lover of babies: I never wanted children, which was lucky because my womb and I parted company in 1974 and that was the end of that. But my first entrance to Nonnatus House was to be with an armful of babies, lovely to look at, but heavy to carry and often uncooperative.

My feelings about children haven't altered; I'm constantly warned to keep my language pure when the under tens are on set. It was both a delight and a relief when Mother Mildred became Mother Superior and had slightly less to do with babies and more with being a fount of irascible wisdom at the service of the order. It was the beginning of a delightful professional experience which is still continuing. I hadn't known Jenny Agutter, who is the mother of the company. She welcomes all new cast members with warmth and humour.

Call the Midwife was a reunion with Judy Parfitt (Sister Monica Joan), whom I first met in Los Angeles at Eric Matthews' dinners in the Valley. She is a larky girl when not dressed as a nun – and politically miles away from me. Usually I steer clear of the Brexit divide, but Judy is different; I have to have her in my life. She's eighty-five and from Yorkshire. More active than I am, sharp as a button, she continues to delight me both as herself and when she enters her character, playing with compassion and gentleness the ageing nun the nation has taken to its heart.

I based my character of Sister Mildred on a nun I met as a child in Oxford. There was a Carmelite convent just around the corner from 'the hovel' and I often met the two lay sisters, Sister Anthony and Sister Aloysius, on my daily walk to school. Curious about their lives inside the order, as was my wont, I had struck up a relationship with Sister Anthony.

One day, she told me she had mentioned me to her Mother Superior and then asked if I would like to meet her. I was only nine and said I'd better ask Mummy and Daddy first. My parents agreed and one afternoon I was invited for tea at the convent at four o'clock.

Carmelites are strict, closed-order Catholics, not like the Anglican Nonnatus House. I was led into a small room with a set of bars right across one wall. After a few moments a lady in full habit entered and sat down on a chair behind the bars. I moved my seat closer to see her better and we started to talk. She was totally practical and completely normal, a middle-class lady, very professional, like a lawyer or counsellor, with considerable authority. She told me she came from Liverpool and had been to the Liverpool GPDST High School, the sister school of my Oxford High.

I noticed her shoes were rather strange and I commented on it. She told me that the nuns of the order made all their own. I laughed and showed her my smart Clarks sandals; 'I couldn't make shoes for anything,' I told her. I remembered that because I thought it was the weirdest thing. But she herself was utterly direct, down to earth, without any sort of spiritual nonsense. I never forgot her and I modelled my Mother Superior on her.

I turned up to the first day of filming with a bag of my snack of choice – whole, raw Spanish onions. When I first peeled then chomped into one, everyone grimaced, imagining, I suppose, how ghastly it must taste. But I just munched away. I couldn't understand what all the fuss was about. I have eaten raw onions all my life – I like the taste. I like radishes too. The sharper the better in my book. They make my eyes water but I don't mind (same with curries). I don't know if it's good for the constitution or not, but it's sensible in winter because my onion habit tends to keep people away from me, so I catch fewer colds. True, I'm slightly less popular in the make-up trailer.

I had to be taught everything about Christianity and midwifery. Ann Tricklebank, our endlessly conscientious producer, arranged for on-set 'nun tutorials'. Being Jewish, I didn't know how to cross myself properly. Mummy had stopped me from reading the New Testament. Plainsong was quite beyond me, so I mimed when we were in chapel, just like when I was on Broadway. And getting dressed was a marathon; who knew that under those dark blue habits there were so many layers of costume? Thank goodness I was allowed a dresser; she knew which bit went where. The programme is scrupulously accurate in every department. I'm still wearing the wedding ring on my right hand (nuns are the brides of Christ) so that I'm ready for the call when it comes again.

As the benignly bossy Mother Mildred, I did shake things up a tad at Nonnatus House. For a start, I asked Ann to provide a loo on wheels, close to set, to placate my frequent micturition. I also commandeered handyman Fred Buckle's van – Ann immediately understood I was unlikely to 'do' bikes like the young nuns and midwives. Anyway, I think a Mother Superior would travel around the Poplar cobbles more decorously than that – and I couldn't ride a bike in a nun's habit without breaking my neck; it's a long time since Cambridge when I cycled everywhere.

A particularly memorable episode was the Christmas one in 2019. Usually, we shoot at Longcross Studios, an old speedway test track in Surrey, where Nonnatus House has been cleverly adapted from a lovely Edwardian manor house. Heidi had thought of Malaysia as the location for this Christmas special. But probably for logistical reasons, it was moved to the Isle of Harris in the Outer Hebrides. She is nothing if not flexible! That was fine, I love Scotland and we were going in March, far from the months of the midges.

What no one had reckoned on were the freak storms and cloudbursts which descended. The wind really whipped across the island, and the frigid temperature made it feel like December. Acting is hard at the best of times, but dripping wimples proved a definite health hazard. A sodden habit is a particularly dreary garment to spend the day in. One of the many places we shot in was a church at the top of a steep hill, looking out to sea. The tempest roared, the rain poured, as I struggled up the path fully costumed, only to arrive in the sublimely beautiful but *freezing* church. I've only been colder when I walked along the Great Wall of China one December.

In another scene, the midwives visit the late-Neolithic Callanish Stones but we could hardly see in front of our own faces for the howling storm. None of us could hear the other speaking, so Jenny Agutter and I had to look carefully to see if the other's mouth was still moving before we spoke the next line through chattering teeth. I don't think I've ever laughed as much at being so uncomfortable for such a long time – not a loo in sight. However, after work we stayed in unusual luxury at Amhuinnsuidhe Castle. This amazing place was built in 1865, but the dining hall fulfilled every fantasy of gracious living and for a week we midwives, erstwhile of Poplar, thoroughly relished the delicious food and frequent drams served to us after work. One teatime, I asked for an onion with my Welsh rarebit and they just sprinkled bits on top. I had to explain I wanted a whole one, raw, on the side. Happily, such was the level of service at this extraordinary retreat that the chef complied with alacrity and good grace. (I discovered that a previous chef working there had been my darling Rosemary Shrager from *The Real Marigold Hotel*.)

It was a glorious, if rain-soaked, week and Harris is the most beautiful place I've ever been to. Despite the appalling weather, when you're with good people the sun always shines and every one of my dear midwives warms my atheist soul.

Being Jewish

W hat is an English Jew? And does it matter? It's no exaggeration to say that every day of my adult life I've thought about the Holocaust. When I was seven years old, my father's refugee patients would show me the numbers on their arms. 'What is that?' I asked them. I don't remember their answers; they said nothing that stays in my mind or hinted at horror. But, of course, inevitably, I learnt as I grew up about the camps, the Nazi infamy, the lines at Auschwitz where Mengele made his selections of left and right. It's part of my life. It fuelled my genealogical hobby, now an obsession. It has also coloured my feelings about the world that let it happen, and makes me sharp at spotting antisemitism, even in a mild form. (Thought: is there a 'mild' form?)

I feel intensely Jewish. It's the first adjective I apply to myself, it's how I introduce myself to new people. I watch the reaction, always primed to notice a flinching, an embarrassed smile, or a little laugh, unusually high-pitched. It is my belief that the English don't like Jews and never have. After the Second World War, it wasn't possible to *express* antisemitism, but some eighty years on, once again, antisemitism has become quite common. Most English Jews (and we number less than 0.57 per cent of the population) are law-abiding, middle-class and fit seamlessly into the suburban world. Yet, because of Israel, because of Netanyahu and the way he's behaved, the band-aid over antisemitism has been ripped off. Watching events in Israel, people feel that it's all right now to voice antisemitism. Violence against Jewish graves and shops and synagogues is on the rise, and so I have become more strident in talking about being Jewish, forcing people to absorb it, challenging them to deny their prejudice.

I'm militantly secular – religion has caused so much horror in the world – but I believe in tradition; I want to honour the past, honour my parents, my ancestors and all those who died, and so I follow many of the Jewish practices. To this day, I am a member of two *shul*s (the Yiddish word for 'synagogue') in South London: an Orthodox synagogue in Streatham with friendly Rabbi Myers, plus I can't resist the delightful Chabad rabbi of Battersea, Rabbi Moshe Adler, a young American, and his family of three children and sweet English wife, who wears a *sheitel.*[*] They have treated me with warmth and frequent offers of hospitality, as I am a woman alone – most people are in couples.

I fast on Yom Kippur (and always have), maintain the dietary restrictions during Passover (no leavened bread etc.), and have never eaten bacon, shellfish of any kind, ham or pork in any guise – not even at a restaurant. I may not believe in God, but I'm very proud of my roots: they nourish me. I'm fascinated by the pull of Judaism and its culture – the food, the jokes, the vitality, the suffering, the guilt and the history – it's all part of who I am and what I've inherited. The fact of my being Jewish informs the whole of my life. It informs connections with people. More than anything else, being Jewish informs my actor's aesthetic: emotion is always trembling on the brink for every

---

[*] A wig – Orthodox Judaism forbids a married woman to show her natural hair to anyone other than her husband.

Jewish woman. It comes with the territory, and it's very useful as I don't have to delve to find joy, despair, laughter and tears.

Why, being so militantly atheist, do I want to be Jewish? Why do I still belong to a synagogue everywhere I live? In LA, I was a member of Beth Ohr, a liberal reconstructionist synagogue in the Valley with the most delightful rabbi. Straight out of Central Casting. Rabbi Michael Roth was an elderly Hungarian exile, with a wise face and a strong accent. When I confided in him about my lack of faith, he said, 'Miriam, don't worry, I don't know if I believe in God, either. Who knows? But for me, it's better that I do, so I carry on.' That's unusual; I don't know any other rabbi who would say that. He was insightful and compassionate. He had a wisdom and open-mindedness that was both reassuring *and* illuminating. That's what you hope for in a rabbi.

As a secular Jew, I can't accept the beliefs but I love the rituals. I asked Rabbi Adler to bless a *mezuzah* for my front door: a piece of parchment inscribed with a specific Hebrew prayer from the Torah, enclosed in a slim, rectangular, decorative case and affixed to the doorpost of Jewish homes to fulfil the *mitzvah* (Biblical commandment) to 'write the words of God on the gates of your house'. As you go into your house, you're supposed to put your hand on it and kiss it. (If you watch the TV series *Shtisel*, you'll be very familiar with this tradition.) I wanted to demonstrate to the outside world that I was a Jew.

My parents were, of course, believers. They were not Orthodox, but they were observant: Judaism was part of the armour that helped them to deal with the problems of the world. We belonged to the Oxford Hebrew congregation and I attended the synagogue school, where I learnt about the Torah, and Hebrew. A lot of the members of the synagogue were London refugees like my parents, and yet the Jewish community in Oxford was not a warm one. It was a curiously split community, mirroring the rest of the city: you had the Jewish intellectuals, the dons, people like Cecil Roth who was a very important member of the synagogue, but the actual president was a trader in the market called Mr Bloom. Indeed, snobbishly, my mother regarded a lot of the Jews of Oxford as rather common people.

We had Friday night dinners at home. Mummy sometimes lit the Sabbath candles. We didn't observe the Sabbath the way that really Orthodox people do, so it was like a normal Friday night and Saturday in every respect – we listened to the radio, went shopping, or I went out with friends – and we could ring our doorbell whenever we wanted.

Shabbos lunch was usually a roast chicken, and Mummy also fried fish in olive oil and matzo meal, instead of the more usual flour which non-Jews use. Matzo meal is made of very finely ground crackers – if you ever fry fish, you should always use either matzo meal, or matzo flour, not real flour, because it's much finer. I like chopped liver, smoked herrings, smoked salmon. And cheesecake. And something that Mummy used to do called *gribenes*: scraps of fatty chicken, and the skin fried up to a crisp in olive oil with onion and garlic and bits of fried egg and fried vegetables – it's absolutely delicious. So, in that sense, being Jewish was part of our lives. I am neither a good nor frequent cook – but if I do cook, it will always be something Jewish – soup or chicken. I'm primarily a culinary Jew.

I have always relished being Jewish. We went to synagogue on the three holy days in the Jewish calendar: Yom Kippur which is the Day of Atonement and the holiest day of the year; Rosh Hashanah, the

New Year; and Passover. Passover was the most important event of the year. Passover celebrates the deliverance of the Jewish people from slavery in Egypt and is the equivalent of Christmas, and a similarly family orientated occasion, but with less over indulgence and slumping – it's a much more active, communal event. If you like – and if you believe – Passover is a party with God attending.

My friends and cousins invite me for Passover. Everybody wants to make it festive and delightful, the food to be as good as possible: along with the ceremonial fare, there's a feast, usually involving matzo ball soup, *gefilte* fish, baked salmon, roast beef, or some delicious chicken recipe, accompanied by all manner of scrumptious vegetable side dishes. And, of course, there's invariably a choice of several exquisite puddings.

During lockdown, I joined a Zoom *Seder*, but it's not the same, because it is in essence a very intimate, sharing, joyous event. There are prayers throughout the meal, interspersed with stories and lots of songs; you clap, it's gay, it's happy. Everybody present at the *Seder* is supposed to contribute (it's difficult to be a passive Jew), and the youngest child at the table asks four questions. The first is, 'Why is this night different from all other nights?' Another is, 'Why on this night do we lean, and on all other nights we don't lean?' to imply that we are safe together, we can relax. If a rabbi is hosting the *Seder,* they invite each of the guests to talk about something meaningful that's happened to them in the last year. Even though I'm a secular Jew (and now most Jews in England are secular), we draw on the memory of rabbis of the past and on our joint history. We remember the *shtetel*s, where our ancestors came from, where people eked out an existence, yet they always celebrated Passover.

When the communities were destroyed during and after the Second World War, those who survived would club together, find each other wherever they were, and write a memoir of their village, a Yizkor book. They listed the names of the people they remembered; what the main street was like, the people in the shops and what the shops sold; what market day was like; and the name and description of the landlord who owned most of the property in the area. They tried to recreate, in these memory books, everything that had been destroyed, the world that they knew as children that had now been lost for ever.

They couldn't bear the thought that all the people they had known had disappeared without trace, and nobody knew their names, and nobody knew that they lived, they were just obliterated. That's what these books are to prevent. The Jews have become the people of these books of memory, and in nearly every village, or *shtetel*, that was destroyed, even if there was only one person left, they would create the memory book.

Through the Jewish Genealogical Society, I organised the collection of money for the Grodno (my paternal family town) memory book to be translated. That's how a lot of people find out about their ancestors; you look up the ancestral village online and see that there is a memorial book for that place. In England, you have parish registers; but the Jewish people who lived in those villages – and there were millions of them – are gone: the towns laid waste, the inhabitants murdered, even the gravestones of their dead destroyed. Those who were not Jewish remained, often annexing the properties that were left by the Jews. When you visit those little towns now, some of them are terrified because they think you've come to take back their houses.

We Jews have always been outsiders. That gives you a certain energy and also, of course, a certain insecurity. Most Jewish families are traditionally very close-knit, something the Jewish community encourages. But now people are 'marrying out', as we call it, and there are fewer and fewer of us. Under threat, we Jews tend to stick together in order to try to preserve a Jewish community and its traditions. There are many Jews who don't know anybody who *isn't* Jewish. They interact with other people in the course of their day-to-day lives, but the people who come to their homes, who they count as friends, who they go to football matches with, who they play bridge with, are all Jews. That's why many Jewish people send their children to a Jewish school. They don't want them to be assimilated – whereas my parents *did*. Thanks to my school and my university, my friends come from all walks of life. In that sense, I grew up with one foot in each camp.

The insularity of some Jewish communities, of course, is a reaction to our people being destroyed. Christians are under threat in many places, I know that, but they haven't been under threat in the way that the Jews were. Jewish people have always felt that others wanted us dead and 'disappeared'. Why Hitler, in particular, wanted that I don't know. And millions joined him in his crusade to eradicate Jews from Europe. Like most Jews, my family lost relatives in the Holocaust. It's something I cannot forget, it's there all the time. People were murdered in their millions because they were Jews, and you can't 'get over' that: you can't forget it. It has been a shadow across my entire life, and I think nearly all Jews would say that. Every time I go in a train, every time I have a shower ... I think about those people, and I am torn with horror and rage and pity for them.

When we were filming *Yentl*, Barbra Streisand arranged a coach trip to Theresienstadt. It was the most sobering and overwhelming experience. Theresienstadt had been a concentration camp, not an extermination camp. It looked like an out-of-season caravan park: a memorial to the banality of evil. There was nothing there that could alarm you or make you realise how people suffered there. In fact, I later found out that some of my relatives had died there.

Much, much later on, about five years ago, I went to Auschwitz. It made me extremely angry and feel helpless at the same time. Of course, like Theresienstadt, the long barracks, where people were so cruelly housed, were all cleaned, but the manifold tragedies that had occurred there weigh on you. It was a hateful place. It left me feeling as if I didn't want to laugh ever again. There are collections of hundreds of thousands of suitcases and umbrellas, and shoes – millions of pairs of shoes – behind windows, and you realise that each is a skeleton of a person: a human being wore those shoes and carried that case and that umbrella, and within hours of arriving at Auschwitz, they were just ashes. It was an efficient death factory.

It had also been made into a tourist destination. People were eating ice creams and looking at the death chambers, walking around taking snapshots of each other. 'There's no business like *Shoah*-business,' as they say. I wanted to scream at them, 'My cousins died here. How would you like that?' It is as if the horror of what happened doesn't sink into people, they try not to see it, but they *must*: that's why it's there – for us to be aware, and not let it happen again. This is what can result when some people become 'less important', when it's frighteningly easy to take life away.

Neither Hitler, nor the many previous centuries of pogroms, succeeded in our eradication, however, and that's one of the reasons why I'm so outspoken. I push being Jewish down people's throats; it's my way of saying: 'Hitler didn't win, I'm still here and I'm still saying

I'm a Jew, so you *can't* ignore me. *I'm here.* I can't let it be. Why should I let it be when, in my lifetime, six million people were murdered, because of it? How can I hide my head and duck down behind the parapet?

So much energy has been focused on the concept of Israel, the return to Zion, the 'Homeland'; and when people are trying to destroy you – and not just trying but succeeding in destroying you – you cling on to the chance of life and hope, and a continuation of the family and the people and the nation. But when the Zionists reclaimed Israel, they didn't take into account the Palestinians who were already living there. What were they supposed to do? Were they supposed to disappear? That's where, as a people, we Jews fell down, and where Hitler won. He changed us from being a compassionate nation into a destructive, uncaring and inhumane one. The tragedy of the Palestinians is just as much the tragedy of the Jews.

Choosing My Side

Since I met the Hodgkin family, I've always been political – now more than ever. I thought I was a middle-of-the-roader, but I veer towards the left. Since Brexit, politics consume me; I never thought that I would feel so alienated from my own people, from my country.

We have now in power a government, chosen by a relatively small number of people, of almost unparalleled incompetence, whose probity is in doubt, whose lack of diligence has killed thousands of people, and whose majority in Parliament prevents their being held to account.

Like Alastair Campbell, in his recent article in the *New European*, I am puzzled by the lack of *rage* in the country. Racial prejudice fuelled the Brexit blindness. And my heart bleeds for Britain, particularly for the young. We are part of Europe; the knaves who bamboozled the nation into thinking otherwise will deserve the damning verdict of history, but I won't be there to see it. This is truly Scoundrel Time.

I don't look back on the British Empire with any sense of pride. We were taught at school that the Empire was marvellous, giving India trains and cricket and saving the savage Africans from the eternal fires of damnation and all that – and that was simply wrong. Some British people don't like facing the truth of our colonial past and that's part of the problem; they don't want to be re-educated about our long history of exploitation and cruelty. Those people have always thought of England as the best country in the world. Well, it isn't. It was cruel and greedy and unjust, much like the rest of the world, and the aftermath of Empire has given rise to a hateful legacy of racism.

The English are not open to the outside, or to outsiders.

My parents were good people, but they were conservatives. They believed in Winston Churchill and thought Ernest Bevin was a terrible man – they thought he was an antisemite, and that may have been true. They weren't extreme right-wingers but *always* voted Tory. They brought me up to be a good Tory too.

After spending so much time in the company of Liz Hodgkin's large, vociferous and opinionated household, I challenged my parents – although I knew they wouldn't change. As soon as I could vote, I voted Labour and with only one exception, on which more later, I've been a Labour voter all my life.

I engaged in politics when I was at Cambridge. I was active in the Anti-Apartheid Movement, even more so than in nuclear disarmament, which was the major 'cause' of my generation. The appalling injustices and deliberate cruelty white South Africans imposed on their black countrymen was what first ignited my activism. Even my parents agreed with me about that. Our cousins from South Africa had stayed with my grandparents before Mummy got married. She remembered the way they threw their clothes on the floor, expecting a servant to pick them up.

I have always felt an outsider – as did my parents, and they passed it on to me; it's one of my most powerful emotions growing up. I felt I knew well what it would be like to be black and to be shut out from the world that everybody else was enjoying. The unfairness of the apartheid regime enraged me and that's why I volunteered to work in the campaign office in London and went to demonstrate outside South

Africa House, something I did many times. Many years later, after Mandela had been released, Antony Sher and I were invited to a function at South Africa House; it was strange to be walking as a guest into the place that had become a symbol of everything I hated.

After Cambridge, as soon as I got my first professional acting jobs in theatre, I became a member of the actors' union Equity. When I first joined the BBC Radio Drama Repertory Company, I was elected to the audio committee and served on it for over thirty years. Eventually, I was elected to the Council. Since then, I have always been an active and vocal participant in my trade union.

At that time, in the late sixties and throughout the seventies, Equity was sharply divided on how best to fight apartheid. A growing list of international playwrights, including Daphne du Maurier, Samuel Beckett, Tennessee Williams, Muriel Spark and Arthur Miller signed a declaration through the Anti-Apartheid Movement in London, refusing performing rights for their plays to all theatres in South Africa where discrimination was practised on grounds of colour.

I agreed, I felt that artists and sports people should *refuse* to work there – we had to name and shame the South African government by boycotting all commercial artistic engagement in the country.

As an Equity Council member, I attended all the meetings. Vanessa Redgrave was never a member of the Council, but she and her brother, Corin, regularly spoke at the annual general meetings with fire and fluency – both superb speakers without notes. I first worked with Vanessa in 1972. Ted Heath was in Number 10; in Equity likewise, the right wing was in power: people like Marius Goring and Nigel Davenport and Leonard Rossiter. Leonard was a bastard: a good actor, but a nasty, spite-driven man. With all those right-wing actors flexing

378

their muscles, the Workers Revolutionary Party faction were the great opposition, and so Vanessa became an important element in the deliberations.

Vanessa was quite retiring, except when there was anything political going on, and then she would harangue you from morning till night. I didn't know her well but, intoxicated by her articulate conviction, I started to join her at the WRP meetings.

When you were interested in politics in those days – and I suppose for some people it is still the case – you had to go to meetings. You wanted to stand up and be counted, and I was no different. I soon became a signed-up member, though whether I joined the WRP *literally* because of Vanessa, I don't know.

Not long after I became a member, the WRP annual summer camp was held in an enclosed field by the Blackwater estuary in Essex; naturally I went along. Gerry Healy, the leader of the WRP, was an unpleasant, devious chap; he was dangerous in fact. There were talks and discussions in a big tent and Gerry would lecture us all about how to move England to the extreme left. I'd never been to that sort of political meeting before, and it was not appealing. Most of the other camp attendees clearly found it rousing: I found it threatening and nasty. I realised then that this wasn't my idea of a left-wing revolution, but the summer camp was in a beautiful place, and Vanessa and people like Frances de la Tour were there, so I stayed. In the morning, I thought I'd go for a walk with a chum. When we arrived at the fence enclosing the camp, a man with a gun was guarding the gate. He said, 'Where do you think you're going?' I said, 'For a walk.' He said, 'Oh, no. You can't leave.' I said, 'What do you mean we can't leave? We want to go for a walk.' 'Well, you can't. That's against the rules,' he said. 'No one can leave the camp.' And he put his hand firmly on his gun. 'All right, love, keep your hair on,' I said and we went back to the Red House, our revolutionary hostel. Although I stayed to the end of that particular jamboree, that incident marked the end of *my* workers' revolution.

———

I couldn't stand Thatcher but she fascinates me. I always say she did more harm to England than Hitler, she certainly destroyed our Union but she had a unity of vision, a commitment to her perception of the world, that was remarkable in many ways. I hate her for what she did to England, but I would like to have met her and talked to her. She thought that Britain could be run like a grocer's shop. Well, it can't.

I've become more political as I've got older; I haven't mellowed – I've billowed. I don't feel like being accepting and understanding, I want to fight more. I'd prefer not to be political, but how can one help it with such a collection of nasty people in charge?

Until Brexit, in elections, I always voted Labour; then, in a local election, I voted for the Lib Dems, because they were against leaving the European Union. For me, that was the great failure of the Labour Party, and of Corbyn. The result was legions of voters in the north of England turning out for Brexit – which meant voting for Boris Johnson – and these were people who had always voted Labour. They bought the Tories' Brexit lies wholesale and look where it's got us.

It's upsetting to feel out of touch with people you thought you understood. Somehow, we on the left have to reach them again. And I don't know how you do that. It's the injustice of things that infuriates me. I can't bear it when I see people doing well who ought not to be – Philip Green, for example, should be kicked, and instead he's in Monte Carlo living the high life. I particularly mind about him because he's a Jew.

Corbyn not only made gross mistakes in his stance on Brexit but also in his attitude to the antisemitism row within the party. Of course there is antisemitism in the Labour Party but nowhere near as much as people say. Undoubtedly Corbyn handled it badly and I regret it, because he's a good man and no antisemite. Antisemitism, however, is widespread in the Tory party, but that's never mentioned. The actions of the Israeli government have exacerbated British antisemitism. Now people can express anti-Jewish opinions with impunity, conflating anti-Jewish and anti-Zionist sentiments as if they were the same. It is cunning and deliberate, and I will continue to oppose it with all my strength.

Brexit is the biggest catastrophe of my adult life. The fact that my European citizenship has been taken away from me by this crowd of charlatans and rascals is appalling. I cannot understand it; it's a madness that has overwhelmed the nation. Prejudice and racism abound. There could easily be a pogrom in this country now. It could be against Jews, or more likely against Muslims; it could even be against the traveller community. There are too many people boiling with hate and resentment, and it is alarming.

I'm getting angrier and more disappointed with the world as I get older. I'm shocked at the effect that Johnson and his cronies have had on our lives. I love British culture but the beauties of our country are being corrupted and destroyed. I am particularly horrified by this government's vindictive attacks on the BBC, under the guise of protecting free speech. Boris Johnson is like Trump: a ruthless, dangerous narcissist, drunk with power.

———

To some extent, my documentaries have allowed me to connect to people at the opposite end of my political spectrum. They have helped me to see people in their entirety. My 2017 documentary *Miriam's Big American Adventure*, for example, took me on a road trip through the American heartland from Chicago to New Orleans, meeting real people from both sides of the tracks.

The American South is a courteous place, but many of the people are still racist and abusive. Many of them call themselves Christians – evangelicals. I call them 'evil-gelicals'. The true message of that great socialist Jesus Christ hasn't got through to them. Why are some Americans afraid of Mexicans? Why do they not see them the way that I saw them – as a clever, artistic, funny, proud people? Why do they believe the lies? I always try to reconcile the two halves of the people I meet. I am compelled to do it, especially when I profoundly disagree with them; I have to try to understand.

Many of the people I met were sweet, but lacked powers of analysis. We need to encourage people to think critically about their country and its relation to the world. I am still in touch with the Flanders, one of the American families I met in 2017. They are evangelical Christians and creationists yet nonetheless I know that they are good people. Jennifer Flanders cried real tears for me because I'm an atheist and I'm going to hell. How can I explain to her that not only am I not going to hell, but that there is no such thing? But I keep trying, and so does she.

More recently, I did a conversation piece with Vanessa Redgrave in the *Guardian*. We talked about theatre mostly but of course politics came into it. After the piece was published, I looked at the comments online. Most were complimentary, but one said: 'Two antisemites talking to each other. No, thank you.' I am not an antisemite, and neither is Vanessa. That, however, is what happens when you criticise Israel; you're instantly persona non grata. You're not allowed to be critical of Israel, although Israel deserves criticism of the most severe kind. The Law of Return states that any Jew, born anywhere in the world, can go and live in Israel. No Palestinian can. That is *wrong*. Let us see the humanity in the Other; let's not start with terror and murder. When you go to Israel, visit Palestine too. See for yourselves how Israelis behave to the Palestinians. It is not acceptable.

I believe that people have to face up to the moral implications of their actions, and not sit on a fence, and I've made my choice. I don't sit on the fence. I don't want to be somebody who says, 'On one hand . . . and then on the other hand . . .' My country right or wrong doesn't work for me. I'm on the side of Humanity; if I see a wrong, I feel I must do my best to right it. That is who I am.

Speaking Out

Four days before my eighth birthday, David Ben-Gurion, the head of the Jewish Agency, proclaimed the creation of the State of Israel. I remember the cautious celebrations at home.

My parents were troubled by Zionism, more because they felt that Jews having their own country would increase antisemitism, rather than from a sense of the wrong done to the Palestinians. Because of my public refusal to support the State of Israel, I have become unpopular with other Jews. It's difficult not to be a Zionist when you're Jewish; there are many who think I'm betraying my people. I've been vilified on social media, labelled a fascist, an antisemite, a terrorist, a self-hating Jew. I'm not welcome in certain parts of North London, where my relatives live. Eyes narrow, heads turn away briskly when I enter the synagogue or the kosher restaurant; conversation stops. Last year, my lovely cousin, Rabbi Roderick Young, invited me to his Zoom *Seder*. Another participant, when she noticed my name, put on the Zoom chat that she couldn't stay at the same table as me. And she left. Roderick was upset, so was I. I'm not sure what she gained by her action.

My position on Israel has lost me friends. Naturally this makes me sad, but I have to tell the truth: I've seen with my own eyes how the State of Israel is abusing the Palestinians. I doubt the removal of the accused ex-prime minister Netanyahu will change the situation. He is on trial for corruption charges. He is not alone: since 1948, one president, one prime minister, eleven ministers, seventeen Knesset members and one chief rabbi have been found guilty of various offences, from rape to bribery, and been fined or imprisoned. It is a shameful record; it proves that the wrong people are being elected into government. Israel is not alone in that!

About twenty-five years ago, when I performed *Dickens' Women* at the Jerusalem Festival, I went to Gaza. When I left the safety of the UN vehicle, I was stoned by the children in the streets. I wasn't hurt and I wasn't angry. I understood that to them I was part of the reason they lived in squalor in this overcrowded prison. I have met many wonderful people in Israel then and since, who work hard to try and make things better, but in Gaza I saw the terrible fate of the Palestinians who live there. The poverty is shocking. I was told that Israeli settlers come down from their concrete houses up in the hills into the valley where the Palestinian farmers were working their land and throw dirt in their water system. I saw the results of their deliberate vandalism. The brutality of their attitude towards the Palestinians was appalling. I didn't think Jews could treat others in this way, but sadly the abused have become the abusers.

When I left the country, I was interrogated unpleasantly by Israeli security. It was a frightening experience – they wanted me to name my Palestinian friends. Of course, they have a right to protect their country, but those methods are unacceptable.

In 2012, I went back to Palestine for ten days with Karl Sabbagh, a half-Palestinian friend from my Cambridge days. On the West Bank, we went to Birzeit University near Ramallah, where I met students in a faculty room with their professor. It was a strange experience because, of course, Palestinians nearly always guess that I'm Jewish, so automatically think of me as Israeli. They seldom get the chance to see an ordinary Jew, because the only Israelis they encounter are armed and wearing a helmet, a visor or some sort of uniform. A student looked at me and said, 'You are Jew?' I said, 'Yes.' She said, 'And you are here? Are you not afraid?' I told her that I wasn't frightened. 'I am sympathetic. I am somebody who is pro-Palestinian and trying to help. I don't believe you would attack me just because I'm a Jew.' The students looked at me with amazement.

Hebron was a sad place. The Jews who live in the houses above the market throw rubbish down onto the Palestinians below, so they'd had to rig up a kind of net above the market stalls. It was a Jewish holiday when I was being shown around, and the ultra-Orthodox males – decked out with their *shtreimels* (fur hats) and their side curls, and those old-fashioned black satiny overcoats with a belt – were strutting like peacocks down the middle of the pavement. They walked right through any Palestinian who was coming their way, pushing them off the pavement and into the gutter. I saw this with my own eyes.

My hope is that if I can get Jewish people, *my people*, to see the Palestinians as human beings, people with longings and disappointments, and fears and joys, maybe they can cross that divide. It's about understanding how *you* would feel if soldiers came and pushed you out of your home, destroyed your orchard and the farm that your family had owned for hundreds of years, and made you feel like vermin in your own country. I keep saying to British Zionists: 'Please – just go and look for yourself.'

Compassion has always been a Jewish tradition. We are urged to be a compassionate people, but when it comes to the Palestinians, all our compassion evaporates. Jews are taught, like Christians, to love your neighbour as yourself, to treat the stranger with respect and kindness, and yet, here, the opposite is true.

The appalling acts of Palestinian and Arab terrorism are not ignored by me. I loathe them and will never defend such things. Their cruelty, insanity and continual murder are facts. But ask yourselves: *Why?* I don't acknowledge the claims of history. I care about *now*, the present. That land must be shared, people must be treated equally. It *is* possible, if the will is there; if the Diaspora Jews brought pressure to bear on the Israeli government, attitudes could change. Jews in Europe and America are beginning to realise what is going on. Slowly, too slowly, the tide is turning. Israel must *change*, or it will destroy itself.

It would be much easier not to speak out. My support for Palestine has brought me great heartache, but I can only speak my truth. Whenever I raise money for Jewish causes, which I do frequently, people say to me, 'Now, Miriam, don't be controversial.' How can I not be controversial? It's like my parents not wanting me to be a lesbian: they're asking me to be another Miriam. I *can't* accept that something wrong is being done in *my* name. I am a proud Jew, I fight antisemitism wherever I see it. I'm not a believer, but I adore the culture I spring from, and honour it.

I believe people can change; Truth is not hard to see if you open your eyes.

A Right Royal Reception

The funny thing is that I am a socialist, but I get excited by royalty. I know it's inconsistent, but it's always been about people for me. I don't believe it when people say they don't care about the royals.

The Queen is almost exactly fifteen years older than me and I clearly remember her Coronation. At the time I told myself I'd never forget it and I never have. Over the years I've played various queens, including her great-great-grandmother, Victoria – more than once. But that was the nearest I had got.

So when the invitation arrived to attend the reception for British Book Week at Buckingham Palace, I was thrilled. Everyone connected with the world of books was invited; I was there in my capacity as a reader of audio books. As always, when lovely things happen, I wished my parents had been alive to *kvell*. Everything they had worked for, every sacrifice they had made, was to make my life better. At last, despite my rackety choice of profession (Daddy never did quite come to terms with acting), despite my lack of Jewish doctor husband and children, despite my odd friends and unusual lifestyle, I was finally fulfilling Mummy's dream of 'meeting the best people'.

My old schoolfriend Brigid Davin had been invited too and we went by taxi to the palace. One of her colleagues, a Scottish representative of the Booksellers Association, came also. I had dressed more thoughtfully for once; it was an indoor party so I felt it would not be impolite to forgo wearing a hat (I look like a mushroom in a hat).

We had a sticker for the taxi windscreen, so we were waved in by the policeman on duty and sailed through the famous gates and rolled up to the entrance in the courtyard behind. Smiling equerries opened the taxi door and we stepped out, to be guided to the very large reception hall where hundreds of people thronged and buzzed. I felt this might be my opportunity to fulfil a dream: I approached one of the equerries lining the red and gold walls and said, 'Excuse me, do you think it would be possible for me to meet the Queen? I would so love to.' He looked down at me (they are all tall) and said, 'Oh, yes, it's perfectly possible. You simply locate Her Majesty in this melee, form a semicircle, smile, and if Her Majesty sees you smiling in her direction, she will approach and talk to you.'

You can understand that however portly one is, forming a semicircle on one's own is challenging. Brigid wasn't interested in meeting Her Majesty, and she went off to find an ashtray and a seat, so I went with her Scottish friend to hunt down the Queen.

The crowd was huge and noisy but, despite her being tiny, about my height, we immediately spotted the Queen, looking exactly as she should, with a helmet of iron-grey hair and her handbag clamped like a grenade to her elbow. We quickly shuffled into a semicircle, using a Trooping the Colour technique, and pasted rictus smiles on our faces. In a few moments, Her Majesty turned in our direction, saw that we were smiling and came towards us; others soon followed to join our semicircle.

Unbelievably, Her Majesty the Queen was standing in front of me. 'And what do *you* do?' she asked.

That was where I made my first mistake: meeting the royals does tend to make people daft. Instead of saying like any normal person,

'Your Majesty, I am an actress who records audio books,' I took a deep breath, and declared, 'Your Majesty, I am the best reader of stories in the whole world!' Her Majesty looked at me wearily, rolled her eyes heavenwards, sighed and turned away to my Scottish friend, who was standing next to me. She said to him, 'And what do *you* do?' He replied, 'Your Majesty, I'm an academic trying to help dyslexic children to read. We've discovered that if the letters on the page are printed in different colours and if the pages themselves, the paper, is of different colours, it helps the children to absorb the information more quickly and easily.' Listening beside him, I couldn't help joining in: 'How fascinating!' I said. 'My goodness, I didn't know that.' At which, Her Majesty turned back to me and said sharply, 'Be quiet!' The 't' of 'quiet' was especially crisp.

Everyone looked down, trying to contain their embarrassment at my gaffe. Undeterred, I spoke again: 'I'm so sorry, Your Majesty, I got carried away with excitement.' The Queen rolled her eyes – again – sighed and, deciding to ignore my remark, started to talk to our semi-circle: 'This morning I went to a girls' school in North London, and I was most fascinated to attend the literature class there, and watch the girls being taught by a most expert teacher. And clearly her passion for the subject was what illuminated it for them. They were not particularly interested in literature. Indeed, sadly, very few people are these days. But I could tell that it was what she was communicating to the class that was holding their attention . . .'

I was keen to respond so, once more ignoring her request for my silence, I blurted: 'But, you see, Your Majesty, we are so lucky to be born English and to have English as our first language, because we have the finest literature in the world. And we can read it in the original. We don't need translations to read Shakespeare and Dickens and Keats and Wordsworth and Shelley and Browning and Mrs Gaskell and the Brontës and Jane Austen . . .' I was going right through the syllabus. I could sense the Queen was getting a bit restless. I stepped closer to Her Majesty, recklessly warming to my theme: 'You see, Your Majesty, we are so lucky that we're born English, that English is our language. Imagine, for example, Your Majesty, if we had been born' – I paused, searching for a country that I assumed didn't boast much of a literature and I came up with – 'Albanian!'

Well, that was altogether too much for the Queen. I supposed it smacked of the political. Alarm crossed her face and she moved away, anxious to put some distance between herself and this clearly crazed woman. Clutching the handbag even more closely and murmuring 'Yes, yes' vaguely to herself, she disappeared into the throng.

———

In 2002, another thick, creamy-white envelope, embossed with the royal insignia, was delivered, announcing that I had been awarded an OBE for Services to Drama.

A lot of people were quite surprised, none so more so than me. Some people think that because of my political views, I shouldn't have accepted my OBE. Of course, I shouldn't have; I know that. It goes against everything I believe in, but I most certainly wasn't going to turn it down.

When you get 'the nod', you're not supposed to tell anybody, and I didn't. But the only way I could keep it to myself was to go swimming; I swam on my back and whispered happily into the chlorine-scented air, 'I've got an OBE. I've got an OBE!' Against all the odds I had made it, I had been honoured by the Establishment.

As the Queen was observing mourning for her mother who had just died, it was Prince Charles who performed the presentation at Buckingham Palace that day. And as he pinned on my gong, he said, 'Oh, I am so delighted to be able to give you this.' I was delighted too, because we have got to know each other a little over the years. I think perhaps he enjoys my enthusiasm more than his mother did: he has done more than anyone to make me a royalist.

I have to say I think Australia should choose to be a republic, but I would be very happy to have King Charles. It all started when HRH wrote me a lovely letter out of the blue about my 1998 unabridged audiobook of *Oliver Twist*. It was four pages in his own handwriting. Of course, I wrote back. I always write in pen, on good writing paper. I never take a copy.

I feel protective about Prince Charles. We have met a handful of times over the years but I was amazed when Lindy my agent rang to say, 'Prince Charles has invited you to go and spend three nights at a house party in Sandringham.' I said, 'Give over, that's nonsense.' She said, 'No, really, they contacted us because they didn't know your home address. They've sent a long list of all the things that you might need to wear.'

I decided to go by train – I wasn't going to take my Nissan to Sandringham with all those Rolls Royces. Then I thought, 'Well, I'd better go First Class, because that shows that I know how to behave.' I had decent clothes to wear on the journey, but decided to wear my trainers on the train. I thought, 'I'll just wear those and then when I get out, I'll put on smart shoes.' Thanks again to Hodge, I was properly kitted out, even down to the required ballgown. She had even upgraded my handbag to one of those posh Longchamp totes, and I put the court shoes and my bits and bobs in that.

As we approached King's Lynn station, I changed my shoes, putting my trainers in the Longchamp bag. I teetered down the platform in my uncomfortable, polite heels to be greeted by a gentleman in a dark suit and an elegant, smiling lady. I shook hands with the gentleman. 'How kind of you to meet me, thank you so much.' That was my first mistake: he was the chauffeur.

The smiling lady and I got into the car. She introduced herself. I didn't catch her name and asked again. I didn't catch it the second time, but let it pass. The whole way to Sandringham, which was about twenty-five minutes, she chatted away to me in the friendliest way imaginable, but her upper-class accent was so inpenetrable that I couldn't understand a single word. I just kept nodding, looking interested and saying, 'Oh, goodness, yes!'

Eventually we passed through some imposing, iron gates and along an immaculate gravel drive to the house itself, a Victorian country mansion, three storeys high, with a sloping tiled roof and lots of windows, the pointing in the red brickwork in perfect condition. A line of uniformed members of staff stood waiting to receive us. They took the luggage out of the boot of the car, and my Longchamp bag with my trainers and socks, and somewhat shabby wheelie case, were whisked off.

We were ushered inside to a drawing room, which had a lovely, cosy, country-house feel. All the other guests were assembled. There were about eighteen of us. I immediately recognised Stephen Fry, Michael Morpurgo, Jeremy Paxman, David Hockney, Sir Antony Sher and his partner Greg Doran, Peter Shaffer, Lord Gowrie and his wife, and Mrs Drue Heinz – of the 57 varieties of Heinz. I was particularly thrilled to see David Hockney; I'd always wanted to meet him.

After about half an hour or so, Prince Charles and Camilla joined us, and the prince went in turn to every single person and welcomed them. When he came to me, I got a hug, then he said, 'There's something I want to show you. Here, come with me.' I followed him, and there in the entrance of the house was a curious chair. It was a big leather chair, but it wobbled – it seemed not to be properly stable on the ground. He said, 'I want you to have a look at that. What do you think it is?' So I said, 'Well, it looks like a big fireside seat, or a sofa, or something.' He said, 'No, it's a weighing machine.' Prince Charles explained that when Edward VII, his great-great-grandfather, had his house parties, he would weigh each of his guests when they arrived, and then he would weigh them again when they left: and if they hadn't put on weight during their stay, he felt that he had failed as a host. He showed me the original weighing book with all the famous people, their weights noted alongside. What a terrifying thing to see as a guest! I said, 'I hope you're not thinking of weighing me!'

The next day was the annual flower show at Sandringham. Thousands of people come from all over England to see the royal party at the flower show. It was a blisteringly hot summer's day. After breakfast, I went back up to my room but I couldn't find my sunglasses. And I couldn't find my trainers. I hunted all around in my room and realised then that they must have been in my Longchamp bag, which obviously hadn't come up with the rest of my luggage. The staff had made a judgement: the smart luggage goes with the smart lady, and not, alas, with me. I didn't know quite what to do about it, but everyone was waiting downstairs to go off to the flower show, so I rushed to join the rest of the party.

The flower show was great fun and I was delighted to hear people shouting, 'Miriam, Miriam!' And I waved back in regal fashion, because I was part of the royal party, after all. After the show we had an al fresco lunch in the grounds. At the long table I sat next to Prince Charles, and opposite the smiling lady with the white-blonde hair and the elongated vowels I'd met at the station. It turned out that she was Lady Solti, widow of Georg Solti, the music director of the Royal Opera. And she was wearing my sunglasses. Yes, *my* sunglasses! I was dumbfounded, but not for long. I realised the only thing to do was to say straight out, 'Where did you get those sunglasses?' Lady Solti took them off, and said, '$@%^$£&?' which in translation (I believe) was, 'Oh, are they yours?' I replied, 'Well, yes. I think they are.' It turned out that I was correct: the servants *had* made a judgement about me and my tatty suitcase and decided that my smart Longchamp bag couldn't possibly belong to me and had taken it to Lady Solti's room instead. They'd unpacked everything, and she had assumed sunglasses were provided for guests. Once she realised they were mine, she immediately handed them over. I liked her very much, and knew that in other circumstances we would have been quite friendly. She had no 'side'.

The weekend continued swimmingly, so much so I even went swimming with Camilla at Holkham Sands. Prince Charles and Camilla are cracking good hosts; the food is spectacularly good – I went to the kitchens and was given a doggie bag of the grouse to take home. I will never forget it, especially a supper under the stars, sitting with Stephen Fry and Tony Sher, after which Prince Charles entertained us in the drawing room with a monologue written by Barry

Humphries. The prince is a fine actor, he had a superb Aussie accent and he made us all laugh.

I think he's a good man who cares a great deal for the country, and I can't bear the horrid things people write about him and the other members of the royal family. I don't talk politics with him, I don't think it's fair, but I'd a damn sight rather he ran the country than the incompetent buffoon who sits in Number 10.

Spliced

B astille Day 1968 was the First Fuck – for Heather and me, that is. It's fifty-three years ago and the joyous memory ignites me still. Through the years we have made our lives together and apart. It was essential for me to live in an English-speaking country and essential for Heather to live in a Dutch-speaking country, accessing the archives for her work. She and my old Cambridge ADC lighting-man beau, David Bree, met and liked each other and they bought a house together on Amsterdam's Prinsengracht canal. And the years went by and the laws got sharper and we realised that although we didn't believe in 'marriage' as such – and the thought of referring to one another as 'wife' makes me feel sick – without a formal civil partnership, should one of us fall ill, no hospital or doctor would release information to the other. It seemed the obvious thing to do and we decided that doing it in England was probably easiest.

Lambeth Town Hall was to be the venue for our nuptials. I had decided the date should be 26 June 2013, seventy years to the day after my parents' wedding. Heather would come over shortly before and I had to leave for a job in Australia on 17 July. Our very close friends, my Australian lawyer and his wife, Sandy and Dianne Rendel, who happened to be visiting London at the time, would meet us at the town hall and be our witnesses. My favourite restaurant is Brasserie Zédel, opposite the Piccadilly Theatre in Sherwood Street, and I invited Denise, my beloved assistant, and my best friend, Carol Macready, to join us after the ceremony. I had no idea what was involved but I went to the register office and booked the day and the table at Zédel. It was deliberately low-key.

On the appointed day, my long-time driver, Dave Pask, arrived at my house, beautifully suited and booted to take us to the town hall. On arrival, we waited in the anteroom until someone asked us which fiancée was the bride and which the groom? Heather is intensely private and found the whole thing mortifying rather than moving. She nearly expired with horror at the question, and I tried to explain that we didn't quite see it like that and it was myself and the other lady who were getting a civil partnership. We were led into another room and the extremely courteous lady registrar explained that this was NOT to be our Splicing Day but only our Answering Questions Day, preparing for another future date to be arranged. 'But I've booked a table, can't you do it today?' I asked. 'No, I'm so sorry. This is the process we have to observe,' the registrar said kindly. I contained my rage; no point in fighting with officialdom, especially such a pleasant example of it, but what it meant was that after we had gone through the history of our relationship from 1968 to the present day, showed our passports and birth certificates and signed various documents, my little 'Unwedding Party' went to Zédel, claimed our table and had a merry time. To say I felt a right twat doesn't quite convey the depths of my squirming; of all things to fuck up, this was the worst. At least I'd been able to rearrange the Actual Day for two weeks hence, according to the rules. It *had* to be 16 July, the latest possible date before my departure for Australia. The Rendels wouldn't be there, alas, they'd already have had to return to Australia, but Dave Pask and Denise and Carol bravely agreed to attend Take Two. Carol and Denise were the new witnesses.

Dave turned up punctually, again suited and booted, and he drove us four ladies to the town hall. We were all hysterical with laughter. We went together into the main room – there were flowers everywhere. The same nice lady was officiating. She made a very good speech, not religious at all (we were glad of that) but expressing a pleasure in our happiness, and wanting us to realise the seriousness of what we were doing. She shook hands with Heather and me, wishing us every happiness, and off we scooted for the Second Lunch at Zédel, just Heather and me and Carol and Denise. As it turned out, on my arrival in Australia I was taken straight to hospital with a wandering gallstone and given intravenous antibiotics. But it didn't matter: all I could think about was the fact that we were well and truly spliced – TWICE!

Getting Older

Getting older is a hideous experience. I'm not someone who believes old age is a blessing – bollocks! It's fucking awful and you get through it as best you can. I'm glad I only have to do it once.

No one ever tells you about how things change as you get older. It's one of those topics that people avoid talking about until it's too late and you are old too. That's when you realise that it's going to be such an effort bending over to pick something up, you might as well not bother. You change, and what you want changes. I get extremely irritated by it – I don't mean in the superficial sense of mourning my youthful good looks: I refer to the general sagging and wrinkling, the age spots and skin tags, the sprouting of facial hair. Some of my friends have had plastic surgery and Botox, but that's not for me. My face has always been a pleasant one; I have a winning smile and good eyes. The wrinkles which have appeared are the honourable traces of my life: laugh lines rather than frown lines.

My body is taking its revenge. The years of overeating and under-exercising have resulted in a belly of gargantuan proportions. I am ashamed of it. And my bladder is weak, or is it my sphincter? All I know is that I have about ten seconds to get to the loo. I always carry a spare pair of knickers: when this book is finished, I've promised myself a course in pelvic firmness. Apparently, it can be done, so I live in hope.

Although I was never sporty, as a young person I was not unfit. Until the inexorable passage of time took its toll, I had health, vigour and stamina. I've always loved water, and for forty years I swam every day. I wasn't a good swimmer; I was, in fact, a *pathetic* swimmer, but at least I did it.

When I was a child, my parents forbade me to join in school swimming lessons: they were frightened of polio as many believed that swimming was where children caught the disease. In 1955, Jonas Salk invented the polio vaccine and the world breathed more easily, much as we're doing now facing the horrors of COVID-19 and the sensible ones rushing to get their jabs. (Don't mention anti-vaxxers to me; that is not a sane opinion to hold.) Eventually, however, I persuaded my parents to let me learn to swim – at school, we had our lessons in the River Cherwell. From that moment on, swimming was my sport. In London, I used to swim in the Marshall Street Baths in Soho, or sometimes at the Queen Mother Sports Centre in Victoria. Mary Wilson, Harold Wilson's widow, used to swim there, and also Jennifer Paterson, one of the 'Two Fat Ladies'. We always knew when she was in, because she was a baritone and she sang, 'Pomty pom, pomty pom' in stentorian tones as she dried herself in the cubicle.

My local pool, on Clapham Manor Street, is one of my favourites, as it's easy to step into. I hate pools where they have only perpendicular metal ladders, so you are required to be a climber as well as a swimmer. And I prefer to swim in the open air; if Tooting Bec Lido and Brockwell Lido were heated in the winter, I would be so happy. My favourite pool in the world is the Carnegie Memorial Pool in suburban Melbourne, but alas, it's being redeveloped (a word which strikes terror into me – next to 'cancer', my least favourite word is 'developer'), until at least May 2023.

My daily swim was marred only by selfish swimmers. Pool Nazis are usually men, who pound up and down the lane, ignoring anyone nearby while they splash, hit and kick with impunity. There is no excuse for not looking around to see who else is in the pool.

In my seventies, I was diagnosed with benign positional vertigo (BPV) perhaps caused by water getting into my ears. That sadly brought an end to my daily dips. My poor body was used to swimming, so when I stopped, it gave up too and went to pot. I've had skeletal problems, osteoarthritis, and a knee replacement operation since. The latest blow is spinal stenosis, a debilitating condition which makes it difficult to walk or even stand for any amount of time without severe pain.

Consequently, I've become physically nervous, though I think that's something that comes to all of us with age: while I never liked my body much, I used to trust it, and now I worry it'll let me down and so I move about the world, anxiously and carefully. I walk with a stick, and if people get too close, and their droplets could infect me, I wave the stick in their faces – and mostly, they keep away.

———

The worst thing about ageing, obviously, is the great sorrow of losing friends – as you grow old, people you have loved and imagined would always be there start, with wretched regularity, to leave your life. I've loved writing this book, but the saddest part has been revisiting the losses.

It's not all doom and gloom, however. There are perks of age. People listen to you more. They don't see you – you're invisible when you're in the street – but if they're sitting talking to you, they think you're wiser and you're going to be talking sense because you're old. It may not be true, but still . . .

Also, you stop giving a damn. When I get into a tube train and I want to sit down and there are no seats, I say: 'Please, may I sit down?' Once I was so exhausted and a man was sitting down right in front of me. When he didn't stand up to offer me his seat, I just plonked myself on his lap! He was surprised, then really quite angry, but he got up pretty quickly. He didn't stay under the Mighty Margolyes for long!

On another occasion, quite recently, I was at Waverley Station in Edinburgh when my back went into spasm. The pain was too much to bear but there were no empty seats nearby, so I asked this young guy for his seat. He was on the phone and I shouldn't have interrupted, I realise that, but there was nowhere for me to sit and I really needed to rest my back. I said to this young man, 'Would you mind if I had your seat?' 'What? What? I'm on the phone, for Christ's sake,' he snapped. 'There are seats over there. Go over there!' Then he went back to his phone conversation.

I had a bottle of water with me. I took off the cap and I poured it on his head. He got up then! A woman saw; she came over and she said, 'I saw what you did. That's a common assault! You assaulted that man!' I said, 'Madam, I'm in pain and I needed somewhere—' 'I don't care,' she interrupted. 'You assaulted that boy. I'm going to get the police.' She returned with a transport police officer. By now, the young man, just a little bit damp, had disappeared, but I explained what had happened: that I'd emptied some water on the man's head when he had refused to offer me his seat, to which the officer said, 'Oh, dear, that doesn't help matters, does it?' I agreed, and then I saw that my train was coming in, so I just got up and walked away. The policeman didn't come after me, and I wasn't arrested, so in a sense, I got away with it.

Usually I'm quite sweet, but I was so angry with that young man. How dare he! He was at least fifty years my junior. I've noticed that the people who do offer their seat are usually women. Men rarely bother; they pretend to be too engrossed in a newspaper to notice if someone needs to sit down. But good manners still matter. You should always be as polite, careful and caring to people as you possibly can be. But if people are nasty and cruel, then fuck it – they've got it coming.

My spine may be unstable and my knees are giving up, but I'm not. That's the benefit of being a character actress. My looks have changed over the years, but as I was never beautiful, I'm no less beautiful now. I get more work, if anything. In the last five years, I've co-starred in Frog Stone's BBC Four sitcom *Bucket*, in which I played a foul-mouthed and flatulent septuagenarian from hell (NAR – No Acting Required), ticking off my daughter and my bucket list of must-dos before I snuff it. (By the way, that's an example of the literary term 'zeugma', which I've always longed to use.)

More recently, I've been busy on stage at the Park Theatre in London playing *Sydney and the Old Girl*, and in Melbourne taking on Maggie Smith's great hit, *The Lady in the Van*. (I was so nervous about taking on the role that I went round to Alan Bennett's house to get his blessing. He reassured me that it didn't matter I was so short. I'm also realising what is now *not* possible for someone of my age. There is a sadness in accepting I will now never play Masha in *The Three Sisters*, for example. But I'd advise everyone to look at the footage of Gwen Ffrangcon-Davies reciting Juliet on TV when she was nearly one hundred years old. It will give you hope.

———

I'm too old for a lot of things, but I'm not too old for everything. I've been fortunate my career has opened up surprisingly well in the last fifteen years. Documentaries have become an important new strand in my professional life. I enjoy talking to complete strangers. When I need to sit on a park bench, I go to where someone's sitting. Most people like to pounce on an empty bench, but I long for human communion – that to me is Holy Communion. I love talking to people, and asking them questions. They're giving me a present of their stories. Talking, listening, learning what it's like to look through the eyes of another soul. That's what I relish about being a 'documentary person'.

It started in 2005 with *Dickens in America*: ten episodes for BBC Two directed by Richard Shaw. Both Dickens and I had unexpectedly gone to America in the middle of our careers and following in his footsteps, I felt I understood the man and the writer better than before. And it seemed we shared an opinion about America. He had written: 'this is not the Republic of my imagination'. His delight in the new democracy had soured. But I had to wait for eleven years before my next foray into dockos. In 2016, I did a little morning programme about the NHS in Scotland and got a smashing review in the *Guardian* (the headline ran: MORE MIRIAM MARGOLYES

PLEASE)[*] and I took part in the first *The Real Marigold Hotel* documentary. The BBC sent me, singer Patti Boulaye, former newsreader Jan Leeming, chef Rosemary Shrager, dancer Wayne Sleep, former Doctor Who Sylvester McCoy, comedian Roy Walker, and former World Darts champion, Bobby George, to live for three weeks in a luxurious private mansion in Jaipur, to see if we could contemplate retiring there.

E. M. Forster wrote that when you go to India you come face to face with yourself and I hoped that would happen, but I found that the heat proved too difficult for me. I wasn't keen on the lack of flush toilets beyond the confines of our hotel. The caste system and the disparity of wealth was equally hard to stomach. In one day we visited both the slums and the palace of the royal family in Jaipur. The striking thing was that the standard of politeness and grace was exactly the same in both milieux. The people of India – their courtesy, energy and intelligence – are remarkable; I'd love to go back, despite my disgust at their prime minister, Modi. He's one of the evil men of the world.

When we won the Grierson Award for Best Constructed Documentary Series, it opened the door for more series, and I have travelled to many more foreign places since, meeting geishas and tango dancers and pandas, making many new friends along the way. The documentary-makers threw me together with an unusual selection of vintage celebrities, mostly delightful.[†] And I discovered I loved

---

[*] Thank you, Julia Raeside. We've never met but you made me very happy.

[†] The only one I definitely wouldn't want to stay in touch with, was Stanley Johnson, Boris's father, who has achieved a surprising eminence, but, sadly, proved the adage that the rotten apple doesn't fall far from the tree.

making documentaries. You don't have to learn lines, you have a licence to be inquisitive and to travel the world – with somebody else paying.

And in learning more about the world, I've learnt much more about myself, which has led to documentaries about fatness and death, subjects that most people avoid talking or even thinking about. But for me, no subject is off limits. I believe strongly that being able to talk about *everything* is the only way to face our demons and it is why I decided to confront the subject of dying. I went to see my parents' grave in Wolvercote Cemetery. Jews are pragmatists. We don't bring flowers when we visit a grave; we bring a stone. Flowers die like people, stones don't. As soon as I arrived at Mummy and Daddy's burial place, however, I realised that, stupidly, I'd only brought one stone; so with real chutzpah, I had to nick one from a nearby grave. I hope Daddy doesn't mind that it was just a little stone, but it was like that in life too – Mummy was big and he was little. I think they would have approved of *Miriam's Dead Good Adventure*, which I made precisely *because* I'm terrified of death. I hoped it would help me to be less frightened. And to some extent, it did.

A good death, to me, means that you die in bed, hopefully without pain, surrounded by people you love, and you can smile at them, close your eyes and go. That's what I long for. But, as the last eighteen months have shown, you can't count on anything. So many people have died in isolation wards, without being able to see their loved ones. The pandemic has even removed the therapeutic side of funerals. Funerals don't work on Zoom: the whole point is the living, breathing people. I want to see all my friends and fellow mourners and be able to talk and sing and cry together, sharing our memories of the person we are there to honour. And experience the black humour, finding joy in those shared memories of the dead, that's what I love most about funerals. I think laughter is better than God.

———

I think of myself as in the autumn of my life – it's my favourite season. I like the idea of ripening, maturing into my prime. I hope I have learned on my journey, but I still want to keep improving. I have always resisted any kind of meditation, self-contemplation or spirituality as an indulgence. But now I've reached eighty, however, this might be an appropriate moment to look into my soul rather more critically – and *learn*. The goal of life is to end up wiser. But more importantly, I think it should be to end up kinder, both to yourself and everyone around you (unless, of course, their surname happens to be Johnson).

Dirty Talk

I hope this isn't the first chapter you turn to, but I wouldn't blame you if you did. I realised while writing this book that I haven't directly tackled the thing that has brought me the most notoriety late in my career: dirty talk. I am now better known for my naughty stories than almost anything else.

It's not out of character. As you may have picked up from this book, I've always enjoyed talking about sex. In Newnham Old Hall dining room at breakfast, I could be relied on to spill the beans on whomever I had sucked off the night before. While no penis has ever been inside me, I have always been amused by them. Even now, I find myself looking at where the penis bulges in men's trousers. It's such an odd dangler to have – something hanging outside yourself. Our naughty areas are contained, for the most part, *within* our bodies, but men have to deal with this extra stalk. It's a fascinating subject that people simply don't discuss enough.

When I had my first proper lesbian relationship with Marion, she was mortified to find out that I was discussing everything (all our ins and outs!) with the rest of the cast. She thought that a private life should remain just that. But it was such a gobsmacking revelation to me that I wanted to share everything I'd learned. Sex isn't so much part of my life now, but I like remembering it and talking about the things I used to do when I had it.

From the very beginning, I always wanted to connect with

people using language and humour and sometimes naughtiness. I hope people will like me, but if they don't, I want them to notice me. I've always asked, 'How old were you when you had your first fuck?' It's a good way of getting a reaction: because sometimes, if you prick people, they respond genuinely, and that's what I seek: a genuine response.

I delight in the whole physical aspect of life, and find sex and penises, vaginas and knickers, and lavatories and farting, hugely funny. And breasts. I love talking about breasts. They make me laugh. In general, when I'm at a loss for conversational gambits, I fall back on a subject I know people enjoy hearing about, which is SEX, even when it is slightly dirty – which it almost always is with me. I know I'm capable of being outrageous, but I don't do it *all* the time; at home I'm quiet and boring, preferring to subside into a book or into the computer. I do not have a public persona. I don't assume sweetness for the camera; I'm the same person no matter where I go or what company I'm in. But, like everyone else, I judge which facet of my personality will suit a particular situation and present it. To that extent, I am calculating – but never to conceal, only to reveal.

My friends, of course, knew exactly what I was like, but it only dawned on the wider world when I started appearing regularly on chat shows. The first time I was invited on *The Graham Norton Show* was in 2012. Beside me on the sofa was a charming young man called will.i.am. I didn't know who he was, but he was a lovely fellow and I was pleased to meet him. When will.i.am started using the word 'like' in the way that Americans do – unfortunately everybody's doing it now – I gently pointed out that the continual repetition of the word was a waste of time and proceeded to give him a short grammar lesson on the subject.

Thankfully, will.i.am took it well. I didn't set out to be funny, though. I just wanted to explain why that word should not be used in that way. It still grates when I hear it misused so often. I've lost the battle to stop people saying it, but I won't stop fighting. (I joined the Apostrophe Protection Society, as that little mark is also rapidly becoming another lost cause. It's a war I'm still fighting but on my own now as, sadly, the society has closed down.)

will.i.am practically fell off the red sofa when, at Graham's prompting, I told the story of an incident during my last show in Edinburgh. I was walking home late after work one night, through the Meadows – the large open field just behind the university area – when I heard a rustling above me (I'm so short, almost everything is above me, actually). I looked up and in the tree I saw a young man in military uniform, vigorously masturbating. I watched him for a moment, just to make sure I had fully grasped the situation, and then said, 'What on earth are you *doing*?' I felt concerned for him, so I asked, 'What is your occupation?' I thought a few questions might take his mind off it. He replied, 'I'm a soldier.' I asked, 'In the military Tattoo?' 'Yes,' came the reply. I said, 'Come down at once.' He clambered down. I said, 'What's the matter with you? You can't do that. You know you can get into trouble doing what you're doing? You could destroy your career. What rank are you?' I think he was a corporal. I said, 'Now look, I will help you out with this one, but you must go home after, and remember you are a soldier. You'll get into a lot of trouble if anyone catches you up a tree doing that again. Or indeed anywhere.' I then gave him a helping hand, so to speak, and off he went. He was charming and, I must also say, grateful.

I'm going to add to this story something I didn't say on TV, because

I thought it might brand me as a sex maniac, which I'm not. But after the soldier had said cheerio, I was cleaning my hand when I heard someone saying, 'Miriam, do you remember me?' I turned around and, sitting on the bench nearby was a sweet boy I'd known in Oxford, a Nigerian called Winston. He said a bit cheekily, 'I saw how you helped that young man; what about me?' Well, I didn't want to be accused of discrimination, and I liked Winston, so it turned out that night I killed two birds for the price of one. I felt good, they felt good; truly, what's the harm? No animals were hurt in the process.

Back to Graham Norton. When one of the other guests exclaimed, 'Jesus, Miriam!' I simply said, 'He was a soldier, and you've got to support the troops.' Their assumption that because I care about correct language that my days of thinking and talking dirty would be far behind me, was not only erroneous, but downright offensive.

It is the absolute truth that when I go on that show, I genuinely do not know what I'm going to say. We have a telephone chat with a researcher a few days before and they ask me what I want to talk about, but I've no idea then and I tell them so. I prefer things to be spontaneous; I like the freedom Graham gives his guests. He is the most charming host, genuine, quick-witted and generous. All his guests feel the same – he makes it into a party. Perhaps I do go a little far; I remember the lovely Stanley Tucci saying plaintively, after one story: 'I just want to be on a programme that airs!' As an American actor, he's used to much more buttoned-up chat shows where people go on to plug something, but are determined not to give too much of themselves away. He couldn't believe the BBC would actually broadcast the words I was speaking. My appearances on all the talk shows are fraught with danger because my language is often foul. I've been reported to Ofcom several times. I know I swear too much and I'm constantly being reminded to keep it clean. I regret I offend – it's a bad habit I got into very early. But saying 'fuck' and 'shit' and 'cunt face' isn't as bad as racism or selling drugs. Get real!

I enjoy a chat, and if I can pop a bit of sex into it, I don't think there's any harm. Not a lot of gay women front up on TV, so I hope I give courage to young dykes to be proud and confident. If you tell the truth – and I always do – you shame the devil.

The Final Curtain

My grandmother Flora gave me a gold brooch shaped like a star that was almost like a talisman – an emblem of what my family thought of me. My mother always believed in me; when I was starting out, she gave me strength. She said, 'Go forward. Don't look at what other people are doing. Think about the road ahead. What matters is what *you're* doing. You are gifted. You will go far; have faith.' And because I believed and trusted her, I did.

One of the best moments of a performance is waiting in the wings after the curtain has descended, when you know you have given your all, remembered every line and cue and the audience has responded as you hoped, laughing at the right moments and being moved at others. There is always a hush and a caught breath as you wait for their reaction. It's not like that with books. I don't have a clue how the various acts and scenes of my life have gone down with you, my dear reader – I hope you've enjoyed reading it. I've enjoyed living it. But now I realise my days, like these pages, are numbered.

William Saroyan wrote: 'Everybody has got to die, but I have always believed an exception would be made in my case . . .' Given its inescapable nature, therefore, I want to do it well. In interviews now, I'm always asked, 'Are you scared of Death?' Of course, I fucking am! Absolutely shit-scared most of the time. But death itself is just the end of things; it's the dying that's the problem. The last two years have been particularly difficult to bear. As a fat, old person, the threat of the pandemic is immediate and real. During lockdown, I wouldn't even leave the house to go to a shop; I was too nervous. That may be why I'm so rude and noisy a lot of the time – I'm trying to keep the Grim Reaper away. And so far, it's working.

When I became the patron of the Coffin Club, based in Hastings, they persuaded me to try their one-size-fits-all coffin to prove the lid would stay on, even over my enormous breasts. It did. I am happy to confront the things that many people prefer to overlook. In *The Life and Death of Peter Sellers*, my lovely stand-in, Margery Lyons, awkwardly asked me if I'd mind actually getting into my character's coffin as she couldn't face it. I didn't mind at all. I *will* mind when it's no longer optional, however.

Let me tell you though, I'm not even close to being done. At eighty years old I've kept (most of) my marbles and my career is still going strong. And if my work has entertained people, that makes me happy. I'm determined to keep stretching myself. I mustn't fall back on the easy things. That's my main aspiration, because after a certain point, people think you can't do it, so you have to prove you can. So, for instance, while I love reading biographies, I left writing my own till this year and it turned the house arrest of lockdown into a great adventure, remembering all the people and experiences, good and bad, naughty and nice, I've come across in the last four score years.

One of the problems about being old today is that with the advances of technology, if you're not computer literate you are excluded from modern life and thereby disenfranchised. A lot of my friends don't use Zoom, WhatsApp and the other connecting technology because they don't know how to – some of them can't even turn on their smart televisions. My pet project, which I've tried to start a few times, is to present a government-run initiative on TV, to help older people use computers. I believe, in addition, that there should be a nationwide army of young people who volunteer to go in and help us oldies to set up our technology and teach us to use it properly. 'Sponsor a Nanna' is what I'd call it. It's vital to have some technology for everyday life and it's scandalous that those big, rich tech giants haven't started one. If you read this, Bill Gates or Mark Zuckerberg, get in touch.

I'm still new to a lot of technology but for an eighty-year-old I'm not bad. I have a desktop computer, a laptop, and an iPad. I have my own website and I visit Facebook; it's proved useful in my genealogical quest, allowing me to track down distant relatives. And, of course, being stuck in Italy during the pandemic, I was an enthusiastic Zoomer; at the moment I'm doing twenty Zoom calls a week. It's difficult to keep track sometimes.

I won't have anything to do with Twitter, though. Limit myself to 280 characters? Ridiculous.

———

As long as my body holds out, I would love to travel the British Isles, tracking down as many of my old friends as I can, not descending on them – I'd find a hotel – but just seeing again the people I've loved and worked with. I want to do more dockos in Australia and I'd love to visit the elephants and rhinos I've adopted in Africa and give them a hug. And I long to make a programme about Israel and Palestine, getting enemies to meet and discover their humanity together.

Yes, as I hurtle towards incontinence and immobility, there is still fun to be had. Extraordinary proof of this was given to me on my eightieth birthday this 18th of May. I had intended to spend it quietly, with Mahnaz, my dear friend of over sixty-five years, and have a delicious Persian supper and a videocall with her sister, Shanaz, in Vancouver. After the meal Saleem, Mahnaz's son, connected his computer to my TV. Shahnaz appeared, we had a grand talk and then, quite suddenly, without warning, eighty-five of my closest friends bubbled up right in front of me on the screen,[*] all laughing and talking at once (try telling actors to mute themselves). I couldn't believe it, especially when Richard E. Grant made an adorable speech, everyone shouted 'Hear hear', then Bobby Crush tuned up his piano and Stephen Fry led the crew into a heartfelt (if not wholly tuneful – it's very hard for eighty-five people to sing in time) chorus of 'Happy Birthday' and I overflowed with happiness and realised that my life's achievement was there on screen, in the friends I'd made and kept through the years.

Best of all, my beloved Heather, has remained my rock and anchor throughout the roller-coaster ride of my life. Now you've read the stories (those the lawyers have allowed me to retain) of my adventures across the last eighty years – you might be as surprised as I am, that she has chosen to stick by me. I have been blessed. This much is true.

---

[*] Masterminded by my amazing assistant of over twenty years, Denise Wordsworth.

Acknowledgements

Georgina Laycock and Rose Davidson must be first in this list. They guided me through the writing of this book, gently but firmly. They call themselves editors, in reality they have needed to also be babysitters and care workers. No words can express my gratitude. My mistakes are mine, all the good bits they honed and burnished. Dear ladies – thank you.

All the other names here have been kind to me over the last eighty years. It's a long list, and horribly incomplete, but I want to pay tribute to those who have particularly helped me along the way:

Jan Adams, Stefania Alboretti, Sally Alekna, Ann Alexander, Bernice Alexander Jones, Robin Amadio, Irma Anita & Remo Ricci, Moira Armstrong, Jane Asher, Rowan Atkinson, Caroline Barker, Glen Barnham, Libbie Barr, Sheila & Laura Benson, John Bett, David Bitel, Joyce Blair, Becky Brand, Jo Brand, David Bree, Simon Brett, Juliet Brightmore, Sheila Brill, William Broadhead, Simon Callow, Gabriella Capisani, Macey Carsey & Tom Werner, the casts of *Wicked* and *Me and My Girl* (you know who you are), Daniela Cesarei, Kathy Chalfant, Paul Cheifitz, Greg & Julie Chittick, Ann Churchill-Brown, Katerina Clark, David Clews & all at Two Four, Mike & Linda Cochran, Denise Coffee, Sarah Collier, Justin Coober-Lake, Suzanne & Walter Coppenrath, Jill Corner, Deb Cox, Laurie Critchley and all at Southern Pictures, Nora Crook, Blanche D'Alpuget & Bob Hawke, Kay Daniels, Lucy Darwin, Luca Deidda, Judi Dench, Ken & Tina Danziger, Essie

Davis, Hugues Delage, Marian Diamond, Lady Anne Dodd, Simon Draper & Alicia Kerr, Fiona Eagger, Diana Eden, Barnaby Edwards, Ros Edwards, Ben Elton, Kate Feast, Helen Ford, Francesca Franco, Stephen Fry, Sophy Gairdner, Robb Gardner, Diane Gelon, Marie & Bobby George, Jo & Ellen Gerber, Peter Geschiere, Jon Gilbert, Joy & Don Glover, Jean Gooder, Joan Goodman, Dean Grant, Richard E. Grant & Joan Washington, Beryl Green, Waris & Shama Habibullah, Jackie Haliday, Lady Nickie & Sir Peter Hall, Paul Hamman, Roger Hammond, Margo Harley, Ken & Joan Harrison, Michael Haslam, John Henshall, Patricia Hodge Owen, Liz Hodgson, Ong Hok Ham, Olivia Homan, Jennifer & Don Howard, Charlotte Hutchinson, John Hyslop, Gloria Jacobson, Jonathan James-Moore, Martin & Ros Jarvis, Peter Jarvis, Marie & Dan Jessel, Mark Jones, John Jordan, Richard Jordan, Joel Keating, Rabbi Jonathan Keren-Black, Michael Kilgarrif, Lindy King, Tom & Kate Kinninmont, Neil & Glenys Kinnock, Robert Kirby, Alan Knight, Peter Lavery, Jeremy Lawson, Iain Leighton, Ruth Leon, Penelope Lerner, Annabel Leventon, Sue Limb, Mrs Lipsey, John Lloyd, Susan Loewenberg, Sylvester McCoy, Andrew McKinnon, Leigh, Margi & Elaine McLaughlin, Leith McPherson, Carol Macready, Ruth McVey, 'Chuck' Mallett, Jill Margo, Natasha Morgan, Robin Morgan-Bentley, Mary Murnane, Genni Nevinson, Michele & Graham Newstead, Graham Norton, John Norton-Smith, Valda & Ronnie Norwitz, Biddy O'Brien, Rohan Onraet, Judy Page, Jack Palladino, Dave Pask, Jose Patterson, Robert Paul, Mark Pawsey, Christine Payne, Biddy Peppin, Stewart Permutt, Rose Pickthall, Nigel Planer, Rosella Pugliese, Pamela Rabe, Saul Radomsky & Oded Schwartz, Esther Rantzen, Carol Regan, Sandy & Dianne Rendel, Griff Rhys Jones, Vanessa Robb, Michael Robinson, Rabbi Michael Roth,

Acknowledgements

Karl & Sue Sabbagh, Susan Sampliner, Valerie Sarruf, Alexei Sayle, Gerald Scarfe, Phillip Schofield, Arlene & Larry Schwartz, Kenneth See, Paolo Serafini, Wendie Shaffer, Alan Shallcross, Roy & Ann Sharples, Tony Sheffield, Richard Simpson, Professor Michael Slater, Don Smith, Susan Smith, Ellinor Sokole, Peter Sokole, Nancy Stieber, Sandra Sutherland, Louis Theroux, Marina Thurairatnam, David Timson, The Hon. Hilary Todd, Janet Todd, Claire Tomalin, Jenny Topper, Ann Tricklebank, Selwyn & Carol Turiansky/Torrance, Mahnaz Vaillancourt & Shahnaz Amanat, Kerry Washington, Philip & Wendy Watson, Dudley Werner, Ann Whitehead, Sallie & Dave Wille, Enyd Williams, Holly Willoughby, Dan & Sallie Wolsoncroft, Rabbi Roderick Young . . . And last, but by no means least . . . my wise, kind, generous and infinitely patient personal assistant of twenty-two years, Denise Wordsworth.

Thank you so much. I couldn't have done it without you.

Credits

Text

Extract from 'May-Day Song for North Oxford' by John Betjeman from John Betjeman, *Collected Poems*, reproduced by permission of John Murray (Publishers). Extracts from *Blackadder*, reproduced by permission of Richard Curtis and Ben Elton.

Pictures

Author's collection: inset 1, pages 1–7 above; inset 2, pages 2 above left, 3 above left; inset 3, page 8 above. Drawings from the Form Magazine produced by Miriam's year at OHS © Biddy Peppin: inset 1, pages 4 top left and 5 above right.

Alamy Stock Photos: inset 2, pages 2 middle and below/Donald Cooper, 3 below/Donald Cooper, 5 above right/AF Archive, 6 above/©TriStar Pictures/Everett Collection, 6 below/Geraldine Overton © Carsey-Werner/Everett Collection, 7 below/© Columbia Pictures/Everett Collection, 8 above/Photo12, 8 below/AF Archive; inset 3, pages 1 below/© Warner Brothers/Everett Collection, 2 below/ Everett Collection, 5 above and middle/PA Images. BBC Photo Library: inset 2, page 4 above. Conrad Blakemore/ArenaPAL: inset 2, page 5 above left. Henrietta Butler/ArenaPAL: inset 2, page 5 below. Getty Images: inset 2, page 4 below/Don Smith/Radio Times; inset 3, pages 3 above/Ken Hively/Los Angeles Times, 3 below/Robbie Jack/ Corbis, 4 below/Anwar Hussein Collection. Photo by Charles Green: inset 3, page 2 above. © Tristram Kenton: inset 3, page 4 above. Neal Street Productions/BBC One: inset 3, page 5 below. Jennifer Robertson and Lynne Fletcher/Kyte Photography: inset 3, page 8 below. © Gerald Scarfe: inset 2, page 1 below. Shutterstock: inset 1, page 8 below/ITV; inset 2, pages 1 above/ITV, 7 above/Alastair Muir; inset 3, page 6 above/Lukas Coch/EPA. © Vinod Singh Photography: inset 3, page 7 above. © Don Smith: inset 2, page 3 above right. © Southern Pictures: inset 3, page 6 below. Stearn's Cambridge: inset 1, page 7 below. Duncan Stewart: inset 1, page 8 above. Still © Company Pictures: inset 3, page 7 below. WILLIAM SHAKESPEARE'S ROMEO + JULIET © 1996 Twentieth Century Fox. All rights reserved: inset 3, page 1 above.

Index

Adler, Larry 278
Adler, Rabbi Moshe 368, 369
Age of Innocence, The (film) 318, 330–4
Agutter, Jenny 362, 365
AIDS 144
Alboretti, Ruth 272
Aleandro, Norma 308
Ali, Tariq 27
Allen, Patrick 137, 210
Almost Australian (TV documentary) 358–9, 360
Amadio, Robin 269
Amateur Dramatic Club (ADC) 101, 103–4
Andrews, Susan 99, 267
Angell, Nick 209
Ann Summers 138–41
antisemitism 5, 22, 367–8, 381, 383
apartheid 377–8
Armstrong, Gareth 218
Armstrong, Moira 267, 268
Ashenden, Peter 235–6
Ashton-Smith, Lady Joan 190
Assenheim, Naomi 93
At the Eleventh Hour 277–8
Atkins, Eileen 177
Atkins, Robert 115
Atkinson, Rowan 283, 284–5, 288

auditions 273, 274, 310–11, 326–7, 342
Augustine, Carole 215–16
Aukin, Liane 271
Austin, Derek 15
Australia 156, 256, 298–9, 353–60
Awakening, The (film) 361
Ayres, Sue 252

Babe (film) 220–1, 357
Baddeley, Hermione 186, 190
Baddeley, John 210
BAFTA (British Academy Film and Television Awards) 318, 333–4
Bailey, David 190
Bain, Ron 308
Balcon, Jill 332
Barclay, Humphrey 115
Barenboim, Daniel 264
Barr, Roseanne 313
Bates, Kathy 303, 335
Baxter, Stanley 213–14
BBC Drama Repertory Company 65, 117, 120–1 122–3, 126–8, 157, 378
Beadnell, Maria 291, 294
Beatty, Warren 145, 319–21, 325, 327
Beckett, Samuel 204, 207, 378

Being Julia (film) 325
Bening, Annette 325
Bennett, Alan 404
Berlin, Sir Isaiah 79–81
Betty Witherspoon Show, The (radio
 show) 279
Blackadder (TV series) 283–4,
 285–9
Blackman, Enid 166
Blair, Joyce 172
Blair, Lionel 172
Blessed, Brian 283, 284
Braden, Kim 166, 168
Bradley, David 348
Branagh, Kenneth 321–2, 347
Branch, Margaret 261–5, 268
Breath of Fresh Air, A (radio play)
 126
Bree, David 103–4, 397
Bridges, John 117, 120–1
Briers, Richard 204
British Council 296–7
Broadbent, Jim 283, 284
Broadhead, William 231
Broadmoor 100–1
Broadway 113, 246–7, 285
Brooke-Taylor, Tim 115
Brooklyn Academy of Music (BAM)
 248
Brooks, Ray 210
Brown, Nigel 115
Brown, Tom *see* Stevens, C. E.
Browne, Coral 122, 306
Browne, Roscoe Lee 221
Bucket (TV series) 404
Buckingham Palace 388–91
Bullfinch Productions 200–1

Burton, Tim 322
Buscemi, Steve 318
Butcher's Wife, The (film) 321
Byrne, Patsy 288–9

Cadbury's Caramel Bunny (TV
 advertisement) 216
Call the Midwife (TV drama)
 361–2, 363–5
Cambridge University Social
 Services Organisation
 (CUSSO) 100–1
Cameron, Audrey 127
Campbell, Alastair 376
Carsey, Marcy 312–13
Carson, Jeannie 306
Carson, Johnny 301–2
Cavanaugh, Christine 220
Chadbon, Tom 196, 197
Channing, Carol 309–10
Chapman, Graham 115
Charkham, Esta 250
Charles, HRH Prince of Wales 28,
 392–3, 394, 395–6
Cheifitz, Paul 16
Chester, John 173
Christie, Anne 29
civil partnership 397–9
Claire, Irene 165
Clark, Katerina (Katy) 150–2, 267,
 353
class 12–13, 31–2, 55–6, 114, 134–5,
 211, 330–1
Cleese, John 113, 115
Clinton, Bill 305
Cloud 9 (Churchill) 202–3
Coffin Club, Hastings 415

Cohen, Ruth 82, 107–8
Collings, David 218
Comic Strip Presents, The (radio show) 283
Coltrane, Robbie 308, 348
Columbus, Christopher 346
comedy 277–83
Conservative Party 55–6, 377, 381
Cook, Lesley 101, 102, 103, 105–7
Copp, Alan 214
Corbyn, Jeremy 380, 381
Corner, Jill 99
Couric, Katie 301
Courtney, Stella 187, 188
COVID pandemic 163, 401, 407–8, 414–15, 417
Covington, Julie 202–3
Coward, Sir Noël 205, 353
Crane, David 303–4
Crayford, Helen 295
Cryer, Barry 280
Crossroads (soap opera) 273–5
Crush, Bobby 417
Curtis, Richard 283
Cusack, Cyril 292
Cushman, Robert 193
Cuthbertson, Iain 148

Dance, Charles 302, 303, 324
Dance of Death, The (Strindberg) 185
Danes, Claire 336, 337, 338–9
Daniels, Kay 271
Dartland, Dottie 316
Dastor, Sam 104–5
David Copperfield (Dickens) 294, 299

Davies, Betty 127
Davin, Brigid 388, 389
Davis, Warwick 347
Day-Lewis, Daniel 332
de la Tour, Frances 194, 201, 379
Dead Again (film) 322
Defeating Mrs Dresden (BBC play) 121–2
Deirdre (Epstein) 64
Dench, Dame Judi 324–5
Desert Island Discs (radio series) 134
Devlin, Diana 81
Dharma & Greg (TV series) 312, 316
DiCaprio, Leonardo 336, 337–9, 340
Dickens, Charles 12, 290–1, 405; *see also Dickens' Women*
Dickens in America (TV documentary) 405
Dickens' Women (one-woman show) 112, 127, 182, 244, 269, 271
productions 293–9, 385
directors 202–5, 206–7, 212–13, 215
Disney World 342–3, 344
Dodd, Ken 281–2, 315
Donovan, Patricia 197, 201
Donovan, Terence 215, 233
Drew, Bryan 137, 208, 216–17
du Pré, Jacqueline 263–5
dubbing 218–21
Dunlop, Frank 293

Earp, Susan 106–7
Eban, Abba 166

Ed and His Dead Mother (film) 318
Eden, Diana 166
Edinburgh Festival 113, 251–2,
    253–4, 293, 295, 298
Edzard, Christine 291, 292, 293,
    321
Elizabeth II, HM Queen 53, 388,
    389–91
Ellam, Harry 292–3
Elliott, Tommy 165
Elton, Ben 286, 288
End of Days (film) 323–4
Endgame (Beckett) 204–5, 206–7
Enfants du Paradis, Les (film)
    175
Enter Solly Gold (BBC play) 143
Equity 167, 199, 200–1, 378
Essex, David 181
Esslin, Martin 127–8
Evans, Dame Edith 177

Family Guy 283
farts 276–7
Fazan, Eleanor 188
Feast, Kate 186
Feldman, Marty 278
Ffrangcon-Davies, Gwen 405
Fiddler on the Roof (musical)
    164–70, 172–4
Fielding, Fenella 157
Fields, Gracie 12, 30
Flaming Bodies (Wilson) 180–1
Fletcher, Mandie 286–7
Flood, Kevin 121–2
Fool, The (film) 321
Footlights Club 113–16, 117
Frannie's Turn (TV show) 312–17

Fraser, Sonia 112, 250–1, 252, 254,
    256, 299
    Dickens' Women 271, 293, 294,
    295
French, Dawn 69, 209, 242
Freud, Clement 279
Frost, David 113, 114
Fry, Stephen 113, 180, 288, 395, 417

Gairdner, Sophy 99, 108
Gallimore, Patricia 123, 128
Gascoigne, Bamber 118
Gay Yids 130–1
Gertrude Stein and a Companion
    (Wells) 90, 250–9, 357
Gillard, Julia 358
Gillies, Carol 271
Girls of Slender Means, The (TV
    series) 103, 267–8, 354
Glasgow 4–8, 33, 35–6
Glen-Doepel, William 122
Gloomsbury (radio show) 282
Godley, Adam 196
Golan, Menahem 300, 301
Gooder, Jean 110–11
Goodman, John 313
Gordon, Noele 274–5
Goudsmit, Lex 168–9
Grade, Michael 285
Graham Norton Show, The (chat
    show) 2–3, 309, 349, 410–12
Grant, Richard E. 333, 335, 417
Gray, Elspet 283
Great Gatsby, The (film) 339
Green, Philip 381
Green, Robert 269
Greenwood, Joan 291

Greer, Germaine 113, 353–4
Grenville, Cynthia 165
Griffiths, Trevor 168
Grint, Rupert 348–9
Guilt Trip, The (film) 328–9
Guinness, Alec 291–2, 293, 340
Gummer, Joan 63–4

Hack, Keith 191
Hall, Sir Peter 181, 248
Hamlet (Shakespeare) 65, 126
Hammond, Roger 271
Hare, Doris 171–2
Hare, Mollie 165, 171
Harris, Isle of 365–6
Harris, Richard 347, 348
Harrison, Carey 145
Harrison, Eric 305–6
Harrison, Joan and Ken 272
Harrison, Rex 246, 247
*Harry Potter and the Chamber of
    Secrets* (film) 346–52
*Harry Potter and the Deathly
    Hallows* (film) 351–2
Haslam, Michael 295
Hawke, Bob 298–9, 357
Hayes, Patricia 292
Healy, Gerry 379
Heath, Edward 189, 191, 378
Helmsley, Leona 304
Hemingway, Ernest 251
Hendra, Tony 115
Henn, Tom 110
Hepworth, Marise 137, 138
Hervey, Grizelda 125–6
Heston, Charlton 361
Hewitt, Sean 166, 167

Heyman, David 346
Heyman, Norma 351
Hickey, Tom 204, 205, 207
Hockney, David 393, 394
Hodge, David 140
Hodge, Patricia 267–8, 300–1, 392–3
Hodgkin, Dorothy 56–8
Hodgkin, Liz 47, 56–8, 64, 267,
    377
    Cambridge 97, 99, 105, 118
Hodgkin, Thomas 56–8
Hogarth, Catherine 294
Hogarth, Mary 294
Holborough, Jackie 274
Hollywood 160–1, 308–11, 312–18,
    319–28
Holocaust 1, 13, 220, 367, 373–5
homosexuality 130–1, 144
Hooper, Jim 203
Hopkins, Anthony 334
Horne, Kenneth 279
Howards End (BBC play) 122
Humphries, Barry 353, 395–6
Hurt, William 308
Hussein, Waris 304, 306
Hutchinson, Bill 168

I Love You to Death (film) 308–9,
    321
Importance of Being Earnest, The
    (Wilde) 248–9
Importance of Being Miriam, The
    (one-woman show) 10, 354
India 296–7, 406
Irons, Jeremy 325–6
Israel 92–6, 367–8, 375, 381, 383,
    384–7

Jackson, Glenda 194, 195, 196–7, 198–9, 201
Jackson, Tony 126, 210
Jacobi, Derek 291, 293, 321
Jam and Jerusalem (TV series) 69
James and the Giant Peach (film) 322–3
James, Clive 114, 353, 354
Jarvis, Martin 210
Jarvis, Peter 252
Jason, David 280
Jewish Chronicle 278
John, Augustus 85–9
Johnson, Boris 380, 381–2
Johnson, Stanley 406, 408
Jones, Gemma 351
Jordan, Richard 298
Joseph, Lesley 251
Judaism 4, 6–7, 11, 90–2, 173, 368–73, 384; *see also* antisemitism; Holocaust; Israel
Julius Caesar (Shakespeare) 65
Just a Minute (radio show) 279

Kane, Carol 247
Karlin, Miriam 164
Kasdan, Lawrence 308, 309
Katkov, Nina 51, 65
Katsaros, Andonia 166, 170
Katzenberg, Jeffrey 315
Kauffman, Marta 303–4
Kaufman, Laura 99, 272
Keating, Paul 299
Keaton, Diane 321
Kennedy Centre 344
kibbutzim 93–6

Kick Up the Eighties, A (TV show) 308–9
Killing of Sister George, The (Marcus) 107
King, Lindy 302, 345, 392
Kingsgate (Kent) 36–7
Kline, Kevin 308
Kristen, Anne 146–7, 148
Kwouk, Burt 218

Labour Party 377, 380, 381
Ladies in Lavender (film) 324–5
Lady in the Van, The (Bennett) 404
Lansbury, Angela 306
Latham, David 255
Lavery, Peter 230–1
Lear, Norman 296, 303–4, 312
Leavis, Frank 109–10, 111–12
Leavis, Queenie 109, 110, 111
Lee, Susan 118
Leno, Jay 302
Lenya, Lotte 186
Lerner, Penelope (cousin) 28
lesbianism 61, 71, 130–1, 144–9, 250, 256–9, 359
  coming out 157–61
Life and Death of Peter Sellers, The (film) 254, 415
Limb, Sue 282
Lindsay-Hogg, Michael 195–6, 198, 199
Lipman, Maureen 214
Little Dorrit (film) 291–3, 300
Lloyd, Norman 306
Loach, Ken 25
Loewenberg, Susan 296

London 11, 14, 119–20, 129–33, 187, 231–4
Long Day's Journey into Night (O'Neill) 185
Lorre, Chuck 312, 313, 314–15, 316
Lortel, Lucille 255
Los Angeles (LA) 292, 300, 302–6, 307–8, 369; *see also* Hollywood
Luhrmann, Baz 198, 318, 335, 336–7, 338, 340
Lumley, Joanna 322, 323
Lushington, Mark 271
Lynch, Sean 187
Lynn, Johnny 166
Lyon-Maris, Paul 352
Lyons, Margery 415

Macbeth (Shakespeare) 103
McBurney, Simon 204–5, 206–7
Macready, Carol 397–9
McDougall, Gordon 293
McGuire, Biff 306
McInnerny, Tim 283, 288
Mackay, Mrs 171–2
McKellen, Ian 160
McKeown, Allan 309
McKinnon, Andrew 269, 298
McNeill, Dorelia 85–6, 87, 89
Maddern, Victor 189
Magee, Patrick 194, 196, 198
Malta 123–4
Mandabach, Caryn 313
Manikin Cigar (TV advertisement) 215–16
Mantello, Joe 276
Margaret, HRH Princess 182
Margolyes, Doris (aunt) 6

Margolyes, Evalyn (Eva) (aunt) 6, 35–6
Margolyes, Jacob (Jack) (uncle) 6, 8, 33–4
Margolyes, Joseph (father) 4–5, 6–11, 18–20, 21–3, 119, 161–2, 407
  Berlin 79–80
  Cambridge 107–8
  character 27, 28–31, 86
  coming out 158, 159
  medicine 25–6, 53
  money 229
  politics 377
Margolyes, Miriam 21–3, 26–7, 33–7, 75–8, 409–13
  age 400–8, 414–17
  Age of Innocence, The 330–4
  arrest 222–8
  At the Eleventh Hour 276–7
  Australia 353–60
  BBC 120–2, 126–8
  Blackadder 283–4, 285–9
  Broadway 246–9
  Cambridge 79–84, 97–108, 109–12
  Call the Midwife 361–2, 363–5
  civil partnership 397–9
  Crossroads 273–5
  documentaries 382, 405–7
  dubbing 218–21
  Endgame 204–5, 206–7
  family 59–60
  Fiddler on the Roof 164–70, 172–4
  Footlights 113–16
  friendships 266–72

Margolyes, Miriam (cont.)
  Gertrude Stein and a Companion 250–9
  Harry Potter series 345–53
  Hollywood films 319–28
  Israel 92–6, 384–7
  Judaism 90–2, 367–75
  lesbianism 144–9, 157–61
  life modelling 85–9
  Little Dorrit 291–3
  London 129–33
  men 69–71, 72–4
  OBE 28, 391–2
  politics 376–83
  property 229–37
  puberty 67–9
  Romeo + Juliet 335–41
  royalty 388–91, 392–6
  school 38–47, 48–51, 55–6, 62–6
  Sutherland, Heather 150–7, 397–9
  theatre 175–85
  therapy 260, 261–5
  Threepenny Opera, The 186–93
  USA 300–6, 307–11, 312–18
  voice-overs 138–41, 208–17
  weight 238–45
  White Devil, The 194–201
  see also *Dickens' Women*
Margolyes, Muriel (aunt) 33–5
Margolyes, Philip (grandfather) 5–6, 8–10
Margolyes, Philippa (cousin) 33, 34, 35
Margolyes, Rebecca (grandmother) 5, 6
Margolyes, Ruth (mother) 4, 12–15, 17–20, 23–4, 26–7, 119, 407

Berlin 79–80
Cambridge 107–8
character 29, 30–2, 262–3
coming out 158–60
death 161–3
education 75
family 58–9
housework 28
John, Augustus 85–6
Judaism 369–70
Miriam 21–3, 32–3
money 229
Oxford 25, 52–4
politics 377
puberty 67–8
theatre 176
voice 134, 136
weight 239–41
Marks, Alfred 280
Marks in His Diary (radio show) 280
Martin, Barry 173
Martin, Catherine 337
Martin, John 298
Marvin, Blanche 255
Mason, Ronnie 128
Matthews, Geoffrey 210
Mayall, Rik 283, 308
Meager, Pam 292
Melia, Joe 186, 189
menstruation 67–9
Merkelis, Rita 166–7
Metropolitan Museum (NYC) 252–3
Mexico City 337, 339
Michigan Womyn's Music Festival 256–8

Milian, Tomas 316
Miller, George 220
Miller, Liz 99
Miriam's Big American Adventure
  (TV documentary) 382
Miriam's Big Fat Adventure (TV
  documentary) 244–5, 270
Miriam's Dead Good Adventure (TV
  documentary) 407
Mitchell, Norma 238
Modi, Narendra 406
money 200–1, 229–37, 247–8
Monich, Tim 332
Monkey (TV series) 218–19
Monkhouse, Bob 143
Monty Python (TV show) 114
Moore, Demi 321
Morgan, Fidelis 201
Morgan, Natasha 251–2, 255, 256
Morison, Patricia 306
Mother Teresa 297
Mount, Ferdinand: *Cold Cream* 27
Muir, Jinty 118
Mulan (animation feature) 342
Mullard, Arthur 186, 189–90
Murray, Wendy 304
My Left Foot (film) 332

Narizzano, Silvio 250
Neill, Sam 334
Netanyahu, Benjamin 367, 384
Newnham College, Cambridge 56,
  80–3, 97–108, 109–12, 117–18
Nimmo, Derek 172
Noel, Wendy 137, 138, 208–9, 211,
  216
Noonan, Chris 220, 221

Norrington, Sir Arthur 42
Norton, Graham 276–7; *see also*
  Graham Norton Show, The
Nunn, Trevor 103, 115

Oddie, Bill 115
Old Vic theatre 194, 196
Oliver Twist (BBC drama) 293
Oliver Twist (Dickens) 290, 294,
  392
Olivier, Sir Laurence 185, 206, 309,
  348
oral sex 71, 73, 101–2
Oremus, Stephen 246
Orpheus Descending (Williams) 178
Orton, Joe 279
Oxford 21–2, 25–7, 52–5, 369–70
  Somerville College 80–1, 82,
    83–4
Oxford High School 38–47, 48–51,
  55–6, 62–6, 68–9, 83
  friendship 266–7
  religion 91–2
  voice 134–5, 136

Pacific Heights (film) 321
Palestine 57, 96, 375, 383, 384–7
Palladino, Jack 272
Palmer, Tony 118–19
Parfitt, Judy 362
Park, Robin 272
Parker, Robert 209
Parton, Dolly 276–7
Pask, Dave 398–9
Passover 7, 368, 371, 384
Pasternak Slater, Catherine 43, 44,
  56, 83, 267

Patterson, Jennifer 401
Pawsey, Mark 296–7
Peaky Blinders (TV drama) 313
Pfeiffer, Michelle 332
PG Tips (TV advertisement)
  213–14
Phillips, Andy 199
Phoenix, River 308
Phoenix Theatre (Leicester)
  145–8
Picasso, Pablo: *Portrait of Gertrude
  Stein* 252–3
Pinter, Harold 190
Pitt Club 104
Planer, Nigel 283
Plater, Alan 171
Plowman, Mary 135, 136
Plowright, Joan 308, 309
politics 55–6, 57–8, 105, 189,
  376–83
pornography 138–41
Postlethwaite, Pete 339–40
Previn, André 200
Price, Vincent 306
property 229–37, 357–8
Proudfoot, Donald 168
Pryce, Jonathan 194, 197

Queen and I, The (radio play) 127,
  317–18
Quick, Diana 187, 188
Quinn, Patricia 187, 188

Rabe, Pamela 256, 257, 258–9
Rachman, Peter 129
racism 376, 377–8, 381
Radcliffe, Daniel 348–9, 351

radio 122–3, 124–8, 134, 278–9,
  280; *see also* BBC Drama
  Repertory Company
Radomsky, Saul 131
Rantzen, Esther 277
Ray, Ted 279
Real Marigold Hotel, The (TV
  documentary) 405–6
Redgrave, Corin 378
Redgrave, Lynn 248
Redgrave, Vanessa 178, 186, 188–9,
  192–3, 266, 378, 383
Reds (film) 319–21, 327
Reeves, Keanu 308
Rendel, Sandy and Dianne 397, 398
Rhys Jones, Griff 280
Richardson, Tony 186
Rickman, Alan 347, 348, 352
Rietberg, Countess Elisabeth von 108
Rigby, Terry 248
Rix, Jamie 282
Robertson, Patrick 187
Robinson, Tony 283, 288
Romeo + Juliet (film) 198, 318, 335–41
Roseanne (TV series) 313
Round the Horne (radio show) 279
Rosenthal, Jack 326
Rosh Hashanah 370–1
Ross, Annie 186, 187–8
Rossiter, Leonard 378
Roth, Cecil 370
Roth, Rabbi Michael 369
Routledge, Patricia 122, 157
Rowling, J. K. 349, 352
Royal Court theatre 202–3
Rubinstein, Shirley 171
Ruby, Thelma 169

Rush, Geoffrey 254
Ruskin School of Art 70, 85
Rutherford, Jonathan 296
Ryan, Madge 194
Ryder, Winona 332, 333
Rylance, Mark 204, 205

Sachs, Andrew 218
St Margaret's Bay (Kent) 235–7
Sandeman, Hanna and Simon
 (great-grandparents) 13,
 16–17
Sandringham 392–6
Sands Films 292
Sargent, Stefan 209
Saroyan, William 414
Sarzin, Ann (cousin) 356
Saul, Christopher 166, 168
Saunders, Jennifer 69, 209
Sayle, Alexei 283
Scarfe, Gerald 293
Schlesinger, John 321
Schofield, Phillip 361
school plays 64–6
Schwartz, Oded 131
Schwarzenegger, Arnold 323–4
Scofield, Paul 105, 122, 157
Scorsese, Martin 330–1, 333
Scott, Terry 143
Selick, Henry 322–3
Sentimental Journey (radio
 documentary) 13
Sessions, John 282
sex 69–71, 103–4, 142–3, 214–16,
 409–10, 411–13; *see also*
 homosexuality; lesbianism;
 oral sex

*Sexy Sonia: Leaves from My
 Schoolgirl Diary* (voice-over
 tape) 140–1
Seyler, Athene 311
Shabbos (Sabbath) 4, 6–7, 370
Shakespeare, William 56–7, 65, 66,
 103, 126
Sharma, Madhav 168
Shaw, Fiona 332, 348
Shaw, Richard 405
She Stoops to Conquer (Goldsmith)
 181–2
Shephard, Richard 271–2
Shepherd, Jack 103, 194, 197,
 199–200
Sher, Sir Antony 203, 378, 393–4,
 395
Shooman, Sadie 171
Shrager, Rosemary 366, 406
Shrapnel, John 271
shtetels (villages) 371–2
Sinden, Donald 181–2
Slater, Michael: *Dickens and Women*
 294–5
Sloman, Roger 308
Smith, Anthony 278
Smith, Arthur 13
Smith, Don 268
Smith, Dame Maggie 63, 135, 179,
 280, 324–5, 333, 334
 Harry Potter films 347, 348,
 351–2
Smith, R. D. (Reggie) 127
Smith, Susan 160–1, 296, 302–3,
 307–8, 317
Sokole, Peter 272
Solti, Lady 393, 395

South Africa 16–17, 377–8
Spielberg, Steven 310
Springfield, Dusty 130
Stack, Peggy 44–5
Stack, Vera 42, 44, 83, 136
Stafford-Clark, Max 202–4
stage fright 179–81
Stallings, Rex 173–4
Stand Up, Virgin Soldiers (film) 195, 319
Steadman, Alison 282–3
Stein, Gertrude 250, 251, 252–3; *see also Gertrude Stein and a Companion*
Stevens, C. E. 76–8
Stockman, Olivier 292
Stoll, Rosalind 130
Stone, David 247–8
Streisand, Barbra 326–9, 373–4
Stringle, Bernie 214
Stuart-Clark, Chris 115–16
Stuart, Isobel 167
Supervía, Conchita 30
Sutherland, Heather 2–3, 145, 150–8, 160, 161–2, 168, 170
    Australia 354, 355–6, 357–8
    civil partnership 397–9
    therapy 263, 265
    swimming 401–2
Sydney and the Old Girl (O'Hare) 404
Sydney Festival 254
Syfret, Rosemary 82

Tamm, Mary 268
Tate, David 210

television 136–7, 208–9, 285–7, 312–16; *see also* BBC Drama Repertory Company; individual shows
Ternan, Ellen 294–5
Thatcher, Margaret 56, 380
theatre 29, 30, 63, 101, 103–4, 175–85, 269
    directors 202–5, 206–7, 212–13, 215
    Footlights 113–16
    see also individual productions
theatrical digs 170–2
therapy 260, 261–5
Theresienstadt concentration camp 373–4
This Morning (TV show) 361
Thomas, Dylan 134
Thomas, Heidi 361, 365
Thompson, Emma 322
Thomson, David 126
Thorndike, Daniel 280
Thorndike, Dame Sybil 81, 280
Three Sisters, The (Chekhov) 405
Threepenny Opera, The (Brecht/ Weill) 186–93
Timson, David 295
Tinbergen, Niko 43
Tobin, June 125
Today Show (TV show) 301
Todd, Hilary (Billy) 157, 158
Toklas, Alice B. 250, 251, 256
Tomalin, Claire 294
Toms, Carl 182
Tonight Show, The (TV show) 301–2
Topol 164, 168
Tosh, Ben (uncle) 58, 59

Tosh, Buffy (cousin) 16, 58, 60
Tosh, Doris (cousin) 58
Tosh, Jack (Jacob) (cousin) 58
transgender 76–8
Trebilcock, Julio 166
Tricklebank, Ann 364
Truelove, Anna 43–4, 56, 83, 267
Tryingham Hall 243–4
Tucci, Stanley 412
Tuscany 2, 155, 230–1
Tydeman, John 127, 272
Tynan, Kenneth 118

Ubu Roi (Jarry) 293
Ullman, Tracey 308–9
United States of America 254–9,
    296, 298, 300–1, 381–2, 405;
    see also Broadway; Los Angeles
University Challenge (TV show)
    117–18
Ustinov, Sir Peter 236

Vaughan, Frankie 91
Villiers, James 194, 197, 201
Vinogradov, Anton 72–4
voice 127, 134–7
voice-overs 136–7, 208–17, 138–41,
    309–10; *see also* dubbing

Wacks, Jonathan 318
Wall, Max 292
Walters, Doris (aunt) 14, 17–18
Walters, Flora (grandmother)
    13–14, 18, 19, 414
    Oxford 52, 53, 58–9
Walters, Augusta (Gusta) (aunt) 14,
    16, 17–18, 58, 59

Walters, Jacob (uncle) 14
Walters, Julie 180–1, 348
Walters, Ruth Sandeman *see*
    Margolyes, Ruth
Walters (Sandeman), Sigismund
    (Siggi) (grandfather) 13–16
Wanamaker, Sam 81
Warburg, Maria 218
Washington, Joan 335–6
Water Margin, The (TV series)
    218
Waterman, Dame Fanny 171
Watson, Emma 348–9
Webster, John 194
Weise, Marion 293
Welles, Orson 196, 213
Wells, Win 250, 251
Werner, Tom 312–13
Westbury, Marjorie 125
Westwood, Chris 256
White Devil, The (Webster)
    194–201
Whitehead, Annie 99
Whitelock, Dorothy 82, 109
Whitfield, June 143
Whitlam, Gough 357, 359
Wicked (musical) 183, 246–8
Widowing of Mrs Holroyd, The
    (Lawrence) 184
will.i.am. 410–11
Williams, Enyd 127
Williams, Kenneth 193, 279–80
Willis, Bruce 321
Willoughby, Holly 361
Wilson, Mary 401
Wilson, Stella 301, 333, 334
Wimbush, Mary 126

Windsor, Barbara 186, 188–9,
191–2, 193
Winters, Shelley 305, 311
women 114, 137, 291; *see also*
Dickens' Women; lesbianism
Wood, John 209–11
Woods, James 311
Woodthorpe, Peter 218
Woolf, Henry 190
Wooman, Lovely Wooman, What a
Sex You Are! see Dickens'
Women
Wordsmiths of Gorsemere, The
(radio show) 282–3

Wordsworth, Denise 397–9,
417
Workers Revolutionary Party
(WRP) 189, 379–80
Worth, Jenny 361
Wright, Norman 121

Yentl (film) 326–8, 373–4
Yiddish 13, 79, 90, 91
Yom Kippur 7, 368, 370
Young, Rabbi Roderick 384
Young Ones, The (TV show) 283

Zionism 92, 95, 375, 384